Ethnic Conflict and Civic Life

Ethnic Conflict and Civic Life

Hindus and Muslims in India

Ashutosh Varshney

Yale University Press

New Haven & London

Set in Adobe Garamond type by The Composing Room of Michigan, Inc., Grand Rapids, Michigan.

Printed in the United States of America.

Library of Congress Cataloging-in-Publication Data

Varshney, Ashutosh, 1957–
    Ethnic conflict and civic life : Hindus and Muslims in India / Ashutosh Varshney.
        p.   cm.
    Includes bibliographical references and index.
    ISBN 0-300-08530-3 (cloth : alk. paper)
    1. Communalism—India.   2. Ethnic conflict—India.   3. Hindus—India.
    4. Muslims—India.   5. India—Politics and government—1947–   I. Title.
    DS422.C64 V37   2001
    954'.0088'2971—dc21

                                                                2001046526

A catalogue record for this book is available from the British Library.

The paper in this book meets the guidelines for permanence and durability of the Committee on Production Guidelines for Book Longevity of the Council on Library Resources.

10 9 8 7 6 5 4 3 2 1

Contents

Preface

In the summer of 1990, I decided to take a leave of absence from political economy, the field to which most of my previous research and writing had belonged. After completing my doctorate at MIT, I had just finished my first year of teaching at Harvard. Feeling a little exhausted, I was looking for an intellectual change. An insurgency in Kashmir had recently broken out, and I thought I would spend the summer studying it. The aim was to learn something on a new subject and write an article. I did later publish a journal article, but little did I know that I was also taking decisive steps toward a whole new research project that would keep me occupied for the next seven to eight years. Although this book is not about the ethnic insurgency in Kashmir, its origins lie in the sojourn I took that summer studying it.

I am often asked why Kashmir had such influence on me, shaping my research life for much of the 1990s. My answer has always been the same. The emotional intensity I encountered in the Kashmir valley not only overwhelmed me but also aroused deep intellectual curiosity. Until that time, my fieldwork had dealt with the politics of economic policy. Compared to that experience, the loss, pain, and suffering I witnessed in the Kashmir valley appeared to belong to an entirely different realm of life, a realm not easily amenable to a standard political economy inquiry. I saw children who had lost their limbs, families that had lost their children, and yet people were willing to fight a war of insurgency. Their inner selves, they argued, were at stake, and they were prepared to suffer a lot of pain for dignity, identity, and self-respect.

The intellectual challenge—after such interviews—became quite obvious to me. Can we, I asked, do a social science of pain, suffering, loss, and death experienced in ethnic or communal conflict? If I had not been a social scientist, perhaps I would have framed the challenge differently. But having been trained as one, I thought my comparative advantage lay in social science, not in constructing ethnographies or writing fiction. Extending the arena of research beyond Kashmir and in search of greater generalizability, I decided to concentrate on Hindu-Muslim conflict, asking why Hindus and Muslims had riots in some parts of India but they conducted their lives reasonably peacefully in others. I sought to understand the sources of communal violence.

Answering this question was not easy. Considerable retooling of my training was required. I read books on religion, took classes in religious law, and spent months sampling the vast literature on ethnic conflict. All of this required a huge investment of time. Two fellowships—one from the MacArthur Program of Social Science Research Council and another from the United State Institute of Peace—allowed me to go on leave from Harvard. Later, substantial grants were also made by the Ford Foundation and Harvard University—which allowed me to travel to India many times, conduct a survey, hire research assistants, and free up time for writing. Finally, as director of the Harvard Academy of Area and International Studies, Samuel Huntington financed a semester's leave to enable me to make substantial progress on writing. I am also grateful for a summer fellowship to the Wilson Center in Washington.

The list of friends and acquaintances who helped me in India is very long, but I would especially like to acknowledge what I learned, or the help I received, from Imtiaz Ahmed, Ashis Nandy, Balwant Reddy, Achyut Yagnik, Amitabh Kant, the late V. Rajagopalan, Mohd. Aslam, Gangadhar Menon, M. G. S. Narayanan, the late Ashok Priyadarshi, M. K. Gahrana, the late Praveen Visaria, Ghanshyam Shah, Saiyid Hamid, Nasir Abid, Suraiya Ali, Rudra Mohanty, Nayeem and Rafat Quadri, M. A. K. Anwar, P. Sasi, Devesh, Masooma Khatoom, Mark Tully, Prabhash Joshi, Mark Robinson, Dhirubhai Sheth, Abid Hussain and Julius Ribero. During research, Delhi's India International Centre and Center for the Study of Developing Societies provided warm hospitality. And in the United States, the late Myron Weiner, Samuel Hunting-ton, James Scott, Stanley Hoffmann, Jagdish Bhagwati, John Harney, Steven Wilkinson, Rina Verma, Sanjay Reddy, Samhita Patwardhan, Manjari Maha-jan, and Karthik Muralidharan provided help, guidance, or inspiration.

Presentations based on this book were made at the annual meetings of the American Political Science Association and at seminars and symposia at the fol-lowing universities and institutions: the University of Chicago, Columbia Uni-versity, Harvard University, JNU, the University of Michigan (Ann Arbor), MIT, Notre Dame, Oxford University, the University of Texas (Austin), the University of Toronto, Uppsala University, Yale University, and the Ford Foun-dation (Delhi). For comments, criticisms, and suggestions, I would like to thank Hans Blomkvist, Paul Brass, Kanchan Chandra, Partha Chatterjee, Pradeep Chhibber, Robert Hardgrave, Donald Horowitz, Atul Kohli, David Laitin, Roderick MacFarquhar, Scott Mainwaring, Anthony Marx, Bhikhu Parekh, Elizabeth Perry, Robert Putnam, Lloyd and Susanne Rudolph, Manoj Srivasatava, Alfred Stepan, Steven van Evera, Sidney Verba, Yogendra Yadav, Crawford Young, and three anonymous reviewers for Yale University Press.

After almost ten years' work, it is my hope that this book will provide some new insights on ethnic conflict and also a way to peace.

Part I Arguments and Theories

Chapter 1 Introduction

In this book I seek to establish an integral link between the structure of civil society on one hand and ethnic, or communal, violence on the other. To be more precise, the focus is on the *inter*communal, not *intra*communal, networks of civic life, which bring different communities together. These networks can, in turn, be broken down into two parts: associational and quotidian. I call the first *associational* forms of civic engagement and the second, *everyday* forms of civic engagement. Business associations, professional organizations, reading clubs, film clubs, sports clubs, festival organizations, trade unions, and cadre-based political parties are some of the examples of the former. Everyday forms of engagement consist of such simple, routine interactions of life as Hindu and Muslim families visiting each other, eating together often enough, jointly participating in festivals, and allowing their children to play together in the neighborhood. Both forms of engagement, if robust, promote peace; contrariwise, their absence or weakness opens up space for communal violence. Of the two, the associational forms turn out to be sturdier than everyday engagement, especially when people are confronted with the attempts by politicians to polarize ethnic communities. Vigorous associational life, if intercom-munal, acts as a serious constraint on the polarizing strategies of political elites.

Although some of the key terms used above—"civil society," "civic life," "ethnic," "communal"—are discussed in great detail in the next chapter, let me briefly specify what I mean by them. Since scholars and activists do not use these terms in the same way, a clarification of how I have understood and de-ployed them will help pre-empt speaking across different conceptual registers.

By "civil society," or "civic life," I mean the part of our life that exists be-tween the state on one hand and families on the other, that allows people to come together for a whole variety of public activities, and that is relatively in-dependent of the state. Civil society is not a non-political but a non-state space of collective life. Moreover, in its non-state functions, it can cover both social and political activities. Soccer leagues, playing-card societies, and philately clubs may be social, not political; but trade unions and political parties are pri-marily the latter, not the former, though in the process of playing their political roles, they may also provide social platforms for people to come together. Both types of organizations are parts of civil society, so long as they are independent of the state.

A special note may be taken here of the double role of political parties. They constitute an important component of civil society in a multiparty democracy but not in a one-party system. In the latter, political parties become an ap-pendage of the state, losing their civic functions. Since India is a multiparty democracy, its political parties are part of the nation's civil society, along with its unions, business associations, reading clubs, film clubs, NGOs, and so on.

What about the terms "ethnicity" and "communalism"? There are two dis-tinct ways in which the term "ethnic" is used. In its narrower sense, "ethnic" means "racial" or "linguistic." This is the sense in which the term is widely un-derstood in popular discourse, both in India and elsewhere. For example, for politics and conflict based on religious groupings, such as Hindus and Mus-lims, the principal subjects of this study, Indian scholars as well as bureaucrats and politicians since the British days have used the term "communal," not "eth-nic," reserving the latter primarily for linguistically or racially distinct groups.

There is, however, a second sense in which ethnic groups are defined in the so-cial sciences. This usage is broader in its implications. As Horowitz argues,[1] all conflicts based on *ascriptive* group identities—race, language, religion, tribe, or caste—can be called ethnic. In this umbrella usage, ethnic conflicts range from (1) the Protestant-Catholic conflict in Northern Ireland and Hindu-Muslim conflict in India to (2) black-white conflict in the United States and South

Africa, (3) Tamil-Sinhala conflict in Sri Lanka, and (4) Shia-Sunni troubles in Pakistan. In the narrower construction of term, (1) is religious, (2) racial, (3) linguistic, and (4) sectarian. The term "ethnic" often in the past would have been reserved for the second and, at best, third conflicts, but not extended to the first and the fourth.

Exponents of the broader usage disagree with such distinctions. They argue that the form ethnic conflict takes—religious, linguistic, racial, tribal—does not seem to alter its intensity, longevity, passion, or relative intractability. Their emphasis on the ascriptive and cultural core of the conflict, imagined or real, and they distinguish it primarily from the largely non-ascriptive and economic core of class conflict. Ethnic conflict may have an economic basis, but that is not its defining feature. Irrespective of internal class differentiation, race, language, sect, or religion can define the politics of an ethnic group. Contrariwise, class conflict tends on the whole to be economic, but if the class to which one is born is also the class in which one is locked until death, and this happens to be true for large numbers of people, then class conflict does acquire ascriptive overtones. Following Horowitz, it is now well understood that the latter characteristics apply not to ethnic systems in general but to ranked ethnic systems, such as the United States of America during the period of slavery, South Africa during apartheid, and India with its caste system. *Ranked* ethnic systems merge ethnicity and class; *unranked* ethnic systems do not.[2]

The larger meaning, one might add, is also increasingly becoming the standard meaning in the social sciences, even if that is not yet true of politics and activism. I will use the term "ethnic" in this broader sense. In other words, I may distinguish between communal, linguistic, sectarian, tribal and caste categories, but I will not differentiate communal from ethnic. Ethnicity is simply the larger set to which religion, race, language, and sect belong as subsets in this definition.

Thus far, scholars have worked either on civil society or on ethnic conflict, but no systematic attempt has yet been made to connect the two.[3] For all practical purposes, the role of civic networks has not yet been appreciated in the literature on ethnic conflict.[4] How my argument linking the two emerged, therefore, requires some explanation. I start with a puzzle often encountered in the field of ethnicity and nationalism, and how I sought to resolve it.

THE PUZZLE

Sooner or later, scholars of ethnic conflict are struck by a puzzling empirical regularity in their field. Despite ethnic diversity, some places—regions, nations, towns, or villages—manage to remain peaceful, whereas others experience enduring patterns of violence. Similarly, some societies, after maintaining a veritable record of ethnic peace, explode in ways that surprise the observer and very often the scholar as well. Variations across time and space constitute an unresolved puzzle in the field of ethnicity and nationalism.

How does one account for such variations? With isolated exceptions,[5] uncovering commonalities across the many cases of violence has been the standard research strategy. This strategy will continue to enlighten us, but it can only give us the building blocks of a theory, not a theory of ethnic conflict. The logic underlying this proposition is simple, often misunderstood, and worth restating.[6] Suppose that on the basis of commonalities we find that interethnic economic rivalry (a), polarized party politics (b), and segregated neighborhoods (c) explain ethnic violence (X). Can we, however, be sure that our judgments are right? What if (a), (b), and (c) also exist in peaceful cases (Y)? In that case, either violence is caused by the intensity of (a), (b), and (c) in (X); or, there is an underlying and deeper context that makes (a), (b), and (c) conflictual in one case but not in the other; or, there is yet another factor (d), which differentiates peace from violence. It will, however, be a factor that we did not discover precisely because peaceful cases were not studied with the conflictual ones.

In short, until we study ethnic peace, we will not be able to have a good theory of ethnic conflict. Placing variance at the heart of new research is likely to provide by far the biggest advances in our understanding of ethnicity and ethnic conflict. Despite rising violence, many communities in the world still manage their interethnic tensions without taking violent steps.

The argument about the necessity of studying variance leads to another important methodological question: At what level must variance itself be studied? What should our unit of analysis be—nations, states, regions, towns, or villages? What methodologists call a large-n analysis can help us identify the spatial trends and allow us to choose the level at which variance is to be analyzed. The project, therefore, went through all reported Hindu-Muslim riots in the country between 1950 and 1995.[7] The detailed results are presented in Chapter 4. For purposes of identifying larger trends, two results were crucial.

First, the share of villages in communal rioting turned out to be remarkably small. Between 1950 and 1995, rural India, where two-thirds of Indians still live, accounted for less than 4 percent of the deaths in communal violence. Hindu-Muslim violence is primarily an urban phenomenon. Second, within urban India, too, Hindu-Muslim riots are highly locally concentrated. Eight cities—

Table 1.1. India's Most Riot-Prone Cities,
1950–95

	Deaths 1950–95
Bombay	1,137
Ahmedabad	1,119
Hyderabad	312
Meerut	265
Aligarh	160
Baroda	109
Delhi	93
Calcutta	63

Note: These cities experienced a minimum of 50 deaths
in 10 riots over 5 five-year periods.

Ahmedabad, Bombay, Aligarh, Hyderabad, Meerut, Baroda, Calcutta, and Delhi[8]—account for a hugely disproportionate share of communal violence in the country: a little more than 49 percent of all urban deaths (and 45.5 percent of all deaths) in Hindu-Muslim violence (table 1.1). As a group, however, these eight cities represent a mere 18 percent of India's urban population (and about 5 percent of the country's total population, both urban and rural). Eighty-two percent of the urban population (95 percent of the total population) has not been "riot-prone."

Consider another way of understanding the role of local concentrations. Two cities alone in the state of Gujarat—Ahmedabad and Vadodara—account for nearly 80 percent of the total deaths in the state; 88 percent of all deaths in Maharashtra took place in the six worst towns of the state, leaving many more towns untouched; and 80 percent of all deaths in the state of Andhra Pradesh occurred in the city of Hyderabad. All these states had many more cities that were peaceful than were violent, and state-level aggregate data on deaths were simply artifacts of riots in a handful of cities. Given such high local concentrations in urban India, the large-n analysis clearly establishes the "town or city" as the unit of analysis.[9] India's Hindu-Muslim violence is city-specific. State (and national) politics provides the context within which the local mechanisms linked with violence are activated. In order to understand the causes of communal violence, we must investigate these local mechanisms.

Following this reasoning, the project selected six cities—three from the list of eight riot-prone cities and three peaceful—and arranged them in three pairs.

Thus, each pair had a city where communal violence is endemic and a city where it is rare or entirely absent. To ensure that we did not compare "apples and oranges," roughly similar Hindu-Muslim percentages in the city populations constituted the minimum control in each pair. The first pair—Aligarh and Calicut—was based on population percentages only. The second pair—Hyderabad and Lucknow—added two controls to population percentages: previous Muslim rule and reasonable cultural similarities. The third pair—Ahmedabad and Surat—was the most tightly controlled. The first two pairs came from the north and the south. The third came from the same state, Gujarat, sharing history, language, and culture but not endemic communal violence. All of these cities, at this point, have a population of more than 500,000, and the biggest, Hyderabad, is a metropolis of more than 4.2 million people.

Why was similarity in demographic proportions chosen as the minimum control in each pair? Both in India's popular political discourse and in theories about Muslim political behavior, the size of the community is considered to be highly significant. Many politicians, especially those belonging to the Hindu nationalist Bharatiya Janata Party (BJP), have argued that the demographic distribution of Muslims makes them critical to electoral outcomes in India. Muslims constitute more than 20 percent of the electorate in 197 of 545 parliamentary constituencies in the country. In a first-past-the-post system, wherein 30–35 percent of the vote is often enough to win a seat in multicornered contests, these percentages make the Muslims electorally highly significant.[10] The higher the numbers of Muslims in a given constituency, argue politicians of the BJP, the greater the inclination of centrist political parties to pander to their sectional-communal demands, and the lower the incentive, therefore, for Muslims to build bridges with the Hindus. Thus, according to this argument, "Muslim appeasement," based on the significance of numbers in a democracy, is the cause of communal conflicts in India.[11]

That Muslim demography has political consequences is, however, not an argument confined to the Hindu nationalist BJP. Leading Muslim politicians also make a demographic claim, though they reverse the causation in the argument. The higher the numbers of Muslims in a town, they argue, the greater the political threat felt by the leaders of the Hindu community, who react with hostility to legitimate Muslim anxieties about politics and identity. An unjustified, even self-serving, opposition on the part of Hindu leaders, they argue, is the source of communal hostilities.[12] Thus, both extremes of the political spectrum heavily rely on demography for their explanations.

These popular arguments are, to some extent, shared by social scientists as well. Rudolph and Rudolph, for example, argue that when a town or constituency has a Muslim majority or plurality, Muslims typically favor confessional parties, not the centrist, intercommunal parties.[13] Muslims support centrist parties when their share of the population or electorate is small in a town or constituency. Smaller numbers make it rational to seek the security of a large, powerful mainstream party.

Can one find cases—cities or constituencies—where similar demographic distributions lead to very different forms of political behavior? Selecting from a larger sample of such cases, this study seeks to do precisely that. As described above, it compares three pairs of cities where a rough similarity in demographic proportions coexists with variance in political outcomes: peace or violence.

THE ARGUMENT

What accounts for the difference between communal peace and violence? Though not anticipated when the project began, the pre-existing local networks of civic engagement between the two communities stand out as the single most important *proximate* cause. Where such networks of engagement exist, tensions and conflicts were regulated and managed; where they are missing, communal identities led to endemic and ghastly violence. As already stated, these networks can be broken down into two parts: *associational* forms of engagement and *everyday* forms of engagement. The former ties are formed in organizational settings; the latter require no organization. Both forms of engagement, if intercommunal, promote peace, but the capacity of the associational forms to withstand national-level "exogenous shocks"—such as India's partition in 1947 or the demolition of the Baburi mosque in December 1992 in full public gaze by Hindu militants—is substantially higher.

The Mechanisms

What are the mechanisms that link civic networks and ethnic conflict? And why is associational engagement a sturdier bulwark of peace than everyday engagement?

One can identify two mechanisms that connect civil society and ethnic conflict. First, by promoting communication between members of different religious communities, civic networks often make neighborhood-level peace possible. Routine engagement allows people to come together and form temporary organizations in times of tension. Such organizations, though short-run, turned out to be highly significant. Called peace committees and consist-

ing of members of both communities, these organizations policed neighborhoods, killed rumors, provided information to the local administration, and facilitated communication between communities in times of tension.[14] Such
neighborhood organizations were difficult to form in cities where everyday interaction did not cross religious lines or where Hindus and Muslims lived in
highly segregated neighborhoods. Sustained prior interaction or cordiality allowed appropriate crisis-managing organizations to emerge.

The second mechanism allows us also to sort out why associational forms of
engagement are sturdier than everyday forms in dealing with ethnic tensions. If
vibrant organizations serving the economic, cultural, and social needs of the
two communities exist, the support for communal peace not only tends to be
strong but it can also be more solidly expressed. Everyday forms of engagement
may make associational forms possible, but associations can often serve interests that are not the object of quotidian interactions. Intercommunal business
organizations survive by tying together the business interests of many Hindus
and Muslims, not because neighborhood warmth exists between Hindu and
Muslim families. Though valuable in itself, the latter does not necessarily constitute the bedrock for strong civic organizations.

That this is so is, at one level, a profound paradox. After all, we know that at
the village level in India, face-to-face, everyday engagement is the norm, and
formal associations are few and far between.[15] Yet rural India, which had more
than 80 percent of India's population in the early 1950s and still contains more
than two-thirds of the country's people, has not been the primary site of communal violence. In contrast, even though associational life flourishes in cities,
urban India, containing about one-third of India's population today and less
than 20 percent in the early 1950s, accounts for an overwhelming proportion of
deaths in communal violence between 1950 and 1995.

Why should this be so? Chapter 2 presents a detailed explanation. Informal
engagement may often work in villages in keeping peace, but it does not in
cities, which tend to be less interconnected and more anonymous. Size, it can
be shown, reduces the effectiveness of quotidian interaction. Associations are
critical when village-like intimacy is impossible.

Organized civic networks, when intercommunal, not only withstand the exogenous communal shocks—partitions, civil wars, desecration of holy places
—but they also constrain local politicians in their strategic behavior. If politicians insist on polarizing Hindus and Muslims for the sake of electoral advantage, they can tear the fabric of everyday engagement apart through the organized might of criminals and gangs. In all violent cities in the project, a nexus of

politicians and criminals was in evidence.[16] Organized gangs could easily disturb neighborhood peace, often causing migration from communally heterogeneous to communally homogenous neighborhoods. People moved for the sake of physical safety. Without the involvement of organized gangs, large-scale rioting and tens and hundreds of killings are most unlikely, and without the protection afforded by politicians, such criminals cannot escape the clutches of the law. Brass has rightly called this arrangement an institutionalized riot system.[17]

In peaceful cities, however, an institutionalized peace system exists. When organizations such as trade unions, associations of businessmen, traders, teachers, doctors, lawyers, and at least some cadre-based political parties (different from the ones that have an interest in communal polarization) are communally integrated, countervailing forces are created. Associations that would suffer losses from a communal split fight for their turf, making not only their members aware of the dangers of communal violence but also the public at large. Local administrations are far more effective in such circumstances. Civic organizations, for all practical purposes, become the ears and arms of the administration. A synergy emerges between the local wings of the state and local civic organizations, making it easier to police the emerging situation and prevent it from degenerating into riots and killings. Unlike violent cities where rumors and skirmishes, often strategically planted and spread, are quickly transformed into riots, such relationships of synergy in peaceful cities nip rumors, small clashes, and tensions in the bud. In the end, polarizing politicians either don't succeed or eventually stop trying to divide communities by provoking and fomenting communal violence. Figure 1.1 represents the argument diagrammatically.

This argument, it should be noted, is probabilistic, not law-like. It indicates the odds, but it should not be taken to mean that no exceptions to the generalization would exist. Indeed, pending further empirical investigation, law-like generalizations on ethnic violence may not be possible at all. For example, a state bent on ethnic pogroms and deploying the might of its army may indeed institute veritable ethnic hells. My argument, therefore, would be more applicable to *riots* than to *pogroms* or *civil wars*. A theory of civil wars or pogroms would have to be analytically distinguished from one that deals with the more common form of ethnic violence: riots.

Indeed, perhaps the best way to understand the relationship between civic life and political shocks is to use a meteorological analogy. If the civic edifice is *interethnic and associational,* there is a good chance it can take ethnic earthquakes that rank quite high on the Richter scale (a partition, a desecration of a holy place, perhaps a civil war); if it is *interethnic and quotidian,* earthquakes of

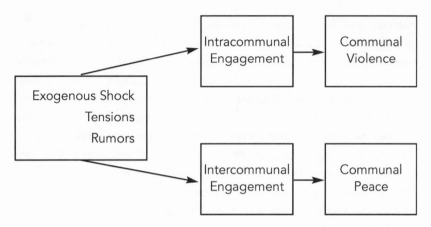

Figure 1.1 Communal Violence and Peace

smaller intensity can bring the edifice down (defeat of an ethnic political party in elections, police brutality in a particular city); but if engagement is only *intraethnic,* not interethnic, small tremors (unconfirmed rumors, victories and defeats in sports) can unleash torrents of violence. A multiethnic society with few interconnections across ethnic boundaries is very vulnerable to ethnic disorders and violence.[18]

Much of the existing literature, as analyzed at length in Chapter 2, focuses primarily on the role of political elites, but it does not assess the role of civic networks in facilitating or constraining elite strategies. Elite behavior is typically explained in two ways. The so-called instrumentalist scholars of ethnic conflict argue that such conflicts are a consequence of the attempts by political leaders to create a winning political coalition, whether or not politicians believe in the intrinsic value of ethnicity. If so, why do politicians polarize communities in some places but build bridges in others, even if it can be shown that polarization will serve their interests? By contending that the politician's efforts to carve out a majority coalition is embedded in the pre-existing institutional framework of politics, the second argument seeks to fill this gap. In multiethnic societies, institutional frameworks—federalism or unitarianism, consociational or liberal democracies, single-member or multiple-member electoral districts, mono- or multiethnic political parties—tend to produce very different political strategies. Some of these systems privilege ethnic accommodation, others favor ethnic polarization. Institutional frameworks can, thus, be linked to communal conflict or peace. Constitutional or institutional engineering matters, predisposing political elites toward predictable forms of behavior.

The argument of this book shifts our attention from political institutions and elites to the structure of civic life. It does so not because institutional designs are irrelevant or politicians do not strive for a winning coalition, but because the same institutional framework of the polity can generate very different maximization drives by politicians. The institutional framework sets up the broad parameters of political strategies, not the actual strategies within a broad cluster permitted by the framework. The same political party, for example, may choose to polarize ethnic communities in one place but not in others, and even if it seeks to polarize, it may not succeed in engendering ethnic divisions. It can be shown that structures of civic life constrain political strategies and their outcomes. Given a thick civic engagement between Hindus and Muslims, polarizing political strategies often fail.

These claims, one might add, are quite analogous to a famous economic debate on international trade, with which a useful comparison can be drawn here. In economics, the theory of comparative advantage is often contrasted with the theory of strategic trade.[19] Given endowments of skills, capital, labor, and natural resources, the comparative advantage theory says, a country will develop specialization in a certain class of goods, but it cannot tell us exactly what goods the country will excel at producing. Using such a theory, one can say that Canada will not develop a specialization in coffee and India in the foreseeable future will not easily export airplanes. But the comparative advantage theory cannot explain why Germany developed an advantage in luxury cars and mechanical engineering and the United States in mass-consumption cars and electrical engineering. The theory is good at a high level of aggregation, not for specific, disaggregated phenomena.

Analogously, consistent with the expectations of the institutionalists, if India's electoral system alone were to shape the strategies of political parties, it would be hard to explain the striking differences in the strategy of the same political party in different cities. Consider the behavior of Hindu nationalists as an illustration. Because their ideology has often questioned the loyalty of Muslims to India and presented India as a Hindu nation, the Hindu nationalists are often associated with Hindu-Muslim tensions and hostilities. In the cities studied in the project, however, they polarize Hindus and Muslims in Aligarh and Hyderabad but not in Lucknow. In the city of Calicut, even when they tried to create long-lasting Hindu-Muslim divisions in the 1920s, they did not succeed. Contrariwise, even though building Hindu-Muslim unity was the ideological centerpiece of the Congress Party in the twentieth century, it can be shown that its politicians have not shied away from a polarizing strategy in the city of Hyderabad or Aligarh. It is not the overall institutional framework of the polity that determined their local behavior, but the structure of local civic life.

How did my project discover the causal role of civic networks? In order to establish causality, a modified technique of "process-tracing" was applied to each pair of cities. Process-tracing works backward from the outcome—peace or violence—step by step, asking what led to what. It can be shown that process-tracing, as applied to one case, may not necessarily establish causality. The argument about the desirability of variance, summed up earlier, is also applicable to why case-based process-tracing can give us history but not necessarily causality. Therefore, a modification was applied to the technique. *In each pair,* we asked whether similar stimuli led to different outcomes in the two cities and then identified the mechanisms that transformed the same trigger into divergent outcomes. Civil society emerged as a causal factor from such comparisons, even though it was not the initial hypothesis. If we had studied only violent cities, where interconnections between Hindus and Muslims were minimal or absent in the first place, we would not have discovered what intercommunal civic links could do. A controlled comparison based on variance, thus, could turn process-tracing into a solid method for establishing causality.

Between 1990 and 1993, when India went through its worst phase of Hindu-Muslim violence since the country's partition in 1947, nasty rumors, tensions, and small clashes between the two communities marked all towns in the project, including the peaceful ones. In the city of Lucknow, a mere 80 miles away from Ayodhya, where the mosque was destroyed in December 1992, symbolically charged and sacrilegious provocations that have regularly precipitated riots in Hyderabad were also tried out by those who wished to instigate riots. A *sadhu* (Hindu holy man) was killed, and a rumor circulated that a Muslim had killed him; it turned out that a Hindu had actually killed the holy man. Pork was thrown into a mosque, presumably to show that Hindus had done it; it was discovered that a Muslim had done it. Events of this type in Hyderabad were woven into the "narrative" of Hindu-Muslim antagonism and used as an occasion by politicians to make provocative speeches, leading to retaliatory violence. In Hyderabad, this pattern has been repeatedly in evidence since the 1970s. In Lucknow, the district administration was able to catch the culprit quickly in each case and present him before his own community, the peace committee, and the press. The trouble-makers in Hyderabad, on the other hand, were rarely caught.

Thus, the same provocations had different outcomes. Why? It is at this point that the value of local networks of intercommunal engagement can be appreciated. As reported at length in Chapter 7, lacking formal contracts, so many Muslims and Hindus are interlocked in daily economic relationships in Lucknow that peace committees at the time of tensions are simply an extension of the pre-existing local networks of engagement. A considerable reservoir of social familiarity is formed out of the daily economic interactions between Muslims and Hindus. Routine interaction facilitates contact between the two communities; rumors are squashed through better communication; and all of this helps the local administration keep peace.

City-level peace committees are ineffective in Hyderabad city. Most Hindus and Muslims do not meet in a civic setting—economic or social—where mutual relations can be formed. One can actually live one's entire life in Hyderabad's old city without spending more than a small amount of time with members of the other community.[20] Lacking political support at the top and networks below, even competent police and civil administrators watch an unfolding riot helplessly. Peace committees, when formed, consist essentially of civic-minded citizens or are imposed from above by the local administration and consist of local politicians already committed to polarization. Such peace committees are effective only in some neighborhoods where everyday contacts between Hindu and Muslims have managed to stay robust despite the remarkable deterioration in Hindu-Muslim relations in the old city. In the city as a whole, such small successes are unable to neutralize the polarizing machinations of politicians and parties.

The other pairs in the project witnessed similar processes. The difference lay in neither the absence of religious identities nor in experiencing tensions, provocative rumors, and small clashes. The presence of the intercommunal networks of engagement was decisive; intracommunal networks did not contain or stop violence.

Endogeneity and the Underlying Causation

Before we accept the argument about the importance of civic engagement, two more questions must be explored. First, how can one be sure that the causes and consequences are not being mixed up in the analysis above? Did communal violence destroy the Hindu-Muslim civic networks in riot-prone towns, or did the presence of such networks prevent riots from occurring? In other words, do we have a case of endogeneity here? Second, process-tracing is good for establishing short-run causality. Is the underlying causation different from proximate causation? Are there historical forces that explain the vitality or absence of civic networks? What emerges if we turn the "independent variable" of the

short-run analysis—civic networks—into a variable to be explained historically?

The city of Surat, the third historically peaceful city in the project, partially
helps us address the problem of endogeneity. In Surat, a nasty riot took place
after the destruction of the Ayodhya mosque. It was the first such riot in nearly
seventy years. An overwhelming proportion of violence, however, was confined
to the slums and shantytowns. The old city witnessed some arson and looting
but no deaths. All deaths during the riots took place in the shantytowns. Subjected to the same stimuli, the pre-existing social networks accounted for the
variance within the city.

Surat has gone through an industrial boom in the past 20 years, becoming
the small industry capital of India. Of the cities having more than a million people, Surat has registered among the highest growth rates in population since
1980. Migrants from within and outside the state have poured into the city and
settled in the shantytowns. Working in small industrial units and unprotected
by the labor laws of the Factory Act, most of these migrants work exceptionally
long hours, returning to the slums and shantytowns only to sleep and eat.
There are few institutionalized settings for building civic ties.

When the mosque came down in Ayodhya in December 1992, the slums
were the site of awful brutality and violence. In the old city, peace committees
were quickly formed. Hindus and Muslims who had lived side by side for years
and had participated in the old city's business and social life came together to
lower tensions. The business associations of Surat are especially integrated.
Their members live primarily in the old city. They were able both to set up
neighborhood watch committees and deploy their own resources in checking
rumors and communicating with the administration. As a result, the local administration was more effective in the old city than in the industrial shantytowns where civic networks were entirely missing and criminals were freely
available for savagery and violence.

What about the long-run causation? Have the Hindu-Muslim civic networks
always been robust in peaceful towns, directing their Hindu-Muslim politics
and making it possible for them to withstand exogenous shocks?

Historical research conducted in the cities demonstrates that civic networks
—associational and quotidian—determined the outcome in the short-to-
medium run, but in the long run intercommunal networks were politically
constructed. Much of India's associational civic structure was put in place in
the 1920s during the freedom movement against the British. That decade was a
transformative moment because mass politics emerged in India under Ma-

hatma Gandhi's leadership. Politics before that was highly elitist. The Congress Party before Gandhi was a lawyers' club, which made constitutional arguments for more rights with the British in the Queen's English.

Gandhi seized control of the movement in 1920 and quietly revolutionized it by arguing that the British were unlikely to give independence to India until the masses were involved in the national movement. Gandhi was not simply interested in political independence from the British but also in the social transformation of India. He argued that independence would be empty unless India's social evils were addressed, drawing attention initially to three primary objectives: Hindu-Muslim unity, abolition of untouchability, and *swadeshi* (buy India, wear Indian, think Indian). To these were later added several other projects of social transformation including women's uplift, tribal uplift, labor welfare, and prohibition. In the process, a whole host of organizations came into being between the 1920s and the 1940s. The associational structure of India before Gandhi was minimal. The foundations of India's associational civic order were laid by the Gandhian shift in the national movement.

The biggest organization, of course, was the Congress Party, which led the movement politically and developed cadres all over India during the 1920s. The argument about social reconstruction also created a second set of organizations, the voluntary agencies. The Congress Party was primarily political, and organizations that dealt with education, women's issues, the welfare of the tribals and "untouchables," self-reliance, and the homespun movement were immediately concerned with their social projects.

The civic order that emerged was not identical in different places. The movement had greater success in forging Hindu-Muslim unity in towns where a Hindu-Muslim cleavage had not already emerged in local politics. India's towns had been having elections for local governments since the 1880s. If local politics emphasized some other cleavages—for example, caste cleavage among the Hindus, or Shia-Sunni divisions among the Muslims—then the Congress Party and Gandhian social workers found it easier to bring Hindus and Muslims together in the local civic life. If, however, Hindu-Muslim differences were the dominant axis of local politics, the national movement could not build integrated organizations with the same success. Once such organizations were put in place, however, they acquired relative autonomy from politics. Depending on how integrated or communal they were, they began to create very different pressures in politics.

To sum up, the role of intercommunal civic networks has been crucial for peace at a proximate level. In a historical sense, however, a space for them was created by forms of mass politics that emerged in the 1920s all over India.[21] Historical reasoning, therefore, requires that we draw a distinction between proximate and underlying causation.

For problems of endogeneity, this reasoning suggests a twofold conclusion, too. In the long run a transformative shift in national politics laid down India's associational civic order. In the short-to-medium run, however, the civic structures put in place by the national movement have in turn been a constraint on the behavior of politicians, for they acquired a life and logic of heir own. Given the thrust of the national movement, the civic constraint on politics was especially serious if building or destroying bridges between Hindus and Muslims was the object of politicians' strategies. The historical lines of causation run from mass movement to civic order to violence or peace.

RESEARCH MATERIALS

The National Level

The large-n analysis of Hindu-Muslim riots is primarily based on a reading of the daily *Times of India,* covering a span of 46 years (1950–95). In case of doubts, reports appearing in other journals were checked. The *Times of India* did have some problems of bias, but these problems, as discussed in Chapter 4, were resolvable.

Moreover, the newspaper was read interpretively, not literally. Newspaper reports do not always distinguish between communal violence, on one hand, and sectarian violence, on the other. At other times, communal riots are simply presented as a clash between two communities. And the term "communal," even if applied correctly, can represent Christian-Hindu clashes, Christian-Muslim violence, or Hindu-Sikh clashes. An interpretive reading of the reports was thus necessary. Unless the labeling of the riot in the newspaper was supported by the description of the symbols and issues involved, to which an interpretive reading was applied, a communal riot was not coded as a Hindu-Muslim riot. Appendix B contains the interpretive protocol used for data classification.

The City Level

Apart from documentary and archival research for the cities, interviews at two levels—elite and cross-section—were conducted. I conducted 25–30 interviews at the *elite* (political, administrative, religious, business, educational) level in each city. To survey the *cross-section* in a methodologically defensible way, a stratified sample of at least 100 households was also drawn for each city.[22] To reach the poor, literacy was used as a principal basis for stratification. Illiteracy is a good proxy for poverty, deprivation, and "subalternity" in India.[23] At least five neighborhoods were then selected in each city—two Hindu-dominated, one violence-prone, the other peaceful; two Muslim-dominated, one violence-prone, the other peaceful; and finally, one or two "mixed" neighborhoods. (In peaceful cities, neighborhoods where tensions recently surfaced replaced the "violence prone" category). Respondents were selected on the basis of literacy. If 50 percent of Muslims and 30 percent of Hindus in the neighborhood were illiterate, the neighborhood sample of 20 interviewees (10 Hindu, 10 Muslim) included 5 illiterate Muslims and 3 illiterate Hindus. This procedure was repeated in all neighborhoods.

A team of two research assistants—one Hindu, one Muslim—was trained in each city, yielding a research team of 12 in six cities. To ensure candor, Muslim respondents were interviewed by Muslim research assistants, and Hindu respondents by Hindus. Each interview was imagined as a two-to-three-hour conversation on questions specified in the questionnaire after rapport had been established through earlier meetings and neighborhood contacts. We thus got more than 700 cross-section interviews in six cities and nearly 130 interviews with elites.

The survey was used for two different purposes. The first was to study Hindu and Muslim attitudes toward politics, administration, police, religion, and history and especially to identify the everyday forms of engagement between the two communities in neighborhoods.

The second purpose was to respond to some standard criticisms of social science research on ethnic conflicts. Unlike works on the functioning of legislatures, executives, and bureaucracies, which typically deal with institutionalized forms of elite politics, research on communalism, ethnicity, and nationalism, which tend to be part of *mass politics,* runs up against a by now popular criticism, especially made by postmodernist critics. The complaint is that even while talking about the masses, our sources on communalism and nationalism end up being highly elitist, or "official." We consult reports of the government. We conduct interviews with a select group of political leaders, educational and religious elites, bureaucrats and police officers. And we read newspapers, which at least in poor countries do not necessarily represent the opinions of the masses. In particular, the use of "official records" on communal violence has been vehemently criticized. It is argued that official records are unreliable, especially when the state itself, both colonial and postcolonial, may be involved, at least partially, as an instigator of communal divisions or violence.[24]

In order to deal with these objections and to collect "unofficial transcripts," I turned my survey, first of all, into a way of collecting brief oral histories on specified questions. This was an unconventional use of survey methods because those who sample rarely collect oral histories, and those who collect oral histories rarely sample their respondents. Forty percent of respondents were more than sixty years of age: the aim was to retrieve local memories of Hindu-Muslim relations in the 1930s and 1940s. Such accounts exist in plenty for the national or the provincial level but not for the town level. Since the city was the unit of analysis in the project, local materials for the 1930s and 1940s had to be created—in part, orally.

Moreover, by using literacy as a stratification principle, I also used the survey to collect the so-called subaltern narratives. Illiteracy, as already argued, is a good proxy for subalternity in India: the illiterate also tend to be very poor. And since much of India is illiterate, a sample stratified according to literacy allowed me access to a substantially large number of illiterate people, especially in the Muslim community, who rarely get interviewed by the newspapers or researchers in a systematic way. To put it differently, through a sampling technique, I sought to "hear the voices of the subaltern," voices that are typically heard by those who focus on one town or one village.[25] If one wants to reach the subaltern in a *multi-town* project, stratified sampling—sampling the same proportion of the subaltern as in the population—is by far the most methodologically defensible way of being representative. To make subaltern voices as authentic as possible, considerable prior rapport was built in order to create a nonthreatening situation for the interviewees.

The survey data have been converted into statistics only where such conversion is more meaningful: for example, in assessing the degree and nature of everyday engagement between communities, or attitudes toward history, personal laws, and administration. Wherever textual summaries were more useful, statistics have not been used.

To sum up, the following kinds of research materials have been used in the study: (1) archival research for historical periods about which historians have not yet written and oral records cannot be created; (2) documentary research for contemporary issues; (3) purposive and focused interviews with the elite in all six cities; (4) stratified survey research for the cross-section, including the illiterate poor, in all towns; and (5) a reading of each day's *Times of India* between 1950 and 1995 to figure out the long-run and large-n distribution of communal violence over a period of 46 years.

THE MODE OF NARRATION

The format of "stylized facts" is a preferred technique of empirical narration in economics, political economy, and security studies. In the analyses of ethnic conflict, this technique does not work well. Concentrating on the "essentials," it tends to present a disembodied and linear narrative, whereas ethnic conflict is neither. For example, violence per se does not have the same meaning in ethnic conflict as do the types of violence, its timing, its targets, and its symbolic significance. Indeed, the dynamics and intensity of ethnic conflict cannot be completely explained unless we understand how decisions are made about which sections of the population should be the targets of violence—women, children, and old people or the able-bodied men; whether festivals and celebrations should be disrupted; whether sacred monuments and places of worship are attacked; whether automatic weapons are used by a few or small weapons by a lot, though each method may kill as many people. We are in a world where considerable planning often goes into the timing, type, and targets of violence, for symbolic violence is often central to ethnic conflict. Ethnicity must be "narrated," and doing so requires more historical and cultural detail than is customary in political economy, economics, and security studies. Heroes, symbols, monuments, and history must form part of the narrative.

The opposite of "stylized facts" is, of course, "thick description," a technique that narrates in splendid detail but is skeptical of cross-case theorization. Believing that we can strike a balance, I use a narrative style that combines the two. I will not present a selection of representative facts first and present the analysis later, as in the stylized facts technique. Rather, the text itself will interweave facts and analysis. Special attention will be paid to issues of symbolic significance: historical events and myths that are anchored or revived in the memory of communities; heroes who acquire the status of legends; monuments that become the focus of collective attention; literature, ceremonies, and festivals that become part of popular culture and folklore. Such analysis requires sensitivity to specific histories of communities and regions.

HOW THE BOOK IS ORGANIZED

Chapter 2 presents some theoretical concerns. Its asks why the existing traditions of inquiry are inadequate for explaining ethnic violence. The literature on ethnicity and nationalism has had four theoretical traditions: essentialism, in-

strumentalism, constructivism, and institutionalism. None of the four traditions accounts for the observed patterns of ethnic violence and peace at the *intra*national level; all seek to explain violence or peace globally or nationally.
Many of the most puzzling features of ethnic conflict cannot be understood
unless we move our analysis below the national level. Explanation at this level
of aggregation requires understanding the patterns of civic life, which tend to
be local or regional.

Chapters 3 and 4 summarize the national trends for political discourse and
Hindu-Muslim violence. Chapters 5 through 11 present materials on the pairs
of cities. Chapter 12 concludes the discussion by situating the findings comparatively and theoretically. It also asks whether interethnic civic networks can be
built afresh or whether they are dependent on historical patterns of ethnic relations.

Chapter 2 Why Civil Society?
Ethnic Conflict and the Existing
Traditions of Inquiry

The existing traditions of inquiry into ethnic conflict can be classified into four categories: essentialism, instrumentalism, constructivism, and institutionalism. All four traditions have a distinguished lineage, but none can account for the local or regional concentrations of ethnic violence. Were India the only country to have such internal variance in the incidence of ethnic violence, we could save the theories by calling India an outlier. But the inapplicability of theories turns out to be more general. Although disaggregated statistics on local or regional dispersions of ethnic violence have not been systematically collected for many countries, the data that we do have—for example, for the United States or Northern Ireland—show roughly the same larger pattern that exists in India.[1] On the whole, ethnic violence tends to be highly *locally or regionally concentrated*, not evenly spread across the length and breadth of the country. Characteristic more of civil wars, a countrywide breakdown of ethnic relations is rare: we tend to form exaggerated impressions of ethnic violence, partly because violence is what attracts the attention of media, not the quiet continuation of routine life. It is more common to have pockets of violence coexisting with large stretches of peace. The inadequacy of all four traditions to account for variance is generic, not specific to India.

In a cumulative spirit of inquiry, we need to take a fifth theoretical step at this stage in our research, a step toward the investigation of links between civil society and ethnic conflict. The virtue of this analytic move is simply that it can explain local or regional variations, whereas the existing traditions do not. Although networks of communities can be built nationally, internationally and, in this electronic day and age, also "virtually," the fact remains that most people experience civic or community life locally. Business associations or trade unions may well be confederated across local units, and business or labor leaders may also have national arenas of operation, but, as members of such organizations, most businessmen and workers in history have been linked to each other on a routine basis in their local chapters. The type and depth of these local networks, whether they bring ethnic communities together or pull them apart, whether the interactions between communities are associational or informal—these are the variables that best explain the patterns of ethnic violence and peace.

I start this chapter with a necessary conceptual clarification between ethnic identity, ethnic conflict, and ethnic violence. In light of this conceptual clarification, I then elaborate on the argument about the inability of existing theoretical traditions to account for the existing patterns of violence and peace. Next I explore the notion of civil society. What aspects of our life should we include in civil society, and what must we exclude? As we shall see, these matters are by no means self-evident. The disputes over how to define civil society have a long and vigorous history. To pre-empt confusion, clarity about what we mean by the term "civil society," especially in the developing world, is necessary. I conclude with a brief conceptual explanation of why certain patterns of civic life contain ethnic violence.

ETHNIC CONFLICT, ETHNIC VIOLENCE,
AND ETHNIC IDENTITY

On the whole, most of the literature has failed to make a distinction between ethnic violence and ethnic conflict. Such conflation is unhelpful. In any ethnically plural society that allows free expression of political demands, some ethnic conflict is more or less inevitable. Indeed, such conflict may be inherent in all pluralistic political systems, authoritarian or democratic. Compared to authoritarian systems, a democratic polity is simply more likely to witness an open expression of such conflicts. The former may lock disaffected ethnic groups into long periods of political silence, giving the appearance of a well-governed society, but a coercive containment of such conflicts also runs the risk, though not the certainty, of an eventual outburst of pent-up frustration when an authoritarian system begins to liberalize or lose its legitimacy. Contrariwise, ethnic conflicts are a regular feature of ethnically plural democracies, for if different ethnic groups exist and the freedom to organize is available, there are likely to be conflicts over resources, identity, patronage, and policies.

The real issue is whether ethnic conflict is violent or is waged in the institutionalized channels of the polity as nonviolent mobilization. If ethnic protest takes an institutionalized form in parliaments, in assemblies, in bureaucracies, or on the streets it is conflict all right, but not violence. Such conflict must be distinguished from a situation in which protest takes violent forms, rioting breaks out on the streets and in the neighborhoods, and in its most extreme form, pogroms are initiated against some ethnic groups with full connivance of state authorities. Given how different these outcomes are, explanations of institutionalized conflict may not be the same as those for ethnic violence and rioting. Further, explanations of rioting may also be different from those for pogroms and civil wars. Ethnic peace should, for all practical purposes, be conceptualized as an institutionalized channeling and resolution of ethnic conflicts. It should be visualized as an absence of *violence,* not as an absence of *conflict.* The world might well be a happier place if we could eliminate ethnic and national conflicts from our midst, but a post-ethnic, postnational era does not seem be in the offing. At least our short-to-medium-run expectations should be better aligned with our realities.

A roughly similar point can be made about the relationship between ethnic identity and ethnic violence. Ethnic identities by themselves do not produce violence; they may coexist with peace conceptualized as above. It is sometimes argued that if ethnic identities could only give way to economic identities, conflicts would be less violent and "civilized." Indeed, "modernization" in the 1950s and 1960s was widely expected to lead to class and occupational differences between human beings, overriding ethnic differences that were deemed relics of a bygone era.[2] Why should economic conflicts be less violent than ethnic conflicts? The underlying intuition is simply that identities tend to be indivisible, whereas a fight over resources is amenable to flexible sharing. If a deal can be struck, splitting shares into a 60-40 or a 65-35 arrangement, a peaceful resolution of conflict is possible. Such bargaining, it is argued, is not possible with respect to ethnicity.[3] With the clear exception of those born of intermarriages,

Christians cannot be turned into half-Jews, and a white person cannot be made half-black. The degrees of freedom being so much lower, clashes based on ethnic identities resist compromise, arouse passion instead of reason, and generate violence.

Is this widely held view correct? It may be right to say that ethnic identities are by and large less amenable to bargaining than are the interests of an economically or occupationally defined collectivity, but we should note that ethnic groups often fight over economic resources, about seats in parliament and schools, about job quotas or affirmative action.[4] Ethnic conflicts, although grounded *in* ascriptive group identities, are not always *about* identities. When ethnic conflicts concern religious laws, places of worship, or icons of special historic and cultural importance, they can indeed be deadly. But when they are about resources, bargains are possible and have often been made in history. At the time of Malaysian independence, the Chinese agreed that, in return for a promise of citizenship and continued Chinese control over the economy, the dominance of the Malays, as sons of the soil *(bhumiputras),* would not be questioned in the polity.[5] In India, after much dithering and political conflict, Delhi agreed in the mid-1950s that the principle of federalism would be linguistic. Each major linguistic group would have a state of its own, while accepting the sovereignty of Delhi. As a result of the agreement, a linguistic reorganization of states took place, which more or less removed what appeared to be a truly violent and seemingly intractable conflict from the political agenda.[6] Such pragmatic bargains are not uncommon in ethnic politics.

All of this is not to suggest that there is no difference between economic groups and ethnic collectivities in politics. The difference is brought out rather clearly when human beings go to extraordinary lengths, including martyrdom, to defend the honor of their ethnic or national group, or when they go on fighting for independence though it is clear that the odds are stacked heavily against them, and independence, if it does come, will come in the very long run, whereas sacrifices will have to be made in the short and the medium run. When the battle is over such matters, the contrast between occupational and ethnic groups can be quite transparent, often distressingly so. Nonetheless, it is worthwhile to remember that ethnic conflicts are not always about identities and are not always violent. And despite having strong ethnic identities, groups can coexist peacefully with others by negotiating and resolving differences in a nonviolent or institutionalized way. To move from ethnic identities to ethnic conflict or to ethnic violence is to make an inadmissible analytic leap. Such leaps have sometimes been made, as we will see below.

EXISTING THEORETICAL TRADITIONS:
WHAT DO THEY EXPLAIN?

Of the four traditions of inquiry identified above, the first two—essentialism and instrumentalism—are set up to explain why ethnic conflicts occur at all, not why they occur when they do and where. Their level of aggregation is almost global: they are deemed to be applicable to all times and all places. The latter two—constructivism and institutionalism—are both more recent and a big advance over the first two. Constructivism explains why *some* ethnic cleavages—black versus white, not Protestant versus Catholic, in the United States; Hindu versus Muslim, not Hindu versus Parsi, in India—become "master cleavages," acquiring remarkable staying power, arousing frequent bitterness, and causing awful violence. But constructivism, as it is practiced, is unable to account for why the *same* cleavage—Hindu-Muslim, black-white, or Catholic-Protestant—is the source of violence in some parts of a country, not in others. Finally, institutionalism, by focusing on the link between types of political institutions on one hand and ethnic conflict and peace on the other, seeks to explain why some political systems manage ethnic conflicts well whereas others do not. Institutionalism also proceeds at a high level of aggregation. It does well when it compares countries having different political systems, but not when it is asked why, within a country, conflict or violence is so unevenly distributed or has so many ups and downs. If political institutions are invariant across the length and breadth of the country, they cannot be the cause of variation across space. A constant cannot explain a variation. Likewise, if they have remained unchanged over time, the ups and down of conflict across time also cannot be explained by looking only at the institutional design.

Essentialism versus Instrumentalism

The debate between essentialists and instrumentalists concerning ethnicity was the first big theoretical axis around which scholars sought to formulate their views and understand the virulence of ethnic animosities and violence.[7] The basic intuition of essentialism is that ethnic conflicts today can be traced back to older animosities between groups; the key proposition of instrumentalism rests on the purely instrumental use of ethnic identity for political or economic purposes by the elite, regardless of whether they believe in ethnicity. The two views are presented as being fundamentally at odds; one focuses on the intrinsic power of ethnic differences, the other concentrates on their instrumental value, political or economic.

This debate has reached a dead end. It leaves too much unexplained, about both ethnic identity and ethnic conflict. Ethnicity can easily combine the two impulses—old animosities can be resurrected—and it can also be a convenient mask for deeper motives. If it is a bit of both and exclusively neither, then the contrast between essentialism and instrumentalism begins to break down.

Essentialism relies on two interconnected arguments, sometimes made together. First, it often refers to primordial or ancient animosities as a cause of contemporary conflict. The animosities are said to be based on inherent differences of race, religion, or culture, and individuals acquire the characteristics of their races, religions, or cultures. Second, it argues that ethnicity inheres in human beings, meaning that all of us inevitably search for, or can easily be made to care for, our ancestry. Either way, conflict results, for a rational calculus is superseded by the emotional ties of blood or by ancient hatreds. Human beings live out not only the positive attributes of the collectivity to which they belong but also its prejudices with respect to other groups. Again and again in history, intrinsic group differences activate prejudices and trigger violence.

More than any other view, this perspective dominates the everyday notions and portrayals of ethnic conflict. Almost any popular account of conflict between Hindus and Muslims, Serbs and Croats, Arabs and Jews, whites and blacks, Catholics and Protestants, Hutu and Tutsi is marked by phrases such as "old animosities," "tribalism," and "ties of blood."[8] In the academic world, too, this view has had its proponents. Clifford Geertz was among the first scholars after World War II to popularize the term "primordialism."[9] More than Geertz, however, Walker Connor has been a leading and consistent advocate of the essentialist view. Man, argues Connor, is a "national, not rational animal." So powerful is the search for origins in human beings that both Adolph Hitler and John Jay, says Connor, were driven to emphasize common ancestry to build their nations. "Blood binds more firmly than business," argued Hitler, and the Americans, contended Jay, are "a people descended from the same ancestors," despite, adds Connor, "the presence of settlers of Dutch, French, German, . . . Scottish and Irish extraction" on American soil in the eighteenth century.[10]

Few scholars subscribe to the essentialist view today. The first problem, and the one most relevant for this book, has already been mentioned. Essentialism makes it hard to explain why, if animosities are so historically deep and so rooted in cultural differences, tensions and violence between groups tend to ebb and flow at different times, or why the same groups live peacefully in some places but fight violently in others.

Another major problem is that essentialism tends not to make a distinction between ethnic (or national) identity on one hand and ethnic (or national) conflict on the other. Both tend to be treated simultaneously. It may well be that for building community feelings, leaders tend to, or have to, emphasize ancestry. Conflict, however, does not necessarily follow. It is one thing to call up an imagined common ancestry *across* ethnic groups, in which case the attempt would be to build bridges. Jay's example would illustrate a bridge-building invocation of an assumed ancestral commonality. It is, however, something quite different to summon the common ties of blood explicitly against an ethnically distinguishable group, in which case the result could well be ethnic hatred and violence. Hitler's attempt would clearly belong to the latter category.

That both Jay and Hitler had to invoke common ancestry implies neither that man is a national animal nor that he is a rational agent—he could be both. Nor do such attempts inevitably re-ignite ancient animosities. If Hindus and Muslims live peacefully in so many cities in India, the reason, I argue in this book, is not that they cease to be who they are in peaceful cities. Rather, despite being Hindus and Muslims, they can have peace. Something other than identity is involved in explaining this pattern. Ethnic or national identity can be a source of meaning and security without implying hatred for another group. These two aspects of ethnic or national identity—positive and negative—are by now well understood and clearly distinguishable.[11]

Instrumentalism is also unable to sort out such variations. It simply argues that building bridges may be in the interest of the political elite at one place and creating cleavages in their interest elsewhere, without showing why interests can be perceived in such dramatically different ways or why the masses should respond to the elite exactly according to the wishes of the elite. If the focus of essentialism is on the intrinsic value of the ties of blood, the emphasis of instrumentalism is on how leaders strategically manipulate ethnicity for the sake of power.[12] This argument has an intuitive appeal because the behavior of many, if not all, political leaders can be cited in support.[13]

The elite may indeed gain power by mobilizing ethnic identity, without actually believing in it, and may therefore behave instrumentally. But if the masses were only instrumental with respect to ethnic identity, why would ethnicity be the basis for mobilization at all? Why do the leaders decide to mobilize ethnic passions in the first place? Why do they think that ethnicity, not the economic interest of the people, is the route to power? And if economic interests coincide with ethnicity, why choose only ethnicity as the central symbol for mobilization?

In principle, an instrumental resolution of these problems exists. Ethnicity can serve as a "focal point" facilitating convergence of individual expectations and hence be useful as a mobilization strategy. The idea of focal points comes from Schelling's seminal treatment of the coordination problem in bargaining. In his famous example: "When a man loses his wife in a department store without any prior understanding on where to meet if they get separated, the chances are good that they will find each other. It is likely that each will think of some obvious place to meet, so obvious that each will be sure that the other is sure that it is obvious to both of them."[14] Ethnicity, in other words, can be viewed as one such focal point for mobilization; it is not valued for its own sake. Some leaders may deploy its potential for mobilization to extract goods and services from the modern sector or to establish power.[15]

The idea of a focal point is not sufficient to explain ethnic mobilization, for it does not distinguish between different kinds of collective action and what their respective costs might be. Ethnic *mobilization* for political action is not the same as ethnic *coordination* for economic and social activities. By providing a social occasion, festivals may indeed bring people together even if not every one appreciates the ritual meaning of celebration or mourning; and by forming mutually converging trust, geographically spread ethnic kinsmen are also known to have supplied credit in long-distance trade without a prior explicit contract between trading partners.

But the analogy of a focal point cannot be extended to group action when the costs of participation for the masses are very high. By its very nature, ethnic mobilization in politics is group action not only in favor of one's group *but also often against some other group.* An increase in the rights and power of one group often means a diminution in the ability of some other group or groups to dictate terms, or it may mean a sharing of power and status between groups where no such sharing earlier existed. Ethnicity in *intra*group social or economic transactions is thus very different from ethnicity in *inter*group political conflicts. The former illustrates the value of ethnicity as a focal point; the latter presents problems of a different order. When an individual provides credit to ethnic brethren without an explicit contract, incarceration, injury, or even death is not the likely cost he bears in mind. Such costs are not unlikely in ethnic or national conflicts.

For something to be manipulated by a leader when death, injury, or incarceration is a clear possibility, it must be valued as a good by a critical mass of people, if not by all.[16] A purely instrumental conception of ethnicity cannot explain why ethnic identities are mobilized by leaders at all.[17]

Constructivism and Postmodernism

Over the past ten to fifteen years, the study of ethnicity has been profoundly influenced by constructivism. In terms of disciplines, going through "the ferment" are "history, anthropology and literature."[18] With the partial exception of political philosophy,[19] political science has paid little attention to this literature. Part of the constructivist inspiration has come from postmodernism, but postmodernists are not the only constructivists. At varying levels, scholars as diverse and "unpostmodern" as Eric Hobsbawm, Linda Colley, and Benedict Anderson have shared the constructivist view, and demonstrated how so many identities that we take for granted today were quite recently constructed in history.[20]

That the formation of ethnic or national identities is a modern phenomenon is what unites constructivism and postmodernism. How exactly such identities come into being, what factors play the most important role, and whether "facts" can be separated from "representations" are the issues that separate them. In the analysis below, I treat them together unless the discussion concerns a matter that divides them.

An important clarification needs to be made before we proceed further. Does the claim that our contemporary identities as Hindus or Muslims, as Jews or Christians, as Tibetans or Han Chinese are modern by any chance mean that there were no Hindus, Muslims, Jews, Christians, Tibetans, and Han Chinese in pre-modern times? Such a claim would obviously be quite absurd, and that is not the constructivist contention. The claim simply is that identities in premodern times tended to be face-to-face and operated on a small scale. Ordinary people rarely interacted beyond their local environments. Conflict, when it emerged, was managed locally, and identities were considerably flexible. Extralocal communities did not include "the people"; such larger communities consisted primarily of the ecclesiastical elite and the court-based aristocracy and nobility.[21]

Modernity changed the meaning of identities by bringing the masses into a larger, extralocal framework of consciousness. It made identities and communities wider and more institutionalized. In what has become a classic constructivist argument, Colley shows how shared Protestantism, opposition to France, and the benefits of empire managed to dissolve the bitter historical disputes between the Scots and the English and led to the construction of a British identity in the eighteenth and nineteenth centuries.[22] And in Benedict Anderson's

Imagined Communities, one of the most influential texts on nationalism today, the emphasis is on how modern technology and a modern economic system—the printing press and capitalism, to be more precise—made it possible to have imaginations about large, popular, and secular communities based on language that overtook the premodern, extralocal, religious communities of clergymen and aristocratic dynasties.

If the modern construction of large, "popular" identities brings constructivists and postmodernists together, their explanation of why and how this comes about separates them. Postmodernism makes a threefold claim: that power relations are deeply implicated in the formation of knowledge;[23] that much of what passes for objective or scientific knowledge, especially in the human sciences, is basically a narrative constructed by the knowledge elite and promoted by the institutions of power; and that such narratives create social, political, and cultural effects of their own. Alternative forms of knowledge were suppressed throughout history, for they were associated with pre-modern ways of knowing and patronized by those who had very little power in society.

What do these highly abstract claims about knowledge have to do with ethnic or national identities? Postmodernists emphasize the construction of group categories by the knowledge elite, its promotion by centers of power, and its effects on "the people." For example, the census, a modern instrument of categorization, would typically ask the masses whether they were (a) Hindu, (b) Muslim, or (c) Christian, even if the masses felt their culture borrowed from all three and their identities were an intersection of (a), (b), and (c). Fuzzy identities, even when real, were not registered as such and were instead split into lucid, modernist categories. Furthermore, if public policy, based on such census groupings, allocated patronage, public offices, or state grants, then the very act of census categorization would begin to create larger identities. This, postmodernists argue, is what happened in the developing world during the colonial period.

Such categorization, according to postmodernists, was not innocent or scientific. The power elite created some categories, not others. The selectivity was based on their preconceptions of what the building blocks of a society were or on a calculation of what divisions would maintain their power. For postmodernists, thus, the only narratives that acquire staying power are those promoted by the elite.

Unpostmodern constructivists disagree. Benedict Anderson would not argue that nationalism as a "master narrative" arose, in the West or elsewhere, merely because it suited the interests of the elite. If anything, he argues that by

involving the masses and posing challenges to the existing dynastic and ecclesiastical elite, nationalism sought to undermine the old order.[24] Modern technologies of imagination are not available only to the knowledge and power elite
but also to the people at large. They can be deployed to construct alternative
ethnicities, alternative nationalities, alternative identities, some of which may
undermine the existing order. The knowledge elite may indeed construct narratives that in turn create newer identities, but the process is not one-way. They
may also have to construct categories and narratives that are closer to ground
realities. Both processes can create enduring national and ethnic identities.

Another critical difference between the constructivists and the postmodernists concerns the possibility of discovering facts in contemporary ethnic
conflict and violence. The latter, say the postmodernists, has become horribly
tangled in discursive "contestations" and politically manipulated "representations." Trivial incidents between *individuals*—a black and a Korean American,
a black and a Jew, a Hindu and a Muslim, an Arab and a Jew—are inserted by
interested organizations and people into the available "master narrative" of antagonism between *groups,* which leads to retaliation, counter-retaliation, and
violence. The real issue here is not what happened but how it was used, or ficti-
tiously produced, given the availability of a narrative of antagonism. It is impossible, say postmodernists, to establish the truth about what happened,
about the cause and effect, in ethnic conflict and violence. Indeed, facts and
representations cannot be separated.[25] The facts necessary to make causal arguments simply cannot be culled from the morass of representations. It follows
that in matters such as identity conflicts, standard social science is impossible.
The best that the social scientist can do is contest the discourses or representations that "harm" the "common people," not seek after facts or causes and effects.

Unpostmodern constructivists do not believe that facts are impossible to
establish or that the insertion of trivial incidents into available prisms of interpretation in many situations is enough to suggest that it can be done everywhere and at all times. Whether facts can be established is an empirical question, not a theoretical one.

With respect to postcolonial societies such as India, the principal constructivist claim is that the major contemporary ethnic cleavages were a creation of
the colonial power and, given the immense power of colonial masters, such divisions have endured and will last for a long time. "Modern colonialism,"
writes one of the best practitioners of the constructivist genre, "instituted enduring hierarchies of subjects and knowledges—the colonizer and the colo-

nized, the Occidental and the Oriental, the civilized and the primitive, the scientific and the superstitious, the developed and the underdeveloped. . . . [T]he colonial rulers enacted their authority by constituting the 'native' as their inverse image . . . not because of the colonizer's bad faith but due to the functioning of colonial power."[26]

Thus, there is no "scientific knowledge" about the origins, rise, and spread of Hindu-Muslim antagonisms; rather, there have only been "discourses" or "narratives."[27] In the hands of the British, a primordial antagonism between Hindus and Muslims dating back centuries became the "master narrative," even though there was evidence of their coexistence.[28] Primordial antagonism was not the "truth" about Hindus and Muslims. It was constructed and promoted as such by the British, partly because it suited them to split India into its two largest religious groups and partly because the natives, argued the British, could not constitute a modern nation—they could think only in terms of pre-modern religious communities. Hindus and Muslims may have existed before the British came to India, but these names did not refer to large, political entities. They only signified small, personal, and village-based cultural entities.

Second, as already stated, the master narrative has over time become the lens through which even small clashes between Hindus and Muslims have been interpreted.[29] Trivial incidents between *individuals* turn into battles between the two *communities,* for these incidents come to be, and have often been, "contextualized" or "represented" in terms of the master narrative, lending excessive rigidity to communal divisions and directly contributing to rising levels of communal violence.[30]

In what ways are these arguments different from essentialism and instrumentalism?[31] Do they advance our understanding of ethnicity or ethnic conflict? What might their pitfalls be? In order to explain the contemporary power of ethnic cleavages, essentialism referred to old animosities or to the pull of ancestry. It was unable to see how the episodes suggesting old animosities might have been selectively retrieved by the knowledge elite, ignoring the many instances of cooperation and coexistence.[32] The argument is also different from instrumentalism. For instrumentalists, ethnicity is basically a mask for a core of interests, and as interests change, so do the masks. Constructivists show why some identities, rooted in popular consciousness, endure and do not easily change. To call such identities masks is to undervalue their endurance and not understand their historical basis. The fact that they are constructed does not mean that they are not *deeply* constructed. Often identities do not change even if interests do.

Is this argument relevant to the problem at hand? Can it explain the regional or local variance in ethnic violence? The basic constructivist argument for ethnic violence in developing countries is that the colonially created master narratives, by making insertions of trivial incidents into those larger narratives possible, lead to violence. The explanation provided for the formation of ethnic *identity* is thus also extended to ethnic *violence*. Whatever one may say about the constructivist explanation for modern identity-formation, its extension to violence does not make sense. Hindus and Muslims in the peaceful cities studied in this project were just as sure of their identities as were the Hindus and Muslims in the violent cities. The same incidents that were inserted into the communal narrative and led to violence in riot-prone cities were managed quite well by the peaceful cities.

If it is true that ethnic violence tends to be unevenly distributed and pockets of violence coexist with vast stretches of peace, then invoking the ubiquitous power of a systemwide, nationwide master narrative as an explanatory device will not do. Either there are several master narratives in a country, one hegemonic in some regions and others powerful elsewhere, or some other locally based factors intervene between the potential power of narratives to cleave society and generate violence and the actually observed patterns of violence.

To conclude, by focusing on specific histories in an attempt to explain why some ethnic cleavages acquire political and emotional salience and become master cleavages in the process, the constructivist arguments have advanced our understanding of the macrocontexts of ethnic conflict and peace. But by failing to deal with variance across time and space, they have left unresolved the local issues, whose autonomy appears not to be flattened entirely by the larger forces. Something intervenes between the master narratives and actual violence, skewing the patterns and making it impossible to read off violence from the macrocontexts. That civic life constitutes that variable is the main argument of this study.

Institutionalism

In the literature available so far, the institutional arguments are best able to deal with why ethnic conflicts emerge, subside, or remain dormant. These are also arguments that, unlike constructivism, have flourished in political science. The central idea of the institutional theories of ethnic conflict is that there are clearly identifiable connections between ethnic conflict or peace, on one hand, and political institutions, on the other. It matters whether multiethnic societies have consociational or majoritarian democracies, federal or unitary governments, single- or multi-member constituencies, proportional representation or a first-past-the-post electoral system. Each of these institutional alternatives can be shown to be linked to ethnic peace or violence.

Ethnic pluralism, it is argued, requires political institutions—forms and rules of power-sharing, types of constituencies, varieties of voting systems, party systems—different from those that are appropriate for ethnically homogeneous, or at any rate ethnically undivided, societies. An uncritical transference of institutional forms regardless of whether a society is marked by ethnic divisions can be a serious cause of ethnic conflict. Contrariwise, an institutional choice suited to the ethnic map of a society resolves, or at any rate mitigates, conflict.

Institutions do not simply specify procedures, rules, and sites for political contestation; they also begin to generate predispositions to outcomes, given the number and size of ethnic groups. If there are only two ethnic communities in a country, if the minority community is more or less evenly distributed across constituencies, if voting takes place entirely on grounds of ethnicity, and if a first-past-the-post system exists, then it can be easily demonstrated that even a minority as large 40–45 percent of the population, constituting a plurality, can be entirely excluded from political representation. Such a majoritarian system is very likely to produce a permanent and sullen minority community. Much passionate conflict, even violence, can be expected.

The lineage of such reasoning goes back to the simple but influential formulations of John Stuart Mill. Considering the political and ethnic context of the nineteenth century, Mill had argued that multiethnic societies did not need and could not successfully have a British-style democracy. He believed that for a democracy to function a nation must exist, by which he meant common loyalty to a political center. A multiethnic society, he contended, must be subjected to the tutelage—including, if necessary, colonial tutelage—of a "civilized" or more politically advanced ethnic group; otherwise order could not be maintained and ethnic conflicts would repeatedly break out. Whether India under the British, the Bretons and the Basques in France, or the Scots and the Welsh under English tutelage, the problem was similar and the same principles of tutelage by the superior group would apply, at least until such time as a civic consciousness aimed toward a political center, not an ethnic group, was born: "Nobody can suppose that it is not beneficial to a Breton or a Basque of the French Navarre to be brought into the current of ideas and feelings of a highly civilized and cultivated people—to be a member of the French nationality . . . than to sulk on his own rocks, the half-savage relic of past times, revolving in his own little mental orbit, without participation or interest in the general movement of the world. The same remark applies to the Welshman or the Scottish Highlander, as members of the British nation."[33]

Few would support colonial tutelage today, but the arguments about whether multiethnic societies can or should have British-style majoritarian democracies continue to reverberate. Indeed, theories proposing a link between institutional forms and ethnic conflict have acquired remarkable sophistication in the past three decades. There are disputes in this literature, but they are about what kinds of political institutions would resolve or exacerbate conflict in multiethnic societies. That identifiable links between institutions and ethnic conflict exist is either considered self-evident or not seriously questioned.

Of the many arguments in the field, those of Arend Lijphart and Donald Horowitz tower over the institutional landscape.[34] Lijphart's lifelong work is associated with a novel idea in political science: that of consociationalism.[35] Though the idea itself has gone through several versions, the basic thesis remains unchanged.[36] Lijphart argues that, in order to be successful and to preempt or reduce ethnic conflict, democracy in a plural society requires elite compromise. A plural society is defined as one in which the various ethnic groups are segmented and have little criss-crossing. Elite compromise can best be assured by a political system that works on intergroup consensus, not intergroup competition. A consensual democracy of this kind can be called *consociational*. It has four features: a grand coalition of ethnic leaders in government, a mutual veto given to each, group proportionality in decision-making positions, and segmental autonomy with respect to matters such as education, language, and personal laws. The small European democracies of Austria, the Netherlands, Belgium, and Switzerland were the key empirical referents for Lijphart.

Calling this institutional scheme more a normative wish than an empirically sound generalization, Horowitz argues that grand coalitions cannot work well if they are not grounded in electoral incentives. The elite should have an incentive to compromise on ethnic matters. If a system requires statesmanship on the part of the elite, it makes too great a demand for its success. Most political leaders, says Horowitz, are neither statesmen nor capable of statesmanship. Making it impossible for political parties to win power unless they make appeals across ethnic barriers is the best institutional intervention in an ethnically divided society. Horowitz's best example is the Malaysian political system, which creates incentives for elite compromise (and he proposes a roughly similar system for post-apartheid South Africa).[37] The exact institutional proposal will, of course, differ, depending on how many groups exist in a society and how segmented and cohesive they are. But, he believes, the principle of "electoral incentives for ethnic compromise" can guide us well.

That the institutional literature has advanced our understanding of ethnic conflicts is beyond doubt. In a multiethnic society in which ethnic groups are geographically concentrated, greater federalism, for example, can indeed be shown to be more appropriate for ethnic peace than a unitary political system. But the institutionist view does run into a problem.

If the political system and institutions are the same right across the length and breadth of the country, institutional arguments cannot by definition account for why *different parts of a country* tend to have very different patterns of ethnic violence and peace. Using national-level concepts and analysis, we can, in principle, explain why country A, rather than country B, tends to have more ethnic violence, but we can't explain the regional or local variations within the same country. For an institutional explanation of local or regional variance to work, the electoral designs or political institutions must themselves vary locally or regionally. If a whole polity is either majoritarian or consociational, or the electoral system throughout the nation is first-past-the-post or based on proportional representation, then our explanation will have to move to a lower level of aggregation. Likewise, we cannot understand the causes of national-level variations across time in a given country if the political institutions in that country do not change—from unitary to federal, for example, or from majoritarian to consociational. Something other than the institutional configuration of the polity will be necessary to account for variations in violence over time.

Let me summarize the basic argument made in this section. Pitched at a high level of aggregation, the four existing traditions of inquiry into ethnic conflict are either unable to account for variance per se, as is true of essentialism and instrumentalism, or have not dealt with variance below the national level, as is the case with constructivism and institutionalism. These traditions also tend not to make a distinction between conflict and violence. Conflict is not necessarily violent. It can take an institutionalized form if ethnic demands for higher political representation, affirmative action, or personal laws are pursued in assemblies, elections, bureaucratic corridors, and nonviolent movements and protests. Finally, although in principle these traditions would distinguish between ethnic identity and ethnic violence, in practice they often do not. If ethnic violence is to be explained, it is assumed that ethnic identity has already been formed, whereas it can be shown that conflict itself is identity-shaping and may have been created for that reason by ethnic partisans. Contrariwise, sometimes explanations for identity-formation are plausibly given, as by constructivists, but it does not follow that conflict thereby would inevitably result. For greater progress in our understanding of ethic conflicts, we need to go beyond these theories. We not only need systematically to compare cases of peace with those of violence, but also to move analysis below the national level of politics. We need variance as well as greater disaggregation in our analytic categories.

CIVIL SOCIETY: WHY, WHAT, AND HOW

Civil society is the missing variable in all available traditions of inquiry. If included, it begins to explain, as essentialism could not, why "long-run" animosities do not embitter relations between the same ethnic groups everywhere: why, for example, in Northern Ireland, civic interconnections between the Protestants and Catholics make the community of Dunville peaceful, but in Kileen/ Banduff and in the Upper Ashbourne Estates, where there is virtually no interaction between these groups, violence is frequent.[38] Civic links, if they exist between ethnic groups, also resolve the unanswered puzzle of instrumentalism, namely, why, even though political elites may try to use ethnicity for political purposes and wish to cleave societies along ethnic lines, they are unable to do so everywhere. In fact, they may not find such efforts sensible at all, and may instead put together winning coalitions in non-ethnic ways. If the electorate is interethnically engaged, the politicians may be unable and unwilling to polarize. And finally, depending on the nature of civic life, the link between ethnic conflict and institutional designs, on one hand, and the connection between ethnic violence and master narratives, on the other, breaks down. Civic engagement between communities tends to be local or regional, whereas the existing traditions of inquiry are national or global. Without an investigation of civic life, the power of long-standing hatreds, of the political elite, of political institutions, and of master narratives can be overstated.

If it is so critical to group relations, what kinds of interactions and links between citizens would constitute civic life? And how exactly does civil society contribute to peace or conflict?

Civil Society: Purposes or Forms?

The concept of civil society, though highly popular and much revived in recent years, remains intensely contested. According to the conventional notions prevalent in the social sciences, "civil society" refers to the space in a given society that (a) exists between the family level and the state level, b) makes interconnections between individuals or families possible, and (c) is independent of the state. Many, though not all, of the existing definitions also suggest two more requirements: that the civic space be organized in *associations* that attend to the cultural, social, economic, and political needs of the citizens and that the associations be modern and voluntaristic, *not ascriptive.* Going by the first requirement, trade unions would be part of civil society, but informal neighborhood associations would not. And following the second requirement, philately clubs and parent-teacher associations would be civic but not an association of Jews in defense of Israel or a black church.[39]

Should we agree with the latter two requirements? Can nonassociational space also be called civic or part of civil society? Must associations, to form part of civil society, be of a "modern" kind—voluntaristic and cross-cutting rather than ascriptive and based on ethnic affiliations? These questions are not simply theoretical. In many societies, group-based but informal activities—sports, entertainment, festivals—are often part of the space between the state and family life. And the same is true of ethnic associations, whether they are black churches in the United States, right-wing Jewish groups in Israel, or an exclusively Hindu group such as the Vishva Hindu Parishad (VHP), existing both in India and in the Indian diaspora all over the world. All of these groups would meet the first definition of civil society, but none would meet the second. Are they part of civil society or not? Why should informal but group-based activity of citizens be excluded from civil society? Why should ethnic or religious associations not be included?

A great deal of controversy exists on these points. Both informal and ascriptive activities are considered by many leading civil society theorists to be traditional, whereas civil society is modern. The modernity of civil society is, of course, quickly qualified, since not all modern political systems have civil societies. Attacking ascriptive hierarchies and privileges, undermining religion, and instituting a secular order, Communist polities were modern, but the state penetrated all sites of organizational life: hospitals, universities, operas, theater, and literary societies. When Tomas, the doctor hero of a Milan Kundera novel, published a short essay criticizing the bureaucratic structures of his Prague hospital, a hospital administrator gave him the choice of quitting surgery altogether or withdrawing the article and issuing an apology for straying from the ideologically correct Communist path in the 1960s Prague.[40] Kundera's hero, of course, was not entirely fictional. Most observers of Communist societies recognized the realism of the situation. Its civil society humbled and infirm, the state in Communist Czechoslovakia was all-powerful, decimating freedom of expression as well as the institutions that might allow such freedoms. Modernity is a necessary but not a sufficient precondition for the rise of civil society.

The modernist origins of civil society were originally attributed to Hegel's nineteenth-century theoretical formulations.[41] In recent years, however, the revival of a modernist notion of civil society, it is often suggested, is due to debates in eastern Europe and the English translation of Habermas's *The Structural Transformation of the Public Sphere*.[42] Because the concept of civil society has been so important to political philosophers, they have been its primary explorers in recent times.[43] In comparison, although the need for it should be quite clear, analytic work on civil society in the more empirical fields of the social sciences has not been as voluminous.[44] Only a systematic empirical investigation of the associational and nonassociational forms of civic life can show whether the functions and forms normally attributed to them in the normative literature are also actually observable.

Normative conceptualizations are, of course, not confined to political philosophy. A normative tenor marks scholarship on civil society as a whole. Consider Ernest Gellner, whose writings on the subject have been plentiful as well as influential. "Modularity," argues Gellner, "makes civil society," whereas "segmentalism" defines a traditional society.[45] By "modularity" Gellner means the ability to rise beyond traditional or ascriptive occupations and associations. Given a multipurpose, secular, and modern education, and given the objective availability of plentiful as well as changing professional opportunities in posttraditional times, modern man can move from one occupation to another, one place to another, one association to another. In contrast, birth assigned occupation and place to traditional man. A carpenter in traditional society, whether he liked it or not, would be a carpenter, and all his kinsmen would be carpenters. He would also not generally be involved in an association; and if he were, it would most likely be an ascriptive guild of carpenters. In such a "segmental" or traditional society, freedom of will with respect to associations, occupations, or places of living would neither be available nor encouraged, and an ethnic division of labor would exist. An agrarian society, argued Gellner, might be able to avoid the tyranny of the state for, in view of the decentralized nature of the production structure, the low level of communication technology, and the relatively self-sufficient character of each segment, the power of the state would not be able to reach all segments of a traditional society. But that does not mean that such a society would be "civil," for instead of a "tyranny of the state" it would experience a "tyranny of cousins": "It thrusts on to the individual an ascribed identity, which then may or may not be fulfilled, whereas a modern conception of freedom includes the requirement that identities be chosen rather than ascribed."[46] Civil society, concludes Gellner, is not only modern but also based on strictly voluntary, not ethnic or religious, associations between the family and the state.[47]

Traditional "Tyranny of Cousins" Versus Modern "Civility"?

Both empirically and conceptually, there is an odd modernist bias in the formulations above. Tradition is considered intolerant and incorrigible beyond redemption. And modernity is assumed to promise and deliver such a great deal that much that may be valuable and highly flexible in tradition, including pluralism, is simply defined out of consideration, and much that may be subversive of free will and "civility" in capitalist, if not socialist, modernity is also, by definition, ruled out of court. Even if choral societies in twelfth-century northern Italy were making it possible for people to connect, their inclusion in civil society *before the rise of modern capitalism,* according to this perspective, is unwarranted.[48]

Each of the major claims in the modernist conception of civil society can be empirically challenged. First, the argument that ethnic or religious associations are ascriptive is only partially correct. A remarkably large number of studies, both in the West and in the developing world, show that ethnic and religious associations combine ascription and choice. Not all Christians have to be members of a church in a given town; not all blacks in a neighborhood are members of a black church; not all members of a caste or linguistic group have to participate in a caste or linguistic association. Moreover, it has also been widely documented that ethnic associations can perform many "modern" functions, such as participating in democratic politics, setting up funds to encourage members of the group to enter newer professions, and facilitating migration of kinsmen into newer places for modern occupations and modern education.[49]

Many ethnic associations are undoubtedly bigoted with respect to outgroups as well as tyrannical to their own cousins, but that does not exhaust the range of ethnic organizations or the variety of ethnic activities. In many societies in which ethnic groups are arranged hierarchically and some ethnic groups have historically faced prejudice, the ethnic associations of such groups are known to have been among the most effective organizations to fight for ethnic equality in the workplace, politics, and schools.[50] A large number of Jewish associations in the United States, "lower-caste" organizations in India, Moroccan and Algerian groups in France, and black organizations in contemporary South Africa have performed such roles with considerable distinction, if not always with great success. Similarly, many churches and religious organizations—for example, in Poland and Latin America—are known to have fought the state for democracy and freedom. The forms of association may have been traditional, but the goals pursued were highly modern.

Taking pride in one's ethnic group and working for the group does not, ipso facto, make one "uncivil." It matters what the aim of such ascription-based group activity is. That is not a theoretical but an empirical question. Paradoxically for Gellner, modularity for their group is what many ethnic associations may seek, realizing how important it has become to leave traditional callings and move to modern occupations. Moreover, the ethnic form of association may also be based on a highly modern consideration: low transaction costs. It is less difficult to get people together on grounds of similarity than difference, and once such association is formed, perfectly modern goals may be pursued: making organized but nonviolent demands on the political system, teaming up with organizations of different groups to make a "rainbow coalition" in politics, providing support for entrepreneurship in their community.[51]

In short, the idea that ethnicity or religion is equal to traditionalism and therefore can't perform the functions of civic organizations—allowing people to come together, making public discussion of issues possible, challenging the caprice or misrule of state authorities, promoting modern business activities— has too many exceptions to be considered empirically admissible. Whatever one may think of ethnic associations in general, at least the ethnic associations that meet the functional or purposive criteria specified by normative arguments should be considered part of civil society.

A similar objection can be raised with respect to informal associations or activities. In much of the developing world, especially in the countryside and the small towns, formal associations simply do not exist. That, however, does not mean that civic interconnections or activities are absent. The sites of civic interactions range from the generally predictable—in that such sites made a public sphere possible in eighteenth- and nineteenth-century Europe as well—to the highly particular and culturally specific. The predictable sites are the neighborhood or village commons, the playground, the halls for entertainment and community functions. Group interaction is not confined to them, however, and may also mark some culturally specific sites: the festival venues where people not only participate in a religious activity but also build connections for secular purposes such as politics; the sidewalks where those returning from work habitually walk together and talk, not simply about the weather but also about organizational structures in the workplace, markets, films, festivals, and politics; the village pond where women not only wash clothes and exchange views about families but discuss schoolteachers, landlords, and village politics; the milkman's depots where men and women buy milk each morning as well as talk about children, relatives, local government, cultural trends, and national politics; the only television center of a neighborhood or village, where families come together to watch news, stories and films; and in societies in which alcohol drinking is not frowned on, the village or neighborhood pub where people socialize, discuss, make friends, and connect with one another.[52]

In the 1930s, a major civic movement in southern India, leading to "reading rooms" in the state of Kerala and turning later into a statewide library movement, was born in the neighborhood tea shops, where people used to come together in the evening, read newspapers jointly, and comment on politics and culture. Watching how many cups of tea were consumed over intense discussions, the tea-shop owners would, of course, be delighted by the business that emerged as a result, but the small groups would also find a common public site for discussion as well as fun. Newspapers in the 1930s were expensive: only a few could buy newspapers individually.[53] Sites of this kind may not be associated with formal organizations, immediately or ever, but they allow people to perform many of the activities that formal civic organizations do: connect, talk, share views, formulate strategies for school exams and local politics, and develop a perspective not only on local but also extralocal politics.[54] Indeed, popular, as opposed to elite, culture often takes this form in many parts of the developing world.[55]

If what is crucial to the notion of civil society is that families and individuals connect with others beyond their homes and talk about matters of public relevance without the interference or sponsorship of the state, then it seems far too rigid to insist that this takes place only in "modern" associations. Empirically speaking, whether such engagement takes place in associations or in the traditional sites of social get-togethers depends on the degree of urbanization and economic development, as well as on the nature of the political system. Cities tend to have formal associations, but villages make do with informal sites and meetings. Further, political systems may specify which groups have access to formal civic spaces and may form organizations and which ones may not. Nineteenth-century Europe provided the propertied classes access to a whole range of political and institutional instruments of interest articulation; trade unions for workers, however, were slower to arrive.

Some of the spirit of these remarks is conveyed in the commentary generated by Habermas's distinction between the "lifeworld" and the "system" in *The Structural Transformation of the Public Sphere*. In its original formulation, the distinction indicated a radical rupture between the significance of everyday interaction and interaction made possible by institutions and organizations. The latter, according to Habermas, was associated with the modern public sphere. Everyday interaction, as it were, made life, but organized interaction made history.[56] The new history written about the popular struggles of women, peasants, workers, and minorities—those not formally admitted to the public sphere in much of nineteenth-century Europe and America—suggests the limited utility of Habermas's distinction.[57] Indeed, in his more recent positions, Habermas has all but dropped the radical distinction he drew earlier.[58] Street-corner activity can now be viewed as a serious civic form as well, if more organized and institutional civic sites are not available—generally or to some specific groups.

The point, of course, is not that formal associations do not matter. Compared to everyday forms of engagement, as I argue in this book, associations are undoubtedly a much more robust form of sustained and effective civic interaction between individuals. Associations do not exist everywhere, however, for the need for formal associations is not obvious, nor access to them universal. An absence of associations stops neither villages nor the subaltern from participating in a public or political discourse. Nor, in the absence of modern associations, do disputes in the villages turn into violence more often. Indeed, rural India, as reported in the previous chapter, was the site of less than 4 percent of all deaths and roughly 10 percent of all Hindu-Muslim riots in India between 1950 and 1995. Peace was maintained not because of associations but because everyday civic engagement between Hindus and Muslims was enough to keep potential rioters away. In cities, however, such everyday engagement was not enough, and associations were required.

When villages become towns, towns turn into cities, and cities are transformed into metropolises, people begin to travel long distances for work, face-to-face contact is typically not possible beyond neighborhoods, and associations become necessary not only for civil peace but also for many economic, social, and political aims and interactions. We should not look for associations where the need for them is not pressing or where access to them is difficult for some groups. We should, instead, look at the alternative civic sites that perform the same role as the more standard civic organizations do.

To conclude, at least in the social and cultural settings that are different from Europe and North America, if not more generally, the purposes of activity rather than the forms of organization should be the critical test of civic life. Tradition is not necessarily equal to a tyranny of cousins, and capitalist modernity does not always make civic interaction possible. At best, such dualities are ideal types or are based on normatively preferred visions. Empirically speaking, tradition can often permit challenging the cousins if existing norms of reciprocity and ethics are violated. Similarly, even capitalist modernity may be highly unsocial and atomizing if people in inner-city America stay at home and watch MTV instead of forming neighborhood watch groups or attending to the abandoned children's homes.[59] Informal group activities as well as ascriptive associations should be considered part of civil society so long as they connect individuals, build trust, encourage reciprocity, and facilitate exchange of views on matters of public concern—economic, political, cultural, and social. While doing all of this, they may well be connected with interethnic violence, though intraethnic peace may be maintained. But that is to be established empirically. Theoretically, one should not assume that ethnic associations promote tyranny of cousins or interethnic violence.

TYPES OF ENGAGEMENT
AND ETHNIC CONFLICT

Having clarified the notion of civil society used in this book, let me now proceed to indicate the links between ethnic conflict and civic engagement, both everyday and associational. In the materials presented and analyzed below, it is civic engagement across ethnic groups that turns out to be critical, not civic engagement per se. *Inter*ethnic or intercommunal engagement makes for peace, not *intra*ethnic or intracommunal engagement.[60] Intercommunal engagement leads to the formation of what might be called institutionalized peace systems. Engagement, if only intracommunal, is often associated with what Paul Brass calls institutionalized riot systems.[61]

Mechanisms of Violence and Peace

On the whole, two links can be specified between civic life and ethnic conflict. First, prior and sustained contact between members of different communities allows communication between them to moderate tensions and pre-empt violence, when such tensions arise owing to an exogenous shock—a riot in a nearby city or state, distant violence or desecration reported in the press or shown on television, rumors planted by politicians or groups in the city in order to arouse communal bitterness and passions, or a provocative act of communal mischief by the police, thugs, or youth. In cities of thick interaction between different communities, peace committees at the time of tension emerge *from below* in various neighborhoods; the local administration does not have to impose such committees on the entire city *from above*. Because of mutual consent and involvement, the former is a better protector of peace than the latter. Such highly decentralized tension-managing organizations kill rumors, remove misunderstandings, and often police neighborhoods. If prior communication across communities does not exist, such organizations do not emerge from below. They are typically imposed from above and do not work well because their politician members, though inducted for purposes of peace, may in fact already be committed to polarization and violence for the sake of electoral benefit. Their presence on peace committees is often merely notional.

Second, in cities that have associational integration as well as everyday integration, the foundations of peace become stronger. In such settings, even politicians who would, in theory, benefit from ethnic polarization find it hard to engender ethnic cleavages, arouse widespread bitterness, and instigate violence. Without a nexus between politicians and criminals, big riots and killings are highly improbable. If unions, business associations, middle class associations of doctors and lawyers, film clubs of poorer classes,[62] and at least some cadre-based parties are integrated, even an otherwise mighty politician-criminal nexus is unable to rupture existing links. Everyday engagement in the neighborhoods may not be able to stand up to the marauding gangs protected by powerful politicians, but the organized strength of unions, associations, and the integrated cadres of some political parties—those not interested in ethnic conflict—constitute a forbidding obstacle for even politically shielded gangs. When associational integration is available, the potential space of destructive and violent action simply shrinks.

Civic links across communities have a remarkable local or regional variation. Depending on how different communities are distributed in local businesses, middle-class occupations, parties, and labor markets, they tend to differ from place to place. As a result, even when the same organization is able to create tensions and violence in one city or region, it is unable to do so in another city or region where civic engagement crosses communal lines. Local and regional

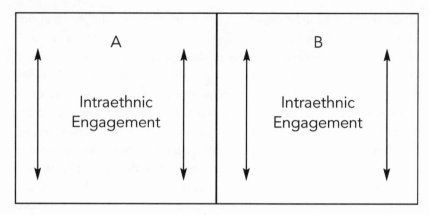

Figure 2.1 Segmented Ethnic Distribution

variation in ethnic violence, its uneven geographical spread, is thus a function of civic engagement, which tends to vary locally or regionally.

These findings significantly change our existing understanding of ethnic conflict. The basic insight, in its simplest form, is diagrammatically represented in figures 2.1 and 2.2. Figure 2.1 contains a raw ethnic distribution of a population, containing two groups, A and B. All existing theoretical traditions have taken A and B as units of their analysis. In essentialism, demographic distributions are carved in stone and, once rolled, have a colliding and destructive momentum of their own. In instrumentalism, ethnic demographic ratios are used by maximizing politicians for putting together winning electoral coalitions. In

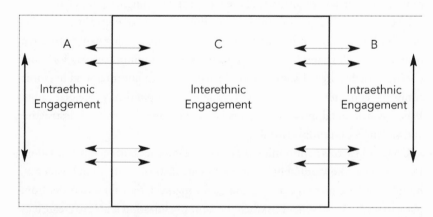

Figure 2.2 Interconnected Ethnic Distribution

constructivism, they are fixed by the colonial power into rock-like solidity, even though centuries earlier fuzziness poured through them, and once given fixity, their effect is the same as in essentialism. And, finally, in institutionalism, these ratios are the basis for judging the peace-making or conflict-engendering properties of political institutions. A consociational system assumes that groups A and B not only exist but are segmental—that is, they primarily interact internally, not across groups. And, finally, a vote-pooling system, à la Horowitz, also assumes that A and B are given, that electoral politics would move along ethnic lines, and that electoral schemes should be created that will make pooling a large fraction of A and B attractive.

Figure 2.2 represents the same ethnic distribution with interethnic civic engagement. Civic engagement shrinks the *effective* size of A and B by making an intersection, C, possible. The latter represents the interconnected space constituted by links across large parts of A and B, a space where incentives and benefits of togetherness as well as fellow-feelings change behavior mapped by the pure, intracommunal case of A and B to a common C. It is no longer necessary to think of electoral schemes for pooling A and B, for A and B already have a large *civic* pool, which is likely to make polarization an unattractive political strategy.

This simple diagram should also indicate that the size of C matters. The larger the C, the lesser the incentives for polarization. Thus, mass-based interethnic organizations, such as trade unions and political parties, are a sturdier civic agent of peace than elite-based organizations, such as Lions Clubs, Rotary Clubs, poetry-reading societies, and philately groups. Similarly, interethnic associations of traders and small businessmen may be more effective than elite chambers of commerce and industry. Chapters 7 and 8 present empirical evidence supporting this claim.

This size-based argument, however, may have to be modified if size is multiplied by resources. Chambers of commerce and industry can deploy their vast resources in informal activities that build bridges by sponsoring cultural festivals, building physical infrastructure in a city, or creating entertainment halls and community centers. Depending on what these activities entail—whether they bring together people of only one community or of many—civic organizations that are small but rich can facilitate a large-scale informal engagement across ethnic communities. Although not as solid an instrument of peace as organizational association, such activities can nonetheless create a larger base of interethnic engagement.

Everyday Engagement,
Associational Engagement

A final question remains. A key argument of this book, already briefly stated, is that associational engagement is a sturdier bulwark of peace than everyday engagement, and although the latter may keep peace in villages, it is rarely enough in the cities. Associations can more easily counter the depredations of politically protected gangs than everyday neighborhood engagement.

Let me give a formal proof for this qualitative argument. In figure 2.3, the relation between size and civic links has been diagrammatically represented,

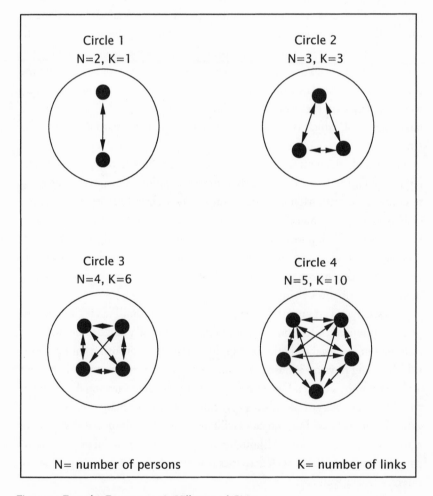

Circle 1
N=2, K=1

Circle 2
N=3, K=3

Circle 3
N=4, K=6

Circle 4
N=5, K=10

N= number of persons

K= number of links

Figure 2.3 Everyday Engagement in Villages and Cities

holding the level of civic engagement constant. How many links will have to be made if we wish to connect each individual with every other individual as we move from villages to cities? Let N represent the number of persons in a village or city and K the number of links that must be made if everybody is to be connected with everyone else. Moving from circle one to four, we can see why associational engagement is necessary in cities.

The four circles in the diagram *increase the size* of the local setting. In circle 1, our diagrammatic representation for a small village, there are only two individuals (N=2); to connect them, we need only one link (K=1). In circle 2, representing a small town, there are three individuals (N=3); we need at least three links (K=3) to connect them all. Circle 3, in which we have four individuals (N=4), can be called a city. We need six links (K=6) if we wish to connect one with all. In circle 4, our diagrammatic substitute for a metropolis, we have five individuals (N=5), and we will need at least ten links (K=10) to connect each of them to everybody else. It would, therefore, appear that, *for a given level of civic density* (in this case, each person connected to everyone else), K rises faster than N. Given density, the number of links rises faster than the number of persons. This whole relationship can be written as follows: $K = N(N-1)/2$.

This formula essentially means that as we move from villages to towns and from towns to cities, compared to the absolute increase in the population, we need many more links to connect the people. This obviously means that cities tend naturally to be less interconnected, and some degree of anonymity and unconnectedness is inevitable.

Since each association or organization can represent a lot of people, organizations end up reducing N in cities and making a lower K viable. That is why everyday engagement may be effective in villages, with smaller Ns, but not in cities, with larger Ns. In order to maintain the same level of civic engagement found in villages, we need associations in cities, not informal and everyday interaction.

CONCLUSIONS

To recapitulate, three arguments have been made in this chapter. First, the four available traditions of inquiry into ethnic conflict are unable to explain the patterns of ethnic violence and peace, which happen to be regional or local, whereas the existing theoretical explanations are set up on a national or global level of aggregation. We need to move from the global or macro to the local, not because the macro factors do not matter but because the local issues have been inadequately understood. Civil society, which by and large tends to be local or regional, is the missing variable in available theories, to which students of ethnic conflict should pay increasing attention. Much that we find puzzling about ethnic violence is explicable if we investigate links between civil society and ethnic conflict. Second, as we take this new theoretical step, the notion of civil society existing in much of the literature must be re-examined. We will go wrong if we expect, especially as we research postcolonial societies with large agrarian populations, modern and interethnic associations to be the only forms of civic activity. We should try to leave questions of forms flexible and focus instead on the purposes of associations. In agrarian settings, this also means that we may have to pay attention to informal modes of communication between citizens, which may perform the same functions in smaller locales such as villages as formal associations do in cities. Finally, everyday and informal forms of civic communication may be sufficient to keep peace in villages, but they cannot have the same effect in cities. Associational civic engagement is necessary for peace in interethnic urban settings.

Part II The National Level

The next two chapters present a *national* overview of electoral and ideological trends, on one hand, and Hindu-Muslim riots, on the other. The purpose is to show that there is a divergence between the national and the local.

After being electorally small for much of the century, the power of Hindu nationalists rose in the late 1990s. But their ideology, focused on Muslim disloyalty to India, did not triumph. In the process of making coalitions for capturing power, they had to make fundamental ideological compromises with the programs of other parties not wedded to Hindu nationalism. More important for our purposes, different cities and areas participated in very different ways in the changing national political climate, many holding on to their peaceful character despite the explosive rise nationally of the Hindu nationalists.

The same is true of the trends in communal violence. Nationally, from 1990 to 1993, communal rioting reached its highest point since the bloody days of India's partition. But the peaceful cities of the project kept peace, even as aggregate national trends showed a remarkable rise in violence—just as they had during 1947–48, when India was partitioned into two countries.

It will become amply clear how localized specific Hindu-Muslim violence is and how autonomous local civic structures can be, once the national picture is examined, followed by a city-based analysis of Hindu-Muslim relations. That there is a relationship between the national and the local may be beyond doubt; that the national overwhelms the local on ethnic or communal relations is, however, a view that must be seriously re-examined, if not given up altogether.

Chapter 3 Competing
National Imaginations

THE MASTER NARRATIVES OF INDIAN POLITICS

There were three master narratives in Indian politics in the twentieth century.[1] By "master narratives" I mean the major organizing devices for *mass politics,* or the leading political idioms that mobilize large numbers of people. Master narratives tell stories that make the critical issues in politics intelligible to the masses. They are ways of putting together popular social coalitions so that politics can be altered and political power won.[2]

Two of the three master narratives of Indian politics—secular nationalism and religious nationalism—speak explicitly about the nation; the third, focusing on caste, does it indirectly in that it aims at rearranging the priorities in politics without explicitly articulating a view of the nation. Although this chapter is about the struggle between the first two narratives, it must also briefly refer to the third, partly because the contestation of the first two has been seriously affected by it. All three narratives have repeatedly generated remarkable passions in politics. They appear again and again as distinctive ideologies in the nation's politics. The basic outlines of these narratives are described below. A fuller investigation of the first two follows thereafter.

Secular nationalism, the first master narrative, is India's "official ideology." It guided the national movement under Mahatma Gandhi and Jawaharlal Nehru and was legitimated by the country's constitution after independence. This narrative evokes the image of nation as a family. All religions (as well as languages and other groups) have an equal place in the national family and as a principle, none will dominate the functioning of the state. The term "secular" here does not mean a radical separation between the state and religion; it simply means that the state will be neutral between the religions, if it does get involved in religious affairs. Secularism, in its Indian usage, has therefore come to mean religious equidistance, not non-involvement. This narrative emphasizes that one's religious faith would not determine citizenship in the country and the rights that go with it; birth in India, or naturalization and acceptance of Indian culture, is the sole criterion. In electoral politics, the Congress Party has been the prime representative of this narrative, though it should be added that agreement with this view extends far beyond the Congress. Most political parties in India subscribe to this view of the nation.

Religious nationalism has been the second master narrative. It has primarily taken two forms: Muslim and Hindu.[3] Muslim nationalism emerged in the first half of the twentieth century. It led to the birth of Pakistan in 1947. The argument for Pakistan was simply that Hindus and Muslims were not two different religious communities but two separate nations. Hindu nationalism can be viewed as the mirror image of Muslim nationalism. Hinduism, according to the Hindu nationalist narrative, is not only the religion of India's majority community but also what gives India its distinctive *national* identity; other religions must assimilate to the Hindu center. Table 3.1 summarizes the distribution of various religions in contemporary India.

Table 3.1. India's Religious Profile

Denomination	Percentage of Population
Hindus	82
Muslims	12.1
Christians	2.3
Sikhs	2.0
Buddhists and Jains	1.2

Source: Census of India, 1991.

What attracted the Hindu nationalists—the presumption about the putative Hindu center of India—was precisely what repelled the Muslim nationalists. According to Hindu nationalists, whether or not Hindus can enjoy legal primacy, they must have cultural and political primacy in shaping India's destiny. The aim of this narrative is not only to emphasize the centrality of Hinduism to India but, when used in politics, to build Hindu unity. Hindus are a religious majority only in a manner of speaking. They are divided internally by multiple caste cleavages.

On the whole, as a conception of the nation, religious nationalism was the chief competitor of secular nationalism in the twentieth century. Muslim nationalism was the *bête noire* of secular nationalists during the national movement. Once Muslim nationalists left India for Pakistan, Hindu nationalists became the principal ideological adversary. In the electoral arena, Muslim nationalism was represented by the Muslim League before 1947 and Hindu nationalism by several Hindu parties. After 1947, the Bharatiya Janata Party (BJP) has been the principal patron of religious nationalism in politics. The party was called the Bharatiya Jan Sangh until 1977.

The third master narrative emphasizes "lower" caste unity. Rather than talk about the nation and the placement of religious or linguistic groups therein, the caste narrative speaks of the deeply hierarchical and unjust nature of *Hindu social order*, an order in which the "upper" castes, always a minority, have traditionally enjoyed ritualistic privileges and superior social rank, and the "lower" castes, always a majority, have suffered the disadvantages of a less dignified, even "unclean," status. Table 3.2 gives us the estimates of upper and lower castes in modern India.

When deployed in politics, an egalitarian restructuring of the Hindu social order is the chief goal of the caste narrative. This has taken two forms: Caste should not determine whether an individual is treated as an inferior or superior human being; moreover, to make up for centuries of caste oppression, affirmative action favoring the lower castes in government jobs should be the primary vehicle of achieving social justice. This narrative, thus, concentrates on India's religious majority, the Hindus. When it speaks of non-Hindu groups, it does so by arguing that both religious minorities and lower castes suffer from discrimination by the higher castes. A lower caste-minorities alliance, therefore, can be constructed in politics.

By principally focusing on the social hierarchy of Hinduism, the caste narrative primarily attacks Hindu nationalism. It does not believe in Hindu unity. It is comfortable with the basic idea of secular nationalism that religion should

Table 3.2. India's Caste Composition

Group	Percentage of Population
Upper Castes	16.1
Other Backward Castes	43.7
Scheduled Castes	14.9
Scheduled Tribes	8.1
Non-Hindu Minorities	17.2

Note: Since no caste census has been taken since 1931, the figures above can be seen as best guesses, not exact estimates.
They are sufficient to show the overall magnitudes, however.
Also, the upper castes in this calculation include the "dominant castes" that are no longer considered deprived, even
though they were ritually not placed in the upper category.
Source: Government of India, *Report of the Backward Classes
Commission* (The Mandal Commission Report), 1980, pt. 1,
vol. 1, p. 56.

not determine the rights and privileges of citizens. But it would add a great deal
more. Disowning the metaphor of a family, it would place social justice at the
heart of politics. As a corollary, it seeks to pit the lower castes against the upper
castes, whereas the secular nationalist narrative would, in principle, make coalitions across castes. The caste narrative was successfully used to mobilize the
masses in the first half of the century in southern India. In the 1980s and 1990s,
its political sweep extended to the north.[4]

All three master narratives have been repeatedly used to organize mass politics in this century—more than any other narrative of India's problems and
solutions.[5] The power of the caste narrative, however, has by and large not
matched that of the other two. The caste narrative has been highly effective at
the state level, but it has not yet put together a nationwide popular coalition in
politics. It has been able to put parties in power at the state level, but it is unable
to aggregate coalitions at the national level. There is a structural reason for
the regional or local splintering. Caste exists all over India, but, experientially
speaking, it is a local or regional entity. There are upper and lower castes in all
parts of the country, but the lower castes in one state may have little to do with
the lower castes elsewhere. Their names, social roles, economic functions, languages, and histories have local or regional meanings, unlikely to be shared by

lower castes in other places. They are all lower castes, but in different ways. Similarly, Brahmins of the south may not be recognized as such by the Brahmins of the north; though each in their respective settings has traditionally enjoyed high status and ritual privileges, each tradition may be different. The caste narrative has a nationwide *resonance,* but it has not been able to achieve a nationwide *aggregation.*

At the present time, the primacy of caste as a narrative of politics is mainly articulated by the Janata or Janata-like parties.[6] Their power in the states of Uttar Pradesh, Bihar, Orissa, Karnataka, and Tamil Nadu is substantial. These regional expressions do add up to a significant national force, but not an overwhelming one.[7]

It may be that the caste narrative will overcome its problem of aggregation in the future. A more odds-on scenario, however, appears to be that it will continue make it difficult for the other two narratives to ignore it, but it will not triumph entirely on its own. How this has already begun to happen will be analyzed at the end of this chapter. It suffices to note here that given its splintering and inability to aggregate nationally, secular nationalism and religious nationalism have been the major ideological protagonists for the shaping of the national political agenda. Of the two versions of religious nationalism, Hindu and Muslim, the latter, as already indicated, triumphed with founding the state of Pakistan in 1947. Since then, secular nationalism and Hindu nationalism have defined the principal arguments about India's national identity.

How has this contestation evolved? In imaginations about India's national identity, there was always a conceptual space for Hindu nationalism. Still, it remained a weak political force until recently, when the context of politics changed. The principal argument of what follows is that the rise of Hindu nationalism can be attributed to an underlying and a proximate base. Competing strains in India's national identity constitute the underlying base. The proximate reasons are supplied by the political circumstances of the 1980s, creating an institutional and ideological vacuum in Indian politics and generating a mounting anxiety about the future of India.

In the remainder of this chapter, I first analyze the key points of difference between the secular and Hindu nationalisms, focusing especially on Hindu-Muslim relations. Next I explain whether Hindu nationalism is a form of Hindu fundamentalism, followed by an investigation of why Hindu nationalism has become such a big force. Concluding remarks discuss the limits of Hindu nationalism in India.

THREE STRAINS AND TWO IMAGINATIONS

India's National Identity
and Hindu Nationalism

Who is an Indian? Deceptively simple, the question is hard to answer, as indeed it is with respect to several other nations in the world.[8] Literature on comparative nationalism suggests that national identities have been based on several principles of collective belonging:[9] language or race (Japan, Germany, and much of Europe), religion (Ireland, Pakistan, and parts of the Middle East), ideology (United States, the former USSR, and Yugoslavia), and territory (Spain, Switzerland, a number of developing nations). One should note that the territorial idea inevitably becomes part of all nation-states but territory does not have to be the defining principle of national identity.

Moreover, in some cases, there may be no clear principle of collective belonging; rather, competing notions of identity may exist, one becoming dominant at one time, the other at a different time. As Stanley Hoffmann argues, there are two competing views about French identity: one based on the French Revolution and the principles of freedom and equality, which brings French identity quite close to the definition of the American nation in terms of freedom and equality, and a second one based on ethnicity, which in French history led to the Vichy regime and to Le Pen in recent years.[10] In the United States, as Samuel P. Huntington has argued, the key constituents of the "American creed"—liberty, equality, individualism, democracy, and the rule of law—have not always existed together, nor can they, for they don't form a coherent logical set.[11]

What turns on the distinctive principles of national identity? Their political implications vary. Some of the most passionate political moments of America have concerned the issues of freedom and equality; just as those in Germany have concerned ethnicity or race. Similarly, competing strains in national identity open up distinctive political logics. Excessive drift in one direction brings forth a reaction, and alternative strains begin to acquire political momentum. A substantial number of French people today feel threatened by the increasing ethnic diversity of France, which is conceptualized by some as a monoethnic society, a conception opposed by others as too narrow and destructive of the principles of the Republic.[12] Similarly, in American history, as Huntington has argued, "Conflicts easily materialize when any one value is taken to an extreme: majority rule versus minority rights; higher law versus popular sovereignty; liberty versus equality; individualism versus democracy."[13]

Since the rise of the Indian national movement, three competing themes about India—territorial, cultural, and religious—have fought for political dominance. The territorial notion is that India has a "sacred geography," enclosed between the Indus River, the Himalayas and the seas and emphasized for 2,500 years since the time of the Mahabharata.[14] The cultural notion is that ideas of tolerance, pluralism, and syncretism define Indian society. India is not only the birthplace of several religions—Hinduism, Buddhism, Jainism, and Sikhism—but in its history, it has also regularly received, accommodated, and absorbed "outsiders"—Parsis, Jews, and "Syrian" Christians (followers of Saint Thomas, arriving as early as the second century, Christianity thus reaching India before it reached Europe). In the process, syncretistic forms of culture[15] (and even syncretistic forms of religions worship)[16] have emerged and become part of India. Apart from syncretism, which means a coming together and merging of cultures, pluralism and tolerance have also existed, with different communities finding their niche in India and developing principles of interaction. *Sarva Dharma Sambhava* (equal respect for all religions) is the best cultural expression of such pluralism. The third religious notion is that India is originally the land of the Hindus, and it is the only land that the Hindus can call their own. India has nearly all of Hinduism's holy places[17] and its holy rivers.[18] Most of India is, and has been, Hindu by religion[19]—anywhere between 65 and 70 percent in the early twentieth-century India and 82 percent today. A great deal of diversity may exist within Hindu society: a faith in Hinduism brings the various practitioners together. India thus viewed is a Hindu nation.[20]

The three identity principles—geography, culture, and religion—have their political equivalents. In political discourse, the territorial idea is called "national unity" or "territorial integrity," the cultural idea is expressed as "political pluralism," and the religious idea is known as *Hindutva,*[21] or political Hinduism. The political notion of pluralism itself has two meanings, dealing with the linguistic and religious issues. The principle of federalism was developed in order to show respect for the linguistic diversity of India: not only would the states be organized linguistically but the ruling party would also be federally organized, leaving enough autonomy for state level party units. The political principle governing religion has two levels. In general, religion would be left untouched so that religious pluralism in society could exist, but if the state did have to intervene in religious disputes, it would do so with strict neutrality. The state would maintain a posture of equidistance, a principle that came to define India's secularism.

These strains have yielded two principal theories about India's national identity: the secular nationalist and the Hindu nationalist. The former combines territory and culture; the latter, religion and territory. In understanding the fundamental differences between the two, a clear distinction between three terms—pluralism, syncretism, and assimilation—is required. Secular nationalism insists on pluralism and syncretism; Hindu nationalism, on assimilation.

Pluralism would indicate the coexistence of distinctive identities (A respects and lives peacefully with B). An example of pluralistic tolerance from Hinduism would be Mahatma Gandhi, whereas Maulana Azad, his colleague during the national movement, embodied pluralistic Islam. Syncretism would signify not a tolerant coexistence of distinctions but a merging of cultures or religions, leading to a new form of culture or religion (A interacts with B, and an amalgam C emerges as a result). In its interaction with Hinduism, Islam, especially Sufism, developed forms of piety and culture that represented Indian as opposed to Arab versions of Islam.[22] Syncretism should also be distinguished from assimilation. Assimilation means absorption into the dominant culture or religion (A merges into B, losing its distinctive identity); syncretism implies a give-and-take between cultures and religions (C represents elements of A and B). Not only have Islam and Christianity developed syncretistic forms in India (as indicated above), but even syncretistic religions (as opposed to syncretistic forms of the same religion) have emerged. Sikhism is a syncretistic religion par excellence, combining elements of Islam and Hinduism and becoming a faith in itself.[23]

For the secular nationalist construction, the best source is Nehru's *The Discovery of India*. Syncretism, pluralism, and tolerance are the major themes of Nehru's recalling of India's history:

> Ancient India, like ancient China, was a world in itself, a culture and a civilization which gave shape to all things. Foreign influences poured in and often influenced that culture and were absorbed. Disruptive tendencies gave rise immediately to an attempt to find a synthesis. Some kind of a dream of unity has occupied the mind of India since the dawn of civilization. That unity was not conceived as something imposed from outside, a standardization . . . of beliefs. It was something deeper and, within its fold, the widest tolerance of belief and custom was practised and every variety acknowledged and even encouraged.[24]

Notice that Nehru, unlike Hindu nationalists, finds the unity in culture, not religion.[25] He has no conception of a "holy land." Ashoka, Kabir, Guru Nanak, Amir Khusro, Akbar, and Gandhi—all syncretistic or pluralistic figures, subscribing to a variety of Indian faiths[26]—are the heroes of India's history in *The Discovery*, whereas Aurangzeb, the intolerant Mughal, "puts the clock back."[27] Like the Hindu nationalists, Nehru does in fact mention a second strain: the geographical one. It is, however, constructed differently—as territory and topos, not as a holy land: "When I think of India, I think of broad fields dotted with innumerable small villages; . . . of the magic of the rainy season which pours life into the dry parched-up land and converts it suddenly into a glistening expanse of beauty and greenery, or great rivers and flowing water; . . . of the southern tip of India; . . . and above all, of the Himalayas, snow-capped, or some mountain valley in Kashmir in the spring, covered with new flowers, and with a brook bubbling and gurgling through it."[28]

Perhaps the best way to illustrate the difference between culture and religion is to cite Nehru's will. Nehru wanted his ashes scattered in the River Ganga, not because it was religiously necessary but because it was culturally appropriate:

> When I die, I should like my body to be cremated. . . . A small handful of [my] ashes should be thrown into the Ganga. . . . My desire to have a handful of my ashes thrown into the Ganga at Allahabad has no religious significance, so far as I am concerned. I have been attached to the Ganga and Jamuna rivers in Allahabad ever since my childhood and, as I have grown older, this attachment has grown. . . . The Ganga, especially, is the river of India, beloved of her people, round which are intertwined . . . her hopes and fears, her songs of triumph, her victories and her defeats. She has been a symbol of India's age-long culture and civilization, ever-changing, ever-flowing, and yet ever the same Ganga. . . . Ganga has been to me a symbol and a memory of the past of India, running into the present and flowing on the great ocean of the future.[29]

To religious Hindus, the River Ganga is sacred. To Nehru, it was part of India's culture and equally dear. The sacredness, as it were, was not literal but metaphorical. Similarly, India's geography was sacred, not literally but metaphorically. The emotions and attachment generated by the geography were equally intense. To draw a parallel and to illustrate further the distinction between religion and culture, the example of Israel can be cited. One does not have be a religious Jew to celebrate and love the land of Israel. Secular Jews may also do that.

That being said, multiple strains in a national identity have their own political implications. An excessive shift toward one of the strains, as already suggested, may produce a reaction. Let us take secular nationalism as an example. If secular nationalists violate the principle of pluralism—let us say, by attacking federalism on the argument that too much federalism weakens national unity—they undermine a serious principle of the nation itself and begin to generate a reaction. Such attacks do not tally with the concerned state's view of the national identity, which has place for the regional identity as well. A man from Tamil Nadu is both a Tamilian and an Indian. Sometimes the reaction takes the form of separatist agitations. And these agitations, in turn, generate concern about territorial integrity. The centralizing "solution" thus worsens the disease. Something like this happened under Indira Gandhi when she repeatedly undermined federalism on the grounds of "national integrity," only to generate separatist nationalisms.

On the other hand, one can also go too far in protecting pluralism. Kashmir was given a special status in the Indian constitution. Delhi was to be responsible only for foreign affairs, defense, communications, and currency; the state government would handle the rest. Other Indian states had fewer powers. The Kashmir arrangement, thus, had the potential of contradicting the territorial principle, if Kashmiris claimed they were still unhappy. Nehru was instrumental in shaping Kashmir's special status, but he himself had to deploy force to quell the vacillations of Sheikh Abdullah, the leading political figure of Kashmir (1947–82), between India and independence.[30]

A second form of pluralism often deemed excessive and therefore harmful for national integrity concerns "personal laws." Should the various religious groups in India be under a common civil code or under their distinct religious laws? If secular nationalists claim that separate personal laws destroy national unity, they generate a reaction in the religious community whose personal laws are at issue. If, on the other hand, they promote personal laws on the argument that such concessions make minorities secure, they set off a reaction in the "majority" community that the state may have gone too far in minority appeasement, opening up fissiparous tendencies and undermining national unity.[31]

From Religion Versus Culture
to Religion as Culture

Pluralism in the secular view is embodied in laws (such as personal laws and protection of minority educational institutions) and in political institutions (such as federalism). Finding a blending of territory and cultural pluralism insufficient, the Hindu nationalists argue that emotions and loyalty make a nation, not politics, laws, and institutions. Laws, they say, can always be politically manipulated. Moreover, a proliferation of pro-minority laws has not led to the building of a cohesive nation; instead, disintegrative forces have regularly erupted.[32] A "salad bowl," according to them, does not produce cohesion; a "melting pot" does.[33] Rather than running away from Hinduism, which is the source of India's culture, one should explicitly ground politics in Hinduism, not in laws and institutions: "The Hindu *Rashtra* [nation] is essentially cultural in content, whereas the so-called secular concept pertains to the state and is limited to the territorial and political aspects of the Nation. [T]he mere territorial-cum-political concept divorced from its cultural essence can never be expected to impart any sanctity to the country's unity. The emotional binding of the people can be furnished only by culture and once that is snapped then there remains no logical argument against the demand by any part to separate itself from the country."[34]

In their conception of Hinduism, however, Hindu nationalists fluctuate between two meanings of Hinduism—a civilization or culture (as the quotation above suggests) and a religion: "Hindu is not the name of a religious faith like the Muslim and the Christian; it denotes the national life here."[35] Continuing in the same vein, L. K. Advani, India's home minister in the Vajpayee cabinet (1998–), once argued that the term "Hindu" being the description of the nation, Muslims can be called Muslim Hindus, Sikhs Sikh Hindus, and the Christians Christian Hindus.[36] Hindu nationalists are right that the term "Hindu," in its original meaning, meant those who lived in Hindustan (the everyday term for India in much of the north). Over the last few centuries, however, it has become a religious term, and "Indian" has replaced "Hindu" for the civilizational or national meaning.[37] Labels do acquire new meanings in history.

The dispute is not simply semantic. The term "Hindu" is further specified by Hindu nationalists. Savarkar, the ideological father of Hindu nationalism, gave a definition in *Hindutva,* the classic text of Hindu nationalism: "A Hindu means a person who regards this land . . . from the Indus to the Seas as his fatherland *(pitribhumi)* as well as his Holyland *(punyabhumi).*"[38] The definition is thus territorial (land between the Indus and the Seas), genealogical ("fatherland"), and religious ("Holyland"). Hindus, Sikhs, Jains, and Buddhists can be part of this definition, for they meet all three criteria. All of these religions were born in India. Christians, Jews, Parsis, and Muslims can meet only two, for India is not their holy land.

Can the non-Hindu groups be part of India? They can by assimilation, say the Hindu nationalists. Of the groups whose holy land is not India, Parsis and Jews, argue Hindu nationalists, are already assimilated, having become part of the nation's mainstream.[39] This leaves us with the Christians and the Muslims. "They," wrote Savarkar, "cannot be recognized as Hindus. For though *Hindustan* (India) to them is the Fatherland as to any other Hindu, yet it is not to them a Holyland too. Their holyland is far off in Arabia or Palestine. Their mythology and Godmen, ideas and heroes are not the children of this soil. Consequently their names and their outlook smack of a foreign origin. Their love is divided."[40]

Ultimately, Muslims and Christians became the principal adversaries of the Hindu nationalists—especially the former, partly because of their numbers and partly because a Muslim homeland in the form of Pakistan after all did partition India in 1947. They made up 25 percent of India before 1947, and even after the formation of Pakistan, they have been the largest minority, about 12 percent of the country's population at this point. Hence the enormous attention given to Islam by Hindu nationalists.[41]

The Hindu nationalist claim is not that Muslims ought to be excluded from the Indian nation. That may be the position of the Hindu extremists. During 1990–93, one only had to hear the tapes of the speeches made by Sadhvi Ritambhara, a prominent Hindu nationalist activist at that time, to appreciate how much hatred the right wing has for the Muslims. Assimilation, however, is the generic Hindu nationalist argument. That is, to become part of the Indian nation, Muslims must accept the centrality of Hinduism to Indian civilization; acknowledge key Hindu figures such as Ram as civilizational heroes, not disown them as mere religious figures of Hinduism; remorsefully accept that Muslim rulers of India between A.D. 1000 and 1757 destroyed pillars of Hindu civilization, especially temples; not claim special privileges such as maintenance of religious personal laws; and not demand special state grants for their educational institutions. Via *Ekya* (assimilation), they will prove their loyalty to the nation. Maintaining distinctiveness would simply mean that "their love," as Savarkar put it, "is divided."[42]

Because of the insistence on assimilation to an India that is, in turn, defined as the land of the Hindus, the intended distinction between culture and religion effectively breaks down. Specifically, the Hindu nationalist ideologues make no attempts to incorporate Muslim symbols into conceptions of Indian culture and history. Akbar, the tolerant Muslim ruler of the Mughal period, does not figure in their list of Indian heroes: Aurangzeb, the intolerant one, represents the Muslim essence. The Hindu nationalist attitude toward the great Mughal monuments such as the Taj Mahal remains unclear. They have objections even to the Muslim names of Indian cities: Aligarh, they sometimes say, should be called Harigarh, Allahabad Prayag, and Lucknow Lakshmanpur.

The Hindu nationalist discourse on Islam is selective and ominous. In India, Islam developed two broad forms: syncretist and exclusivist.[43] Syncretistic Islam was integrated into the pre-existing Indian culture and also contributed to it. Hindu nationalism makes no concession to a famous formulation about India and Islam presented by one of the most prominent Muslim leaders of twentieth-century India:

> I am a Muslim and proud of that fact. Islam's splendid traditions of thirteen hundred years are my inheritance. . . . In addition, I am proud of being an Indian. I am part of the indivisible unity that is Indian nationality. . . .
>
> It was India's historic destiny that many human races and cultures and religious faiths should flow to her, and that many a caravan should find rest here. . . . One of the last of these caravans was that of the followers of Islam. . . .
>
> We brought our treasures with us, and India too was full of the riches of her own precious heritage. . . . Full eleven centuries have passed by since then. Islam has now as great a claim on the soil of India as Hinduism. If Hinduism has been the religion of the people here for several thousand years, Islam has also been their religion for a thousand years. Just as a Hindu can say with pride that he is an Indian and follows Hinduism, so also we can say with equal pride that we are Indians and follow Islam. I shall enlarge this orbit still further. The Indian Christian is equally entitled to say with pride that he is an Indian and is following a religion of India, namely Christianity.
>
> Eleven hundred years of common history have enriched India with our common achievement. Our languages, our poetry, our literature, our culture, our art, our dress, our manners and customs, the innumerable happenings of our daily life, everything bears the stamp of our joint endeavour. There is indeed no aspect of our life which has escaped this stamp. . . .
>
> This joint wealth is the heritage of common nationality and we do not want to leave it and go back to the times when this joint life had not begun.[44]

It may well be true that with the formation of Pakistan, this argument about the relationship of Muslims to India politically lost to the two-nation theory in the 1940s, but it does not follow that all Muslims believed in the two-nation theory. To be truthful one will have to identify clearly different kinds of Muslim responses to India and Indian nationhood, belief in an independent Muslim homeland being only one of them.[45] Many millions of Muslims were not inspired by it even during the 1940s. Syncretistic Islam has produced some of the pillars of Indian culture, music, poetry, and literature.[46] Indian Muslims of various hues have, moreover, also fought wars against Pakistan.

By often flattening all Muslims into an anti-Indian mold, the Hindu nationalists embitter even Muslims who are syncretistic in their religiosity and culture, as well as those for whom Islam is a faith, a way to sustain troubled private lives, but not a political ideology, and who have remarkable pride in India. The political and ideological battle of nationalists may well be against Islamic fundamentalism and Muslim separatism; how can it be against everybody professing faith in Islam? In the Hindu nationalist discourse, these distinctions easily blur. An anti-Muslim hysteria is often its natural outcome.

That there have been some bitter struggles between Hindus and Muslims in India's history is beyond doubt, but that there have also been constructive exchanges between them. *Indian culture is not Hindu; it is simply Indian.* Hinduism is undoubtedly a large component of it, but it is not synonymous with Indian culture and civilization. That is why Nehru used the term "Indo-Muslim" to characterize Indian culture. Others have used the term "salad bowl" or "mosaic." Indian culture conceptualized as a mosaic does not devalue the contributions made by religious minorities to India's history and culture; viewed as a Hindu culture, it does. Hindu nationalism, by invoking the latter, does not allow the minorities, especially the Muslims and often the Christians as well, a meaningful and justly proud role in India's public life.

In secular nationalism, the two terms—religion and culture—are clearly separable, and syncretism and tolerance are properties of all religions and communities in India. Consider the non-Hindu "heroes" of Indian civilization according to Nehru: Ashoka, a Buddhist; Kabir, a syncretistic saint, Muslim by birth; Amir Khusro, a Muslim who pioneered Indian classical music; Nanak, the first Sikh guru; Akbar, a Mughal ruler. A celebration of Indian culture thus does not require being a Hindu. For Hindu nationalists, the two terms—"India" and "Hindu"—are synonymous. In Hindutva, the cultural and religious meanings of Hinduism blend into each other, and the distinction so critical for the secular nationalist disappears.

To sum up, Hindu nationalism has two simultaneous impulses: building a united India and "Hinduizing" the polity and the nation. Muslims and other groups are not excluded from the definition of India, but inclusion is premised on assimilation and acceptance of the *political and cultural* centrality of Hinduism. If assimilation is not acceptable to the minorities, Hindu nationalism becomes exclusionary, both in principle and practice.

It should also now be clear why secular and Hindu nationalisms are ideological adversaries and have remained so for decades. In an ingenious way, Mahatma Gandhi sought to combine Hinduism and a composite view of the Indian nation. Tolerance and pluralism, he argued, stemmed from his religiosity. Being a Hindu and having respect for Muslim culture could easily go together.[47] He frequently referred to his appreciation of Christianity, Buddhism, and Jainism. More important for politics, he never defined India as a Hindu nation:

> If the Hindus believe that India should be peopled only by Hindus, they are living in a dreamland. The Hindus, the Muslims, the Parsis and the Christians who have made India their country are fellow countrymen. . . .
>
> Should we not remember that many Hindus and Muslims own the same ancestors and the same blood runs through their veins? Do people become enemies because they change their religion? Moreover, there are deadly proverbs as between the followers of Siva and those of Vishnu, yet nobody suggests that these two do not belong to the same nation. It is said that the Vedic religion is different from Jainism, but the followers of the respective faiths are not different nations.[48]

Gandhi used the point about the same blood not to present a racial argument for nationhood but only to critique the claim that different religious communities constitute different nations and that religions not born in India could not produce fully loyal Indians. Indeed, to underline the point that accepting Indian culture is all that is required to be an Indian, not religion or race or language, he went on to present a truly remarkable formulation about Indian nationhood: "It is not necessary for us to have as our goal the expulsion of the English. If the English become Indianized, we can accommodate them."[49]

Such broad conceptualizing notwithstanding, Gandhi, of course, could not dissuade Mohammed Ali Jinnah and the Muslim League from making a Pakistan. The failure of Gandhi to prevent the partition of India sent two signals. To the secular nationalists, it highlighted the antinomy between religion and Indian nationalism. To the Hindu nationalists, it reinforced their belief in the complementarity between Hinduism and the Indian nation, on one hand, and a basic antinomy between Islam and Indian nationalism, on the other. "The attitude of the Muslims," argue Hindu nationalists, "was the reason for India's partition, an attitude that the Muslims are different from the Indian nation."[50] Since Gandhi's death, therefore, Hindu and secular nationalisms have been locked in a conflict for political power and for the ideological shaping of India.

The first battle for political and ideological hegemony after independence was won by secular nationalism; the battle today is not so clearly in favor of secular nationalists. The context since the 1980s has changed.

RELIGIOUS NATIONALISM, NOT
RELIGIOUS FUNDAMENTALISM

Created in 1925 in the state of Maharashtra, the RSS (Rashtriya Swayamsevak Sangh, National Voluntary Corps) is the institutional core of Hindu nationalism.[51] The ideological trend, however, goes much further back. Viewed as a way to resurrect India's cultural pride, Hindu revivalism in the second half of the nineteenth century was a response to British rule.[52] This revivalism preceded the national movement headed by the Congress Party in the first half of the twentieth century but could not dominate the movement itself. As explained above, even the devoutly religious Gandhi could not be called a Hindu nationalist. He was a Hindu and a nationalist, not a Hindu nationalist. Gandhi's Hinduism was inclusive and tolerant. Being a good Hindu and having respect for other religions were not contradictory.[53] Inclusion of non-Hindus in the Indian nation followed as a corollary of this position. Gandhi's love for Muslims even during the formation of Pakistan was, for Hindu nationalists, incomprehensible. In 1948, when a Hindu fanatic assassinated Gandhi, Hindu nationalism was set back by decades.[54] In the popular perception, Hindu nationalists became the killers of the Mahatma, the father of the nation.[55] Much of the post-1948 generation was told by parents to keep a safe distance from Hindu nationalists.

The term "religious fundamentalism" is often used to describe the kind of behavior seen in Ayodhya in December 1992, when a large mass of Hindu nationalists destroyed the Baburi mosque. *Sadhus* (Hindu holy men) and religious fanatics are indeed involved in the Hindu nationalist movement. Many religious Hindus also supported the movement as an act of faith. But that was only one side of the movement.[56] More important, the Hindu nationalists are religious *nationalists,* not religious *fundamentalists.* Both groups may share an aversion to a certain kind of secularist, and both may attack groups perceived as recalcitrant. The similarities, however, end there. Unlike the Islamic fundamentalists for whom sovereignty in an Islamic state would reside in Allah, who would swear by the *Shariat,* and who target "heretics" as enemies, the Hindu nationalists are calling neither for Ramrajya (the Kingdom of Lord Ram) nor for a return to traditional Hindu law—nor, for that matter, does Hinduism have a notion of religious heresy. There is no single "correct" Hinduism. The doctrinal diversity of Hinduism rules out the notion of heresy. A few *sadhus* may claim to be orthodox in a strict sense of the term. But that is not the aim of the political mainstream of the movement.

Another argument does not appear to be valid. A large number of commentators have argued that Hindu nationalists represent a turn in Hinduism toward what has been called "the semitic model"—"one book, one God, one sacred city"—instead of its intrinsic pluralism on all of these dimensions.[57] Although certainly trying to organize the Hindus as never before, at no point did the leaders of the Ayodhya movement call for an abandonment of Hinduism's multiple gods in favor of Ram. In fact, the right wing of the movement continues to talk about the "liberation" of the birthplace of two more Hindu gods: Krishna (in Mathura) and Shiva (in Varanasi).

The aim of Hindu nationalists is neither to "semitize" Hinduism nor to enforce religious uniformity and orthodoxy. Rather, it is to create a *political* unity among the Hindus, divided otherwise by the various castes, languages, and doctrinal diversities. One of the most important BJP leaders since the 1980s, L. K. Advani, readily admits that he is not very religious.[58] Nor did the BJP as a party in the 1980s and 1990s consist primarily of religious men. The major tracts of Hindu nationalism clearly state, as Advani argued, that "Indian nationalism is rooted . . . in a Hindu ethos"[59] in which "ethos" is viewed as a cultural term, although the culture itself is defined variously.[60]

In a curious irony, Hindu nationalists are closer to the Muslim nationalists such as Mohammed Ali Jinnah, the founder of Pakistan, than to Islamic fundamentalists such as Maulana Maududi, the founder of Jamaat-i-Islami. Hindu nationalists intensely dislike comparisons with the party that led the movement for Pakistan. The 1947 partition, according to them, was the most traumatic moment of the twentieth century in India. In truth, however, Jinnah's argument was similar, though it was made on behalf of Muslims. A modern man not known for religiosity, Jinnah argued that one did not have to be religious to appreciate the cultural differences between Islam and Hinduism. The cultural distinctiveness of Indian Islam, he stressed, constituted the rationale for a separate nation-state of Pakistan: "Islam and Hinduism . . . are not religions in the strict sense of the word, but are in fact different and distinct social orders. . . . [T]hey belong to two different civilizations which are based mainly on conflicting ideas and conceptions. . . . They have different epics, [and] their heroes are different. . . . Very often, the hero of one is the foe of the other and likewise their victories and defeats overlap."[61]

The dispute over the Ayodhya mosque, thus, was not merely a religious dispute. It was a political contestation over India's national identity.

THE POLITICAL RISE OF HINDU NATIONALISM

Although the principal *ideological* adversary of secular nationalism, Hindu nationalism remained a weak *electoral* force until recently. At no point before 1989 did the Hindu nationalists receive even one-tenth of the national vote (table 3.3). The period 1989–90 was the electoral turning point for them. In 1989, the BJP's share increased to 11.4 percent, and in 1991 to more than 20 percent.

In terms of parliamentary seats, the BJP eclipsed the Congress as the largest party of India in the 1996, 1998, and 1999 elections. In March 1998, it came to power, though in a coalition of 18 parties, and again in October 1999 in a pre-election coalition of 24 parties. It had to develop a broad-based alliance with many parties, most of which did not subscribe to the ideology of Hindu nationalism. Thus, the BJP has come to power, but the ideology of Hindu nationalism has not. Table 3.3 presents the electoral performance of the BJP since independence and compares it to the Congress Party, still the largest party in India in terms of vote share, though not of parliamentary seats.[62]

Equally important, support for Hindu nationalism has by now gone beyond the urban trading community, its customary base, to include villagers and the modernized (and modernizing) middle classes. Hardly known for Hindu religiosity, and Westernized in their life, nearly 30 retired generals, including a Jewish ex-general, joined the BJP in 1991. So did a host of former bureaucrats. For a party customarily associated with obscurantism, it was a moment of great symbolic significance. Since then, the BJP has enjoyed solid support in urban India, receiving roughly 40 percent of the urban vote. Its support in rural India, though substantial, is not as high.[63]

Why have the BJP and Hindu nationalism risen to such prominence? What accounts for the BJP's transformation from a party of the periphery to a party shaping India's political agenda? Why should Ayodhya as an issue have come alive in the 1980s, even though it existed as a potential source?[64]

Three political factors, operating simultaneously, come to mind: (1) rise of separatist movements in the 1980s, threatening to rupture the nation; (2) institutional decay of the Congress Party and an absence of other centrist alternatives; (3) an opportunistic twisting of secular principles in Indian politics.

Table 3.3. BJP and INC National Election Results, 1952–99

Election Year	Percentage of National Vote		Seats Won in the Lok Sabha		
	INC	BJP	Congress	BJP	Total Seats
1952	45.0	3.1	364	3	489
1957	47.8	5.9	371	4	494
1962	44.7	6.4	361	14	494
1967	40.8	9.4	283	35	520
1971	43.7	7.4	352	22	518
1977	34.5	—	154	—	542
1980	42.7	—	353	—	542
1984	48.1	7.4	415	2	542
1989	39.5	11.5	197	86	543
1991	36.5	20.1	232	120	543
1996	28.8	20.3	140	161	543
1998	25.8	25.6	141	182	543
1999	28.3	23.8	114	182	543

Note: Until 1980, the BJP was known as Bharatiya Jan Sangh (BJS). The BJS merged with the Janata coalition in 1977 and 1980, making it impossible to derive good estimates of its popular vote.

Sources: David Butler, Ashok Lahri, and Prannoy Roy, *India Decides: Elections 1952–1991* (New Delhi: Living Media India Limited, 1995) for 1952–91 data; Election Commission of India, *Statistical Report on General Elections, various issues, (National and State Abstracts and Detailed Results)* for 1996, 1998, and 1999.

Separatism in the 1980s

India has seen several separatist movements: in the northeastern states of Nagaland and Mizoram in the 1950s and 1960s and, to some extent, in the southern state of Tamil Nadu in the 1950s. A combination of politics and sheer force was deployed to deal successfully with the first two. As for Tamil Nadu, separatism did not really become an armed insurgency. Elections provided a solution to the problem. "Tamil nationalists" won an election in 1967, started ruling the state, and became part of the democratic political process.

At no point since independence, however, was the *mainstream of Indian politics* so profoundly influenced by secessionary politics as in the 1980s. Rightly or wrongly, the small northeastern states of Nagaland and Mizoram do not—and did not—affect politics in India's political heartland. Punjab and Kashmir, where insurgencies erupted in the 1980s and 1990s, are different. Running flourishing businesses, spearheading a green revolution in agriculture, and well-represented in the Indian army, Punjab's Sikhs were seen as a prospering community and as patriots. A Sikh insurgency in the 1980s was profoundly shocking, generating great anxieties about whether Punjab would stay in India. Moreover, as the armed forces targeted the Sikh militants, the militants themselves killed hundreds of Hindus, making the tragedy even more incomprehensible. Hindu-Sikh relations had been historically quite cordial: until recently, it was possible for the same family to call the son a Sikh and the daughter a Hindu.

Being a Muslim majority state, Kashmir was even more critical, especially for the rise of Hindu nationalism. In 1991, there were between 3 and 4 million Muslims in the Kashmir Valley and more than 110 million Muslims outside the valley in India. An insurgency in the state of Jammu and Kashmir broke out in the Muslim-majority valley, not in the Hindu-majority Jammu. Many Kashmiri militants claimed that theirs was not a religious insurgency, but the popular perception began to change, as the Hindus of the valley, a mere 5 percent of the total population there, left in large numbers for the northern plains. By the mid-1990s, there were very few Hindus left in the valley. A large number of them were living in the refugee camps of Delhi and Jammu. Kashmir has always been at the center of Hindu nationalist politics.[65] With the resurgence of the Kashmir crisis and the migration of Hindus, Hindu nationalism received a new political impetus.

Has the "Secular Project" Unraveled?

THE ORGANIZATIONAL DECAY OF THE CONGRESS PARTY

In twentieth-century India, the principal organizational embodiment of secular nationalism was the Congress Party. Once a powerful organization associated with founding and building the nation, the Congress Party is a rusty, clay-footed colossus today. Nations, as we know, are politically created; they do not naturally exist. Just as peasants were turned into Frenchmen over the course of years,[66] the Congress attempted to turn an old *civilization* into a *nation* in the first half of the twentieth century. Of the other large multiethnic countries in the world, the Communists in the former Soviet Union and Yugoslavia also sought to create nations, but not on the basis of conciliation and democracy.[67] Because their nation-building was based on coercion, it was not clear how deeply a Croat felt for Yugoslavia or how ardent a Georgian or a Balt was for the Soviet Union.[68] The Congress Party mobilized the masses into a national movement, generated pride and belief in India, and most of all, maintained an ideology of nonviolence, an ideology that emphasized that even the British were to be politically defeated, not killed.[69] Although violence erupted periodically, it was not the cornerstone of the national movement.

The mobilization lasted almost three decades. As a result, the idea of India as a nation reached every part of India. By the 1940s, Gandhi and Nehru, and with them the Congress Party, were recognized everywhere.[70] The emergence of Pakistan was the greatest failure of the Congress. The Muslim League could not be won over. Nor could the Muslim League win over all Muslims in the subcontinent—in good part because of the interreligious idea of India so painstakingly promoted by the Congress Party.

In the 1970s and 1980s, the Congress declined as an institution. Electoral success coexisted with organizational emaciation. The decay of the Congress coincided with Indira Gandhi's rise to unquestioned power by the early 1970s. Nehru had used his charisma to promote intraparty democracy, not to undermine it, strengthening the organization in the process. Indira Gandhi used her charisma to make the party utterly dependent on her, suspending intraparty democracy and debate and weakening the organization as a result. Nehru's ideological positions were openly debated in party forums and sometimes rejected. Party elections regularly produced state-level leaders; their democratic victories, even when disagreeable, were respected. Indira Gandhi imposed her positions on the party; she would suspend the state-level leaders, if they dared oppose her; she would nominate state-level leaders, not allowing the state unit to elect its leader. Since this could not be done in a party that elected its office holders, she finally did away with *party* elections.[71] She also tried to suspend national elections, but that attempt miserably failed.[72]

By the late 1980s, there was an organizational and ideological vacuum in Indian politics. Organizationally, the Congress was listless. Ideologically, it was not obvious what it stood for. Professing secularism, its leaders were unafraid to use religion for political purposes. Professing socialism, some of its leaders wholeheartedly embraced the market. The Congress was no longer a party but an undifferentiated, unanchored medley of individuals sustained by patronage. It was a political machine. Most opposition parties followed the Congress lead. They did not have organizational elections either, nor for that matter did they show ideological cohesion.

There were two major exceptions to this institutional rot: the Communist Party of India, Marxist (CPM) and the BJP. The class-based mobilization of the CPM has some inherent limitations in India, making it hard for the CPM to extend its popularity beyond isolated pockets. At the national level, a "disciplined BJP" sought to emerge as an alternative to the Congress.[73] In the popular perception, the BJP came increasingly to be seen as a party that could claim discipline, probity, principles, and organization. Having not been in government, it was not tainted by a lust for power or by corruption. Most politicians and parties looked hopelessly compromised by the end of the 1980s. It is not likely that these images of the BJP will survive as it finally handles the job of governance. Indeed, corruption scandals have already begun to sully its image.

SECULARISM AS A MODERNIST IDEOLOGY

> It is not modern India which has tolerated Judaism in India for nearly 2,000 years, Christianity from before the time it went to Europe, and Zorashtrianism for more than 1,200 years; it is traditional India which has shown such tolerance. . . . As India gets modernized, religious violence is increasing. . . . In the earlier centuries, inter-religious riots were rare and localized. . . . [S]omewhere and somehow, religious violence has something to do with the urban-industrial vision of life and with the political process the vision lets loose.
> —Ashis Nandy, "The Politics of Secularism"

> Social analysts draw attention to the contradiction between the undoubted though slow spread of secularization in everyday life, on the one hand, and the unmistakable rise of fundamentalism, on the other. But surely these phenomena are only apparently contradictory, for in truth it is the marginalization of faith, which is what secularism is, that permits the perversion of religion. There are no fundamentalists or revivalists in traditional society.
> —T. N. Madan, "Secularism in Its Place"

With these words, a powerful argument against secularism, led by Madan and Nandy, emerged in India in the late 1980s. India's secularism is collapsing, according to the "antisecularist" view, not because it has not gone far enough but because it has gone too far. Secularism is a victim of its "official" success.

The antisecularist argument proceeds at two levels—a larger theoretical level and an India-specific level. The theoretical attack on secularism is embedded in the generic critique of modernity now so common in the disciplines of anthropology, literary criticism, and history (especially of the developing world). Secularism, in this view, is a necessary concomitant of "the project of modernity," of science and rationality. Modernity is viewed as facing serious political difficulties all over the world, leading to religious (and ethnic) revivals. The basic flaw of modernity, according to this view, is that it mocks the believer for his morality but provides no alternative conception of what the purpose of life is, what the good life is, how we should conduct ourselves in our families and communities. Politics founded on such a modernist, secular vision suffers from irremediable defects. No means are considered detestable enough so long as they facilitate the realization of political ends. Holding nothing sacred, lacking an alternative source of ethics, and having no internal restraints on political behavior, modernity and secularism denude politics of morality. Because human beings cannot live without notions of right and wrong, the secular and modernist project creates increasing popular skepticism. Moreover, because it also generates condescension toward religion, secularism puts the believer on the defensive, setting off a religious reaction.

Pointing to the origins of secularism, the antisecularists argue that it is a Western concept with foundations in the Enlightenment and Reformation. The Enlightenment heralded the supremacy of Reason over Belief, and by making the individual responsible for his salvation without the intermediation of the church, the rise of Protestantism made the separation of church and state possible. Secularism became embedded in Western culture. There is no similar civilizational niche for secularism in India, argue antisecularists.[74] Religion was, and remains today, the ultimate source of morality and meaning for most Indians.

Communal riots did not take place in traditional India, for traditional religiosity, they also argue, had led to principles of religious tolerance and coexistence. Modernity, on the contrary, has led to two results in the realm of religion and politics: (1) owing to the link between secularism and amoral politics, communal riots in India have increased with the advent of modernity and (2) because secularism puts the believer on the defensive, fundamentalism and secularism have become two sides of the same coin. Principles of tolerance will have to be derived from traditional India as Mahatma Gandhi did, not from modernist secularism, as Nehru did.

This is not the place to engage this argument in detail; for purposes of this chapter, the application of the "modernist logic" to Indian culture and politics is more pertinent.[75] It suffices to note that the view that rationality and secularism lead to a moral and spiritual vacuum in human life is philosophically grounded in the Counterenlightenment, whose themes continue to reverberate in several fields of knowledge: literature,[76] philosophy,[77] social sciences, and even in the sciences.[78] Several thoughtful observers of rationality accept the claim that rationality and science are morally neutral if not empty. As Albert Einstein argued, science and rationality are essentially about "is," not about "ought." Unless morally grounded, rationality can indeed be destructive. Embedded in moral ends, however, it can make a remarkable contribution to human life. Nuclear energy, according to Einstein, is the best example of this reasoning.[79]

For the debate on secularism, then, the key issue is: Can the secular man also be "moral"? Put somewhat differently, are there nonreligious sources of morality? Nandy and Madan question the robustness of "modern ethics." Focusing on the amoral side of secularism alone, they seem to be saying that religious morality is internally grounded, whereas modern ethics can only be established through institutions and laws, which will not be legitimate in and of themselves. Presumably, it is the fear of punishment that will generate compliance with them, not internal controls. To them, traditional interreligious tolerance thus has greater authenticity; modernist tolerance forced by secular laws and institutions is bound to be fragile.

I am not here concerned with whether non-religious, modernist ethics can be authentic and therefore spontaneously or naturally legitimate. I shall concentrate on whether it makes sense to talk about tradition and modernity or traditional tolerance and modernist intolerance in an undifferentiated way.

The antisecularists do not distinguish between different types of tradition or between the various types of modernity. Both Akbar, the tolerant Mughal ruler, and Aurangzeb, the intolerant one, were products of medieval India. Akbar built bridges across communities; Aurangzeb destroyed them. Not only did Aurangzeb repress "infidels" (the non-Islamic religious groups), he also sought to impose religious purity within the Muslim community, targeting "heretics" and "apostates" and killing his own brother, Dara Shikoh, in the process. Shikoh's "crime" was heresy: he used Islam to justify his attempt to combine features of Islam and Hinduism. Religion and tradition can thus be tolerant as well as brutally violent.[80] The embeddedness of tradition is to be distinguished from its tolerance or intolerance.

Varieties of Secularism (and Modernity): Tolerance, Arrogance, Innocence

Similarly, modernity and secularism can come in various forms. Two trends marked the behavior of India's secular politicians in the 1980s. One may be called *secular arrogance,* the other *secular innocence.* As explained below, secular arrogance was best exemplified by Mrs. Gandhi, secular innocence by Rajiv Gandhi. Both of these variants are very different from Nehru's secularism, which can be called *secular tolerance.* Nehru, a modernist, might have held strong reservations about religion, but his private beliefs did not translate either into an arrogant abuse of religion or into an opportunistic acceptance of religion in public life. It is principles in *public life,* rather than cosmologies governing private life, that are at issue here. In their private lives, Nehru and Indira and Rajiv Gandhi may have all been areligious (although there are indications that Mrs. Gandhi turned toward religion in the last years of her life). In their public life, however, they were profoundly different. Secular arrogance and secular innocence, associated with Indian politics of the 1980s, fit the Nandy-Madan view best. It was not preordained that tolerance over time would degenerate into arrogance and innocence.

Secular arrogance is the idea that political power may be used either to coopt the believer or to subdue him. The believer is viewed not only as an object of modernization or secularization—an aim with which a number of modernists including Nehru agreed—but also as a pawn on the political chessboard, which modernists like Nehru never imagined. In its worst form, secular arrogance combines two drives: the use of the believer by the politician for secular, political purposes and the wish to crush him.

This kind of process—the use as well as the crushing—was initiated by Mrs. Gandhi. Her political dalliance with Sikh religious extremism in the late 1970s was dangerous. In order to defeat the Akali Dal, a moderate Sikh party that competed with the Congress in the state of Punjab, she used a religious leader, Sant Bhindranwale. Religious preachers such as Bhindranwale felt that the Sikh community was losing its soul, in part a result of the economic prosperity that the green revolution had brought about.

Indira Gandhi in the early 1980s would not accede to the secular demands of the moderate Akali factions—a greater share of river waters, larger federal investment of fiscal resources, and so on—but she accepted to several demands of the religious extreme—declaring Amritsar a holy city, banning smoking there, and allowing Sikh religious broadcasts over state-controlled radio.[81] Such a policy was in striking contrast to the situation in the late 1950s and early 1960s when religious issues figured in Punjab politics. Nehru refused to legitimate the Master Tara Singh faction of the Akali Dal, associated with *religious* demands. Instead, he strengthened the Sant Fateh Singh faction, associated with *linguistic* demands.[82] He would neither politically trifle with religion, despite his opposition to religion, nor opportunistically legitimate religious leaders in politics.

Indira Gandhi used religion for political purposes, just as Bhindranwale used politics for religious pursuits. She achieved a dubious success in the end.

The moderate Akali factions, her rivals in party politics, were weakened, but the preacher and his men went out of control. Seeking to restore piety, Bhindranwale and his followers targeted the heretics and apostates, then the "infidels." They eventually took shelter in the Golden Temple, the Vatican of the Sikhs, and conducted their religious mission from there. Indira Gandhi finally ordered the army to invade the temple.[83]

The desecration of the Golden Temple soured Hindu-Sikh relations and led to Mrs. Gandhi's assassination by her Sikh bodyguards. June 6, 1984 (the attack on the temple) and October 31, 1984 (Mrs. Gandhi's assassination) began a cycle of desecration and revenge. Even the most patriotic Sikhs felt violated by the desecration. And a large part of the Hindu middle class was equally revolted by the action of the Sikh bodyguards.

Indira Gandhi's motivations remain unclear. Several interpretations are possible. Given her notion of politics and power,[84] she in all probability imagined that state power would ultimately subdue Bhindranwale and that even after a mighty desecration, the enticements of power would either co-opt the Sikh community or crush its "pretensions." She paid for this arrogance with her life, and Hindu-Sikh wounds took a long time to heal. After a decade of Sikh insurgency, Punjab returned to peace only in the second half of the 1990s.

Secular innocence can also spell danger, if combined with India's definition of secularism. In India, as already said, secularism is not defined as a radical separation between the state and church.[85] The founders argued that in the Indian context, keeping the state equally distant from all religions and not letting it favor any one in public policy was the best solution.

Unlike the clarity entailed in a radical church-state separation, secularism as equidistance is a nebulous concept. *Equal distance* can also be translated as *equal proximity.* If it is alleged that the state is moving toward one particular religion, the state, to equalize the distance, can subsequently move toward other religions. Each such equalizing step may be aimed at soothing the religious communities. But the state becomes more and more embroiled in religion. An unstable equilibrium results, breeding distrust all around. Under Nehru, equidistance was not turned into equiproximity. Under Rajiv Gandhi, the opposite happened.

The turning point was the Shah Bano case in the mid-1980s. Shah Bano, a Muslim woman, filed for alimony after being divorced by her husband. The husband argued that alimony was not permissible under Islamic law. Shah Bano sought protection under the country's civil law, not Islamic personal code. The Supreme Court, in its judgment, proclaimed that the country's civil law overrode any personal laws.[86] Faced with a Muslim furor, Rajiv Gandhi first supported the court. Then, to allay Muslim fears, he ordered his party, which held nearly three-fourths of parliamentary seats, to pass legislation in parliament that made the Shariat superior to the civil law in matters concerning marriage, divorce, and property for Muslims. He argued that secularism required giving emotional security to the minorities. A Hindu nationalist storm erupted. Then, the Temple-Mosque site in Ayodhya, closed for years, was opened to Hindu pilgrimage and worship. The aim was to give something to both the Hindu and Muslim communities. Instead, the largest demonstration of Muslims seen in Delhi followed, and riots broke out. Ostensibly trying to equalize its distance from the two religions, the government thus got more and more trapped in religious anxieties and fears.

Twisted Meanings, Embattled Symbols

By the time L. K. Advani, the then head of BJP, led the mobilization to rebuild the Ram temple in 1990, the government's argument that laws were prior to faith had become a contradiction in terms. The superiority of faith over law had already been declared by the government. The secular contention about the superiority of law over faith could not possibly apply to only one community. After agitating for and getting a faith-based personal law, the Muslim leadership could not also legitimately claim that the law was superior to faith. Moreover, the Muslim leadership also showed a lack of political imagination and played into the hands of Hindu nationalists.

So long as the matter was presented as a mosque versus temple issue, the dispute remained religious and could not generate a movement. But when it became a Rama-versus-Babur issue, which is how the BJP simultaneously presented it, it took on nationalistic overtones. In the popular perception, Babur is unquestionably an alien conqueror, whereas Rama is not. Of Turko-Mongol descent, Babur invaded India and founded an empire. Although several of Babur's descendants, especially Emperor Akbar, blended into India's culture, Babur himself remains largely an outsider in national imagination. Contrariwise, though no Hindu god is uniformly popular all over India, for all of Hinduism's pantheism Rama is one of the most celebrated. This fact has made him both a religious *and* a cultural figure. The *Ramayana* (the tale of Rama) is the most popular epic, especially in northern India. And an annual and hugely popular enactment of the tale of Rama *(Ramlila),* in which many Muslims have also traditionally participated, makes Rama part of India's everyday culture. One does not have to be religious to experience the Ramayana culturally in India.

Muslim leaders kept harping on the religious meaning of Ayodhya, refusing to encounter the nationalistic meaning. Worse, the various mosque action committees (and the secular historians) initially argued that Rama was a mythological figure, for there was no historical proof for either Rama's existence or his birthplace. This was a gratuitous argument. Core beliefs of many religions, after all, flourish without proof. How can one *prove* that the prophet Mohammed's hair was brought to a mosque in Sri Nagar? Muslims of Kashmir believe so. Similarly, how can one prove that Buddha left his tooth in Sri Lanka, or that Jesus was born to a virgin? Religious belief does not depend on rational evidence. If the Shariat was the word of God for which no proof was required, as the Muslim leaders had claimed in the Shah Bano controversy, how could proof be sought for a Hindu belief about Rama's birthplace?

The problem was compounded by two more facts. It is widely known that the disputed mosque had not even been used for the previous four decades. Moreover, mosques are also known to have been moved in the past, even in Muslim countries. By repeatedly attacking an article of Hindu faith over a mosque not used for decades, the mosque action committees and Muslim politicians gave the appearance of utter intransigence.

The context thus provided muscle to the BJP's critique of the actually existing secularism in India. It, Advani argued, is a pseudo-secularism; it has meant excessive appeasement of minorities, or what he called "minorityism." The argument was both right and wrong, but the wrong side was scarcely noticed in the politics of the late 1980s.

Muslims, Sikhs, Christians, and Buddhists, added to the scheduled castes and scheduled tribes (nonreligious minorities, viewed as minorities nonetheless), constitute more than 37 percent of India's electorate.[87] In a first-past-the-post, British-style parliamentary system, a 40 percent vote can easily translate into 50 to 60 percent of legislative seats. Moreover, in 197 parliamentary constituencies Muslims constitute between 10 and 50 per cent of electorate, and in another 10, more than 50 percent.[88] That makes them an important factor in determining election results in nearly 40 percent of parliamentary constituencies. Since, according to conventional wisdom, the majority community does not vote as a bloc and the minorities do,[89] there is a temptation in the system for power-seeking centrist parties to develop pro-minority programs. Purely in an electoral sense, India's political system does indeed gravitate toward the minorities, though the minorities may feel that that is not enough, and there is some justice in their claim.

Whatever the objective truth—if there is or can be one—the problem of perceptions dominates discussion. Minorities are visible in India's upper political, bureaucratic, and cultural layers. Roman Catholics and Sikhs have often led the armed forces of India. General Jacob, a famous Jewish general, led India to victory in the 1971 Indo-Pakistan war. Muslims have regularly occupied positions in the cabinet. The man who produced India's first-medium range missile and the nuclear bomb is a Muslim. Muslims have led the national cricket team, a sport that generates national hysteria. Muslims are among the leading classical musicians of the country. Muslim film stars have been role models, even for Hindu youth. Minority educational institutions have legal privileges, enjoying special grants from the government. The constitution gives Kashmir, India's only Muslim-majority state, a special status, making several federal laws inapplicable there even as the rest of the states are bound by these laws. If Muslims remain unhappy, many secularists and Muslim politicians argue, the state ought to do more.

The same set of facts, however, was used to present the BJP story. Muslim film and sports stars, musicians, and scientists are proof that talent matters irrespective of religion and that a largely Hindu society may not be unfair. This argument had a serious flaw. Muslims, despite these special provisions, are among the poorest and least educated community in the country.[90] They are also often the object of police brutality in riots. The problem of perceptions boils down to how many concessions to the minorities are sufficient. There is no objective answer to this question, in India or elsewhere. Muslim politicians and secularists point to the economic backwardness of Muslims and argue for greater assistance. The BJP points to the visibility of minorities in India's political and cultural life, saying that enough is enough.

When secularism was equated with secular tolerance and legitimated by Nehru's principled behavior, arguments that it was the responsibility of the majority community to make minorities secure could be openly made.[91] Despite such open arguments, Hindu nationalists were not able to win against Nehru. When principled secularism—not legitimating religion in political mobilization but maintaining a concern for minority welfare—was replaced by an unprincipled secularism, the secular project began to unravel.

This weakening does not disprove the worth of secularism as a political principle, as Nandy and Madan have argued. Morality and meaning in politics, first of all, do not have to emerge from religion; they can also emerge from a modernist, liberal conception of ethics. Nehru was moral as well as areligious. Moreover, nonreligious ethical behavior can also be politically legitimated, even in societies marked by intense religiosity. Secularism by itself thus does not make one amoral or unethical. If this is how secular politicians of the 1980s behaved, it is not what secularism as a principle entails. This distinction is crucial for explaining the events of the 1980s and 1990s.

Is reviving Nehru's secular modernism a solution of the current difficulties? The defense of Nehru's secularism should not be construed as an argument for its revival. As already indicated, the Nehruvian rationale for secularism relied on certain ideas of political liberalism and modernity. Nehru did not make a case for his project in terms of India's civilization, for which *Discovery of India* laid the groundwork. He wanted Indians to leave their pasts and become modern. Although futures are indeed created, they are not typically created on a clean slate. It is hard for nations to leave their pasts behind. The more pertinent issue is: How does a nation reconstruct its past? Which traditions should be revived, and which ones dropped? Since a nation's past is not undifferentiated, contesting visions are generally available. The political and ideological task is to retrieve that which is valuable and to make this selective retrieval a lived reality. An England could not have been created in India; only a future consistent with one of India's several pasts could have been.

Strictly speaking, Nehru's political pluralism and his opposition to religion are separable. One does not depend on the other. It is possible to reconceptualize secular nationalism by combining Nehru's *political* pluralism with his understanding that India's history is marked by *cultural* pluralism. One does not have to defend political pluralism and tolerance in terms of a modernist liberal theory; one can also defend it in terms of India's historical and cultural traditions. A pluralist democracy and secularism can thus be civilizationally anchored. This vision of politics requires recalling the pluralistic and syncretistic heroes of India's past, explicitly defending a politics and ideology of secularism in cultural terms, and mobilizing the people on the basis of that understanding.

CONCLUSION

With the BJP in power in Delhi since 1998, it might be said that Hindu nationalism as an ideology has finally subdued secular nationalism. That, however, would will be a wrong conclusion to draw. The Hindu nationalists have ended their long isolation in Indian politics and formed governments in Delhi, but they have also been forced to make ideologically distasteful but pragmatically necessary political coalitions. For the sake of power, the Hindu nationalists—after the twelfth and for the thirteenth national elections, held in 1998 and 1999, respectively—had to team up with other parties, several of whom were based among the lower castes and subscribed to the third master narrative identified above—that of caste injustice. The principal enemy of the caste narrative is Hindu unity, which, however, has been one of the primary objectives of Hindu nationalists. Thus, the making of a winning coalition has required that the ideologically pure demands of Hindu nationalism—building of a temple in Ayodhya, a common civil code and no religiously based personal laws for minorities, abolition of the special status of Jammu and Kashmir, elimination of the Minorities Commission—be dropped and a program more acceptable to the lower-caste parties formulated. This is the price the Hindu nationalists have had to pay for making their journey to power. In their moment of glory, they have been ideologically weakened.

Why have the Hindu nationalists had to make such compromises? The widely understood reason is simply that India has a *dispersed,* not a *centrally focused,* ethnic configuration.[92] Since independence, no single Indian identity or cleavage—religious, linguistic, caste—has had the power to override all other identities at the national level. Dispersion of cleavages means that parties emphasizing only one cleavage can win power in states. But, to come to power *in Delhi,* politicians must build bridges and coalitions across cleavages. In short, because of India's multicultural diversity, its politics is oriented toward ideological centrism: a multicaste, multiclass, multilinguistic, and multireligious political platform is necessary to capture power in Delhi. By far the biggest obstacle for the BJP is presented by the northward extension of the caste narrative in the 1980s and 1990s. The so-called other backward castes (OBCs) add up to about 52 percent of India (see table 3.2). After the mobilization of lower castes, no party seeking power can ignore their wishes.

The realities of Indian politics have thus already pushed the BJP toward a center-right ideological position. As Hindu nationalism has grown, it has lost its ideological cohesiveness.[93] The right wing of Hindu nationalism is concerned about ideological purity; the center-right would rather gravitate toward ideological expansiveness in search of power. The latter has so far been able to have the upper hand.

Here, then, lies a principal dilemma for Hindu nationalists. If the extreme right succeeds in making the BJP its appendage, it will kill the party's chances to stay in power; if it does not, the BJP will do better, but Hindu nationalism will edge increasingly toward center-right, compromising ideological purity. Either way, a takeover of Indian politics by the Hindu nationalist *ideology* is highly improbable.

Chapter 4 Hindu-Muslim
Riots, 1950–1995:
The National Picture

This chapter deals with the overall statistics on Hindu-Muslim riots, the so-called large-n of communal violence.[1] Based primarily, though not exclusively, on an interpretive reading of the *Times of India* for forty-six years (1950–95), it compiles the riot data and analyzes them. The purpose is to set the stage for the detailed case studies that follow and to ask three questions in particular. First, how is India's communal violence distributed across the nation? Second, do aggregate data, in and of themselves, support some nationwide explanations? Third, if variance is what we should be studying to develop explanations for communal violence, at what level—state, town, village—should variance be studied? What should be the unit of analysis?

The first section explains why existing figures on communal violence are not analytically helpful, making it necessary to create a new data set. The next section describes how data were compiled, what data sources were chosen, and why. Then the chapter breaks down the 46-year time series (1950–95) into the urban-rural, statewise and city-wise distribution of violence.[2] It also establishes the city as the unit of analysis for case studies of communal violence. The final section "tests" a highly popular explanation for Hindu-Muslim violence, one based on modernity. Is modernity the cause of violence or its solution?

EXISTING STATISTICS: WHAT IS WRONG?

For the post-1947 period, the available public figures on communal violence are of six types: official figures on "communal incidents" from the government of India; the annual reports of the Minorities Commission (since 1978); official inquiries into specific riots; government commissions set up to examine issues relevant to public order, such as the Indian Police Commission; the Indian press; and books and articles written by scholars (who were in some cases granted access to confidential records of the government of India).[3]

All of these sources share three defects: government data are neither complete nor easily available; the data are usually not broken down by town or district; and one cannot confidently say that the definition of a "communal incident" was consistent across time and space.

Large Empirical Gaps

Almost all scholars cite the government statistics on "communal incidents" and deaths. This information is usually supplied by the Ministry of Home Affairs in response to questions from a member of Parliament. The published data in parliamentary (*Lok Sabha* and *Rajya Sabha)* proceedings are then reprinted by various journals, especially *Muslim India,* and newspapers. This haphazard process virtually ensures gaps in historical and geographical coverage.

The reports of the Minorities Commission, which, in principle, can fill these gaps, are unable to do so. Ever since its inception in the late 1970s, the Minorities Commission often requested the Home Ministry to supply data on riots, but as the complaints in its reports make clear, the commission did not receive a positive response for many years. In fact, some annual reports of the Minorities Commission have no statistics at all on the previous year's communal riots. In 1992, the commission ceased to a *recommendatory* institution, instead achieving the higher legal status of a *mandatory* body.[4] As a result, its data for the period since 1992 have become better, but for earlier years, there are serious historical and geographical gaps in the publicly available government statistics.

Excessive Aggregation

Only a few Minorities Commission reports provide us with detailed figures on violence in towns and cities. On the whole, they present aggregate figures for each state. These figures give the impression that communal violence is endemic in states, which have high total figures for incidents and deaths. The truth, however, is that in all of India's states violence is concentrated in a few towns and districts only. State-level aggregation hides too much, not permitting an adequate understanding of how violence is distributed and what its causes might be.

Inconsistent Definitions

Government statistics on communal violence, as they presently exist, also appear to be inconsistent. First, the government typically provides data on "communal *incidents,*" not on "communal *riots.*" The former term encompasses everything from a small-scale scuffle to a pitched battle. A large riot in Aligarh lasting several days might, therefore, contain forty "incidents" according to the local administration but be viewed as a single riot by the residents, by those outside the city, and by Indian newspapers. It seems more important to understand, first, why some cities or districts experience riots so often. We may then wish to know why some riots have forty incidents and others only three of four, depending on whether that question can potentially lead to discovering meaningful patterns.

Second, and just as important, there is inferential evidence for the belief that the definition of a communal incident differs across states or even towns. Some states, such as Gujarat, seem to use a narrow definition that records only serious outbreaks of violence, whereas others such as Andhra Pradesh appear to have included a much wider variety of situations affecting communal relations. For example, the Minorities Commission in 1986 reported that in 1985–86, Andhra Pradesh had 102 incidents, in which 10 people were killed and 108 injured, while Gujarat listed only 60 incidents, in which 230 people were killed and 959 injured.[5]

Two interpretations of the statistics presented above are possible. It may be that the statement is factually accurate; or alternatively, all incidents involving some communal strife, even when no major outbreak of violence took place, were recorded in Andhra Pradesh but not in Gujarat. There is no good way of assessing which of the two interpretations is correct on the basis of government data. A survey of the reports in the *Times of India* for the same time period gives greater credence to the latter hypothesis. In 1985–86, none of the Andhra incidents was considered significant enough by the *Times* to merit a report, whereas a very high proportion of Gujarat incidents were covered: 38 separate incidents with 192 dead.

Interviews with officials of the Indian Administrative Service (IAS) and the

Indian Police Service (IPS)—both in Delhi and in the states—indicate that there is no standard definition applied to the term "communal incident." In fact, the way in which data are collected and reported ensures that Delhi can rarely check the information provided by the state capitals. In the state of Uttar Pradesh, for example, records of communal incidents are passed on from each police station to the superintendent of police, who passes them onto the district collector, who sends them to the state capital in the Fortnightly Demi-Official Report (FDO), which is then forwarded to the Home Ministry in Delhi. Although it appears to be rarely done, the only point in this whole process at which these reports might be checked or questioned is in the state capital, where they can be compared with the reports sent separately to the state government by the Intelligence Department.[6] It is entirely possible that at least for some years, the final figures cited by the government are, for all practical purposes, only an aggregation of figures provided by the respective police stations. The judgment of the station officer may thus travel all the way up to Delhi without any statistical corrections in the intermediate stages.

As a result, we can't be sure of what exactly each incident represents and whether each state, district, or police station is using a consistent set of definitions. If the government were to make more disaggregated information available, we would be able to judge the reliability of its data. As of now, it is unwise to place confidence in their accuracy.

Are Government Statistics Always Unreliable?

It is often said that government statistics are inaccurate in the developing world. Why did we look for government data at all?

Whatever one may say about the rest of the developing world, on a whole variety of political and economic issues the Indian government has continued to produced accurate statistics that have formed the basis of solid scholarship. Indeed, no private agency has yet matched the data-collection resources of the vast government machinery at the village and town levels. For problems such as communal riots, however, these statistics are entirely unreliable.

In order to understand why this is so, let us compare government statistics on communal violence and on some economic matters. In order to determine support prices for agriculture, for example, the government collects cost data at the farm level.[7] According to pre-specified and widely accepted statistical principles of stratified sampling, the statistics are collected by the agricultural universities and released by the Agriculture Ministry for the record books. At each stage between data collection and publication there are many steps of statistical oversight. If the field staff overstates how much fertilizer is used per acre, it is easy to check the mistake. A comparison of prices and quantities used in previous years already exists, generating reasonable expectations about how much fertilizer will be used if its price goes down or up (via the so-called elasticity estimates). The concerned agricultural university either discovers the source of error through a reexamination of the sample, or it is made to do so by the Ministry of Agriculture. Errors creep in, as they do in all studies based on large-scale sampling, but going by the standard statistical principles followed worldwide, the margins of error are low enough to generate usable data.

More important, in addition to internal checks, there also exists a large academic community to question the accuracy of key definitions and figures and develop better methods for using the data. As a result, India's agricultural statistics are, on the whole, not only reliable but widely considered to be the best in the developing world.

No such internal and external checks have been instituted by the government of India to ensure that data on communal riots reflect social reality. The data are neither publicly available to scholars nor subjected to detailed internal checks. If the country's agricultural statistics are so open and reliable, why can't the same hold for data on communal violence?

Interviews with government officials suggest that in their view, statistical openness on riots would result in a misuse of statistics by those who wish to hurt the government or the country. It is hard to understand the rationale for this argument. After all, the unavailability of accurate statistics never stops speculation; it merely makes the speculation ill-informed. In the absence of accurate figures on communal incidents and deaths, fictional overestimates are produced by communally minded politicians. They take on undeserved and exaggerated importance, for they become part of the so-called communal discourse. The extent of violence is overstated, not understated, when reliable estimates are not publicly made available—for, absent good statistics, there is no good way to stop or challenge inflated claims.

By allowing all kinds of overblown estimates to be presented by the overenthusiastic reporters and communally inclined politicians and activists, the secrecy surrounding riot data does not facilitate the containment of tensions or violence, if that is the purpose of maintaining secrecy. The government of India has yet to recognize this ironic and unintended result of its information policy on riots.

CREATION OF A NEW DATA SET

What sources to use in research on communal violence has become a contentious issue in recent scholarly literature.[8] It is, therefore, best to lay out clearly what sources were used, why, and how. Those not so troubled by the debate on sources may wish to move directly to the substantive results summarized in the next section.

If appropriate methodological procedures are adopted, newspapers remain the best nongovernmental source for alternative statistics in India. The project chose the *Times of India* as the primary source. We went through each day's *Times of India* reports since 1950 and noted where the riot took place, whether it was rural or urban, what the reported cause was (election, religious processions, criminal conduct, and so on), whether a link was explicit between local violence and some national event, the total number of deaths, injuries, and arrests, and details about the police and government response before and after the riot. Appendix B contains the protocol used for data classification.[9]

The *Times of India* was selected as the principal source because it is the only newspaper that covers the whole period (1950–1995); unlike the *Indian Express,* the *Statesman,* or the *Hindu* (at least until recently), it has a truly national coverage of Hindu-Muslim violence; and according to our research, it has, unlike several other newspapers, many a time refused to run unchecked rumors about communal violence as stories without having them verified by its reporters on the ground.[10] To be sure, the *Times of India* reporting was not without defects, but the application of some simple methodological principles, as reported below, could remedy the errors.

All national newspapers in India have several editions, each headquartered in a major city. The choice of edition, therefore, raises questions about the representativeness of reportage. The Bombay edition of the *Times of India* was chosen for the database. It was safe to assume, subject to later checks, that the Bombay edition would be a reliable source for what we might think of as "large national incidents" of violence, such as a major riot with four or five deaths (and many more injuries).[11] As a national paper, the *Times of India,* regardless of edition, would try to report all major riots in the country.

Surprisingly, the *Times of India* proved to be a reliable source for smaller riots as well—those in which between one and three persons died. To test whether the Bombay edition overreported riots from the neighboring regions (Maharashtra and Gujarat), the ratio of small riots (one to three deaths) to major riots (four deaths or more) was calculated for all states that saw outbreaks of both. As compared to other states, western Indian states, it turned out, did not have higher ratios.[12] The exercise laid to rest doubts about significant underreporting from distant states.

Below this level of violence—namely, in its reporting of riots in which *only injuries* took place—the *Times of India* did, however, have a strong bias toward incidents in states around Bombay. It underreported events of similar magnitude in other states. Thus, the initial hypothesis about a reporting bias was correct, but the level—injuries versus deaths—at which the bias would work was guessed incorrectly. As a consequence, the statistics reported and analyzed below cover only riots in which one or more people were killed. Lacking confidence in the representativeness of other reports, we excluded injuries entirely from the analysis.

Two other methodological issues need to be clarified. The newspapers were read interpretively, not literally. Newspaper reports sometimes do not make a distinction between intrareligious and interreligious violence, reporting them both as "communal." At other times, communal riots are called a clash between two communities. Finally, the term "communal" can cover a whole variety of clashes: Christian-Hindu (as in the tribal areas), Christian-Muslim (as in the state of Kerala), or Hindu-Sikh (as in the state of Punjab in the 1980s), not simply Hindu-Muslim. A detailed understanding of the variety of religious groups, festivals, and contentious issues in different parts of India was thus needed to classify a communal riot as a Hindu-Muslim one. Unless the description of a riot in the newspaper was supported by a discussion of symbols and issues involved, a communal riot was not coded as a Hindu-Muslim riot. Appendix B also contains the set of interpretive rules followed in the statistical coding and classification.

Finally, when faced with an inconsistency in the numbers of reported deaths between different sources cited in the *Times of India,* the classifying rule was one of using the lower figures, not the higher figures. Minimal numbers were considered superior to maximal numbers for two reasons. First, on subjects that are emotionally and politically charged and where government data are unreliable, we cannot generate an intersubjective consensus on the highest numbers reported, for no scholar can find out exactly how many people died. We can, however, get a consensus that "*at least so many* people died." In calculating deaths in Indian riots, statistical exactitude at a national level (large-n) is impossible, for there are no faultless sources of riot-related statistics for the entire country. Such precision is possible only for selected cities (small-n), where fieldwork and exhaustive investigation of documentary sources can be combined to produce accurate statistics.

The improbability of statistical exactitude, however, does not preclude statistical reasonableness. The latter is possible not only because a consensus that "at least so many people died" can be achieved but also because, methodologically speaking, trend analysis examines *directionality*, not the exact distance of one data point from another. If statistical accuracy is impossible, the minimal acceptable figures can be a good second-best for ascertaining directionality, provided minimal figures are the consistent basis for constructing a time series.

This conceptual reasoning is supported by the fact that the aggregate government data for the 1960s and 1970s show the same national trends as the data compiled through the *Times of India* and reported below.[13] Two different data sets, thus, independently point to the same national trends, though neither can be called exact. Does the same directionality by any chance mean that the decision not to rely on government data was wrong?

Results that are no different nationally do not suggest that the decision to disbelieve government data was wrong. First of all, the similarity is only at the aggregate (national) level. Inconsistent definitions can produce the same overall result as consistent definitions do, if the inconsistencies cancel one another out. More important, the government data are not systematically broken up at the urban, rural, and district levels. Thus, despite similarity in aggregate results, the data set based on the *Times of India* is superior because it is disaggregated at many levels. Having compiled riot-by-riot, city-by-city, state-by-state, and year-by-year records and known how it was done, we can have greater confidence in the reasonableness of the *Times* data set than in government reports that never clearly lay out the procedures of classification. Finally, government reports combine all communal riots in their statistics, including Hindu-Christian, Christian-Muslim, and Hindu-Sikh violence. The *Times of India* reports allow us systematically to exclude all riots not concerning Hindus and Muslims.

To sum up, in the statistics presented below two different kinds of claims will be made. First, wherever absolute claims about the number of deaths have been made, they essentially mean "at least so many deaths." Second, however, whenever statements about *trends* have been made, no such qualification is required. Until greater precision about the actual number of deaths can be achieved, the "second best" is the only strategy open to empirical researchers.[14]

HINDU-MUSLIM VIOLENCE:
WHAT ARE THE TRENDS?

National-Level Trends

Did the all-India pattern of communal violence change between 1950–95? It is generally believed that after the peace of the 1950s, the magnitude of violence has increased since the early 1960s. The statistics, in fact, show no trend at all between the early 1950s and the mid-1970s; the pattern can at best be called a random walk (figure 4.1). After the mid-to-late 1970s, however, we do see an unambiguous and rising curve of violence peaking in 1992, when the mosque in Ayodhya was destroyed. In 1994 and 1995, Hindu-Muslim violence dropped to very low levels. It is perhaps true to say that Hindu-Muslim violence in India has declined since the peak of 1993, but in order for that decline to be called a trend, good data on several more years will have to be recorded. It is a judgment to be made in the future.

Figure 4.2 shows the rural-urban breakdown of reported deaths from 1950 to 1995. It confirms the widespread perception that Hindu-Muslim violence is essentially urban. At less than 4 percent in 46 years, the share of rural deaths in overall communal rioting is minuscule. Underreporting of incidents in rural

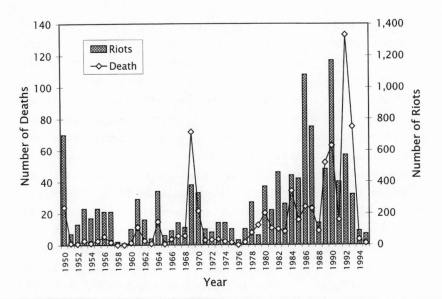

Figure 4.1 Hindu-Muslim Riots, 1950–95

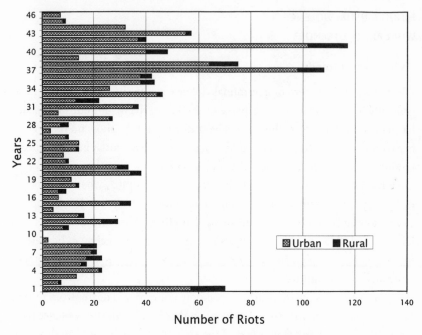

Note: On the y axis, 1 represents 1950, and 46 represents 1995.

Figure 4.2 Rural-Urban Breakdown of Riots by Year, 1950–95

areas may indeed have led to an underestimation of the rural share, but the difference is simply too large to be entirely an artifact of reporting. Even after some underreporting is factored in, it is reasonable to conclude that urban India is the primary site of Hindu-Muslim violence. Put another way, for the rural underreporting completely to undermine the claim that communal violence mainly affects urban India, the underreporting would have to be 15 to 20 times lower than the actual figures. No one intimately familiar with Indian newspapers is prepared to believe such massive underreportage.[15]

It is also sometimes argued that during the Ayodhya movement in the late 1980s and early 1990s communal violence spread to rural India for the first time since the 1947 partition. Figure 4.2 shows that even in the 1960s riots took place in rural India. The Ayodhya movement did indeed provoke a much larger number of incidents—both rural and urban—than in previous years, but it is not true that communal violence in rural areas became increasingly prevalent as a proportion of all violence in the late 1980s. Statistically speaking, the ups and downs of rural communal violence on a base as low as 3–4 per cent of total violence cannot be read as unambiguous or strong indicators of upward or downward trends. It is best to conclude that communal riots have taken place in rural India right since 1947, but the rural share has always been low.

State-Level Trends

A great north-south divide marks perceptions about communalism and communal violence in India. Northern Indian states in general, and Bihar and Uttar Pradesh in particular, are generally believed to be the worst-affected by communal violence. This is partly because, in both popular and scholarly perceptions, the "worst" states are usually seen as those with the greatest total number of incidents and deaths. Therefore the most populous states, even if they have a lower per capita rate of deaths in communal riots, appear to be the most violent. Do significant differences emerge if we compare the aggregate and per capita figures for states?

Figure 4.3 shows the ranking of states when we control for the size of urban population. Uttar Pradesh is not the worst state. The West Indian state of Gujarat, in fact, has the highest per capita rate of deaths in communal incidents, at around 117 per million of urban population. Bihar in the north (78 deaths per million) and Maharashtra in the west (45 deaths per million) also have higher per capita rates than Uttar Pradesh (43 deaths per million). Clearly, communal-

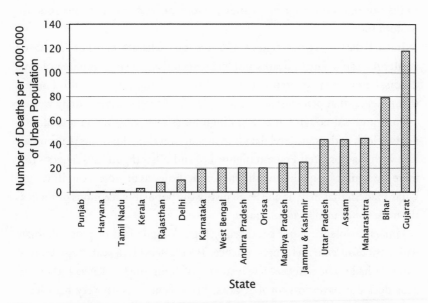

Figure 4.3 Deaths per 1,000,000 of Urban Populations in Riots with One or More Deaths, 1950–95

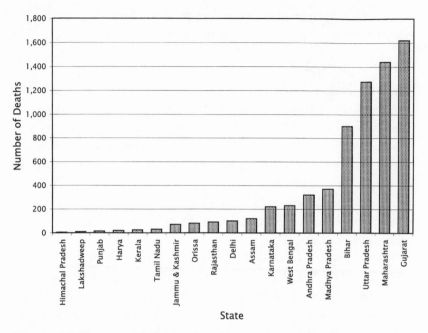

Figure 4.4 Rankings of Total Deaths in States in Riots with One or More Deaths, 1950–95

ism is not primarily a northern Indian problem; it is also a serious issue for western India.

Indeed, the two western states—Gujarat and Maharashtra—not only have a greater per capita rate of deaths and incidents but also a larger number of total deaths in riots than do Uttar Pradesh and Bihar (figure 4.4). Does this finding, then, suggest that perceptions about the levels of violence are entirely wrong?

Not quite. Although Gujarat has high levels of deaths in communal incidents, a look at the state level data for Gujarat over time (figure 4.5) in comparison with that for Uttar Pradesh (figure 4.6) and Bihar (figure 4.7) suggests that there are significant qualitative differences in the levels of violence in Bihar and Uttar Pradesh that may, at one level, justify the popular perceptions of them as the most communally violent states.

Gujarat's violence is not consistently high: long periods of peace alternate with periods of extremely high violence. Twenty-five of 46 years between 1950 and 1995 had no riots or very few incidents of communal violence. Either Gujarat does not have riots, or if it does, the violence reaches very high levels quickly. Contrariwise, the history of communal violence in Uttar Pradesh and Bihar (figures 4.6 and 4.7) is much more consistent. Similarly, Maharashtra

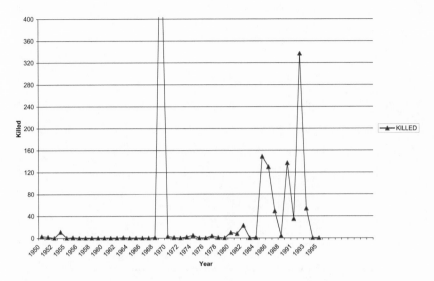

Figure 4.5 Total Deaths per Year, Gujarat, 1950–95

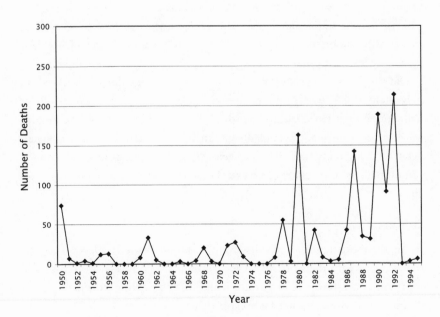

Figure 4.6 Total Deaths per Year, Uttar Pradesh, 1950–95

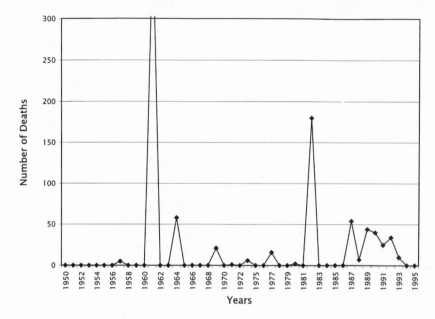

Figure 4.7 Total Deaths per Year, Bihar, 1950–95

(figure 4.8) also has a pattern of consistent violence. There are more years of violence in these states than of peace. In other words, Uttar Pradesh, Bihar, and Maharashtra should be regarded as states "prone" to communal violence. Gujarat's case is one of proneness to *big* violence amid long stretches of peace.[16]

Did the preexisting state patterns continue or change during the Ayodhya movement (1986–93)? Although the violence-prone states discussed above maintained their patterns, it is worth noting that even states where Hindu-Muslim peace normally prevailed were unable to escape the violence engendered by the Ayodhya agitation between 1989 and 1993. Consider trends in the communally peaceful states of Orissa, Rajasthan, and Kerala (figures 4.9, 4.10, and 4.11).[17]

City-Level Trends

By far the most significant results are to be found at the city level. Table 4.1 shows towns with the worst record of communal violence between 1950 and 1995 in increasing order of magnitude (columns 2 to 5). How the orders of magnitude were derived requires some explanation.

The first question in deriving any such measure is: How does one define

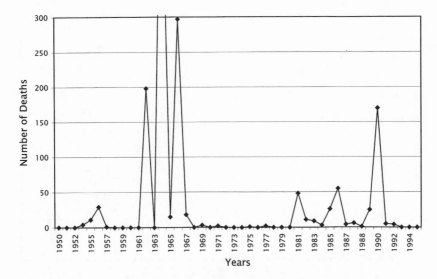

Figure 4.8 Total Deaths per Year, Maharashtra, 1950–95

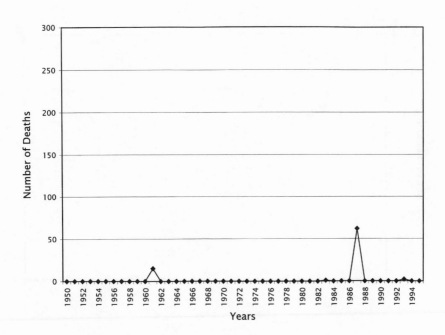

Figure 4.9 Total Deaths per Year, Orissa, 1950–95

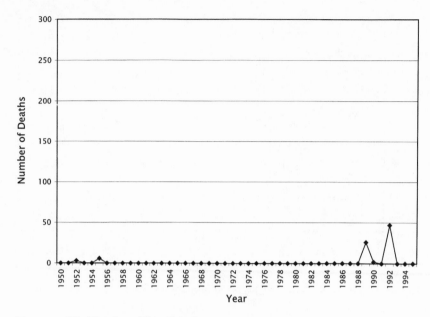

Figure 4.10 Total Deaths per Year, Rajasthan, 1950–95

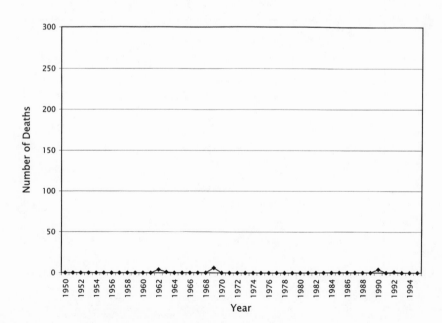

Figure 4.11 Total Deaths per Year, Kerala, 1950–95

"riot-proneness"? There are problems with only using deaths as a measure. Should a town such as Bhagalpur, which had one serious riot in 46 years—but a riot in which scores were killed—be considered more "riot-prone" than Delhi, which has had a large number of riots but very few deaths per riot? One would obviously have to combine intensity *and* persistence. To develop such a composite measure for riot-proneness for the period 1950–95, four simple questions, making the benchmark progressively more stringent, were asked:

a. How many cities in India had at least 3 communal riots, spread over at least 2 five-year periods, in which a minimum of 15 deaths occurred? (table 4.1, column 1);

b. How many had at least 4 riots over at least 3 five-year periods and a minimum of 20 deaths? (column 2);

c. How many witnessed at least 5 riots and 25 deaths over 4 five-year periods? (column 3);

d. Finally, how many had at least 50 deaths in at least 10 riots over 5 five-year periods? (column 4).

These columns can be called RP1, RP2, RP3, and RP4, respectively.

If my reasoning is right, the RP4 category (column 4) was truly riot-prone in the period 1950–95. Of the four categories of riot-proneness constructed, RP4 combines intensity and persistence in a most stringent way. In principle, RP3 (column 3) could also be included in the category of riot-proneness but, as we will see below, the inclusion of RP3 does not alter the primary conclusion that emerges from such an exercise.

The eight RP4 cities account for as many as 45.5 percent of total deaths in urban India and 49 percent of all deaths in the entire country. The RP4 cities hold only about 18 percent of India's urban population, showing how concentrated the country's Hindu-Muslim violence is. Their proportion of the population would, of course, be considerably smaller if urban and rural subtotals were combined. With the latter included, "riot-proneness" would seem to be confined to a mere 5 percent of India's total population.

The riot-prone cities also account for a disproportionate share of Hindu-Muslim violence in their respective states. In the state of Gujarat, for example, the two RP4 cities—Ahmedabad and Vadodara (Baroda)—account for about 75 percent of the total deaths between 1950 and 1995; the city of Hyderabad had more than 90 percent of all riot deaths in the state of Andhra Pradesh; and metropolitan Bombay accounted for 63 percent of all deaths in the state of Maharashtra (and what would be functionally equivalent, the four RP3 towns of Ma-

Table 4.1. Violence in India's "Riot-Prone" Cities as a Proportion of All Reported Hindu-Muslim Violence, 1950–95

RP1: Minimum of 15 deaths in 3 riots over 2 five-year periods	RP2: Minimum of 20 deaths in 4 riots over 3 five-year periods	RP3: Minimum of 25 deaths in 5 riots over 4 five-year periods	RP4: Minimum of 50 deaths in 10 riots over 5 five-year periods	Deaths, 1950–95	% Literate	% Muslim
Bombay	Bombay	Bombay	Bombay	1,137	83	14
Ahmedabad	Ahmedabad	Ahmedabad	Ahmedabad	1,119	79	15
Hyderabad	Hyderabad	Hyderabad	Hyderabad	312	71	34
Meerut	Meerut	Meerut	Meerut	265	61	34
Jamshedpur	Jamshedpur	Jamshedpur		198	81	12
Bhiwandi	Bhiwandi			194	63	53
Surat				194	76	15
Aligarh	Aligarh	Aligarh	Aligarh	160	60	35
Moradabad	Moradabad			149	57	48
Baroda	Baroda	Baroda	Baroda	109	82	11
Bhopal	Bhopal	Bhopal		108	72	28
Delhi	Delhi	Delhi	Delhi	93	77	8
Kanpur	Kanpur	Kanpur		81	72	20
Calcutta	Calcutta	Calcutta	Calcutta	63	78	14
Jabalpur				59	79	11
Bangalore	Bangalore	Bangalore		56	81	14
Jalgaon	Jalgaon	Jalgaon		49	79	16

Sitamarhi				47	n.a.	18
Indore	Indore	Indore	Indore	45	78	13
Varanasi	Varanasi	Varanasi	Varanasi	42	64	24
Allahabad	Allahabad	Allahabad	Allahabad	37	73	22
Nagpur	Nagpur	Nagpur	Nagpur	37	82	10
Jaipur	Jaipur			32	70	18
Aurangabad	Aurangabad	Aurangabad	Aurangabad	30	77	31
Srinagar	Srinagar	Srinagar	Srinagar	30	n.a.	89
Ranchi				29	83	15
Malegaon	Malegaon	Malegaon		23	70	68
Godhra				18	76	40

Deaths in Riot-Prone Cities	4,706	4,359	3,887	3,263
All, India Deaths 1950–95	7,173	7,173	7,173	7,173
Riot-Prone Cities as a Percentage of all India Deaths	66	61	54	45.5
Riot-Prone Cities as a Percentage of all urban deaths	69	64	58	49
Deaths in rural India as a Percentage of all deaths	3.57			

harashtra—Bombay, Aurangabad, Jalgaon, and Nagpur—had 70 percent of all deaths in the state).[18] All of these states had more towns that were peaceful than were violent. Violence, thus, was not concentrated in a particular state but in various cities in different states. The unmistakable local concentration and the relationship between state-level and city-level statistics clearly establish the city as the unit of analysis for a study of the causes of communal violence. India's Hindu-Muslim violence is city-specific. State (and national) politics provide the context within which the local mechanisms linked with violence are activated.

Moreover, popular perceptions about some cities are simply wrong. Until 1993, when horrible communal riots broke out, Bombay, India's premier business city, was often called an island of peace where local energies were mostly spent on cosmopolitan pursuits and monetary gains. This is simply not true. Bombay's modernity and cosmopolitanism have not precluded communal violence. Bombay was among the most communally violent cities even before 1993. Similarly, Delhi and Calcutta, both considered to be peaceful after independence, especially the latter, also have a bad record, though their violence level is considerably lower than that of Bombay. They tend to have small riots but there have been many of them. Delhi and Calcutta benefit from what might be called a scale effect. Given their sheer size, violence in some areas, unless truly ghastly, does not affect routine life in other parts. A riot in Old Delhi does not affect life in New Delhi to the same extent as similar violence would in smaller cities such as Moradabad or Meerut, where practically the whole city can come to a standstill.

Finally, note that all RP3 and RP4 4 towns are the so-called Class I cities of India—in other words, their populations are greater than 100,000. Even in the least violent (RP1) category, there are only two towns—Godhra and Sitamarhi—that are not Class I. Communal violence at its most intense and persistent seems to be a phenomenon of India's larger towns. Communalism may exist in Class II towns (50,000 to 100,000 people) and Class III towns (25,000–50,000), but tensions do not lead to high levels of violence.

Several hypotheses suggest themselves. It may be that communal tensions flare up less in smaller towns, for they lack the relative anonymity of India's largest towns and allow greater routine interaction between Hindus and Muslims. Or, it may simply be that large towns are extremely difficult places for the police to control violence once it breaks out.

In the detailed city comparisons undertaken later in the book, these factors are investigated at length. On a more general level, however, a theoretical debate can be discussed right away. Since larger cities are more modern than smaller towns and villages, it is argued, especially by anti- and postmodernists, that this is enough to show a causal link between modernity and communal or ethnic violence. Is that right?

MODERNITY AND COMMUNAL VIOLENCE

Arguments about the relation between modernity and communalism or communal violence have long been dominant in intellectual circles. By now, of course, the debate has come full circle. Until the 1960s, modernization was considered a solution to the problem of communalism. Over the last decade or so, however, antimodernity arguments have acquired unprecedented popularity. India has had strong advocates on both sides. The customary view, a view that is often associated with Nehru and the Indian left, was that greater modernity would solve the problem of communalism. To the antisecularists or antimodernists, however, modernity is a problem, not a solution.[19]

The Modernists

That a rising tide of rationality and modernization would sweep away the ascriptive identities of religion, ethnicity, and nation—identities that had led to such violence, bloodshed, and ruin in the first half of the twentieth century—was not simply an argument confined to the left. The modernization theory was an article of faith for most intellectuals in the 1950s and 1960s. By the 1970s, it was clear that the expected erosion of ethnicity and religion was not taking place. Since then, the persistence of these identities, despite modernization, has been taken more or less for granted by scholars.[20]

Although few believe in the modernization theory today, a newer form of the argument has emerged of late. In the recent version, the emphasis has moved from economic prosperity to literacy, and, more generally, to "human development."[21] Amartya Sen, for example, has drawn a contrast between Kerala, which has the highest literacy rate in the country and lowest communal violence, and North India, which scores low on literacy and high on riots. Sen argues that literacy and communal violence are related and that improved literacy will lead to lower communal violence or even its gradual elimination.[22]

This argument relies too heavily on a Kerala–Uttar Pradesh or Kerala-Bihar comparison. If we cast our statistical net wider, the argument breaks down. States with the lowest communal violence happen to be at two opposite ends of the literacy spectrum. Kerala and Rajasthan are both among the least communally violent states. Kerala, as is widely known, is the most literate state in India. At 90.59 percent, its literacy rate in 1991 was far above India's overall literacy rate of 52.21 percent.[23] Rajasthan, however, also communally peaceful, is among the least literate. At 38.81 percent, its literacy rate is among the lowest in India. Moreover, states such as Gujarat and Maharashtra have high levels of communal violence coexisting with high literacy rates. At 63.05 and 60.91 percent, respectively, both of these states were considerably above the national average in 1991.

Disaggregation at the city level also yields the same result. The RP3 or RP4 towns in table 4.1 have literacy rates ranging from 60 percent (Aligarh) to 80 percent and above (Bombay, Baroda). The national average for urban literacy was about 70 percent in 1991.[24] Rural India, with a literacy rate considerably lower than that of urban India, is not the primary site of communal violence.

Since, as we move from state-level to city-level data, we can get a large number of observations, it is also possible to run regressions and test the conclusion above more rigorously. Indeed, results of both standard least squares and logistic regressions, as reported in detail in Appendix C, show that literacy has no relation at all to whether a city will be prone to riots.

In short, there is no systematic relationship between literacy and communal violence. For a whole variety of reasons, India ought to improve its literacy levels. But one should not expect that an increase in literacy will reduce communal conflict.

The Antimodernists

How do the data presented above reflect on the arguments of antimodernists or antisecularists? Let us briefly recall the antisecularist view, according to which modernity in its various manifestations—rationality, urbanization, science, and secularism—is the cause of higher religious or communal violence. First, in the garb of a nation-state, modernity tends to flatten the diversity of traditional cultures. Many people resist homogenization, sticking instead to their particularistic roots—be they in religion, language, or culture. India is perhaps the most diverse society in the world. Attempts at homogenizing India are bound to produce violence. Second, modernity attacks the values of a religiously driven society such as India, generating a reaction among the believers: dams, even in a modern age, cannot replace temples of worship. Finally, and most important, modernity, according to antisecularists, makes politicians immoral. Religion used to provide inner controls on human behavior; the modern man considers nothing sacred; in search of power and profit, a modern politician, if necessary, will use communal violence as a strategic tool.

The antisecularist view has been adopted by both antimodernists and post-modernists.[25] Its theoretical grandeur and popularity notwithstanding, it has never been tested. Nor has it ever been indicated what might constitute an appropriate test for the argument, given that the modernity-versus-tradition view, strictly speaking, is an epochal view. It speaks of the modern and pre-modern times, not of shorter time horizons. The latter, needless to add, are more easily testable than the former.

The epochal sweep of the argument may create problems of exact testing, but a proximate test is possible, and it begins to show the cracks in the anti-modernist claim. In his writings, Nandy, among the most influential antimod-ernists of our time, has consistently maintained that the *link between tradition and rural India* is very much alive even today. Modernity has established its hegemony in urban, not in rural, India. The countryside may gradually fall into the trap of modernity, but it remains less afflicted by modernity, and its traditional mechanisms of peaceful resolution of religious disputes are, by and large, still alive. Nandy's argument against the urban-industrial India is unam-biguous: "As India gets modernized, religious violence is increasing. . . . In the earlier centuries, . . . inter-religious riots were rare and localized . . . [S]ome-where and somehow, *religious violence has something to do with the urban-indus-trial vision of life and with the political process the vision lets loose.*"[26]

Does the urban-rural distribution of communal violence support antimod-ernists? It is true that Hindu-Muslim violence primarily takes place in the cities, not in the countryside. But, as shown above, it is also true that as much as 82 percent of urban India is not prone to such violence. Although an overall urban-rural distribution may suggest that modernity, proxied here by urban-ization, may potentially be a cause, a greater disaggregation—that is, an intra-urban distribution—of violence indicates that greater modernity cannot be the reason for higher communal violence.

Urban violence can be examined in yet another way. The most riot-prone ar-eas, as we have seen, are the largest urban centers: the so-called Class I cities, having a population of more than 100,000 people. Moreover, the regression re-sults, presented in detail in Appendix C, also show that the size of the city, mea-sured by its total population, significantly affects the probability that a city will be riot-prone.

Can this observation support the antimodernist claim? The largest cities, after all, are the farthest removed from traditional India, whereas smaller towns maintain, to a considerable extent, the intimacy of village India and arguably its peaceful resolution of religious disputes.

Of the roughly 218 million urban people in India in 1991, 142.14 million (65.2 percent) lived in Class I cities. The population of the eight RP4 cities, all Class I, was about 39.5 million, which was about 28 percent of the total population in Class I cities.[27] Thus, only 28 percent of the overall population of Class I cities lived in riot-prone areas. Even if we extend the definition of riot-proneness to RP3 cities, we find that the aggregate population living there was 37 percent of the total Class I population in 1991. More than 63 percent of the most urban part of the country manages its life in a relatively peaceful manner, broken at worst by an occasional riot.

Once we put this breakdown and the regression results together, an interpretation begins to emerge: the larger the city, the greater the chance that it may become riot-prone, *but it does not have to.* We need to ask why, even though the population size of the city increases the probability that it will be riot-prone, many Class I cities remain calm. The variance within urban India significantly erodes the antimodernist argument.

These tests are unlikely to satisfy the antisecularists and modernists, who may claim that their arguments are deeper. Arguments about modernity, they may claim, are either not reducible to testing, or if tests are conducted, they should cover the pre-modern and modern periods of Indian history, not urban and rural India after 1950. By this logic, only the former can provide a conclusive test.

We only have impressionistic knowledge about communal violence in pre-modern India, whereas a great deal can be said about the modern period, especially the twentieth century. The incomplete evidence that historians have produced shows considerable Hindu-Muslim rioting in the eighteenth century, though the levels of violence do not appear to be comparable to those reached in the twentieth century.[28]

Short of examining exhaustive data, is there a way of resolving the debate? Let us suppose for the sake of argument that the twentieth-century levels of communal violence are indeed historically unprecedented. Would this assumption support antimodernists?

It may well be that the higher levels of communal conflict simply reflect the breakdown of pre-modern ascriptive hierarchies. The rise of equality and self-respect as a behavioral idea can be shown to have undermined caste hierarchies in much of India in the twentieth century: southern India experienced such an erosion in the first half of the century, and northern India is experiencing it now.[29] Is it that religious communities, like caste communities, in traditional India were placed in a hierarchical relationship of lesser and higher worth, of lesser and higher privileges, and such hierarchies were acceptable so long as notions of deference held cultural and ideological sway? If true, then the role of modernity is of a different kind, for it is not the intolerance of modernity or its penchant for cultural uniformity but its attack on ascriptive hierarchies that would cause communal conflict. The former is the argument of antimodernists, not the latter. Indeed, scholars such as Charles Taylor have put the latter idea at the heart of research on ethnic conflict today.[30]

CONCLUSION

If there are enough places that, in spite of modernity, do not have communal violence, and communities in such towns have found a way to solve or coexist with interreligious problems, the explanatory focus will have to shift from modernity to institutions or factors that make it possible for communities to live together and solve their problems in a relatively peaceful manner, instead of expressing them in acts of violence toward one another. These peace-keeping factors will be better able to explain communal peace or violence, not modernity per se. By going into the local history of conflict and peace, the case studies presented in the later chapters confront this issue at length.

Part III **Local Variations**

INTRODUCTION

We proceed now to the three paired cases—a comparison in each case of a violent and a peaceful city having, at the very least, roughly similar Hindu-Muslim proportions in the population. The case materials follow a two-step methodological procedure.

First, we ask why one city has been peaceful and the other violent in recent times. The method of process-tracing is applied to establish how, given similar stimuli or provocations, different kinds of civic networks—intercommunal versus intracommunal, associational versus quotidian—are linked to the divergent outcomes—peace and riots, respectively.

Second, it must be asked whether the relationship observed is merely a correlation or whether civic integration is also *causally* connected to communal peace. This analytically necessary step required investigation of the history of each major civic association found present in the cities researched. It turned out in the process of such detailed historical inquiry that almost all of those associations were born between the 1920s and the 1940s. This finding naturally triggered a question: What was it about the period starting from the 1920s that generated such coincidence in so many cases?

The search for an answer took the inquiry to India's freedom, or national, movement, especially to how the 1920s constituted a transformative moment —socially, culturally, and politically. With the spectacular rise of Mahatma Gandhi and his followers, India's freedom movement, confined to the English-speaking thin upper crust of India before then, became mass-based in the 1920s. The aim of the movement was not simply to wrest independence from the British but, equally important for our purposes, also to reconstruct Indian society. Gandhian ideology was premised on the belief that the British conquest of India was in large part based on India's own internal inadequacies and underlying problems." These had to be fought and Indian society reconstructed just as the battle to oust the British was to be conducted. A mass-based Congress Party was a primary agent of the battle against the British, but it was to be only one of several institutions for social reforms and campaigns.[1]

What would these reconstructive projects be? Gandhian ideology identified several goals: ridding India of Hindu-Muslim divisions and untouchability; building a tradition of self-reliance *(swadeshi);* uplifting the tribals, women, and the downtrodden; and creating educational institutions that could instill pride among pupils, not a sense of shame about being Indian, which British education of Indians and British versions of Indian history had quite successfully done.

Such a massive nation-building project, moreover, was to be carried out in the overarching framework of nonviolence. As is well known, Gandhi was a leading practitioner of "civil disobedience." Violence, Gandhi thought, was not the way to deal with British rule in India. The superior military force of the colonial power could always overwhelm violent acts of defiance, whereas the ruler after a point could not use violence against a people who, while protesting, continued to take blows of the ruler in an organized, disciplined, and peaceful way. Principled nonviolence, Gandhi argued, would produce helplessness in the ruler, for it would make the use of violence self-defeating and morally disgusting. By doing so, it would also build strength in a community. Nonviolent resistance to unjust laws would both defeat the British and build a strong Indian nation.

It should be clear how important education, campaigning, and organizations were for such a nation-building project. India's freedom movement thus was social as well as political. It created a whole range of associations and organizations in India. Indians did interact with one another before that, but pre-

1920 civic engagement was basically an everyday and informal engagement. By creating cadre-based political parties, trade unions, new educational institutions, and new cultural and social organizations, the Gandhian shift in politics laid the foundations of India's associational civic order.

Gandhi is viewed as the father of India, but it is not often realized that he was a master of civic activism and thinking. Gandhi did not have a theory of governance, nor did he trust the state to guide human affairs. His reliance on moral transformation of society meant a lot of civic, nongovernmental activity. In a revealing passage, he wrote: "Political power means capacity to regulate national life through national representatives. If national life becomes so perfect as to become self-regulated, no representation is necessary. . . . In such a state everyone is his own ruler. . . . In the ideal state, therefore, there is no political power because there is no state. But the ideal is never fully realized in life. Hence the classical statement of Thoreau that that government is best which governs the least."[2] This position inevitably led to what in today's language can be called a primary reliance on civil society for governing human affairs and only a secondary reliance on the state.

Given how massive the vision and project were, it is to be expected that Gandhi wouldn't entirely succeed, but neither did he completely fail. All kinds of organizations and campaigns came into being. Anti-British violence was indeed minimal, but Hindu-Muslim violence could not be contained in many parts of India.

The case materials that follow show that different parts and cities of India participated differently in this project of national reconstruction. Why it turned out to be so, why even the extraordinary powers of Gandhi and his followers could not produce "a straight line out of the crooked timber of humanity," and what the implications were in different parts of India—these are the matters of inquiry and analysis in the next chapters.[3]

Part III Local Variations

Aligarh and Calicut: Internal and External Cleavages

Chapter 5 Aligarh and Calicut:
Civic Life and Its Political
Foundations

Before investigating the similarities and differences between the towns of Aligarh and Calicut, let me relate the story of our field research in the two towns. The story bears on a key theme of the comparison: intercommunal trust or communication in civic life.

In order to gather statistics on the Hindu-Muslim breakdown of business ownership in Aligarh, a town in the northern Indian state of Uttar Pradesh, a Muslim member of our research team approached the District Industries Office. A Hindu journalist was sitting there. The project was introduced and a request for data made. A story appeared in the local daily the next day that the CIA was conducting research on Hindu-Muslim relations in India. The newspaper further said that Harvard University, the sponsor of research at that time, was an agent of the CIA. Moreover, the newspaper argued, Muslim research officers were being deployed to gather sensitive information, and a Hindu professor was directing the project from Harvard. The purpose of the project, according to the story, was to discover the causes of riots in Aligarh so that similar riots could be incited in Calicut and other peaceful towns of India. In order to weaken India, the newspaper said, the CIA wanted to instigate widespread Hindu-Muslim violence all over the country.[1]

The research team was unnerved by the banner headlines. Luckily, the national dailies did not think the matter was important enough to carry the story. Research was resumed later in Aligarh. It took some time, however, to allay the fears and instill enough confidence in ourselves that the project could go forward, without such unwarranted and scurrilous journalistic attention.

Several months later in Calicut, a town in the southern Indian state of Kerala, I interviewed E. Moidu Moulvi, a leading Muslim freedom fighter, who passed away in 1995. When I reached the Moulvi's house, I found three reporters and photographers. My purpose was to have the Moulvi recall Hindu-Muslim interactions in Calicut during the freedom movement in the 1920s and 1930s. The role played by the Moulvi during the movement was familiar to me, but little did I realize that the Moulvi was a legendary figure in the city. The newspapers had reporters whose "beat" was to cover the evening of the Moulvi's life. I did not want a public interview, but the journalists requested that they be allowed to stay. They were curious about the research project, about the questions I had for a great political figure of the city, and about his answers.

The next day a leading local newspaper ran a picture of the Moulvi being interviewed by me. The caption read: "A Student of History Meets a Maker of History."[2] Calicut reporters did not think that the purpose of my research was to spread disaffection and violence in their peaceful town, as their counterparts in Aligarh had suspected. They did not ask whether I was Muslim or Hindu. They made a clear distinction between curiosity and suspicion. Indeed, it took very little time to gather information on matters generally considered sensitive in Aligarh. The local business federation gladly shared information on the Hindu-Muslim breakdown of Calicut's trade sector. In Aligarh, it is remarkably difficult to get these figures.

For the Muslims, the two towns are culturally, educationally, and historically significant. Aligarh's Muslim University (AMU) is intimately tied up the modern history of northern Indian Muslims. Since its founding in the 1870s, first as a college, the AMU has been a symbol of the educational and political aspirations of a critical mass of Indian Muslims. Indeed, most scholars of modern India would argue that it is impossible to write the history of Muslim politics in the subcontinent without understanding the role of the AMU. It was the intellectual center of the movement that led to India's partition in 1947 and to the birth of Pakistan. And after 1947, it continued to be the center of higher education for Muslims in northern India, as well as an object of intense political passions and controversies.

Though not exactly comparable to Aligarh's national political significance, Calicut is the center of culture and education for Kerala Muslims. As Aligarh is venerated by northern Indian Muslims, Calicut is respected by Kerala Muslims. It is the headquarters of several leading Muslim institutions and organizations: the Muslim League, the Muslim Educational Society, and the Muslim Service Society. Farook College, the first Muslim college in Kerala, was founded in Calicut. The Calicut University was especially set up to make higher education accessible to Muslims of the area.

Moreover, starting in the 1970s, both cities have developed a substantial Muslim middle class. From both, Muslims migrated to the Middle East in large numbers after the oil price increases of 1973. Profiting from remittances sent home from the Gulf, Muslims have improved their economic standing in both cities. Finally, both have a roughly similar percentage of Muslims in the town population. Muslims have comprised 34–35 percent of Aligarh's population since 1951; in Calicut, their share is 36–37 percent.

Calicut and Aligarh, however, are also a world apart. A deep intercommunal civic engagement marks life in Calicut. Neighborhoods are remarkably integrated, and so is the city's business and professional life. In Aligarh, Hindu-Muslim civic engagement is minimal. Calicut has not had a single communal riot in a century, although it came desperately close to breaking its harmony in 1921 during the so-called Malabar rebellion. Aligarh is infamous for frequent outbreaks of Hindu-Muslim violence. It is among the most riot-prone cities of India identified in table 1.1.

Why do Hindus and Muslims live peacefully in Calicut but not in Aligarh? Two arguments are made in the comparative materials presented here. First, a thick civic engagement between Hindus and Muslims marks Calicut, which makes it hard for politicians to play the politics of religious polarization. Some have tried; most do not, *including politicians who would clearly benefit from such polarization.* The BJP's electoral fortunes are a case in point. The BJP has been a marginal political entity in Calicut. Nothing would benefit the BJP more than antagonism between Hindus and Muslims in Calicut, but the party is unable to create communal animosities. Contrariwise, the BJP flourishes in Aligarh and has often been associated with communal violence. Since independence the politicians of Calicut have, on the whole, built bridges across religious communities. In Aligarh, communal polarization has been the principal political strategy of the BJP and many Muslim leaders, and violence often part of the political calculations.

Second, although they restrain politicians in the short and medium run, the intercommunal civic networks in Calicut were *politically* constructed in the long run. Caste injustice within Hindu society rather than communal antagonism between Hindus and Muslims has historically formed the master narrative of Kerala politics. Caste was more central to the ascriptive hierarchy in Kerala than was religion. Hence ethnic conflict historically took the idiom of caste.[3] Hindu-Muslim politics functioned within a larger context of intra-Hindu caste differences. In Aligarh, the reverse has been true. Communalism has been the dominant political narrative for a century, and caste politics within Hinduism has historically functioned within the larger framework of Hindu-Muslim antagonisms. Communalism in Aligarh emerged because a declining Muslim aristocracy, part of the ruling class in pre-British times, was unable to come to terms with a framework of political participation that relied on elections, not nominations and quotas. Rather than accepting the egalitarian implications of democratic rule, the former Muslim aristocrats wanted to protect their privileges, to which the rising Hindu middle classes were opposed. The Muslim elite wanted a form of consociationalism, which would make them the spokesmen for the entire Muslim community. Their political rivals

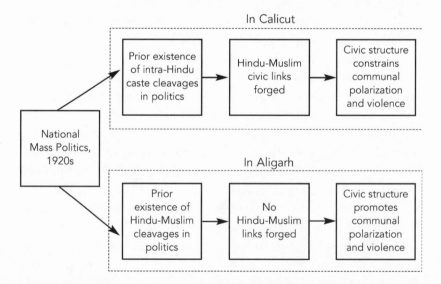

Figure 5.1 Politics, Civic Life, and Communal Violence in Calicut and Aligarh

argued in favor of a majoritarian political system. The latter would not accede to communal consociationalism, and the Muslim elite would not accept majoritarianism. Later, as franchise expanded and mass politics emerged, the consociational argument became part of Muslim mass politics as well. The British, a third important factor in the Hindu-Muslim equation, used the emerging divide among the Hindu and Muslim political elite. Aligarh remained at the center of this larger process.

Figure 5.1 diagrammatically presents the two arguments together. The account below is also organized around the two parts of the explanation above. I first compare Aligarh and Calicut's civic life. Then I turn to its political foundations between the 1930s and the 1940s. Once these foundations were laid, the post-independence phase in politics was marked by a vicious circle of violence in Aligarh and a virtuous circle of peace in Calicut. These circles are explored in the next chapter.

VIOLENCE AND CIVIC LIFE

Similar Provocations, Different Responses: An Example

Between 1989 and 1992, when the Hindu nationalist agitation to destroy the Baburi mosque in Ayodhya led to unprecedented violence in much of India, the two cities responded very differently. Communal tensions did emerge in Calicut, but *all* political parties, including the Muslim League and BJP, supported the local administration's efforts to maintain law and order. The city-level peace committees, formed with the participation of political leaders, were the key tension-management device; in addition, neighborhood-level peace committees emerged between trusting neighbors and neighborhood-level leaders. Unfounded rumors circulated in the town that pigs had been thrown into mosques and temples attacked. Such rumors often lead to riots in several cities in India. In Calicut, the peace committees, and the press, helped the administration squash rumors.

In contrast, blinded by a Hindu nationalist fervor during the Ayodhya agitation, the city of Aligarh plunged into horrendous violence. Unlike Calicut newspapers, which would neutralize rumors after investigating them, Aligarh's local newspapers printed blatant falsehoods in order to incite passions. Two of the largest-circulation Hindi newspapers wrote in lurid detail that Muslim nurses, doctors, and staff of the university hospital had killed Hindu patients in cold blood.[4] Some Hindus were indeed killed outside the university campus,[5] but nobody was murdered in the AMU hospital.[6] The rumors, however, were believed. In the revulsion created by the presumed outrage in the hospital, gangs of Hindu criminals went on a killing spree. Some of them stopped a train just outside the city, dragged Muslims out, and brutally murdered them. Their acts of killing were underreported by the press. Owned and edited by journalists of Hindu nationalist orientation, these newspapers were later reprimanded for unprofessional behavior by the Press Council. The damage, however, had already been done. Gruesome violence rocked the city for several days, leading to at least 75 deaths.

Aligarh's remarkably fragile local mechanisms of peace were insufficient to deal with the situation, as they had repeatedly been in the past fifteen years. The law and order machinery broke down, as it had frequently. And as was true so often before, criminals engaged in killing could not be brought to book. They were not only protected by politicians; they also they had remarkable journalistic connections—Muslim criminals with the Urdu press and Hindu thugs with Hindi press. Effective peace committees could not be formed at the city level in Aligarh, for it was difficult to get the BJP and Muslim politicians together. Rumors would often be started, and played upon, by political organizations. Instead of investigating rumors professionally, the press would print them with utter recklessness.

Contrast the situation in Calicut. On how peace was kept, two points were common to all accounts given by administrators of Calicut between 1989 and 1992 (as well as those who have been posted there since the mid-1980s and dealt with communal tensions). First, politicians of all parties helped establish peace in the town, instead of polarizing communities, as in Aligarh. Second, peace committees were critical to management of tensions.[7] The latter provided information that local political leadership might have had but the administration did not; they became a forum for everybody to speak and express their anger; they gave a sense of participation to all major local actors; and they provided links all the way down to the neighborhood level. With regard to Hindu-Muslim relations, politics became a constructive enterprise in Calicut.

Peace committees in Aligarh have often tended to be intrareligious, not interreligious. They are formed at the neighborhood level to protect the co-religionists from a possible attack from the other communities. They don't facilitate communication with the other communities; they simply raise the perception of risk and harden those who participate in them. The members of these committees take turns to police their community. Intrareligious committees are, by definition, based not on interreligious trust but on a lack of trust. Moving within one's own community, hearing rumors that no one can verify or disapprove, staying up in the middle of the night for weeks together, collecting firearms and other small weapons to ensure that retaliation is swift if attacks are made—these activities fuel, and are reflections of, a communal consciousness, not a consciousness that builds bridges.

Political Strategies and Civic Life

Communalism does exist in Calicut, but its meaning is different, closer to the North American than the Indian understanding of the term. Communalism simply means a regard for one's community in Kerala, not a hatred for the other communities. It does not lead to communal violence. The Muslim League (the League) is a powerful political party. Entirely Muslim-supported, it has repeatedly won elections in Calicut. It has held important ministries in coalition governments at the state level repeatedly since 1967. As a result of its governmental power, it has been able to provide remarkable material and symbolic benefits to the Muslim community including state pensions for Muslim clerics, contracts for Muslim businessmen, a state holiday for Prophet Muhammad's birthday, and creation of a Muslim-majority district. The League seeks and gets Muslim votes, but communal polarization and hatred are not consequences of its politics. When they do emerge, the League moderates communal tensions instead of inflaming them.

Why have Calicut's politicians not polarized religious communities? One might say that being a partner in government, a political party such as the Muslim League had everything to gain from enjoying fruits of power, maintaining law and order, and checking potential violence. But it remains to be explained why the League was not *outflanked* by a Muslim group that blamed it for pulling back exactly when it was necessary to fight for Islamic principles—as when the mosque came down in Ayodhya and when the Tellicherry riots took place north of Calicut in the early 1970s.

A radical Islamic group did indeed emerge. When the League argued that the destruction of the Ayodhya mosque in December 1992 did not require the League's withdrawal from a Congress-led government in Kerala, the religious purists cried foul. Delhi's Congress government, after all, had miserably failed to protect the mosque. Islamic radicals accused the League of betrayal and of placing power over religious pride. A new group, the Islamic Sevak Sangh (ISS) was formed, led by a firebrand religious purist. The ISS embarked on a path of confrontation with the government and with Hindu nationalists.[8] Minor communal violence did break out, but even after several years of campaigning, a period when the wounds of Ayodhya were presumably quite painful, the ISS and its political arm, the People's Democratic Party (PDP), have not been able to register more than a minuscule political presence. Even at a most opportune hour, they have not been able to mount an effective challenge to, much less displace, the League.

Similarly, it remains to be explained why the BJP could not or did not polarize religious communities. Why has the BJP been so ineffective in a state and town where the League in government does everything that the national leadership of BJP would decry as "minorityism" such as public pensions for mullahs, government business contracts for Muslims, an official holiday for Prophet Muhammad's birthday, a Muslim-majority district with its attendant benefits, symbolic and materials, state funds for Arabic education, and quotas for Muslims in government jobs?

In order to create a larger political presence for itself, why does the BJP not turn each act of League communalism into a moment of confrontation? Why does it not convince the Calicut Hindus that the League, its communalism, and its power must be vigorously fought? The BJP leader of Calicut accepts that polarization is in BJP's political interest, for otherwise it may have to continue to be a small player in Calicut (and Kerala) politics. But he is also convinced that his party would not initiate the polarizing process, for it would not like to be blamed for undermining local peace. If the radical Islamic groups launched a violent campaign, however, it would doubtless benefit the party, and the BJP would be happy to respond.[9]

To understand why the BJP is unwilling to polarize Calicut along religious lines (and unable to do so even when it sometimes tries, however faintly), and why the ISS and the PDP have failed to penetrate, even though they have sought to radicalize the Muslim community, one needs to survey the texture of civic life in Calicut. Hindu-Muslim civic integration is so deep in Calicut (and, many would argue, in Kerala as a whole) that to think of polarizing Calicut (and Kerala) along religious lines is to conceive of the virtually impossible. The reverse is true in Aligarh.

The Variety of Civic Networks

Let us first look at the everyday forms of citizen engagement. Nearly 83 percent of Hindus and Muslims in Calicut often eat together in social settings; only 54 per cent in Aligarh do.[10] About 90 percent of Hindu and Muslim families in Calicut report that their children play together; in Aligarh, a mere 42 percent report doing so. Close to 84 percent Hindus and Muslims in the Calicut survey visit each other regularly; in Aligarh, only 60 percent do, and not often. The Hindus and Muslims of Calicut are simply together more often, and they enjoy it much of the time. Aligarh's Hindu-Muslim interactions are comparatively thin. Aligarh's statistics on all of these interactions would be much lower if we had concentrated only on the violent neighborhoods. The peaceful neighborhoods have a more integrated everyday life. That, inter alia, shows that politics has not destroyed civic interaction in all parts of the town, that human beings can still find ways to be human in difficult political settings. Some of the neighborhoods manage to stay independent of the hegemonic political trends in the town.

What about the associational forms of engagement? Much like Tocqueville's America, Calicut is a place of "joiners." Associations of all kinds—business, labor, professional, social, theater, film, sports, art, reading—abound. From the ubiquitous trade associations to Lions and Rotary Clubs, reading clubs, the head-loaders' association, the rickshaw-pullers' association, and even something like an art-lovers' association—citizens of Calicut excel in joining clubs and associations. Religiously based organizations exist, as they do in Aligarh; what is distinctive is the extent of interreligious interaction in nondenominational organizations.

Consider, first, the economic life of the town. Merchandise trade is the heart of Calicut's economy. The town, with a population of about 700,000 in 1995–96, had no manufacturing except the tile industry, which had nine factories and about 2,500 workers in all. About 100,000 people were partially or wholly dependent on trade, and, though exact numbers are not available, estimates indicate that the town had between 10,000 and 12,000 traders.[11] An overwhelming proportion of these traders were members of trade associations—ranging from foodgrain dealers to bullion dealers—which were in turn members of the Federation of Traders' Associations (Vyapari Vyavasayi Ekopana Samithi).

In 1995, as many as 11 of 26 trade associations registered with the federation had Hindu, Muslim, and Christian officeholders: if the president of the association was from one community, the general secretary was from the other.[12] These associations function as civic bodies, refusing to align themselves with the government: "We don't want to enter politics because our unity will be broken. . . . We have debates in our association, so conflicts, if any, get resolved."[13]

Moreover, such is the depth of engagement that many transactions are without any formal contracts. "Our relationships with Muslim businessmen are entirely based on trust. Payments as large as 10 to 15 lakhs ($300,000–350,000) are sometimes due. We send bills, but there are no promissory notes valid in the courts of law. Payments come in thirty days. We work through brokers. There is no breach of trust."[14]

Aligarh also has its traders' association (the Vyapar Mandal). In the late 1980s it had about six thousand members. In the 1970s, it had even acquired a fair number of Muslim members who emerged on the business map after the Gulf migration. The association, however, developed a history of infighting about whether it should support the political party in power, the argument being that supporting a party in power that is favorable to traders would benefit all of them. In the 1980s, it was finally split into two bodies: a "secular" organization and a "nonsecular" one. The nonsecular faction joined the BJP. Muslims traders headed toward the secular faction.[15]

Unlike trade-based Calicut, Aligarh has a significant industrial sector. Aligarh is among the largest producers of locks in India. The lock manufacturing is mostly small-scale, and different units specialize in different parts of the manufacturing process. Can't Aligarh develop an economic symbiosis between Hindus and Muslims through the economy?

It is impossible to estimate the number of people working in Aligarh's lock industry. No surveys have been conducted. It pays to underreport how much labor an industrial unit employs, for the small, informal sector does not have to pay pension and other benefits to its workers under Indian laws. Official statistics are thus entirely useless. Foucault's concept of "popular illegality," as one keen observer puts it, has caught the imagination of Aligarh's lock manufacturers.[16]

We know, however, from ethnographic work that workers are both Muslim and Hindu, and so are the firm owners. We also know that an interlocking intercommunal dependence does not exist. The informal credit market, normally dominated by the Hindu loan-giver *(mahajan),* was the only economic activity on which all Muslim manufacturers used to depend until recently. To ensure that the line of credit from a Hindu creditor to a Muslim manufacturer is not broken in times of communal riots, the frequency of which rose considerably in the 1970s, rotating credit societies have emerged.[17] These are intra-Muslim societies, however. They build trust within communities, not across them. Of late, Muslim manufacturers have also broken into the business of supplying raw materials for lock manufacturing. Though all lock manufacturers obviously depended on raw materials, the trade was previously monopolized by Hindu businessmen. As communal tensions arose, Muslim manufacturers developed sources of supply within their own community.[18]

What about the workers? If the businessmen are not integrated, are the workers? Since workers numerically constitute a larger proportion of the town than the businessmen, interreligious links formed in trade unions can, in principle, more than make up for an absence of such links among the businessmen.

Trade unions hardly exist in Aligarh. Decrepit offices of the local branches of national trade unions, with no staff and few data, greet researchers of labor activities. Calicut has less industry and more trade than does Aligarh, which in principle makes it a less hospitable place for trade union activity. Trade unions, however, thrive in Calicut. The largest are linked to two major national federations: the Confederation of Indian Trade Unions (CITU), which is associated with the Communist Party (Marxist), and the Indian National Trade Union Congress (INTUC), whose political patron is the Congress Party.[19] Both are interreligious. Even though the Muslim League regularly wins elections from Calicut, the STU, a trade union sponsored by the League for the Muslims, is neither as large as the local units of CITU or INTUC nor as vibrant. It is the weakest and smallest of the three. Muslim workers by and large vote for the League, but they tend typically to join INTUC or CITU for protection of their labor rights. The Marxist and atheistic character of CITU does not stop them from joining CITU's unions if they think that CITU will fight better for their right and wages. In the process, they come in touch with Hindu (and Christian) workers, interreligious links are formed, and a Hindu-Muslim division of the workforce does not take place.

A most unlikely site for unionization—porting, or "headloading"—is by far the greatest example of the associational abilities and success of Calicut workers. Distributed over so many shops and small business units, porters in the bazaar are rarely unionized in India. They are in Calicut (and in Kerala). In 1995, there were nearly 10,000 head loaders in Calicut—about 60 percent Hindu and 40 percent Muslim. Most were part of INTUC and CITU trade unions. Since a bazaar exists in Aligarh, these categories of work also do. But Aligarh headloaders have no associations.

A final and highly distinctive aspect of associational life in Calicut concerns its social and educational activities. The city has had an array of film clubs, popular theaters, and science societies. There is nothing unusual about film clubs, for they have been popular all over southern India in general, though not in northern India (except in elite circles of large cities). But societies interested in taking theater and science to the masses are rather uncommon. Even more uncommon have been reading clubs. Kerala today has the highest rate of literacy in India. "Reading rooms," a unique Kerala institution, accompanied Kerala's remarkable rise in literacy and formed deep social networks between the 1930s and 1950s. Young people from most communities would get together several times every week to read newspapers and cultural and political books. The fascinating story of the birth and role of reading clubs has been told by Dilip Menon:

> Between 1901–1931, the rise in the numbers of literate was phenomenal. The growing numbers of schools and the rise in literacy found expression in the numbers of reading rooms that were established both in the countryside and in the towns. . . . One of the novelties in the organization of reading rooms was the [communitarian] drinking of tea, as one person read the newspapers and the others listened. . . . Tea and coffee lubricated discussions on the veracity of the news and of political questions, and a new culture emerged around the reading rooms. It was premised upon sobriety and knowledge rather than drunken companionship transcending consciousness, which characterised the toddy shops. The importance of tea and coffee lay in the fact that they were recently introduced beverages and did not fit into any taboos regarding what could be shared between castes. Tea shops and reading rooms all over Malabar provided common place for people to meet and to drink together regardless of caste [and community]. . . . The reading rooms emerged as central to both formal attempts at organization by the left wing of the Congress as well as local initiatives.[20]

The cumulative outcome of the reading room movement is worth noting. In our Calicut sample, as many as 95 percent of Hindus and Muslims reported reading newspapers—a statistic that is likely to be higher than in most towns in the richer countries of the world. In 1995–96, Calicut, with a population of more than 700,000, had 20 newspapers and magazines![21] In contrast, whereas most Hindus in the Aligarh sample read newspapers, less than 30 percent of Muslims did so. Hindus and Muslims in Calicut get their history from a wide variety of sources—newspapers, history books, radio, and elders. Most Muslims of Aligarh get it from elders. It is quite clear that the AMU, the great symbol of Muslim education, was for Muslim elite, not for the masses. The education movement in Kerala was primarily for the latter.

Civic Engagement, Historical Memories, and Mutual Differences

That there is civic engagement between Hindus and Muslims in Calicut does not mean that there are no problems between the two communities or that prejudices have completely disappeared. Calicut Hindus and Muslims do have some problems with each other, but they have learned to live with differences. Violence, in any case, is not how they would like to express their differences. Institutionalized channels of politics are the arenas of contestation.

Contrasting Hindu-Muslim perceptions of the great Malabar rebellion of 1921 are a case in point. As discussed in the next chapter, the Malabar Rebellion was a cataclysmic event in the areas surrounding Calicut and for Kerala as a whole. It started out as a rebellion against the British in late 1921 but degenerated into Hindu-Muslim violence in which hundreds were killed, thousands injured, and a large number of Hindus forcibly converted to Islam. More than one-third of our Hindu sample called it a rebellion in which the Hindus suffered at the hands of Muslims. Muslims, on the other hand, had a dramatically different version. Not a single Muslim respondent cited a Hindu-Muslim dimension to the Malabar rebellion, calling it a peasant rebellion against the landlords and the British instead.

Differences extend to other areas as well. When asked, "What should the Muslims do which will please you?" nearly one-fourth of the Hindu respondents replied that they should be "more open." About 60 percent resented the way Kerala Muslims treated their women. Nearly 60 percent also thought that the Muslims were "pampered."

The last is a standard BJP argument, yet, as already noted, there is little support for the BJP. Less than 10 percent of the Hindu sample desired that Muslims be "Indians first." In Aligarh, the largest Hindu complaint was not only that Muslims were pampered but that they were antinational. And more than 90 percent of Hindus called the AMU a hotbed of Muslim communalism and antinationalism.

To sum up, despite a significant objection to the Malabar rebellion and a perception of Muslim "appeasement," Hindus and Muslims can form associations, lead integrated civic lives, and get along quite well in Calicut. That they can do so suggests how important intercommunal engagement is. People begin to live with differences, pursue their interests in institutionalized arenas of politics, maintain everyday warmth, and agree on the futility of violence as a way to deal with differences. Moreover, that Hindus suffered at the hands of Muslims in the Malabar rebellion, people feel, is not a reason to implicate every Muslim today in the events of the past. Deep civic engagement dulls the painful edges of historical memories. The depth of intercommunal engagement in Calicut should explain why the BJP can't think of polarization as a strategy and why the Islamic radicals, despite their efforts, are unable to make a break.

HOW CIVIC STRUCTURES CAME INTO BEING

Why and how did Calicut and Aligarh develop such different civic patterns? In order to answer this question, we need to go back to the history of politics in the two cities. Intercommunal civic links, once in place in Calicut, might have seriously constrained political parties having an interest in religious polarization. In the long run, however, variations in civic life were founded on different structures of mass politics in the two towns. In a historical perspective, the pattern and texture of civic life were politically constructed.

The 1920s were a turning point for both cities, as they were for much of India. Mass politics emerged on a national scale for the first time under the leadership of Mahatma Gandhi. The character of India's freedom struggle—or what came to be known as the national movement—was decisively altered by Gandhi. He pulled the elite-dominated Congress Party and the national movement out of their grooves, marked by the dominance of Oxbridge-educated lawyers and a constitutional style of politics. In their place he inaugurated a phase of mass politics, arguing that until the national movement mobilized the masses, it would neither generate enough political pressure against the British nor lead to an inclusive nation. The first nationwide civil disobedience was launched in 1920. For reasons outlined below, it collapsed in 1922, and as it did so, long-lasting patterns of politics emerged in much of India. Both Aligarh and Calicut participated in the movement, but they emerged from its collapse with very different consequences.

In Aligarh a politics of Hindu-Muslim communalism was instituted; near Calicut, Hindu-Muslim violence did erupt, but a politics of caste cleavages and social justice was stabilized. Over the next decades, arguments about Hindu-Muslim differences over the Indian nation and the caste injustices of Hinduism became the master narratives of politics in Aligarh and Calicut, respectively. As explained in Chapter 3, these two narratives are fundamentally opposed to each other. The communal narrative seeks to build Hindu unity and, in its ideological imagination, pits a united Hindu community against a united Muslim community. The caste narrative attacks the desirability of Hindu unity and has little space for Hindu-Muslim cleavages in its political imagination. Instead, it concentrates on the injustices of a hierarchical Hindu social order and seeks to build lower-caste unity, as opposed to Hindu unity. Hindu upper castes, not Muslims, are the key adversary of the caste narrative of politics. Given that these narratives were not confined to elite politics but defined mass mobilization, the communal narrative polarized Hindus and Muslim in civic life, and the caste narrative brought them together, polarizing the upper and lower Hindu castes instead.

How did two different narratives of politics acquire hegemony in the two cities in the 1920s and after? How did they lead to variations in civic structures? These questions constitute the focus of the analysis below. The main claim is that the pre-existing ascriptive hierarchies of the two places were different when Gandhi launched the first civil disobedience movement in 1920. Legatees of the Mughal ruling class, a Muslim elite dominated the local social structure at Aligarh (and in much of northwestern India). Since the deep south of the country was not penetrated by the Mughal Empire, a Hindu Brahmin elite took the same place in Calicut (and much of southern India) as the Muslim aristocracy did in Aligarh. When, in an attempt partially to indigenize local governments in the nineteenth century, the British widened the franchise to include property ownership, literacy, and taxation, the basis for rule ceased to be high social birth. Those born to privilege, even if socially powerful, had to contest for political power and authority. Dominance based on high social birth was challenged from below. In Aligarh, the challenge to the Muslim elite came from the rising Hindu merchant castes, and in Calicut, the Brahmin elite faced a rising lower-caste mobilization. When mass politics arose, the former became generalized into a politics of Hindu-Muslim differences and the latter into intra-Hindu caste differences.

Those mobilizing Hindus and Muslims in Aligarh and lower and upper castes in Calicut put in place a whole range of civic institutions: cadre-based political organizations as well as educational, social, and economic associations. The aim was to institutionalize their vision of politics as deeply in society as possible. Civic life before mass politics was mainly traditional; it followed ascriptive lines. There is not much evidence of *mass-based or large middle-class associations* before the twentieth century in much of India.[22] Informal and everyday engagement, based in the neighborhoods, was the primary mode of civic interaction. Such interaction, on the whole, took three forms: It could cross communal lines, if Hindus and Muslim lived together as they did in many towns; it could also cross caste lines for festivals and economic life, but such interaction remained vertical, with Brahmins or upper castes functioning as patrons and members of the lower castes traditionally having the role of clients and dependents; finally, a large part of social interaction was intracaste, as leading members of one caste helped others of their own caste in social and economic spheres. *Associational life* in India took off with the rise of mass politics. Not only were caste and communal associations formed in large numbers, but intercaste and intercommunal organizations also came into being. Mass politics in Aligarh developed a civic pattern based on the former; Calicut, while having caste and communal associations, also developed a large number of intercaste and intercommunal organizations. Different civic orders thus came to stay in Aligarh and Calicut.

The discussion below starts with a brief description of the national context of politics in the 1920s and 1930s. It then shows how the two towns inserted themselves in national politics and what patterns of politics and civic life emerged.

The National Context of Politics

For the civil disobedience campaign of 1920–22, Gandhi emphasized nonviolence and a joint Hindu-Muslim mobilization of the masses. Both groups fighting together against the British, he argued, held greater political promise than Hindus and Muslims fighting against each other while the British watched. Germany's World War I alliance with the Ottoman sultan, caliph to much of the Muslim world including India, had already brought many religious Muslims directly in conflict with the British, who, along with the French and the Russians, had declared war on the Turko-German alliance.[23] Before the second decade of the century, Muslim elite politics had been pro-British. Between 1915 and 1920, the adversarial relationship of British government with the Turkish caliph (heading the Ottoman Empire at that time) provided a chance to bring Hindus and Muslims together. Gandhi seized the opportunity and convinced the Congress Party to launch the first civil disobedience movement in 1920. Reflecting its dual purpose—expression of sympathy for the Muslims and fighting the British—it was alternatively called the Khilafat (*Khalifa* being the Indian term for the caliph) and the noncooperation movement.

Remarkable Hindu-Muslim unity was created for some time.[24] But a religion-based mass mobilization eventually would release uncontrolled passions. By early 1922, ferocious violence had erupted in several parts of India—against the British in some places and between Hindus and Muslims in others. Nonviolence was clearly dying—partly because the masses could not keep their emotions under control and partly because Muslim clerics did not believe in nonviolence as a creed, only as a method. To pre-empt further violence, Gandhi ended the movement in March 1922. Nonviolence, he argued, demanded greater courage and strength than killing adversaries, and an independence born of violence was scarcely better than servitude.

The end of the Khilafat movement led to the worst period of communal rioting seen in India up to that time.[25] Fearing further violence, the Congress temporarily withdrew from mass mobilization. The organizational gap at the mass level was filled by religious revival groups of Hindus and Muslims. These groups were more interested in proselytization than in freedom from the British. Arya Samaj, the leading Hindu revival organization of the time, started a campaign for reconversion *(shuddhi)* and unity *(sanghthana)*. The aim was to reclaim "low-caste" Hindus who had embraced Islam, voluntarily or due to coercion, and increase Hindu unity. Alarmed by the reconversion drive of the Samaj, Muslim clerics in turn launched the conversion *(tabligh)* and organization *(tanzim)* movements.[26] Literature offending religious sensibilities was vigorously promoted.[27] Lives of religious leaders were threatened.[28] Between 1922 and 1928, according to British records, 112 communal riots took place in India, in which 450 lives were lost and 5,000 persons were injured.[29]

Growth in communal violence convinced the Congress leadership that religious revival organizations had been the principal agents of violence. To renew efforts at an integrated mass mobilization and to challenge the British, preparations for another civil disobedience movement began in 1929. Learning from his earlier mistake, Gandhi would not choose a religious issue for the new campaign. He selected British monopoly over the making and selling of salt in India as his symbol for mass mobilization. That Indians in their own country, he argued, were not even allowed to make and sell salt was a measure of British insensitivity to the Indians. The elemental message of salt *satyagraha* (civil disobedience) generated remarkable mass enthusiasm, but there was an asymmetry between the Hindu and the Muslim response. With one striking exception,[30] Muslim participation in the civil disobedience movement was, on the whole, not vigorous everywhere.[31] Communal consciousness, it would appear, had already gone quite far by the 1920s.

Between the two civil disobedience movements, when the masses were first mobilized on an unprecedented scale in India, enduring political trends in the various regions and towns emerged. Aligarh was a full participant in the larger trend toward communal rioting. Calicut also went through a shorter but concentrated period of communal violence. It was, however, soon overwhelmed by intra-Hindu politics, built around issues such as civil rights for the lower castes. The nationwide civil disobedience movements had sought to standardize politics all over India, but they could not completely overwhelm the salient local or regional issues in politics. The second civil disobedience movement was more successful than the first in challenging the British, but it could not really build

Hindu-Muslim bridges in Aligarh nor displace caste issues from the political agenda of Calicut. A new pattern was set in the 1920s for decades to come.

HOW COMMUNALISM EMERGED IN ALIGARH

Declining Muslim Aristocracy, Rising Hindu Merchants, and the British

Before the middle of nineteenth century, Aligarh was a military outpost manned by "the service gentry"—the class that served the Mughal Empire as its governing and security arm in areas outside Delhi. The gentry administered the area, performing the roles of the customary judge *(mufti)*, the traditional police officer *(kotwal)*, and the medieval recordkeeper *(kazi)*. In exchange for services to the emperor the gentry received titles to land, which enabled its members to become feudal landlords *(zamindars)* and exercise a great deal of local power.[32] On the whole, the gentry was Muslim, and the elite culture of Aligarh was heavily influenced by Persia. Persian was the language of the Mughal court.

Recent historiography, especially the highly influential work of Chris Bayly, shows how communalism emerged in the sociopolitical structure outlined above.[33] As the Mughal Empire declined and the British took over northern India in the nineteenth century, a significant diminution in the power of the Muslim gentry took place, a decline that was accompanied by a corresponding rise in the wealth and power of merchants, who were mostly from the trading Hindu castes. Persian ceased to be the official language in 1836, hurting the class trained in that language to perform their official functions. And, with domestic and foreign trade rising under the British, merchants began to accumulate wealth. The arrival of railways quickened commercialization in the 1860s, making trade and commerce more mobile and less dependent on local power structures. Looking down on business as an inferior occupation and on commercial culture as far too plebeian an enterprise, the Muslim gentry was not ready for the exploitation of new economic opportunities.

Accepting British rule as a fact of life, Syed Ahmed, an aristocrat of Mughal ancestry, knighted later by the British government and fondly remembered as Sir Syed by Muslims all over the subcontinent even today, realized that Muslim decline would be irreversible unless Muslims gave up their traditional learning methods, participated in the modern education system, and sought British help for it. Taking to modern education sooner, the emerging Hindu middle class had already surged ahead educationally.

The British found it expedient to cultivate the Muslim aristocracy. For the stability of British rule, an alliance with the erstwhile aristocrats who still had considerable, though declining, social power seemed better than their persistent sullenness.[34] By the 1880s, when a nationalist movement surfaced, the need for such an alliance became only too obvious. The British calculated—rightly—that if the loyalty of Muslims, the second largest religious community in India, could be secured through its elite, it would make for an effective counter to the Indian National Congress, which claimed to represent all Indians.

The Aligarh Muslim University, which would have profound implications for India's Hindu-Muslim relations, was the child of this alliance. Under Sir Syed's leadership and with British collaboration, the Muhammadan Anglo-Oriental College, as AMU was called initially, was founded in 1877.[35] Its aim was to provide modern education to Muslims. Revenue-free land was provided in Aligarh by the British government.[36]

In the 1940s, AMU became closely associated with the Pakistan movement. "Often in a civilized history," writes Agha Khan III, a patron of AMU in the early twentieth century, "a University has supplied the springboard for nation's intellectual and spiritual renascence. . . . The independent, sovereign nation of Pakistan was born in the Muslim University of Aligarh."[37] And in the famous words of Mohammed Ali Jinnah, "the father of Pakistan," AMU became "the arsenal of Muslim India," training a large number of Muslim politicians, intellectuals, and activists.

Given its role as a center of modern Muslim education, its British links, and its intellectual leadership of the Pakistan movement in the 1940s, AMU became mired in passionate political disputes, both in Aligarh and beyond. For the Hindu nationalists, always in doubt about Muslim loyalty to India, AMU became an institution to be reviled, implicating in their view the entire Muslim community whose pride it came to symbolize;[38] for the Muslims who would become part of Pakistan, AMU became a center of liberation and pride;[39] for Muslims who stayed in India, it became a source of ambivalence, frustration, and often considerable pain,[40] and the same was true of the non-Muslim leaders of the Indian national movement, especially those who had sympathy for the problems of the Muslims.[41]

In the first half of the century, the biggest political product of AMU was a political party, the Muslim League. The League was born as a political organization in 1906. Its leaders were primarily AMU graduates. The aims of the League included promoting "among the Muslims of India feelings of loyalty to the British government" and protection and advancement of "the political rights and interests of the Muslims of India."[42] Pleading with the British rulers for what we could call a consociational political arrangement today, the League sought a Muslim quota in the administrative and judicial services and in municipal boards and legislative chambers.

The League soon achieved an important victory. In 1909, the Morley-Minto reforms were unveiled, outlining the structure of electoral competition for legislative councils in India. Muslims would have *separate electorates,* more or less in accordance with their proportion in the population.[43] Moreover, Muslims would not only vote in Muslim electorates where only their co-religionists could contest, but also in general electorates where candidates of all religions could vote and run for office.

Separate electorates institutionalized Hindu-Muslim differences in politics, leaving a trail of bitterness. To the Muslim League, however, separate electorates simply recognized the differences that already existed and were a response to genuine Muslim anxieties about getting electorally drowned in a majoritarian Hindu sea. Be that as it may, they began to privilege religious distinctions in electoral politics. It was a victory for the Aligarh ideology of Muslim politics.

Impact on Civic Life

With this background, it is not surprising that the collapse of the Khilafat movement, which had sought to build Hindu-Muslim bridges, would lead to a cleavage between a Muslim *university* and a Hindu-majority *town*.[44] Two kinds of organizations started playing a significant local role: Hindu organizations such as the Arya Samaj and Muslim organizations such as the Muslim League and Tabligh.

The Arya Samaj found a solid constituency in the commercial classes of Aligarh. In institutions of local power such as the municipal government, the rising Hindus merchants had clashed with a declining Muslim aristocracy. They resented Muslim aristocrats who, though land-based and economically eroding, wished nonetheless to hold on to the political power and social position inherited from Mughal rule.[45] Moreover, having a Muslim university, Aligarh was in many ways an ideal venue for Arya Samaj activity.[46] The Arya Samaj grew tremendously in the town, becoming the focus of civic life of middle-class Hindus and trying to make headway into poorer classes, too, through a campaign of proselytization.

Muslim civic life moved in a parallel direction. One could, in fact, speak of two different kinds of civic lives for the Muslims—at the elite and the mass levels. The gap between the elite and masses in Aligarh was considerably greater among the Muslims than among the Hindus. Muslims had an upper and a lower class: Hindus had developed a substantial middle class through trade. Both Muslim groups moved in the communal direction.

Aligarh Muslim University was the focus of Muslim elite life. Unable to break the hold of Muslim communalists and British loyalists on the levers of power in the university, the AMU-based leaders of the Khilafat movement decided to establish a new university, the Jamia Milia Islamia. It would later be called the home of *nationalist* Muslims,[47] and Aligarh the home of *separatist* Muslims. The nationalist Muslim university later moved to Delhi. It is possible counterfactually to argue that if the Khilafat leaders of Aligarh had continued to stay in the mainstream of AMU, a different atmosphere would have resulted. Feeling pessimistic about the possibilities of a less communal politics, however, they left AMU. Some students and teachers continued to be part of nationalist politics, supporting the Congress. Moreover, in the 1930s, socialism and communism also began to influence students and faculty, leading to the emergence of some of the finest left-wing Urdu poets and literary figures of India.[48] On the whole, however, the older ideology of loyalty to the British returned.[49] The organizations and tendencies promoting Muslim communalism and Muslim loyalty to the British simply could not be displaced.

Increasingly in the 1930s, AMU became the intellectual and political headquarters of the League.[50] The trends after the mid-1930s depleted the reserves of intellectual, political, and cultural dissent in the university. In 1939, backed by the university administration, the All India Muslim Student Federation was founded in the university, inaugurating a new phase of ideological correctness on campus. The 1940 Pakistan Resolution of the Muslim League—which declared that Muslims were a separate nation and needed an independent state of their own—was accepted by the Students Union as its official ideology. Dissenting teachers were dismissed by the university, veiling of the female staff and students was introduced, college magazines began to censor articles, and a youngsters' league was formed to train children. The strong winds of political and ideological correctness thus reduced the civic life of the Muslim elite to a communal ghetto, leading to a rupture of links with the Hindu elite of the town. In the 1945–46 elections, AMU students vigorously campaigned for the League in Aligarh and several other parts of India. In 1946, ideological and communal fury came together to produce the worst pre-partition rioting in Aligarh. University students attacked the visiting national president of the Congress Party, Maulana Azad, who, despite being a Muslim, had never supported the Pakistan movement. They also "burnt the local cotton and *gur* (unrefined sugar) market and became a terror to the Aligarh Hindus."[51] The town was awfully polarized. Several small riots earlier had taken place: in 1925 and 1927[52] and also in 1931, 1936, and 1937–38. But the 1946 riots were unparalleled in their fury and destruction.

At the mass level, too, this kind of politics did not lead to the creation of intercommunal associations and organizations. Unlike Calicut in this period (as explained below), Aligarh did not witness the emergence of labor unions, caste associations, or reading clubs for the masses. Nor were Aligarh's cadre-based political organizations mobilized across the religious divide. The Arya Samaj, an organization with a solid middle-class base in the town, was openly communal, and so was the Tabligh on the Muslim side. Involved in mass politics in the 1920s, these two organizations promoted competitive proselytization for years, escalating communal bitterness all around. The Muslim League, an elite organization in the 1920s, also took to mass politics in the late 1930s. It developed a cadre of workers and networks reaching down to the lower middle classes. Given the separatist ideology of the League, these cadres were engaged in aggravating Hindu-Muslim differences, not in bridging them.

In principle, the Congress Party could have stemmed the communal trends in politics and civic life. Of the cadre-based organizations with a presence in the town, it was the only one ideologically committed to Hindu-Muslim unity, and it could have created civic institutions that brought communities together. Aligarh Congress, however, did not rise to the challenge. Founded in 1920, the party did participate in the noncooperation movement.[53] And by the time the second civil disobedience movement was launched in 1929, the Congress in Aligarh had expanded into the countryside, becoming a large cadre-based political organization. But factionalism between the urban and the rural wings rocked the party. The city faction was dominated by the urban trading community, in which Arya Samaj enjoyed considerable influence.[54] Since the Congress was both a party and a movement, it did not disallow simultaneous membership of Congressmen in the Arya Samaj on one hand and Muslim League on the other. The argument simply was that all kinds of people had to be brought together under a common umbrella, and the more people joined the Congress movement, the greater would be their commitment to a composite nationality. The strength of this argument in different places depended on whether the Congress ideology of a composite nation or groups subscribing to a communal view of the nation dominated the local wings of the party.

In Aligarh, a considerable intersection developed between Hindu nationalists and Congress activists. The factionalism was so strong and the drive to build a movement bringing Hindus and Muslims together so weak that a leader of the stature of Nehru was asked to investigate the affairs of the party in Aligarh. From his inquiries, Nehru emerged pessimistic about the reconstructive possibilities of Aligarh Congress.[55] The local realities of Congress politics and organization were far away from the ideals sketched out by the national leadership of the party.

CASTE INJUSTICE AS A MASTER NARRATIVE IN CALICUT

Muslims and Islam in Kerala

The state of Kerala, where Calicut is located, has three parts: the north is called Malabar, the midlands Cochin, and the south Travancore. Calicut has been the leading city of Malabar. Long part of a multireligious land, Muslims in the 1990s constituted about 23.3 percent of Kerala's population,[56] 36 percent of Malabar, and 38 percent of Calicut. The Christians, concentrated in Cochin and Travancore, make up about 19.3 percent of the state's population. The Hindus, spread all over the state, form approximately 57.3 of Kerala's population.[57] Malabar Muslims are called *Moplahs,* sometimes also written as *Mappillas.* In Malayalam, the language of the state, the term means "the great child."

In occupational terms, the Moplahs have evolved into two large groups. In the coastal areas and towns, trading has been their main economic activity. Vaishyas, the traditional commercial castes in Hinduism, were absent in the Hindu society of southern India. Moplahs, Jews, and Christians filled that gap. The Moplahs came to be viewed as *the* business community of Malabar (the Christians occupying the same place in the midlands and southern Kerala). Indigenous conversions to Islam, especially of lower castes, created a second group of Moplahs, a group on the whole poorer, comprising small farmers and agricultural workers. Depending on the class and location, thus, the Moplahs are rich as well as poor and part of both urban and rural life.

There are several differences between Moplahs and the northern Indian Muslims that bear on the Aligarh-Calicut comparison. Unlike northern India, where Aligarh is located, Kerala was never ruled by the Moplahs.[58] Moreover, northern Muslims never developed a business class, whereas, for centuries, Moplahs have been the leading business community of Malabar. Northern Indian

Muslims were either the ruling elite, who developed their own highly influential Persian cultural styles, or, alternatively, the poorest of the poor speaking local dialects and participating in the syncretistic rural cultures.

Moplah immersion in the culture of Kerala goes beyond Hindu-Muslim *rural* syncretism.[59] Moplah integration is also linguistic. Unlike the court-based northern Muslim aristocracy, rich urban Moplahs did not develop a distinctive language. Urdu, the language of urban Muslims of northern India, never acquired popularity in Kerala. The Moplahs adopted not only the language of Kerala but also the indigenous script. Even the religious texts of Islam were translated into Malayalam.[60]

The story of Moplah integration contains an awkward subplot, however. As India's national movement reached Malabar in the 1920s, a horrendous turn in Hindu-Muslim relations took place. An insurgency against the British was transformed into a Hindu-Muslim conflagration, leading to a large number of killings, forced conversions, and desecrations of holy places. Yet, instead of suffering a permanent legacy of bitterness, Malabar overcame the aftermath of animosity.

Calicut, the city in our study, is just north of the center of Malabar rebellion. Exogenous shocks such as this one have often transformed Hindu-Muslim relations elsewhere in India. Why did they not in Calicut and Malabar? It is this anomaly, a happy one, to which I turn.

The Malabar Rebellion of 1921

Like elsewhere in India, a joint Hindu-Muslim mobilization was launched against the British at Calicut in early 1921. By the middle of 1921, however, Congress leaders had lost control over the movement, and Muslim clerics *(tangals)*, who participated in the movement to protest against the British treatment of the caliph in Turkey, had become the principal leaders of the Moplahs. Motivated by religious concerns, they fought to revive the Turkish caliphate.

In August 1921, what started as a peaceful protest turned into a violent rebellion against the British and, subsequently, degenerated into prolonged Hindu-Muslim strife. It took the British six months to suppress the rebellion. By the time the smoke cleared and British rule was reestablished, according to official figures, 2,339 rebels had been killed, 1,653 wounded, 5,955 captured, and 40,000 had surrendered.[61] The numbers should indicate the depth of the rebellion. The rebels managed to reach the outskirts of Calicut several times, but British control over the city remained intact.[62] Urban Moplahs, the merchants, did not participate in the rebellion, but such a large upheaval breaking out only a few miles south of the city could not but affect feelings in Calicut. A large number of Hindu families took refuge in Calicut, telling tales of "Moplah atrocities."[63]

Moplah violence had several aspects. First, the rebels attacked British government offices after the British entered an important Moplah mosque—the Tirurangadi mosque—which had, according to the British, become a hideout for Khilafat activists and their violence-inciting clerics.[64] Another event, known as the "train" or "wagon tragedy" of November 1921, has acquired the status of a legend. About a hundred Moplah prisoners were put in a goods wagon for transportation to a prison camp. When the wagon was unlocked at a train station ninety miles away, prisoners were found dead and others seriously ill. Suffocation was the cause of the deaths. The train was unfit for human transportation owing to lack of ventilation. "Beyond a few chinks in the walls and flooring, there [was] no other entrance for air," making the van "practically a closed box."[65]

The landlords constituted the second object of Moplah attacks. Rural Moplahs in southern Malabar were primarily poor tenants, landless agricultural workers, and small traders. The lords were mostly upper-caste Hindus.[66] Third, and most important for our purposes, many Hindus were forced to convert to Islam, and those who resisted were put to death.[67] Desecration and displacement accompanied the rebellion. At least one hundred Hindu temples were attacked or broken.[68] It is generally agreed that the rebellion acquired an unambiguous Hindu-Muslim edge as it progressed, despite its anti-British origins in the Khilafat movement.[69]

Why Did the Malabar Rebellion Not Leave a Legacy of Communal Violence?

The Malabar rebellion was the first big blow to the Hindu-Muslim unity being constructed by the Indian national movement under Gandhi's leadership.[70] The Congress feared more communal violence and began to develop cold feet about mobilizing the Muslims. Moreover, as already stated, campaigns for competitive proselytization, in which the Arya Samaj and several Muslim religious groups participated, also came into being in the 1920s.

Ironically, Malabar, which was instrumental in touching off the new period of communalization and communal violence, did not experience any more Hindu-Muslim riots. In Malabar, a Hindu-Muslim divide did emerge,[71] but religious bitterness progressively declined. From an all-India perspective, the developments in Malabar were counterintuitive. Communal rancor and violence increased in many parts of India, but not where violence originated. Why?

The principal reasons have to do with the pre-existing social hierarchy of Hinduism, its grave caste injustices, and an emerging lower-caste mobilization. India's freedom movement did not introduce mass politics to Malabar. Mass politics there had already taken the form of intra-Hindu struggles over caste, led by lower-caste organizations. Civil rights of the lower castes, especially with respect to pollution, temple entry, and greater access to educational institutions and government employment, were the key issues. Hindu-Muslim issues simply could not match the passions aroused by caste inequalities and injustice. A restructuring of mass politics took place. Communal bitterness increasingly disappeared from the political space. Politics, memory, and emotions were reconfigured.

How this happened can best be illustrated by cataloguing the failed efforts of the Arya Samaj in Calicut. In both towns, as the noncooperation movement collapsed and as the Congress party withdrew temporarily from mass politics, communal organizations such as the Arya Samaj stepped into the void. The Samaj, matched by Muslim organizations of a similar kind, caused great communal rivalry and bitterness in Aligarh. In Calicut (and Malabar), the Samaj did make a determined entry, but its campaign was stillborn. Given the British suppression of Moplah clergy, a Muslim proselytization campaign such as the tabligh had no chance in the aftermath of the Malabar rebellion. The Samaj, in other words, had a whole political terrain to itself. Yet it failed to communalize Malabar.

A Stillborn Arya Samaj

The scholars and observers of the Arya Samaj agree that the Malabar rebellion was a turning point for the Samaj: it directly led to the reclamation *(shuddhi)* and Hindu unity *(sanghthana)* campaigns.[72] Forced conversions in Malabar revived Samaj fears that Hindu society was far too "disunited" and "tolerant" to withstand the proselytizing streak in Islam. The fact that traditional Hinduism did not subscribe to the concept of proselytization was, to their minds, a weakness, not a strength. Proselytization, the Samaj argued, was necessary, and so was greater Hindu unity. "Hindus are comparatively weak and cannot protect their religion and women. Unity and goodwill can exist only between two equally strong parties."[73] For Malabar Hindus, the Samaj pledged to "start a movement for the reclamation of forcibly converted Hindus and persuade the caste groups to receive them back. Moreover those persons who have been forcibly converted and whose homes have been destroyed have to be given adequate help."[74]

The Samaj headed toward Malabar for the first time. It "reclaimed" several recent converts to Islam, but it was unable to establish a stronghold. Language was part of the problem. In northern and western India, where Hindi was widely understood, the Samaj's emphasis on Hindi was adequate for its religious work. The language of Malabar was Malayalam, not Hindi. The Samaj did not have the adequate literature or personnel for a campaign in Malayalam.

Given its linguistic inadequacy, the Samaj needed powerful indigenous support groups. In Aligarh, the rising Hindu commercial classes provided a base for Samaj activities. In Malabar, the situation was different: Moplahs were the *merchant* class. The Hindu merchant castes of the north were generally absent in the deep south, where Hindu social structure had the Brahmins on one end of the spectrum and lower castes on the other. Christians were the merchants of southern Kerala, the Jews and the Christians the merchants of the midlands, and the Moplahs the merchants of the north. With its message of Hindu unity, the Samaj could not have possibly created a base among the Christians, Jews, and Muslims.

A non-Muslim option was in principle available in the trading sector. Paradoxically, it turned out to be the biggest stumbling block for the Samaj. A large Hindu caste, the Ezhavas, traditionally engaged in "toddy tapping" (production of fermented liquor) and therefore considered "polluting" by the Brahmins, had experienced considerable economic mobility in the closing decades of the nineteenth century.[75] The upwardly mobile Ezhavas had left their traditional occupation behind and formed a sizeable business class in Malabar cities, including Calicut.[76] A self-respect movement had already come into existence. The Ezhavas were rebelling against the indignities of Hindu social order and fighting for their civil rights. They could not be mobilized for Hindu unity.

A Battle for Civil Rights

Sociologists agree that caste hierarchies did not acquire the same rigidities in the north as in the south; lower-caste humiliations were never as extensive in the north, and Brahminism was rarely as ritualistic, hegemonic, and overpowering. The Ezhavas were not only considered untouchable but also "unseeable"; northern India did practice untouchability but not unseeability. Indeed, the catalogue of everyday humiliations for the Ezhavas was painfully long in Kerala:

> They were not allowed to walk on public roads. . . . They were Hindus, but they could not enter temples. While their pigs and cattle could frequent the premises of

the temple, they were not allowed to go even there. Ezhavas could not use public wells or public places. . . .

An Ezhava should keep himself at least thirty-six feet away from a Namboodiri and twelve feet away from a Nair. . . . He must address a caste Hindu man as Thampuran [My Lord] and woman as Thampurati [My Lady]. . . . He must stand before a caste Hindu in awe and reverence, assuming a humble posture. He should never dress himself up like a caste Hindu; never construct a house on the upper caste model. . . . [T]he women folk of the community . . . were required, young and old, to appear before caste Hindus, always topless.[77]

By the time the Malabar rebellion broke out, the Ezhava protest movement was already in existence. Led by a famous Ezhava saint, Sri Narain Guru, sometimes called the Gandhi of Kerala, the movement aimed at self-respect and education. Self-respect entailed withdrawal from toddy tapping, a movement into modern trades and professions, and a nonviolent attack on the symbolic order. Since they were denied entry to temples and were only allowed to worship "lower gods and spirits," the Ezhavas, the Guru said, would have their own temples, in which they would worship "higher gods" to whom they would offer flowers and sweets, not animals and liquor reserved for the "lower gods." To improve their economic and social status, they would educate themselves. And to facilitate all of these activities, they would set up an organization. "Strengthen through organization, liberate by education" was the motto.

An organization called the Sree Narayana Dharma Paripalana-yogam (SNDP) had been set up in 1903. It would play important roles in social, educational, and political affairs. In 1916, an Ezhava temple was built in Calicut, financed by prospering Ezhava traders and consecrated by the Guru. In 1918, an Ezhava conference in Calicut called on the Ezhavas to boycott all temples and shrines that prohibited their entry. The movement gathered further strength in the 1920s. By that time, the Ezhava middle classes "had very consciously defined themselves as a community apart, centered on their own circuits of worship, rather than as Hindus."[78]

The Samaj plea for Hindu unity made no sense to the Ezhavas. Overcoming quotidian insults inflicted by Hindu upper castes, especially the Brahmins, was much more important to the Ezhavas than fighting a battle with the Muslims. The Ezhavas were the largest Hindu group. The Arya Samaj could not earn their respect and admiration.

Seeking other local patrons, the Samaj sought to cultivate the erstwhile Calicut princely families, the Zamorins, thinking they would help propagate its message of Hinduism in danger. The Zamorins in turn summoned the Brahmins for help.[79] The Samaj was right in thinking that Malabar Hindus were awfully divided. But the Brahmins were not the agents of unity. They were precisely the principal objects of Ezhava anger. The Samaj could not have built Hindu unity through the Brahmins.

In the end, the Arya Samaj was unable to put down roots in Calicut and Malabar, for caste antagonisms occupied the same place in Malabar as religious antagonisms in the north. The best summary of why the Samaj failed is provided by the most formidable mobilizer of lower castes in twentieth century Kerala:

> The Arya Samaj and other Hindu communal organizations came and started their work in Malabar, first by way of affording relief to Hindu refugees fleeing from the areas of the rebellion, then by reconverting those Hindus who had been forcibly converted to Islam by the rebels and ultimately going to the extent of converting Muslims to Hinduism. The Muslim intelligentsia was terror-stricken because of the post-rebellion repression. . . . They could do nothing but remain sulking for the time being. . . . It is true that this did not lead to communal tension and communal riots so familiar to the people of North India. [The Arya Samaj] did not catch the imagination of the people here. . . . The main reason is that the Hindus here are so caste-ridden, the caste-rules regarding their mutual social relations so rigid, it is extremely difficult to create a real sense of Hindu solidarity. The low-caste people felt more at home with the Muslims and Christians than with their co-religionists. . . . *The main form of communalism [here] was caste against caste, and not Hindu versus Muslim.*[80]

A Restructuring of Mass Politics and Its Impact on Civic Life

With the Samaj unable to find a niche in Malabar, the region's politics was decisively restructured in the 1930s. The key issue was social justice, defined in terms of the civil and economic rights of the lower castes. Entry into temples—for all lower castes, including the Ezhavas—and an attack on the social deference system concerning dress and access to public roads and more equal access to education drove the civil rights campaign. Simultaneously, tenancy rights and greater lower-caste access to government employment spurred the mobilization for economic rights.

The two campaigns—social and economic—could be merged in Malabar because the social and economic hierarchy had a clear correspondence. The Brahmins and the Nairs were more educated and held most of the land and government jobs. In Malabar, for all practical purposes, the caste and class narratives of social justice were two sides of the same coin.[81]

The foundations of a new civic order in Calicut, described above, were laid in the 1930s and 1940s. The left wing of the Congress Party created a remarkably large number of peasant unions, labor unions, and lower-caste associations that became the locus of education and struggle. They educated lower-caste peasants and workers through reading clubs and night classes and also preached a message of struggle against oppression.[82] These mass-based organizations brought a large proportion of Kerala's non-Brahmins under their umbrella.

By 1940, the Communist Party of Kerala was born in Malabar.[83] It was an outgrowth of the left wing of the Congress. In the 1946 elections, the Communists won 25 percent of popular vote in Malabar.[84] Although still not as popular as the Congress, they were a rising force and had clearly established a large presence. Most important, by repeatedly emphasizing the issues of social and economic justice, mobilizing the subaltern, organizing networks of education and camaraderie among them, and exerting pressure on the Congress, left-wing politicians reshaped the discourse of Malabar politics and forged an array of civic institutions—unions, associations, and clubs—incorporating the masses.

CONCLUSION

Given the social hierarchies of Kerala, caste injustice and civil rights of lower castes became the master narrative of Kerala politics, in contrast to Aligarh, where Hindu-Muslim differences took on the same importance. In Calicut, the upper- versus lower-caste construction of politics triumphed over the Hindu versus Muslim construction, whose theoretical possibility had been created by the Malabar rebellion. A large number of civic associations and cadre-based organizations were spawned by the votaries of lower-caste politics in Calicut, whereas the civic organizations of Aligarh took an increasingly intracommunal form. Hindu-Muslim civic engagement was given a solid associational foundation in Calicut's new organizations, which attacked the hegemony of upper castes, not of a Muslim elite, as was the case in Aligarh. Intercommunal civic life flourished as a by-product of the caste-based framework of mass politics. Contrariwise, intracommunal links became deeper and deeper as mass politics in Aligarh took a communal form. The varied civic orders in the two cities, thus, had very different political foundations.

Chapter 6 Vicious
and Virtuous Circles

If the major puzzle of pre-1947 Calicut politics was that the Malabar rebellion did not leave a bitter communal legacy, another paradox marks the city's (and the region's) post-1947 politics. The Muslim League, a political party representing the Muslim community, has acquired remarkable power over the past three decades. It has held a number of ministries in state government since 1967 and used its governmental participation to deliver a large number of benefits to the Muslims. Yet a "Hindu reaction," or Hindu-Muslim bitterness, has not come to the fore. Incidents of communal violence have been few and far between in the region and entirely absent in the city of Calicut.

In contrast, communal antagonisms developed during the national movement have deepened in Aligarh, and a great deal of communal violence has taken place. The AMU—owing to its involvement with the Pakistan movement and its symbolic importance for Indian Muslims—has kept Aligarh's links with national politics alive in two ways. What happens to Muslims in Aligarh, and especially to the AMU, has national ramifications. Moreover, Aligarh's tenuous communal relations have also made the city vulnerable to Hindu-Muslim violence elsewhere in the country. Aligarh has often been on the edge. The Hindu nationalists as well as the mainstream Muslim politicians have played a polarizing role in the city. They have exploited the narrative of communalism, seldom trying to contain its spread.

In Calicut (and the state of Kerala), caste has continued to be the dominant idiom in politics. The Muslim League's politics functions within the larger caste framework. It has been perceived as a *communal* party but not as a *polarizing* party. The distinction between good and bad communalism is often drawn in Kerala. Good communalism stands for advocating the interests of one's community; bad communalism entails spreading bigotry. The League has been associated with the former, not with the latter. Good communalism has become part of the routine politics of Kerala, where all communities, religion- or caste-based, organize to lobby the state for sectional benefits. Further, in times of Hindu-Muslim tensions, the League has so far consciously played a moderating role.

Why have the politics in Aligarh and Calicut been so different? After 1947, a vicious circle of violence has come into existence in Aligarh: there have been few civic links between Hindus and Muslims, and electoral politics has been communally oriented, too. In contrast, a virtuous circle of peace exists in Calicut: civic links between Hindus and Muslims are robust, and electoral politics, despite the presence of a Muslim League, has not ruptured them either. Civic life and electoral politics have fed into each other in both cities, in a violent direction in Aligarh, and toward peace in Calicut.

In Aligarh, the civic networks of intercommunal engagement, once weakened by the pre-1947 history of Hindu-Muslim politics, made it easier for politicians to be divisive and even have links with criminals who perpetrated acts of violence. Several criminals, seen as warriors or saviors, became heroes in the process. An "institutionalized riot system" was born, as politicians, thugs, civic organizations, and the local press formed parallel Hindu and Muslim communal networks that thrived on communal propaganda, rumors, and violence.[1] The law and order machinery often broke down; and the Hindus and Muslims developed even greater distance than before, forming ties only within their own communities rather than across communities.

The major civic developments of post-1947 Aligarh can be summarized as follows. By far the biggest development was communal segregation in the education system. The city's Hindu elite, in reaction to the Muslim character of AMU and its pro-Pakistan history, established colleges of their own. The student body and faculty in these colleges are overwhelmingly Hindu. Once placed in such institutional spaces, thousands of young people, who could have interacted with Muslims, lost the opportunity to do so. The AMU, the richest educational institution in the city, does accept Hindu students, but their numbers simply don't compare with those in the primarily Hindu colleges of the city. Even primary and secondary education remain highly segregated. Muslims have an abysmally low level of literacy, and a large proportion of those who do learn to read and write go to schools set up by the AMU, where Hindu pupils don't register. Few cities in India have the kind of segregated education one sees in Aligarh. As a corollary, the associations in these institutions—of teachers, staff, and students—are primarily intracommunal, with token representation from the other community.[2]

As for the professionals, there are too few Muslim doctors and lawyers to make professional associations a strong enough agent of peace.[3] And in the city's economic life, religion has continually interfered with business. For some time, trade and business associations of the city tried to weather communal tensions and integrate businessmen from both communities, but the effort did not succeed. Trade associations were broken along political lines, rather than business lines.[4]

Finally, at the level of mass-based, citywide organizations, very little has happened to facilitate integration. Labor unions are practically nonexistent and the Congress Party, which brought large masses together in various parts of the country, remains organizationally weak, continuing a pre-1947 trend. Aligarh was among the first cities of the state where the Congress Party lost elections after independence and among the first where the Hindu nationalists built a solid organization and electoral presence.

A recent change may finally turn out to be promising. As a new middle class among the lower Hindu castes has emerged and the caste-based narrative of politics has spread to Aligarh, a restructuring of politics has become a clear possibility. If caste-based politics does become dominant or hegemonic in the city, it may well undermine the communal institutionalized riot system, and put in place a new civic engagement between Hindus and Muslims. There are some signs of it already, but it is still too early to make confident predictions.[5]

In Calicut, by contrast, an institutionalized peace system is in place. Intercommunal civic life has ensured that electoral politics remains free of divisive Hindu-Muslim issues, and vice versa. The restructuring of mass politics in the 1930s created space for Hindu-Muslim civic links to be formed. In the 1950s, 1960s, and 1970s, these links were strengthened further. Reading rooms were turned into a massive library movement. A popular science and theater move-ment took ideas from the classroom to the masses and ideological education to the streets.[6] All kinds of workers—from the informal to the formal sector—were organized into unions.[7] A new integrated chamber of business came into being, and more trade associations were formed. Unlike Aligarh, a remarkable literacy drive, which will soon bring 100 percent literacy to Calicut, was spear-headed by integrated schools and colleges; this drive brought Hindu, Muslim, and Christian youth in regular contact with one another. Finally, the left-wing movement became bigger and the Communists, after giving up violent insur-rection as a political strategy, came to power several times through elections. Their organizations after 1947 have been larger, the cadres more numerous. In fact, much of the popular science and street theater movement has been led by the left-wing cadres.[8]

Calicut's intercommunal civic depth has restrained politicians from polariz-ing religious communities, even though the pro-Muslim activities and power of the Muslim League, in theory, provide room for communal propaganda to pro-Hindu parties, on one hand, and the League's inability to distance itself from governmental power, even when religious principle are compromised, al-lows right-wing Muslim organizations to launch radical religious campaigns, on the other. Neither the BJP nor the right-wing Muslim organizations have been able to penetrate Calicut and the surrounding region.

WHAT KIND OF UNIVERSITY?
WHAT KIND OF TOWN?

The Logic of Polarized Local Politics

There are few university towns, in the typical American sense, in India. Aligarh is one of them. It is a university town with a difference, however. Its economy is not built around the university, but the university is the principal reason for Aligarh's fame. Locks and building materials, the town's main industrial prod-ucts, simply do not compare with its university.

The town has a large Muslim population, but it is predominantly Hindu. The university has a significant proportion of Hindu students and faculty, but it is mostly Muslim. Famous though AMU is, attracting Muslim students from all over India and also the Middle East, the town has a troubled relationship with the university. More than 90 percent of Hindu respondents in the Aligarh sample acutely dislike AMU, calling it a den of communalism and bigotry.

The hostility of the town toward the university creates enormous problems for the town's mostly poor Muslims. The better-off Muslims of AMU live in the spacious university campus and its surrounding areas. The town Muslims live in crowded neighborhoods. At 56.4 percent, Aligarh's literacy rate in 1991 was below the national urban average of about 70 percent.[9] It is generally accepted that Muslim literacy in the town is considerably lower, although, in the absence of a religious breakdown of census data on literacy, precise figures cannot be given. A prosperous Muslim middle class did emerge in the late 1960s, its size growing after the option of migration to the Gulf opened up in the 1970s. Craftsmen and workers earlier, Muslims began to own small lock factories. By and large, however, the Muslim masses have continued to be fruit and vegetable sellers, sweepers, small mechanics, butchers, washermen, weavers, and factory workers in the unorganized sector.

For poor Muslims, AMU, only 2–3 miles away from the town, is truly a distant land.[10] They needed primary and secondary schools close to their neighborhoods, not a university made for the former aristocrats and gentry. Even though they are looked down upon by the Muslim elite for their "low-caste" origins[11] AMU and its elite have become an integral part of the lives of the Muslim poor. University students fight battles for Muslim cultural pride, but it is the poor Muslims who are the principal targets in riots. The university is well-guarded, because if it were attacked by Hindu townsmen, the vocal section of Muslims, at least in northern India, would be indignant. A monument of cultural pride, if "desecrated," would have serious political consequences. No government in Delhi, unless it is an entirely Hindu nationalist one, can easily allow the town to attack the university.

Muslims living in the town are not so fortunate. They are not well-guarded. The police force does not care. It rarely prevents attacks on them, even though they have had little to do with the university's origins or its policies. Since they lack a voice that can represent them, being a Muslim has become inextricably intertwined in politics with being a partner in the AMU legacy—in the eyes of Hindu nationalists and their many sympathizers. A passionate dislike for the university that was the "arsenal of Pakistan" rubs off on the poor Muslims. They are able to defend themselves only in the few neighborhoods where, despite Aligarh's overall atmosphere, everyday links with the Hindu neighbors remain intact, or where the neighborhoods have become entirely Muslim and developed strong self-help mechanisms. For the town Muslims, it has been hard to break the nexus between being a Muslim and being considered a supporter of AMU. They would need a leadership of their own, which they do not yet have.

The issues for Hindu nationalists are somewhat different, though the results are equally polarizing. Either most Muslims in town are seen to be implicated in the AMU project or, by essentializing Muslims as Muslim, not categorizing them as poor or rich Muslims, and forming politics on that basis, the Hindu nationalists force an increasing identity between the "low" and the "high" Muslims, the so-called *ashraf* and *ajlaf*. These two political tendencies—a Muslim one that links AMU with Muslim pride and a Hindu nationalist one that also does precisely that—make it hard for politicians to create a space for a Muslim identity independent of AMU in the town's politics. The town Muslims have not created an alternative identity and the town Hindus, by their actions, have not allowed one to emerge. A preposterous equation—that AMU represents all Muslims—has stuck.

Just as not all Muslims are supporters of AMU, Hindus are not all Hindu nationalists, even in a town as polarized as Aligarh. Three large groups, two of them Hindu, have determined the evolution of town's post-1947 politics: the Muslims, the rich Hindu trading castes, and the scheduled castes. The percentage of Muslims and scheduled castes in the town population has hovered around 34–35 and 14–15 percent, respectively.[12] The census does not report caste data beyond the scheduled castes, making it difficult to derive precise estimates about the size of trading castes. The traders' share of the population is often stated to be 21 percent. If this percentage is right, these three groups—the Muslims, Hindu traders, and the scheduled castes—would account for about 70 percent of the town population. Hindu traders, a large, rich, and influential group in the town, have increasingly supported the Hindu nationalists.[13]

For almost two decades after independence, AMU was the most contested issue in the Hindu-Muslim politics of the town. Since the early 1970s, two big changes have taken place. A new middle class has emerged among the Muslims, which has made Hindu-Muslim conflict bloodier. If the Hindu nationalists target the town Muslims to avenge what happens in the university, there is a new Muslim middle class to hit back. A middle class among the lower Hindu castes has also come into being. It is caught between two impulses. Given the hierarchy of Hindu social order, it dislikes the upper Hindu castes and can lead the lower castes against the upper, but it also remains divided on Muslims. The ways in which this has complicated local politics is analyzed below. We begin with a discussion of the first phase, when AMU was the biggest, and for all practical purposes, the only issue in the Hindu-Muslim politics of the town.

The University and the Nation

After 1947, there was a large Muslim exodus from Aligarh to Pakistan. In 1941, Muslims constituted 45.5 percent of the town's population; by 1951, only 34 percent of the population was Muslim. Much of the exodus was from the middle classes.[14] A large number of university professors, administrators, and students left for Pakistan. The Muslim League ceased operations in the aftermath of partition, and the Muslims who remained in the city started voting primarily for the Congress. The Congress was an adversary of the League before independence, but whatever the ambiguities of the party before 1947, it provided the greatest bulwark against a possible rise of Hindu nationalism after independence. Members of the League who did not migrate to Pakistan switched to the Congress. To reduce bitterness among the Muslims, and to win them over, the party welcomed them. It won the Aligarh assembly seat in the first two elections (1952 and 1957). It easily subdued the Hindu nationalists, still reeling from Gandhi's assassination. The Hindu nationalists received only 9 and 13 percent of the city's vote in the 1952 and 1957 elections in the city, respectively (table 6.1), but those vote shares were considerably above their national share. Aligarh was not yet conquered by Hindu nationalists, but their presence was not insignificant.

With power in their hands, the secular nationalists of the Congress Party took control of AMU. They made it into a "central university." A central uni-

Table 6.1. Aligarh Assembly Elections

Year	Congress Vote (%)	Hindu Nationalist Vote (%)	Janata or Janata Type Parties Vote (%)
1952	59.4	9.2	NA
1957	50.1	13.5	NA
1962	31.5	6.4	NA
1967	25.5	38	NA
1969	37	22.2	24.37
1974	37.4	18.2	14.3
1980	28.2	30.1	NA
1985	39.5	17.2	35
1989	10.9	46.4	NA
1991	6.2	47.3	37.9

Note: In 1977 it was not possible to distinguish the vote shares of non-Congress parties.
Source: Various Election Commission Reports, Lucknow.

versity has a privileged status in India. "State universities" are dependent on the often precarious financial health of state governments. They are nearly always short of resources; a central university rarely is.

A series of secular nationalist and government-appointed heads of AMU, called vice chancellors, sought to reform the university. They filled up the faculty with leftist professors, Hindu and Muslim, inviting them from all over India. Leftist Muslims, sidelined by the Pakistan movement, found a new institutional home. A parliamentary amendment in 1951 opened the "University Court," the highest decision-making body, comparable to a board of trustees, to non-Muslims. Islamic theology was deleted as a requirement for Muslim students. Measures to promote greater integration among Hindu and Muslims included: desegregation in university dormitories (hostels) to allow Hindu and Muslim students to live together; introduction of coeducation to allow women to study at AMU; celebration of national festivals; and attempts to rewrite Indian history to de-emphasize the religious and communal dimensions and highlight the socioeconomic aspects.[15] AMU's first vice chancellor after independence was clear about the political aspects of the enterprise: "The way Aligarh works, the way Aligarh thinks, the contribution Aligarh makes to Indian life in its manifold aspects will largely determine the place Muslims will occupy in the pattern of Indian life. The way India deals with Aligarh will largely determine the shape of things in the future national position of the Muslims."[16]

The "shape of things" began to evolve before long. By the mid-1950s, relentless bickering between the leftists and the conservatives on the faculty turned the university's attention away from research and teaching and led to several incidences of violence perpetrated by Muslim students and staff opposed to reform.[17] By the mid-1960s, it was clear that at least the vocal and politically influential sections of the Muslim community were not in favor of reform. Attempts to change AMU were increasingly given up, even as its status as a central university and its government funding remained unchanged. Teaching and research, the main purposes of a university, became increasingly peripheral.

Why was university reform so difficult? A large Muslim minority, despite the creation of Pakistan, was still in India. For them, AMU was not only a birthplace of Pakistan but a center of modern education that they had created. The latter was a matter of pride, whereas the former engendered guilt and shame in many and indifference in others. Being an institution of such contrary emotions, AMU did not allow a neat resolution of Muslim sympathies.

As a result, the problem of the secular reformers was as follows: If they did not "secularize" AMU's policies, syllabi, power structure, and atmosphere, they would only reward the intellectual and ideological bastion of the Pakistan movement with generous central funds. But if they went too far in restructuring it, they would risk alienating the Muslim community. Where lay the balance between too much restructuring and too little change? Where lay the line between attacking "the arsenal of Pakistan" and hurting Muslim pride? Secular nationalists kept looking for ways to reform AMU but not hurt Muslim pride. It was not clear how one could do both.

Only two sets of people had clarity about what to do: the Hindu nationalists, who would either let AMU atrophy or dissolve its Muslim character,[18] and the Muslim right, which defined any change in AMU's functioning as an assault on Muslim culture and society. Others struggled with ambiguities and nuances, but their ambiguities could not preclude the polarizing process.

The Town's Reaction: Distrust and Violence

A UNESCO survey did some valuable research on the university-town relationship in the early years of independence. When "a middle-aged Hindu resident of Aligarh entered the university precincts for the first time in 1948, [he] was pleased to discover a fine educational institution within two miles of his house."[19] For much of his life, AMU was a "hostile territory." "We have heard of the university, but we have never been there," answered nearly half of the Hindu respondents in the 15–18 year-old group in the UNESCO survey.[20]

The incidents sparking riots and tensions in Aligarh between 1950 and 1970 are summarized in table 6.2. In this whole period, only one incident of communal violence—in 1954—was unrelated to AMU. Events there would typically be reported prominently by the local press, and the students of the new Hindu colleges would retaliate disproportionately. In 1950, upset that the singing of India's national anthem reportedly was interrupted by some Muslim students at AMU, Hindu students stopped a passenger train, killing several Muslim passengers and assaulting Muslim residential areas and citizens in the town.[21] In 1956, said the local newspaper in bold headlines, AMU students had insulted the Gita, a holy book of the Hindus, to "avenge" the way Prophet Muhammad was allegedly described in a recently published Hindi book. Rioting followed.[22] In the spring of 1957, the local rags repeatedly wrote lead stories on how Pakistani agents were being trained in AMU and non-Muslims were being harassed.[23] In 1961, a clash between Hindu and Muslim students in the AMU Student Union elections led to riots in the town, which spread to many other parts of India and made 1961 the worst year of violence in the country

Table 6.2. Communal Tensions and Violence in Aligarh, 1950–70

Year	Reported Cause
1950	Hindu students stop passenger train, kill several Muslim passengers, and assault Muslim citizens following interruption of national anthem at AMU.
1954	Dispute between fruitseller and customer
1956	AMU students reported insulting of the Gita, a holy book of the Hindus, to avenge insulting remarks about the Prophet Muhammad in a popular book.
1961	Clash between students in AMU Student Union elections
1966	Government's attempt to increase powers over AMU
1969	Hindu applause for visiting cricket team at AMU

Source: The Times of India, various issues.

since 1947.[24] In 1965, AMU students assaulted the university's pro-reform vice chancellor, bringing themselves and their institution greater disrepute. In 1966, the government's attempt to increase its powers over AMU's functioning caused disturbances; and in 1969, applause by some Hindu students for the visiting cricket team of Punjab University made trouble. The university was frequently in turmoil and frequently in the news. There was a relentless quality to its political battles.

POLITICS SINCE THE 1970S: A NEW MUSLIM MIDDLE CLASS

An Institutionalized Riot System

In the early 1970s, AMU ceased to be the only bone of contention in Aligarh's Hindu-Muslim politics. The polarization of the two communities did not stop, however. In fact, Aligarh developed a nexus between crime and politics. On the whole, communal violence became bloodier, nastier, and more frequent in this period. Criminals of both communities were evenly matched. Protected by politicians, they also developed allies in the local Hindu and Urdu press catering to the city. Violence increasingly stemmed from within the town. Of the many incidents of violence since 1971, developments within AMU were linked to only two riots (table 6.3), one in May 1979 and another in December 1990.

A new Muslim middle class has arisen in the town. It emerged in the infor-

Table 6.3. Communal Riots in Aligarh Since 1971

Year	Month	Reported Cause
1971	March	Arrest of Hindu nationalist student leader at the time of elections
1972	June	Hindu seven-year-old knocked down by a Muslim scooter driver by accident
1977	October	Cause insufficiently reported
1978	October	Clash between Hindu and Muslim wrestlers
	November	Retribution for previous violence
	December	Retribution for previous violence
1979	May	Clash between Hindu nationalists and AMU students going on a train to protest in Delhi
1980	August	Police fires at a Muslim protest, rioting three times in two weeks
	September	Arrest of two local journalists
	October	Random stabbing
	November	Muslims attack the Provincial Armed Constabulary
1982	July	Cause insufficiently reported
1983	March	Stone throwing by Hindu religious processionist
1987	June	Police arrest of a Muslim
1988	October	A market shutdown called by Hindu nationalists for Ayodhya march
1990	November	Tension due to the Hindu nationalist march for Ayodhya
	December	False rumors of Hindu patient killed in AMU Medical College Hospital
1992	December	Desecration of mosque in Ayodhya
1994	March	Random stabbing

Source: The Times of India, various issues.

mal economy, especially small industry, where most Muslims found work. The size of the class expanded as the post-1973 Gulf oil boom afforded new opportunities. Between 1965 and 1975, only four small industrial units producing locks were owned by Muslims. By 1976–80, thirty-three such units were Muslim-owned, and by 1981–85, eighty-seven units.[25] This transformation was primarily brought about by the earnings made possible by the temporary but large-scale Muslim migration to the Gulf. The new Muslim prosperity, however, did not bring peace to the city, nor can it be held entirely responsible for the absence of peace. Overwhelmingly poor until then, the town Muslims simply developed the muscle and financial capacity to take the Hindu nationalists on.

The evidence of a nexus between crime and politics first emerged in the 1971 riots. As the Muslim candidate of the Congress Party for parliamentary elections seemed set to lose, Muslim criminals went on a rampage, burning and looting shops and hurting and shooting innocent people. A Judicial Inquiry Commission instituted by the Congress government of Uttar Pradesh concluded that the "unruly elements" of the Muslim community were responsible for the riot, and the Congress candidate simply stood by, doing nothing to control the situation even though he had the power and connections to do so.[26]

The year 1978 provided by far the most striking evidence for the nexus between politicians and criminals. The riots of 1978 were touched off by a match between two professional wrestling schools (*akharas*), one Hindu and one Muslim. Subsequently, a Hindu wrestler was stabbed by some Muslims. The stabbed wrestler died in a hospital. Even before an official postmortem could take place, the body was snatched by the wrestler's supporters, carried in a long procession, and taken through Muslim neighborhoods. Slogans threatening collective revenge resonated throughout the procession. It was the job of the police to procure the body from the hospital for postmortem; it never did so. It turned out that the wrestler was part of a Hindu nationalist organization, and the latter at that time was part of the ruling coalition in Delhi, as also in the state capital (1977–79). Hindu nationalists had taken the procession out.[27] Riots continued for months. Retaliatory violence alternated with the curfews, showing remarkable preparation on both sides.[28] Evidence that riots were part of factional infighting within the Janata ruling coalition was powerful, though not direct.[29]

In 1980 there were pitched battles between Muslims and the Provincial Armed Constabulary (PAC), the paramilitary security organization of the state government. Since the PAC was widely viewed by Muslims in Aligarh and elsewhere in Uttar Pradesh as anti-Muslim, they started relying more and more on Muslim criminals for protection.[30] In August 1980, Muslim mobs attacked the PAC. The mobs were led by individuals described as thugs by the police and as liberators by the town Muslims.[31]

Lower Hindu Castes and Communal Violence

With the recent rise of lower-caste based parties in Aligarh, this institutionalized riot system may unravel. Though caste injustice was always present as a narrative around which politics was, and could be, organized, it could not earlier overpower the communal political mobilization in the city.[32] The caste narrative is now beginning to challenge the Hindu-Muslim cleavage as the principal axis of politics in Aligarh. Lower-caste parties have finally galvanized

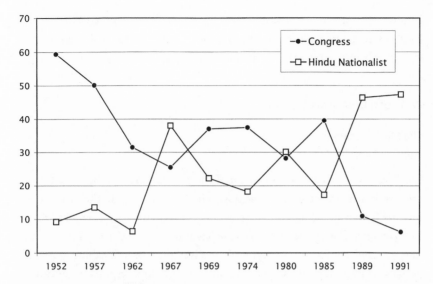

Figure 6.1 Aligarh Assembly Elections

their constituency with the promise of affirmative action.[33] Hindu nationalism and affirmative action have emerged as two competing modes of political mobilization. The Congress, not clearly identifiable with either, has been relegated to virtual irrelevance. By the early 1990s, the Congress looked electorally insignificant in the city (fig. 6.1). In the elections of 1989 and 1991, the Congress polled a mere 11 and 6 percent of the city's vote, respectively; the BJP polled 46.4 and 47.3 percent; and the lower-caste parties 38 percent (see table 6.1).

The political forces of the lower castes know that if they let communal riots take place, a Hindu-Muslim polarization will continue to exist, and communal passions will crowd out their agenda.[34] Muslims are seen as an important part of the anti–upper caste coalition. Being more than 30 percent of Aligarh and 17 percent of the state, the Muslims are an important vote bank. For three decades after independence they largely voted for the Congress. The lower-caste parties have of late been a better option for them: these parties are likely to lower communal violence and may at some point in the future also include the Muslims in affirmative action programs.

It is not clear, however, whether the lower castes will eventually come under the larger Hindu umbrella of the BJP, or go en masse for a Muslim–lower caste alliance. There are internal differences among the lower castes,[35] and some continue to be uncomfortable with the idea of an alliance with the Muslims.[36] Which way the bulk of the lower castes go will also decide the fate of Hindu-

Muslim relations in the city. As of now, the civic links between Hindus and Muslims are tenuous. Just as it did in Calicut, only a major political transformation is likely to reshape civic life in Aligarh.

CAN COMMUNALISM BE GOOD?

The Muslim League and Alliance
Politics of Kerala

Muslims have made up 18–21 percent of the population since the formation of the Kerala state in the 1950s (table 6.4). The Muslim League (the League) has repeatedly won an average of 8–10 percent of seats in the state assembly. Except for 1987–91 and 1996–2001, the League has also ruled the state as a member of the governing coalition. It has typically received three or four cabinet posts, especially education, public works, and industry. All three, especially education, are important for patronage.

Kerala has developed a party system in which the Congress and the Communists occupy roughly equal space, but each needs support to form a government. The alternation in power depends on what alliances are struck. In a system such as this, being small has an advantage. If a small party merges with the Communists or the Congress to participate in government, it loses its identity; if it stays separate but forms an alliance, it can participate in government and retain its identity. By following the latter strategy, it can also increase its bargaining power, for withdrawal of a small party can often undermine governments. The League has followed this strategy and carried the advantages of being small. The League's power, thus, results from the alliance politics of Kerala.

While in government, the League has been able to provide many benefits to the Muslim community, both symbolic and material. As part of a Communist-

Table 6.4. Religious Communities of Kerala as a Percentage of Total State Population

Year	Muslims	Hindus	Christians
1951	17.50	61.60	20.80
1961	17.90	60.80	21.20
1971	19.50	59.40	20.10
1981	21.20	58.10	20.50
1991	23.33	57.28	19.32

Source: Census of India, various years.

led government between 1967 and 1969, it was able to carve out a Muslim-majority district, Malappuram, from Calicut and neighboring areas in 1969. The ostensible argument of the League was that Calicut was too unwieldy a district; smaller units would provide the people easier access to the district administration. It can, however, be shown that the attempt was primarily to create a Muslim-majority district, headquartered in an area that was the center of Malabar rebellion and a place of pilgrimage for Malabar Muslims.[37]

The League also managed to revoke a state regulation requiring government permission to construct or renovate mosques and succeeded in reserving 10 percent of government jobs for Moplahs.[38] Moplahs were among the last communities to take to modern education. Compared to the Nairs, Christians, and Ezhavas, fewer Moplahs were in government employment.[39] Job quotas were, therefore, of great significance to the community.

The League has always laid claims to the Education Ministry. Unlike most governments in India, the Kerala government since independence has spent between 30 and 40 percent of its budget on education. The Education Ministry, as a result, offers remarkable powers of patronage. Using such powers, the League's education minister was able to establish a university in Calicut.[40] He also created positions for teaching Arabic in schools for Muslim pupils and provided grants for the study of Arabic and Islamic history.[41]

Symbolically, the most remarkable victory for the League was the government's announcement in 1973 that the Moplahs who participated in the Malabar rebellion would be given the title of "freedom fighters." The title carried a state pension as well as benefits for the rebels and their dependents. The state recognized *all* rebels, including those who were not convicted of attacking British property, as freedom fighters.[42] Finally, during its stint in power between 1982 and 1987, a scheme of government pension for Muslim clerics was also approved.

Hindu nationalists call these concessions a sign of "minority appeasement." Yet they have not been able to launch a serious campaign against the League's communalism and power. Part of the problem is that the tight economic and social links between Hindus and Muslims provide no space for a large-scale communal mobilization of the Hindus. Another, related part is that pro-Muslim decisions are seen as part of Kerala's routine patronage politics. Because caste has been the main cleavage of Kerala, the meaning of the League's communalism is not the same as in much of the north and the west. All caste groups use the state for sectional gains. For the purposes of politics, Muslims have become yet another caste. Their moves are not seen as linked to nationalism. The framework of meanings and interpretations is highly regional and influenced by the dominant regional narrative of caste. To better understand how tight the links between Hindus and Muslims are, and how a regional narrative of politics transforms meanings of actions that would constitute a threat in the north and west, we need to look at the ideology of social justice and how it has operated in post-1947 Kerala.

Social Justice and Party Politics

Kerala's politics continues to be dominated by an ideology of equality and justice, an ideology that coexists with and draws upon a strong caste consciousness. It is a measure of the success of the Communists that in a society in which nearly 70 percent of Hindu population was defined as untouchable and much of it unseeable, the rules of deference have collapsed within a matter of decades. From being the most hierarchical region of India a century ago, Kerala today is the most egalitarian in the country. The traditional rules of pollution and deference have disappeared, access to education and temples is now unrestricted, the state will soon be 100 percent literate, and feudal landlordism has been abolished. All of this has been achieved in a democratic framework.[43] The land reform legislation, abolishing tenancy altogether and giving ownership titles to former tenants, was unanimously passed in Kerala's assembly in 1969. Even opposition parties, some representing rural propertied groups, did not vote against it. It was a remarkable tribute to how much the Communists had changed the thinking and habits of Kerala.[44]

Still, the Communists have been, to use Gramsci's terms, dominant without being hegemonic. They have set the ideological agenda of the state, and other parties have responded, negatively or positively. Those responding negatively have remained politically and socially viable. Religions have flourished. Kerala has more temples, more mosques, and more churches today than at any time in recent history. The Muslims and the Christians have their own parties. "Looking back," admitted E. M. S. Namboodiripad, the late Marxist theoretician, "I feel one of our key failures has been in understanding issues connected with religious minorities in Kerala. Muslims and Christians are under the predominant influence of religion-based leaders [who] took strong anti-Communist positions."[45]

In areas dominated by Christians and Muslims, the Communists have historically done badly.[46] Thus, nearly 40 percent of Kerala's population—Muslims and Christians—remains beyond the reach of the Communists, for it substantially votes for religion-based parties. Communism has made the greatest sense to caste-based Hindu society. Among the Hindus, support for the Communists has been centered among the Ezhavas and other low or scheduled castes.[47] These castes were historically at the lowest end of the ritual as well as the economic hierarchy.

The League's Formula: Be Small, Be Moderate, Let Caste Dominate, and Stay in Government

There are two linked sources of the League's moderation. First, the focus on caste and social justice may have isolated the Brahmins and the landlords, but it has integrated Hindus and Muslims in social and economic life. Even if it wanted to do so, the League would find it hard to break up civic integration that is decades old. Second, the League has no incentive to do it. Coalition governments moderate its politics. The League can't come to power entirely on its own. If communal tensions got out of control and its cadres were involved, the League would lose. Its alliance partners would raise objections to its continuance in power or in alliance. Its best strategy, thus, is to act moderately. By acting immoderately, it would make itself unacceptable to alliance partners.

As a result, when tensions do mount concerning religious issues, the League tends to cool them. It neither incites Muslims to retaliate, nor does it lead the charge of religious fervor. When anti-Muslim riots erupted in Tellicherry in 1972—one of the few incidents of communal violence in independent Kerala—the League called on Muslims not to retaliate.[48] In 1992, after the Ayodhya mosque was broken, the League faced a crisis. To protest against the Congress government in Delhi, which did not protect the mosque, the Delhi-based parliamentary wing of the League sought to undermine the Congress-led government in Kerala, in which the League was a partner. The state wing of the League chose to split the party but did not withdraw from the government. It argued that the demolition of Ayodhya mosque was a loss to the nation, not simply to the Muslim community.[49] The League knows that it can support Muslim interests best by being in power, not by staying outside.[50] It also knows that it can stay inside a governing alliance if and only if it does not lead Muslims to violence. Finally, it knows that even if tried to incite communal fury, its base, heavily integrated with the Hindus, would find it entirely impractical. A virtuous circle has thus formed. Moderation flows from the structure of political and civic symbiosis.

The four largest groups in the state include two caste communities, Nairs and Ezhavas, and two religious communities, Christians and Muslims.[51] A ma-

Table 6.5. Regional Diversity of Kerala's Population

Region	Hindu	Christian	Muslim
Malabar	62.65%	4.34%	32.96%
Cochin	54.00	34.42	11.50
Travancore	61.18	29.24	8.15
Kerala	60.83	21.22	17.91

Source: Census of India, 1961.

jor survey conducted in 1970 gives us a good sense of the distribution of the four communities: Ezhavas (22.2 percent), Christians (21.05 percent), Muslims (19.5 percent), and Nairs (14.5 percent).[52] The four communities thus account for about 80 percent of the state's population.

Each of these communities has developed a distinct political organization. Christians protect their political interests through the Kerala Congress. The Nairs dominate the Congress; in addition, they have a small political party, NDP, and a caste organization, NSS, which lobbies the government for them. The Ezhavas dominate the Communist Party; they also have a small Ezhava party (Revolutionary Socialist Party, or RSP) and their caste organization, SNDP. All groups want "more employment, more business facilities, more schools, more seats in professional colleges, more berths in the ministry."[53]

So widespread are these activities that *the term communalism has changed its meaning in Kerala.* Discussions of communalism focus on all four major groups. Communalism in Kerala simply means to develop "a feeling of group identity among different communities and to assert its presence in the day-to-day functioning of society."[54] It means community or ethnicity, not politicized religion. It incorporates sectarian activities of caste groups as well. The League's activities are no different from those of the Nairs or Ezhavas.[55]

CONCLUSION

Aligarh's civic life, epitomized by its highly segregated educational system, has been primarily intracommunal, not intercommunal. An intracommunal civic life makes it easy for communal politicians and organizations to function, and with few civic checks on their polarizing strategies, violence often breaks out. A major political transformation, such as the spread of a lower-caste ideology, can potentially change the situation in Aligarh and bring at least the lower Hindu castes and Muslims together, both electorally and in civic life. Thus far the civic structures have offered scope for polarizing politics and violence. Only a major political restructuring will change the situation.

In Calicut, intracommunal links exist, but intercommunal links have also flourished. The city's intercommunal civic engagement makes it hard for polarizing politics to emerge and checks potential violence. Yet, in the end, just as the seeds of intracommunal civic engagement were sown by the inability of the Congress Party to restructure mass politics in Aligarh in the 1920s and 1930s, we also have to remind ourselves that the intercommunal civic life of Calicut was politically constructed. As we saw in Chapter 5, the Malabar rebellion was too brutal a shock in the 1920s. Such exogenous shocks have decisively altered communal relations elsewhere in India.[56] In Malabar, even arch-Gandhians, inveterate believers in the possibilities of human will, had withdrawn from mobilizing the Muslims. It was the left wing of Congress, later turning to Marxism, that redefined the issues of mobilization. It switched to social justice and conceptualized an alliance of the lower castes against the upper castes *within* Hindu society. Over the next few decades, mass politics in Calicut was transformed. Land reform and social justice became the battle cries. A whole series of associations and organizations emerged to propagate the new ideology of social justice, civil rights for the lower castes, and education for all.

Hindu-Muslim civic engagement emerged in Calicut as a by-product of the redefinition of the principal cleavage in politics. It was no longer Hindu-Muslim, but intra-Hindu, issues that dominated politics. Intercommunal civic links may have made it impossible for the Hindu nationalists today to make a dent in the politics of Calicut and Kerala, but the primacy of civic life has a different meaning when a historical perspective is applied. The presence of intercommunal engagement, such a remarkable feature of Kerala's life today, was politically constructed.

Part III Local Variations

Hyderabad and Lucknow: Elite Integration
Versus Mass Integration

Chapter 7 Princely Resistance
to Civil Society

The second pair of cities—Hyderabad and Lucknow—introduces another important dimension of civic life: the difference between civic integration at the level of the elite and the masses. As briefly stated in Chapter 2, this distinction matters for ethnic peace and conflict. If politics is not an arena confined to the elite anymore, and the masses have begun to act as *citizens*, not simply as *subjects*, then mass-level integration is likely to be a stronger bulwark of peace than a mere elite-level integration. The size of the former differentiates it from the latter, making electoral strategies that respond to mass-level integration, or its absence, more likely than the ones that merely concentrate on a tiny elite, important though it may be socially and economically. In addition, this second comparison of cities reiterates a lesson we learned in the first: namely, intragroup divides contribute to intergroup peace. If in the first comparison Hindus were badly divided along caste lines in the city of Calicut, it is the Shia-Sunni conflicts in the city of Lucknow that have been functionally equivalent. By identifying the main enemy within the Muslim community, Shia-Sunni conflicts facilitate Hindu-Muslim integration. To pre-empt confusion, and following the standard South Asia terminology, I will use the term "sectarianism" for the Shia-Sunni divide and "communalism" for Hindu-Muslim conflicts.

In the twentieth century, the Shia-Sunni animosities in the city of Lucknow time and again overpowered the city's Hindu-Muslim differences. In Hyderabad, both Shias and Sunnis exist, but a theoretically conceivable Shia-Sunni split has remained politically dormant. Instead, a Hindu-Muslim divide has been politically active since the 1930s. It is, moreover, a divide that exists primarily at the mass level, not at the elite level. Residing mostly in the newer parts of the city, roughly equivalent to American suburbs, the city's social and educational elite interacts across the Hindu-Muslim divide, but the teeming thousands in the old city, equivalent to inner cities of the United States, have deep Hindu-Muslim divisions. The city's political leaders and their organizations, following the numerical logic of a universal-franchise democracy, are connected more to the mass-level equations than to those prevalent among the tiny social elite.

Before we explore the cities' differences further, let us quickly note their similarities, which initiated the comparison in the first place. Hyderabad and Lucknow have historically been viewed as centers of the so-called syncretistic Hindu-Muslim culture. They were ruled by Muslim princes—called the Nizams in Hyderabad and the Nawabs in Lucknow—for a long time. Hindu and Muslim elites participated in the culture of the court, and they spoke and were instructed in Urdu. Moreover, for decades, the proportion of Hindus and Muslims in the population of these two cities has roughly been in the same range. In Hyderabad, Muslims have constituted 35–37 percent of the population since 1961, in Lucknow 28–30 percent. Each of these proportions would make winning very likely in a first-past-the-post electoral system, if Muslims were to vote as a bloc, if multiple candidates participated in elections, and if the Hindus had internal differences, causing a split in their votes. With such demographic ratios, there is an electoral incentive for Muslim political parties to consolidate the Muslim vote with highly communal appeals, without, however, going so far as to unite the Hindus under a single party.

Indeed, a Muslim party exists in Hyderabad, and large proportions of Hyderabad Muslims, especially in the old city, where a large majority of the community lives, tend to vote en bloc. In Lucknow, however, this theoretical expectation goes wrong, illustrating once again that the existence of ethnic or religious communities does not automatically imply religious or ethnic political parties. The same demographic ratios, given the interconnections across communities, can generate very different forms of politics. In Lucknow, Muslim parties exist but an overwhelming majority of Muslims do not vote for them.

The story of communal violence turns up a still bigger contrast. Lucknow's only major Hindu-Muslim riot of the twentieth century took place in the 1924, so long ago that it is not even part of the city's memory.[1] Lucknow had no riots during the two biggest nationwide shocks in the century: India's partition in 1947 and the demolition of the Baburi mosque in December 1992 in Ayodhya, a town only eighty miles away from Lucknow. Lucknow had tensions and small skirmishes on both occasions, but no riots in which people died. In contrast, its communal peace first broken in 1938, Hyderabad has turned into one of the most riot-prone cities of India. After a turbulent Hindu-Muslim phase between 1938 and 1948, it remained quiet in the 1950s. In the 1960s, it had communal disturbances in eight of ten years.[2] The period since 1978 has been especially violent. Riots have taken place with remarkable regularity, and an institutionalized riot system—connecting politicians, criminals, parts of the local administration, and the press—has come to exist.

Why have the two cities diverged so much? At a *proximate* level, Lucknow's communal peace depends on a civic integration between Hindus and Muslims. By now, Hindu-Muslim links in the economy are extensive at the mass level. When communal tensions arise, these preexisting networks make it possible for Hindus and Muslims to come together and prevent violence. At the elite level, too, such integration exists. In Hyderabad, intercommunal civic links mark the upper layers of society only, not the mass level. And the elite links do not filter down to the mass level. There is a radical disjunction between the two.

At an *underlying* level, the difference in civic patterns goes back to the transformative political events of the 1930s and 1940s. A Shia-Sunni cleavage in politics preceded the rise of the Indian national movement in Lucknow. Pre-British Lucknow was ruled by Shia princes (1737–1856) who struck alliances with the Hindu community, not with the Sunnis, with whom they had a history of doctrinal disputes. Shia-Sunni power relations were not only expressed in elite alliances but also reflected in the city's popular culture. In the great Muslim festival of Muharram, in which the Muslim masses participate by the tens of thousands, the Shia version of the doctrine enjoyed princely patronage and supremacy over the Sunni interpretation. So long as the Sunnis were poor, the doctrinal clash remained politically inactive. As the traditionally poor Sunni community developed a middle class and Shia nobility declined by the end of the nineteenth century, the doctrinal dispute took a violent form. The month of Muharram often brought tensions and violence.

Contrariwise, in Hyderabad, as mass politics emerged in the 1930s, politics was superimposed on Hindu-Muslim, not Shia-Sunni, differences, although in principle, both cleavages were available for politics. The turning point was the refusal of Hyderabad's Muslim prince, the seventh Nizam, to concede popular rule in a state where Hindus constituted a majority of subjects but Muslims dominated the power structure. The prince found the demand that the subjects be viewed as citizens with voting rights and associational freedom appalling, for he believed that he had a dynastic right to rule. Using his authoritarian powers in the last decade of his rule (1937–48), the prince blocked the emergence of mass-level organizations that could have promoted civic integration of Hindus and Muslims. Instead, he relied on the support of a communal political party of the Muslims and its cultural organizations. Even though Muslims were a minority in the state, the Muslim party developed a doctrine of Muslims as a ruling race and launched a violent campaign against the majority community with the tacit support of the prince.

Thus, when mass politics did rock the political calm of the princely state, where politics until then had been primarily about courtly intrigues and princely fancies, it took a communal and violent form. The associational space for intercommunal engagement steadily shrank. Once very different civic structures were put in place in the 1930s and 1940s in the two cities, intercommunal civic checks on Hyderabad politicians were scarcely too strong, and in-

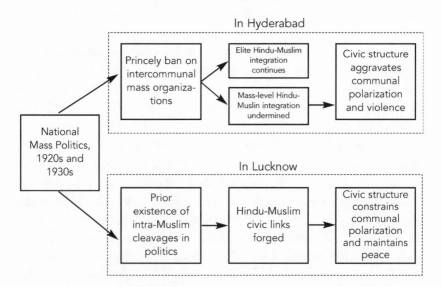

Figure 7.1 Politics, Civic Life, and Violence in Hyderabad and Lucknow

tercommunal civic constraints on Lucknow politicians, even of the Hindu nationalist variety, rarely feeble. Hyderabad politicians, with very few exceptions, have used Hindu-Muslim polarization and violence as a strategic political tool, whereas Lucknow politicians have sought to build bridges in times of communal tension. Figure 7.1 sums up the argument diagrammatically.

I present the argument in two parts in this chapter. The first part compares civic life in the two cities, and the second probes the political foundations of civic life, going back to the 1930s. How Hindu-Muslim relations and the path of politics since the 1950s have depended on the epoch-making political shifts of the 1930s and 1940s is the subject of Chapter 8.

WHAT KIND OF CIVIC ENGAGEMENT?

Economics as Integration,
Economics as Separation

In Lucknow, the biggest source of mass-level civic engagement is economic activity. Although the economic ties between the two communities are vertical—the Hindus are overwhelmingly traders-cum-entrepreneurs, and the Muslims primarily workers—a symbiosis marks their relationship. Neither group can live without the other, except by bearing significant economic costs. In Hyderabad, no such symbiosis exists. On the whole, Hyderabad Muslims have done much better than their Lucknow counterparts: their businesses are bigger and better than those of Lucknow Muslims (tables 7.1 and 7.2), but that has not led to widespread Hindu-Muslim linkages.

Historically, Lucknow and Hyderabad Muslims were primarily in government employment, not in business. A significant fraction of the community was employed by the feudal estate holders (the *jagirdars* in Hyderabad and the *taluqedars* in Lucknow). Many estate holders were absentee landlords, drawing their incomes from land but living an urban life. After Indian independence, Muslim middle classes in both cities migrated to Pakistan in large numbers. The very rich and the poor, however, stayed back in India, the former because they had too many property stakes in India, and the latter because, even if they wished to migrate, their poverty precluded the possibility of migration. A vast majority of Muslims were poor in both cities, and a tiny Muslim elite was quite wealthy, whereas Hindus could be found in all classes—upper, middle, and lower.

How did this economic structure develop after the 1950s? Lucknow's eco-

Table 7.1. Muslim Firms as a Proportion of Total Industrial Firms in Hyderabad

	1983						1994					
	Total	Percentage	Panel C	Percentage	Panel D	Percentage	Total	Percentage	Panel C	Percentage	Panel D	Percentage
Hindu	497	86.28	277	94.53	220	77.73	725	83.14	382	91.82	343	75.21
Muslim	69	11.97	11	3.75	58	20.49	135	15.48	29	6.97	106	23.24
Other	10	1.73	5	1.70	5	1.76	12	1.37	5	1.20	7	1.53

Note: Firms in Panels A and B are the bigger firms of Hyderabad; those in Panels C and D are smaller. The number of Muslim-owned firms in Panels A and B was negligible for the two years presented above. Hence it has not been reported. Muslim firms in Panels C and D, though smaller, are a substantial proportion of the total number. Moreover, the Muslim proportion has risen in both categories. The 1994 figures are higher than the 1983 ones.

Source: Directory, Federation of A. P. Chamber of Commerce and Industry, 1983 and 1994.

Table 7.2. Muslim Firms as a Proportion of Total Industrial
Firms in Lucknow, 1994

	Total	Percentage
Hindu	243	92.7
Muslim	4	1.53
Total	15	5.73

Note: The caluculation above is based on the firms registered with the
PHD Chamber of Commerce and Industry. Many firms are not registered, but there is no good way of estimating how many of them are
Hindu- or Muslim-owned. The proportions above are, however, enough
to show that very few Muslims take to business in Lucknow. Compared
to Hyderabad (see table 7.1), their numbers in Lucknow are very small.
Source: Directory, PHD Chamber of Commerce and Industry, 1994.

nomic developments are relatively straightforward. The embroidered textiles
industry, based on the special skills of Muslims artisans, progressively became
the heart of Lucknow's economy. The industry is known as Chikan and Zardozi: these are two different ways of embroidering clothes. The use of modern
technology is minimal, and there are no factories in the production process.
Rather, it is a huge "putting out system" based on piece wages, and is classified
as an informal or unorganized industry.[3] Embroidery is the distinctive aspect of
the clothing. It is a skill not easily replicable by machines.

How many people work in the industry, and what relationships do they
have? Since the industry is in the informal sector and the numbers of workers
in the informal industry cannot be exactly determined, it is impossible to get
good point estimates about the Chikan workforce, but reasonable interval estimates can be provided. By the late 1980s, the workers numbered anywhere between 75,000 and 100,000.[4]

Let us consider the implications of the statistics above. If we assume a family
size of six to seven members and two workers per family—fair assumptions,
given the descriptions of the industry[5]—about 200,000 to 300,000 people are
by now partially or wholly dependent on the Chikan industry in Lucknow.
Even if 90 percent of the industry's workers are Muslims—an estimate on the
lower side for the sake of argument—it would mean that, numbering 180,000
to 270,000, anywhere between 30 and 50 percent of the entire Muslim population is employed in the industry.

The size of the industry acquires a deeper meaning for Hindu-Muslim relations when we note four more characteristics. First, Chikan workers are over-whelmingly Sunni Muslim, a large number of them women. Second, the traders-cum-entrepreneurs are overwhelmingly Hindu. Since Hindus had his-torically enjoyed a cordial relationship with the Shia community, the existence of Sunni workers in the industry added large numbers of Hindus and Sunni Muslims in a mutually dependent relationship. *Both Muslim sects are thus linked to the Hindus, but not as integrally to each other.* Third, the division of la-bor is informal. There are no wage contracts. Finally, "none of the artisans can do solely all items of work and turn out finished product."[6] Lacking explicit and formal contracts, the entire system works on trust, and each step in the process is dependent on the preceding step.[7] If the tailors don't deliver, printers can't work; if the printers don't, the materials can't be sent to the female em-broiderers. A large network of agents, mostly Muslim, manage the operation in key stages.

In short, an economic symbiosis, marked by trust, has developed between a very large number of Hindus and Muslims in Lucknow. If communal violence took place in the city, argued all the traders interviewed in this study, the econ-omy would simply collapse.

Can Trust Emerge in Vertical Relationships?

One may object to the use of the word "trust" to describe relationships in a ver-tical setting. It has been argued that trust can emerge in horizontal, not vertical, relationships.[8] Although this argument is on the whole right, it may not apply to all contexts. Trust can emerge in vertical networks if an *ideology* supporting hierarchy exists and is part of the consciousness of people engaged in hierarchi-cal networks (for example, India's caste system until recently) or if the vertical relationship is marked by an economic *symbiosis* whereby it is very difficult, if not impossible, for communities to live without each other.

In Lucknow, the latter argument holds. Trust rather than coercion fuels the embroidery industry. Coercion can easily be the basis of power in small-scale, tightly knit villages and neighborhoods, but it will be difficult to show how co-ercion can sustain an economy as large as the one in Lucknow in the absence of laws supporting coercion, in the presence of other economic options, and if multiple political groups exist.

Consider the evidence in favor of social trust. Legal contracts simply do not exist in the industry. Materials worth $15,000–20,000 (a large sum per trader) are nearly always in circulation without any legal paperwork.[9] Thousands of traders participate in the economy, making the market fairly competitive. If they so wish, the middlemen can switch to other traders. Muslim craftswomen can also join cooperatives that have already organized women in the industry, especially under powerful NGOs such as the Self-Employed Women's Association. Many of the women involved in the industry are, from all evidence, quite happy that they don't have to step out of their homes to find work. The orders for embroidery arrive at home, and they can make a living without venturing out for work. For women caught in the system of veiling—an unfortunate system but one difficult to break out of in Muslim South Asia—working at home is an attractive option.[10]

Finally, if workers are mostly Muslim, the number of Muslims workers is large, the bosses are Hindu nationalists, and the bosses do use force and fear to generate compliance, the conditions of political competition in a democracy make such a situation appealing for anti-BJP parties at the local level. We know that the richest traders are BJP politicians. Yet the Congress or other anti-BJP parties have never taken up this issue. Coercion would appear not to rule, at least in a raw and overpowering form.

The point is not that the Chikan industry approximates the perfect-competition economic models and, therefore, no unfairness exists. We know that even when perfect competition exists, the outcomes can be highly unfair if initial conditions are highly unequal.[11] Workers in the Chikan industry, like workers in many informal industries, do not have access to strong unions and clear contracts and therefore do suffer from structural disadvantages. But, given the symbiotic nature of the relationship, the structure is akin to a moral economy. A moral economy is often hierarchical, but such economies are also known to have norms of reciprocity and trust.[12]

The Muslim women don't have to step out of their homes; the middlemen reach them through their ethnic networks; and the traders depend on these transactions to make money. Few pieces of paper pass through the entire operation. Expectations of "good behavior" run the industry, and such expectations are routinely fulfilled. In the process, a large network of trust and engagement is built up between Hindus and Muslims.

The Economy in Hyderabad

Nothing comparable exists in Hyderabad. It is industrially far more advanced than Lucknow. Several large industries, placed in the "organized" sector, exist. But no single industry employs more than ten to fifteen thousand people. And there is no economic symbiosis.[13]

Economically stagnant in the 1950s and 1960s, the Muslim community has received a tremendous economic boost from migration to the Middle East since the mid-1970s. (Migration from Lucknow is many times smaller.) Skilled and unskilled workers have constituted the bulk of Hyderabad's migrants, and the impact of migrant remittances has been primarily felt in the informal sector. Of those registered with the Hyderabad Chamber of Commerce in 1994, there were no Muslim firms in the "large" category. All Muslims firms were in the "small" and "very small" categories.[14] (See table 7.1.) Another study indicates that the informal sector of the city is 65–70 percent Muslim.[15] Muslims dominate trading in shoes, fruit and vegetables, metal scraps, and book binding and constitute a large number of auto mechanics and auto-rickshaw drivers. None of these activities leads to stable and significant trader-customer linkages between Hindus and Muslims. Hindus also exist in most of these categories, and the clienteles tend to form along communal lines. Moreover, associations of traders, when they are built, are formed along intracommunal lines.

To sum up, over the past fifteen to twenty years, rising incomes have *not* locked Muslims into solid economic or associational links with the Hindu community, and vice versa. The two communities have not built a web of intercommunal interdependence.

CADRE-BASED POLITICAL ORGANIZATIONS

Of the conventional mass-level political organizations, trade unions are small and weak in both cities. But cadre-based political parties are powerful. Large, cadre-based political parties, as we know, have the potential to bring people and communities together. In Hyderabad, they link individuals intracommunally; in Lucknow, the links are intercommunal, and the splits that do exist concern the Shias and Sunnis, not Hindus and Muslims.

It is widely known that Muslims in most parts of India embraced the Congress Party after partition. Occasional complaints notwithstanding, the party was committed to a vision of a multireligious India and seemed best placed to fight Hindu nationalism, which, owing to its anti-Muslim postures, was the more threatening. By and large, the Muslims of Hyderabad have departed from this all-India pattern. They have overwhelmingly supported a Muslim party called the Majlis-e-Ittehadul Musilimeen (MIM, or simply Majlis).

Although, in its official statement of purposes and activities after Indian independence, the MIM has talked of the welfare of all "depressed classes," it is for all practical purposes a Muslims-only party. It is cadre-based, its activities are confined to the city of Hyderabad, and it has made no serious attempts to move beyond the city, not even to areas that were under the control of the princely state of the Nizam.[16] In Hyderabad, the MIM has contested elections at all three levels: the local municipal, the state assembly, and the national parliament. It has done best at the local level, its performance occasionally strong enough to make it possible for it to run the local government. Since the 1970s, it has also been winning roughly half of state assembly seats in the city, and since the 1980s, one of two city seats for national parliament.

Although the MIM's local success is clearly a sign that it has responded to Muslim anxieties and feelings, the obverse side of this development should be noted. The decision of most Hyderabad Muslims to stay away from the Congress Party means that the largest organization of twentieth century India, which historically brought Hindus and Muslims together (if not in recent years), has not played its bridge-building role in the city. In fact, the MIM's strength in the city has created fertile ground for Hindu nationalist organizations. In southern India, as noted in the previous two chapters, it is the intra-Hindu caste narrative, not the Hindu-Muslim narrative, that has historically dominated politics, making it hard for Hindu nationalism to find a foothold. Constituting a major exception, Hyderabad was the first city in southern India to witness the rise of Hindu nationalist parties and organizations.

Instead of providing an associational space for Hindu-Muslim engagement, the MIM and the Hindu nationalists have split Hindus and Muslims. The Congress and the Communist Parties, both cadre-based and historically committed to Hindu-Muslim integration, have not been able to counter the polarizing logic of MIM–Hindu nationalist interaction. Indeed, there is evidence, presented in Chapter 8, that in recent years, despite its historical character, the Congress Party has not shied away from making use of communal cleavages in factional battles within the party.

POPULAR FESTIVALS

Festivals are often an important source of civic engagement in societies. Whether July 4 or Saint Patrick's Day parades in the United States or Dussehra or the August 15 parades in India, festivals of various kinds—religious and secular—involve rituals of public participation. Such rituals can often bring otherwise separate individuals into a common civic space. Because they are so central to public culture, festivals can also be the focal points for group assertion, communal disputes, and sectarian contestation. The rituals of participation are thus a double-edged sword. Celebrations of high ideals or of the divine can go together with violence and bigotry.

Unlike towns in the neighboring state of Maharashtra, Hyderabad had no tradition of large, citywide celebrations for *Ganesh chaturthi,* a festival in honor of the Hindu deity Ganesh. Traditionally, Ganesh celebrations were confined to the household or to the neighborhood level in Hyderabad. In the late 1970s, under the leadership of local Hindu nationalists, small Ganesh processions were merged into a truly massive citywide procession. With several hundred thousand participants, the annual Ganesh processions over the past two decades have often been several miles long. Policing such processions is a nightmare. Many personal, commercial, communal, and political scores have been settled, as the processions have marched through key markets, neighborhoods, and institutions.

The first chairman of the Ganesh festival, a prominent Hindu nationalist in the city, openly admits that the purpose of enlarged processions was to demonstrate to the Muslims how united the Hindus could be. It was necessary to do so, he argued, because, riding on the new-found prosperity brought in by migration to the Middle East, the "Muslims had started causing too much nuisance."[17] Their mosques had become shinier and their prayers louder, often broadcast on loudspeakers. Muslims, he concluded, had to be taught a lesson. A mammoth citywide Ganesh festival, on the pattern of neighboring Maharashtra, was the answer.

Not to be left behind, the MIM also engineered a new collective rite for Muslims, called the Pankha procession, in honor of a local Sufi shrine. Sufism, a paradigm of syncretistic Islam and famous for bringing Hindus and Muslims together, was thus turned into a vehicle of communal assertion by the powerful cadre-based Muslim organization of the city. In 1984, the Pankha and Ganesh processions followed in quick succession, leading to the worst communal violence of the decade.

The popular civic arena of festivals has thus been awfully polarized in Hyderabad. Via rituals of religious celebration, interested groups have sought to arouse mass rivalry and contestation.

The Shia-Sunni Dispute and Rituals of Muharram

Lucknow also has been a center of festival politics involving the masses, but the dispute there is between Shias and Sunnis, not between Hindus and Muslims.

The bone of contention is Muharram, a very important month in the Islamic calendar all over the Muslim world. The conflict has two sides: a doctrinal side, which is universal, and an aspect specific to Lucknow, which has charged the doctrinal dispute with special intensity.

Shias all over the world believe that Ali, son-in-law of Prophet Mohammed, was designated by his father-in-law to be his successor. They think that Abu Bakr, Omar, and Osman, the first three caliphs (successors to the prophet), deprived Ali of his right. It was only after the death of Osman that Ali became the fourth caliph, and that too was highly contested by Muavia, the governor of Syria, who was indirectly an appointee of the third caliph. Ali was finally assassinated, and Ali's sons—Hasan and Hussain—were also deprived of the caliphate by Muavia and his son, Yazid. In A.D. 680, after much maneuvering and scheming in the battle of Kerbala, Yazid's forces massacred Hussain and all other male members of his family and army. Only Hussain's little son, Zain ul Abidin, was left, saved by Hussain's sister, Zainab.

Thus, the Shias hold Mohammed, Ali, Hasan, Hussain, and Fatima (Ali's wife and Mohammed's daughter) in the highest veneration. Ali is regarded not as the fourth caliph but as the first imam. The Shias don't recognize any of the caliphs after Ali, instead giving allegiance to the nine imams who succeeded Hussain. Many also view the adversaries of Ali as enemies—not only Yazid, who draws no sympathy from the Sunnis either, but also the first three caliphs, whom the Sunnis revere. For the Sunnis, the first three caliphs were rightful successors. Ali is acceptable to both and Yazid to neither. On three days in the Islamic calendar each year, the Shias commemorate the martyrdom of Ali and Hussain: on the tenth day of Muharram (the first month of the Islamic year), on the fortieth day of Chehlum, and on the twenty-first day of Ramadan (the day Ali was assassinated).

The battle of Kerbala occupies a central place in Shia history, culture, and public rituals. During the first ten days of Muharram, community gatherings *(majlis)* are attended in Lucknow by thousands of people. The purpose is to hear the events of Kerbala rendered by professionals who specialize in the act of narration and recitation and prepare for it for months. In many places, *tazias* (replicas of the tomb of Hussain at Kerbala) are also taken out in a procession for burial. Reverence for Hussain is demonstrated through the majlis, tazias, and expressions of grief.[18]

Since Lucknow was ruled by Shia princes, Muharram came to occupy a truly special place in the city's cultural life. The princes promoted grand public celebrations of Shia history. Princely patronage was responsible for the city's most spectacular buildings, called *imambaras*—literally, the Houses of Imam. Students of architecture use the term "political architecture" for these buildings.[19] The imambaras serve several functions: they keep the tomb-replicas of Hussain during Muharram; they provide grand spaces where elegies and dirges are narrated by professionals to thousands listening; and they are magnificently decorated and lit on the eighth and ninth days of Muharram.

The last is important in that it was done despite the theological view that the splendor of lights disagreed with the sorrow of the occasion. But it was in keeping with the more political idea that the royal imambaras would present a spectacle of the Shia court culture.[20] Indeed, the elegies *(marsiya)* were transformed into veritable art forms under princely patronage, with the leading poets of the land competing and reaching out to large masses of people through Indianized metaphors of sorrow and valor. These elegies, argues C. M. Naim, came to resemble epics, in a religion that actually did not have epics.[21] In short, the Shia princes sought to turn Shi'ism from a *religion* of rulers into the popular *culture* of Lucknow.

The color and drama of Shia Muharram has always invited Sunni displeasure in Lucknow. Much to the dismay of the Sunnis, the pageantry and spectacle resemble those of Hindu festivals. Hindus have also traditionally participated in Muharram in substantial numbers—more for the sake of the spectacle than for the ritualistic expression of sorrow.[22] That is precisely what turning Shi'ism into the popular culture of Lucknow meant, demonstrating the success of the princely project. Second, the devaluation of the first three caliphs in Shia expressions of sorrow—the charge that they were usurpers—is against the faith of Sunnis. To express their displeasure, the Sunnis have often insisted on what has come to be known as *Madh-e-Sahaba* (the companions of the prophet) processions, which include a public recitation of verses in praise of all four caliphs (Abu Bakr, Omar, Osman, and Ali). Objecting to the placement of the first three caliphs in the same category as Ali, the Shias have held out *Tabbara* (curses on the first three caliphs) processions. The public cursing not only expresses a religious belief but was also a practice sustained by the dominance of Shi'ism in Lucknow.

Several organizations have been involved in the dispute, both religious and political. Some have mediated between the Shia and the Sunnis, others have taken sides. The Congress Party in Lucknow has maintained a large cadre base among both Hindus and Muslims for much of the twentieth century, and in recent years, as its power has diminished, the lower-caste parties have played the same role. These political organizations have sought to mediate, and when in power, have often suspended both Tabarra and Madh-e-Sahaba recitations, allowing the rest of the activities. By far the most paradoxical political development, however, has been the support extended by some Shia organizations to the Hindu nationalists in the city. The latter organizations have found the Sunni presence in the Congress more troubling than the idea of supporting Hindu nationalists.

In short, the Shia-Sunni cleavage became deeply rooted in the popular civic and political culture of Lucknow. At the mass level, Lucknow has had little Shia-Sunni civic engagement; Hyderabad, in contrast, has had very little Hindu-Muslim engagement. One shows deep-rooted intragroup divides, the other intergroup cleavages.

CIVIC INTERACTION AT THE ELITE LEVEL

In contrast to the mass-level segregation, Hyderabad's *social* elite seems to have had a great deal of civic interaction across the Hindu-Muslim divide. True historically, such interaction continues to exist today. The social elite lives in the newer parts of the city, which have rarely been affected by communal violence. The old city is where communal violence takes place.[23]

Elite-level integration marks the many clubs of the city, where the social elite wines and dines.[24] Hyderabad also has a substantial number of modern NGOs, which have mushroomed since the 1980s and are led mostly by intellectuals and professionals among the new city's social elite. Many of these organizations are deeply concerned about Hindu-Muslim relations in the old city, and their commitment to building Hindu-Muslim civic links is beyond doubt. Some have actively participated in countering communal violence by forming peace committees or using their own organizations for peace. Others have used their skills and education to write essays in the city's several English-language newspapers or to make films about communal violence, exposing the polarizing strategies of politicians.[25] The problem with this otherwise well-meaning civic activity is simply that the new city intellectuals and activists are not "organically linked" to the old city, whose crowded squalor many of them left behind when their families moved to the newer, more modern neighborhoods. Their peace committees are more able to deliver relief after riots than to preempt riots. Their English-language articles are not read in the old city, where the vernacular press dominates. The films exposing the machinations of politicians and their terrible human costs do not reach the masses of the old city; the metropolitan upper middle classes of India and the cosmopolitan or diasporic audiences in the United States and Britain are its principal consumers.

Similarly, the many institutions of higher education in the new city, which make Hyderabad a nationally important intellectual center, can't easily have the same kind of impact on the old city as the latter's own educational centers. Realizing how important educational institutions can be for building a new generation of cadres and sympathizers, the MIM has founded and is running engineering and medical colleges in the old city. Muslim students have entered these new colleges in large numbers. Since these colleges draw an overwhelming proportion of their student body from the Muslim community, they are also sites of meager Hindu-Muslim interaction.

Lucknow does not have such a dramatic difference between its elite and masses. Just as they are integrated at the mass level, Hindus and Muslims interact a great deal at the elite level as well. The educated Muslims who go into the textile business penetrate the primarily Hindu network of textile traders. Most educated Muslims, however, do not go for business. They seek a government job or wish to work in the courts as lawyers. The city has many openings for them, for it is the state capital, with a large number of government offices, the headquarters of the mammoth Northeastern Railways, an important judicial center, a leading center for scientific research, and a large medical school.

Unemployment among the educated exists, of course, but a significant proportion of educated Muslims is absorbed into these institutions. The railways, for example, are a big source of employment. Muslims constitute about 11 percent of the workforce, much of which is unionized.[26] They also constitute 11 percent of the bar association.[27] Since the city is about 30 percent Muslim, these figures at first may not indicate high integration. But once it is noted that the Muslim literacy rate is considerably lower than that of the Hindus—perhaps less than half—one would expect the Hindu-Muslim ratios in *educated* sectors to be less than 15:85, not 30:70. The Muslim proportions cited above match such theoretical expectations.[28]

Similar results obtain even if we travel up the social scale and concentrate on the former court-based Muslim families. The patrician families were Shia to begin with and heavily connected with the court-based Hindus. Given the historical poverty of the Sunnis in the city, the aristocrats were not socially linked to the plebeian Sunni families.

Ever since the post-independence land reforms terminated the system of absentee landlordism, the former aristocracy has declined. It used to live in the city (and still does), but it had relied on rental income from land farmed by tenants. The bigger tenants became landowners as a result of land reforms, forcing the former aristocrats toward government service, law, and business. Whichever way they went, however, these families became part of the city's integrated business and professional networks. Some have married into Hindu families, creating even stronger Hindu-Muslim bonds.

In short, Lucknow's elite is highly integrated across Hindu-Muslim lines but not along Shia-Sunni lines. Such patterns have coexisted with the mass-level civic integration in the city. In Hyderabad, integration of the social elite is in evidence, but there are deep Hindu-Muslim cleavages at the mass level. The results of such patterns are dramatically different for communal violence.

HOW DID DIFFERENT CIVIC PATTERNS EMERGE?

The civic structures described above were a result of the transformative politics of India's national movement. Each city had substantial everyday Hindu-Muslim engagement until the early decades of the twentieth century.[29] In Hyderabad, such engagement was badly undermined by the arrival of mass politics in the 1930s; in Lucknow, mass politics had the opposite effect, for it deepened Shia-Sunni cleavages but brought Hindus and Muslims together. The key intervening variable in Hyderabad, which destroyed Hindu-Muslim linkages at the mass level though not at the elite level, was the hostility of the prince to demands for popular government. Such demands introduced the notion of citizenship, whereas the prince only believed in subjects, not citizens. His ban on the intercommunal mass organizations that led the demand for popular government and his reluctance to outlaw a Muslim mass organization that supported him had devastating consequences for Hindu-Muslim relations in the city.

Already part of British India since 1858, Lucknow was not under princely rule in the 1920s and 1930s. Since intra-Muslim Shia-Sunni cleavages had already emerged is a big way, the national movement of this period had little difficulty in forging Hindu-Muslim links in associations and organizations. The Muslim masses, as well as the elite, were opposed to close Shia-Sunni relations, not to Hindu-Muslim cordiality.

Princely Ardor for Subjecthood

The royal dynasty that ruled Hyderabad between the seventeenth and the twentieth centuries was called the Nizams. The Nizam's territories were not captured by the British. Rather, they became part of what came to be known as "Princely India," not "British India." About two-thirds of pre-1947 India was directly administered by the British; the remaining third was princely. The prince had power over the day-to-day governance and administration of his territories ("dominions"), but the British were sovereign. Over policy areas and institutions considered critical—especially foreign relations, the armed forces, and fiscal soundness of the state—the British did not typically tolerate princely dissent, exercising ultimate and unquestionable authority.

Communal amity, it is generally argued, marked princely India partly because electoral pressures did not exist there, as they did in British India. Politicians did not have to mobilize Hindus and Muslims to win power; the prince instead would distribute power through patronage, keeping some kind of balance between the two communities. Does this general understanding capture the realities of princely Hyderabad?

Hyderabad under the seventh Nizam is the period most relevant to us. The seventh Nizam, Mir Osman Ali Khan, ruled from 1911 to 1950. As proof of the Nizam's even-handed philosophy, two examples are often cited. Hindus, it is said, were appointed to some of the highest offices by the Nizams.[30] Moreover, in 1923 the seventh Nizam banned cow slaughter in public places, a measure aimed at pleasing the Hindus.

No authoritative history of twentieth-century Hyderabad has yet been written. Oral histories, memoirs, and correspondence, however, abound, providing a rich source of information. Based on these sources, one can make three points. First, Muslims dominated the princely state structure and employment. Second, there is no evidence of a serious Hindu-Muslim divide until the 1920s. Third, the accounts of the 1930s and 1940s, however, present a two-sided picture. Oral histories and recollections that concentrate on the aristocracy of Hyderabad provide evidence of Hindu-Muslim amity at the elite level. But those that recall the events from below present a city (and state) in the throes of communal turbulence.

Muslim Domination of the State

The Nizam's territories were multireligious and multilinguistic, but the Muslims dominated state employment. Although they made up 11 percent of the population (tables 7.3 and 7.4), Muslims constituted more than 75 percent of the police and civil administration, dominating both the officer class and cadres.[31] Moreover, their language, Urdu, was the language of the state, even

Table 7.3. Religious Composition of the Nizam's Police Force

Religious Group	Percentage officers	Percentage others
Muslims	78.3	85.4
Hindus	15.1	10.1
Christians	6.5	4.3
Others	—	0.2

though the mother tongue of nearly 90 percent of the population was not Urdu.[32]

A feudal system *(Jagirdari)* dominated the rural economic and political landscape. The feudal estate *(jagir)* consisted of one or more villages given as a free grant by the Nizam to the grantee as a reward for rendering a special service of a military or civil nature.[33] The Nizam's personal lands *(sarf-i-khas)* accounted for roughly 17 percent of state's area. Their revenue constituted the Nizam's personal income. Of the seven biggest feudal lords, six were Muslim and one was a Hindu.[34]

The industrial sector of the state was underdeveloped, dotted primarily by small industries. Given the feudal values of the time, land ownership, not industrial ownership, indicated status. In the period between 1935 and 1945, 60 percent of the industrialists were Hindu and 19 percent Muslim. Muslims received a preponderant share of public capital, but private capital was primarily Hindu.[35] Given the tiny size of the industrial sector, however, the overall impact of industry on mass incomes or welfare was small. Nor were the industrialists powerful.

Table 7.4. Religious Composition of the Nizam's Civil Administration

Religious Group	Percentage officers	Percentage others
Muslims	83.0	76.7
Hindus	11.3	21.9
Christians	5.6	1.2
Others	0	0.2

Note: The scheduled castes (called "Adi-Hindus" in the Census) are included in the Hindu category.
Source: Calculated from the *Census of India, 1931*, vol. 23, H.E.H. the Nizam's Dominions, (Hyderabad State), part 2, table 11, p. 184.

THREE NARRATIVES: ELITE, COUNTER-ELITE, AND POPULAR

The account above, it may be said, commits a theoretical error. It reads into Hyderabad's past a contemporary consciousness, or uncritically transfers to Hyderabad a form of consciousness that belonged to British India, not to princely India. It reifies communities where none existed. Muslims may have dominated the state, but it is possible that they did that as individuals, not as a community. Did Muslim domination of the state amount to a *community* domination, a case of communal discrimination, or was it merely a domination of Muslim individuals not identified with a community as such? When did the Muslims and Hindus develop a group consciousness in Hyderabad, if at all?

In the best of circumstances, these questions are fraught with interpretive difficulties. In Hyderabad, the problem is more serious, for three different historical narratives are available in the literature.[36] The first of these are elite narratives, showing the existence of Hindu-Muslim peace. Here is a typical memoir based on elite life in the 1920s and 1930s: "In Hyderabad there were no communal hang-ups. People followed their own religious often with a deep religious ardour, but people of different communities lived and worked together without any problems involving religion."[37]

A second narrative, also elite-based, emphasizes communal peace, but in addition it calls attention to a native-migrant (Mulki–non Mulki) cleavage. The Mulkis were the "sons of the soil," the non-Mulkis, migrants in Hyderabad from British India, arrived in the late nineteenth and early twentieth centuries. Occupying many of the key positions in the Nizam's governing bureaucracy, the migrants were the dominant elite in Hyderabad at the end of nineteenth century. Since the sons of the soil sought to challenge the migrant elite, theirs was essentially a counter-elite narrative.[38] By the 1920s, a slowly brewing native nationalism had clearly surfaced in upper echelons of Hyderabad.[39] The native-migrant cleavage was not communal but geographical and migration-based.

A common problem marks both of these narratives as well as most historical accounts based on elite sources. We learn from them a great deal about how the elite—both Hindu and Muslim—functioned, but we are left ignorant about how the common people behaved among themselves or viewed the Nizam's rule. Later in the 1920s and 1930s, a third, more "popular" narrative did emerge.

Based on non-elite (lower-middle and poorer classes) memoirs, this narrative gives evidence of an emerging Hindu-Muslim divide.

Consider the following account of the mid-to-late 1920s, given by Swami Ramananda Tirtha, a leading freedom fighter, a man from a comparatively modest background and also someone who mobilized the middle classes against the Nizam under the Congress banner:

> The parents of the students . . . would narrate what ignominious life they had to pass through. They would speak in low whispers when they complained about the various types of harassment at the hands of the officialdom. . . . To please the masters, they would even don the Fez cap. They were all Urduised, having been taught in that language at the expense of their own mother tongue. They would say that they could not offer worship in a public place. The observance of religious festivities was also frequently tabooed. . . . No newspapers worth the name were published. No meetings could be held. . . .
>
> It was all a communal Muslim hierarchy that controlled life. To be a Hindu meant all humiliation. . . . Muslims of the higher strata enjoyed all privileges and the poor ignorant Muslim felt happy at the idea that his co-religionist was at the helm and that he belonged to the ruling race. Himself in rags he would gloat over the opulence of a section of his race! . . . The administrative machinery was loaded with Muslim aristocracy. Even a superficial view would make one feel how greatly the majority section had been suppressed. No wonder that the Hindus came to develop a slave's mentality. Fear eclipsed all their inner urge.[40]

Thus, what appears as intercommunal harmony in the elite narratives becomes dissimulation in the accounts from below. It is a problem by now fairly well understood in the social sciences. James Scott, for example, has pointed to the relevance of "hidden transcripts" in power-laden scenarios: the weak, he argues, often tell the elite what is safe to utter.[41] The Nizam allowed little freedom of political expression.

Evidence for the authenticity of Tirtha's narrative is easy to provide. The groundwork for the campaign for competitive proselytization that (as explained below) created a storm in the 1930s had been laid in the 1920s, when two sets of rival religious organizations emerged in Hyderabad. The principal Hindu organization was the Arya Samaj (the Samaj), and the main Muslim organization, the Majlis (MIM).[42] The Samaj, since its birth in the 1870s, had been fighting for a Hindu religious revival in many parts of India. According to the Samaj, centuries of "alien" rule—first the Mughal, then the British—had weakened Hinduism, and practices such as idol worship had corroded its spirit.

The Samaj sought reclamation of Hindus, generally from the castes lower in the social hierarchy, who had in the past converted to other religions, especially to Islam and Christianity. The Samaj started a recruitment drive in Hyderabad in the 1920s.[43] To reach out to the masses, it translated the organization's key Sanskrit text, *Satyartha Prakash,* into Telugu, the largest vernacular in Hyderabad at that time. It also opened schools and gymnasiums and printed pamphlets and partisan materials.

The MIM was born in 1926. It sought to unite the various Islamic sects for the preservation of Islam. In addition, it also pledged loyalty to the Nizam and state laws. The initial years were fired by the religious objective of education and conversion *(Tabligh).*[44] Although court-inspired lifestyles continued to mark the lives of Hindus and Muslims at the upper echelons of society, the MIM and the Samaj primarily targeted the middle and poorer classes. The base of society was thus penetrated by organizations aiming to increase religious consciousness, a campaign that not only sought to enhance piety but also aimed at conversions.

A communal transformation of Hyderabad's mass-level consciousness was completed between 1937 and 1948, when mass politics emerged. During that period, the princely state had to deal with four kinds of mass-based organizations: communal Hindu (the Samaj), communal Muslim (the MIM), the nonviolent interreligious (the Congress), and the violent interreligious (the Communists).[45] On the whole, the Nizam suppressed the first, third, and fourth groups and promoted the second.[46] The effects on Hindu-Muslim relations at the mass level were devastating.

Competitive Proselytization

By 1937–38, the religious campaigns initiated a decade earlier culminated in competitive proselytization. The MIM converted Hindus to Islam, and the Samaj engaged in reconversion *(shuddhikaran).* Religious conversions have historically been controversial in India, touching off charges of coercion and fraud even when sufficient voluntarism might have marked the acts of conversion. As conversion became competitive, unrestrained viciousness was added to what in any case would have generated much heat and passion. A leading Urdu daily aligned with the MIM promised to wipe out "all the teachings of the Vedas and the Manusmriti," texts viewed as sacred by many Hindus, and the MIM urged Muslims to kill all those "who disparaged Islam." The Samaj thundered that "Muslims should either be converted to Hinduism or drowned in the Arabian Sea."[47]

Hindu-Muslim riots were by-products of the competitive proselytization. They broke out in Hyderabad city for the first time in April 1938. A small piece of land between a mosque and a temple became an object of dispute. More riots in Hyderabad city followed—in June 1938 and March 1939.[48]

Civil Disobedience

Amid the communal tensions and violence, two political movements emerged. One was led by the Samaj, the other by the Hyderabad State Congress, linked to the Congress Party in British India. Both chose the method of civil disobedience *(satyagraha)*, already popularized by Gandhi all over British India. Fighting for civil rights, especially the right to religious freedom, the Samaj openly merged religion and politics. Institutionally separate and founded on an interreligious principle, the Hyderabad Congress sought to fight not only for civil rights but also for democratic government.

The Arya Samaj's civil disobedience began in October 1938.[49] Thousands came from British India to express support and court arrest. The Hyderabad State Congress launched its own civil disobedience in October 1938. In 1935, the British had already conceded the principle of self-rule at the provincial level in British India. Provincial elections had been held in 1937. In keeping with the emerging trends in British India, the Congress demanded responsible government, with the Nizam as titular head.[50]

The Nizam was ready for some corporatist devolution of power, pursuant to which he would choose the groups to be represented in government, as well as the persons to represent them.[51] He was prepared neither for elective government nor for independent associations of civil society. The independence of associations was anathema to his ideology of rule. He believed in subjects, not citizens. To prevent "dangerous" political currents from entering his state, the Nizam's government banned the Congress within weeks, a ban that was not lifted until eight years later in 1946. This decision, along with his resolve not to ban the MIM, was epoch-making. It shaped Hindu-Muslim relations for decades to come.

The Doctrine of Muslims as a Ruling Race

The mainstream Muslim response to the civil disobedience had two sides: organizational and ideological.[52] The MIM's membership expanded remarkably. Fund-raising drives were launched. "Muslims, attach yourselves to the Majlis," argued the president of Majlis, "make it your own, go wherever it leads you, do whatever it asks you to do."[53] In addition, a voluntary paramilitary organization called the *Razakars* was founded in 1938. Of critical importance a decade later, the Razakars were allied to the MIM as self-defense squads.

By 1940 an explicit ideology also emerged, proclaiming Muslims to be the a ruling race *(haakim kaum)* of Hyderabad state: "Hyderabad does not need any democratic system of Government . . . the Majlis . . . is not prepared to accept any political or constitutional change. . . . The Majlis policy is to keep the sovereignty of His Exalted Highness intact and to prevent Hindus from establishing supremacy over Muslims."[54]

The implications for the Hindus were clear, but the Nizam too did not find the new MIM entirely agreeable. The new doctrine implied that the Nizam as a ruler embodied the collective wishes of the Muslim community. The Nizam preferred an uncontingent title to rule, not one contingent on Muslim wishes. He wanted the MIM's support but found the idea of popular constraints on rule unpalatable.[55] Over time, however, the MIM and the Nizam developed a working relationship. Faced with attacks on his authority by the Arya Samaj and the Hyderabad Congress, the Nizam backed the MIM.

The Catastrophe: 1947–48

By 1946, it was clear that the British would leave India, British India would be handed over to elected governments, and a partition of India into a Hindu-majority India and a Muslim-majority Pakistan would take place. Where would the princely states go? Would they be independent? As far as the MIM was concerned, an independent Hyderabad was the logical culmination of the doctrine of Muslims as a ruling race. Becoming part of an independent Pakistan meant keeping Muslim rule but losing Hyderabad's sovereignty, and being part of a Hindu-majority India was equal to losing both Muslim rule and Hyderabad's autonomy. The Nizam supported the demand. The British, however, advised the Nizam to merge with India and seek the best terms possible within a merger. The Indian National Congress demanded merger and popular rule.[56]

The Razakars, the shock troops of the MIM, became key players in the emerging political equation. They adopted a threefold strategy for the defense of Hyderabad's sovereignty: infiltration of the highest levels of government;[57] an ideological and armed campaign to prepare the Muslim youths psychologically and militarily for a battle with India's armed forces; and a violent campaign to terrorize Hindus as well as Muslim dissenters. Two rabble-rousing themes dominated the campaign: invocations of the spirit of *jehad* against a conspiring India and intimations of a military victory, once the psychic resources of Islam were deployed. "The Quran in one hand and the sword in the other, let us march forward; cut our enemies to pieces; establish our Islamic supremacy."[58]

A reign of terror and paramilitary build-up accompanied the ideological campaign of the Razakars. Consider the testimony of a district-level Muslim official of the Nizam:

> The atrocities committed by the Razakars were ignored. . . . The Razakars were described as defenders of independence. . . . Being in a district I was seeing and also hearing the acts of the Razakars. At many places they had looted the property and burnt the houses of Hindus. At some places they had killed them. General harassment of Hindus was spreading. Whenever the Hindus went from one place to the another they were searched by Razakars. Sometimes their valuables were taken. Panic-stricken but mostly well-to-do Hindus were rushing across the border. Razakars had taken the law into their own hands and were searching the luggage of every Hindu in trains. . . . Some Hindus travelled in Muslim garb.[59]

Moreover, "Government and its officers have been so completely dominated by MIM and they do not take any action against the Razakars. . . . Often in the presence of . . . officers of Government . . . the Razakars commit acts of loot and arson and burn the houses of innocent people and . . . Government officers content themselves by looking on these acts with indifference and . . . sometimes with amusement."[60]

In what was called "police action," the Indian armed forces finally launched an attack on Hyderabad on September 13, 1948. They overran India's largest princely state in a matter of five days. The Nizam agreed to popular rule. Delhi installed him as a titular head. The Razakars too gave in. Hyderabad became part of India, but the legacy for communal relations was awful.

LUCKNOW'S HERITAGE: SECTARIAN STRIFE, COMMUNAL AMITY

After the disintegration of the Mughal Empire (1526–1707), Lucknow was ruled by a succession of Muslim princes, the *Nawabs,* roughly from 1739 to 1857. The princes often resented the British overlordship of the state and powers of interference. The state was annexed by the British in 1856, when direct British rule commenced. A rebellion against the takeover began in 1857. The mutiny was eventually suppressed by the British, many of the palaces destroyed, and much of the city redesigned.[61] In modern Indian history, Lucknow is remembered as the last bastion of resistance to the British.

Local history in Lucknow has never been presented in communal terms.[62] In the list of Lucknow's Muslim rulers, there is no figure like the seventh Nizam of Hyderabad. Like the Hyderabad rulers, most princes of Lucknow did lead lives of utter indulgence and grandeur.[63] Unlike the Nizams, however, none is associated with communalism. Our survey in Hyderabad found that 90 percent of Muslims call the seventh Nizam "secular" and religiously neutral, but only half of the Hindus interviewed saw the Nizam that way, and fully a fourth were willing to call him "communal." The Lucknow survey found no such disputation over Lucknow's princes. Not a single Hindu interviewed in Lucknow called the Nawabs communal.

The principal contestation in Lucknow has been sectarian, not communal. Shia-Sunni riots rocked Lucknow regularly between 1905 and 1909 and between 1935 1942. In Hyderabad, too, the Shia community has lived for centuries.[64] Indeed, before the Nizams Hyderabad was ruled by Shia princes. In theory, a Shia-Sunni cleavage was available there. The sectarian divide, however, did not become politicized. A Hindu-Muslim cleavage did.

The absence of Hindu-Muslim violence in Lucknow is even more puzzling when one considers that the city was an important political center for the Muslim League, the party that, after 1937, symbolized the ideology of Muslim separatism and led the movement for Pakistan. The League for some time was headquartered in Lucknow;[65] some of the leading lights of the League came from Lucknow;[66] many of the critical meetings of the League were held in the city. Still, communal violence did not take place.

Why, then, is Lucknow's history divided along sectarian rather than communal lines? Why has sectarian passion coexisted with communal quiescence? The customary argument goes as follows:[67] The Lucknow princes were Shia. Hyderabad's Nizams were Sunni. The princes, through elaborate public rituals and Shia-inspired monuments, interwove Shi'ism into the popular culture of Lucknow. Nowhere else in India was Shi'ism given such prominence. The well-known doctrinal disputes between Sunnis and Shias, buried when the Shia rule was at its peak, emerged as the objective situation changed. Slowly but surely, Sunnis progressed as artisans and small businessmen. The Shia nobility, their flamboyant life styles unchanged, stagnated on small British pensions or rental incomes.[68] The Sunnis finally asserted themselves in the twentieth century, an assertion resented by the Shias. Frequent violence attended the reversal of fortunes.

Two more arguments—the discursive and the organizational—need to be added to this customary picture. Lucknow's Muslim princes had the fortune of *not* being part of the nationalist or mass politics era. Their rule ended in the 1850s, whereas mass politics emerged in the 1920s and 1930s. It is not clear what they would have done if they had faced mass politics. As it happened, Lucknow's princes were associated with resisting the British, not India; Hyderabad's seventh Nizam, on the other hand, wanted independence and offered armed resistance to the idea of integration with India. The contrast with Lucknow could not be sharper. In popular iconography, the mutiny of 1857, centered in Lucknow, is sometimes called the first war of independence.

Differential discursive possibilities of local histories are, however, not the only reason. The second reason for the coexistence of sectarian passions and communal peace is even more critical. Mass-based organizations and associations played a very different role in the two cities in the 1920s and 1930s. The MIM in Hyderabad was a mass-based party. In the 1930s, it led communal politics, with another mass-based organization, the Arya Samaj, as its adversary and competitive mobilizer. Of the secular parties that could have mobilized the masses in Hyderabad, the Congress was banned, and the Communists were popular, but only in the countryside, and often they were also subject to the Nizam's repression.

In Lucknow, mass politics was led either by the Congress Party, which sought to build Hindu-Muslim alliances, or, as explained below, by the various Muslim sectarian organizations, which led to Shia-Sunni riots. The Muslim League, which fought for independence from India and could have played the same role the MIM had in Hyderabad, primarily drew the support of the propertied and the well-off Muslims. It was an elite party and was outmatched by the mass-based organizations.

To understand this point, consider the remarkable differences between the Hindu-Muslim riot of 1924 and the sectarian riots of 1935–42. The former became an outlier; the latter a trend. The difference lay in organizational involvement and mass mobilization.

The Hindu-Muslim Riot of 1924

A Hindu-Muslim clash over the time of evening prayer, simmering for some time, turned violent on September 13, 1924. The Muslims had earlier complained that the evening *(maghrib)* prayer at the mosque was being disrupted by the devotional music sung in a nearby Hindu temple. Muslims found music before the mosque sacrilegious. The British deputy commissioner separated the two prayer times by five minutes so that the Muslim prayer *(namaz)* could be said before the Hindu prayer *(puja)* began.[69] On September 13, however, "during the progress of the Muslim prayer a number of Hindus went to the temple and attempted to ring the bell there. . . . During the night sporadic fighting began but the position did not become serious till this morning. . . . There has been no mass rioting but small parties of [Muslims] and Hindus have met and fought."[70]

By the morning of September 14, four deaths and about thirty cases of injury were reported. So shocked was Lucknow that there were quick public denunciations of communal violence. Many Hindus went to the deputy commissioner, complaining that "their leaders, if any can be called as such, have placed them in a false position, for it is pretty certain that *Aarti* [Hindu worship] was never performed in the past at the same time as the *Namaz* [Muslim prayer]."[71] Newspapers lamented that "the reputation of this old and historic city with its noble traditions . . . has been stained with blood."[72] Some newspapers investigated the causes of violence. It turned out that some members of a Hindu nationalist organization (Hindu Mahasabha) were interested in creating a communal situation.[73] They did not succeed. Citizen pressure was the first reason for failure. The second was the role of mass-based parties such as the Congress. "There is undoubtedly a desire on the part of the more important men to effect a settlement. . . . The reasons are obvious. They have probably had orders from the Central Congress Committee that the local differences must be settled and settled quickly in order that Lucknow should take part in the more important work of protesting against the [British]."[74]

The Shia-Sunni Violence of 1935–42

Consider how different the Shia-Sunni violence was: its rituals and symbolism, passions, organizational character, and politics. "The orthodox section of the Sunnis," wrote the president of the All-Parties Shia Conference, "condemns [our] celebrations as *bidat* [un-Islamic]. . . . The Shias consider *tazias* to be a cardinal tenet of their faith while the Sunnis think that making imitations of the tombs of the dead . . . is a sin and a prelude to idolatry."[75]

By 1905, almost half a century after the end of princely rule, the Sunnis had begun to insist on what is known as *Madh-e-Sahaba* (the companions) processions, which involved a public recitation of verses in praise of all four caliphs. The Shias had responded with *Tabbara* processions, which included public curses of the first three caliphs. The dispute and the violence lasted until 1909, when a British government committee, headed by Arthur Pigott, determined that Madh-e-Sahaba was an innovation and prohibited its public recitation.[76]

This tradition-validating argument ended up supporting the power relations expressed in the public rituals. The Sunni rituals were an innovation precisely because, under Shia princes, such public expressions of Sunni displeasure were simply not conceivable.

With the emergence of mass politics in the 1920s and 1930s, Madh-e-Sahaba and Tabarra were transformed. Now, even if banned, such processions could be presented in the form of civil disobedience. Gandhi had already shown the power of civil disobedience, and it had acquired legitimacy in much of India. Between 1938 and 1940, the Sunnis arrived in Lucknow in large numbers—from all parts of the state and outside it—to agitate for the right to recite the Madh-e-Sahaba and to court arrest.[77] Next, the Shias followed from various parts of the province to conduct the Tabarra as civil disobedience.[78] The group meetings often attracted ten to fifteen thousand people, the numbers sometimes equally matched.[79] Thousands of arrests were made each year. Riots kept breaking out,[80] and lives and property were lost on a large scale.[81]

The Shia-Sunni civil disobedience movement continued uninterrupted even as the Muslim League started its campaign to unite the Muslims against the Hindus. "The Muslim league is either powerless or unable to control the Muslim masses," argued the deputy commissioner.[82] Given how elite-oriented the League was, it could not match the power of mass-based organizations. As partition approached, several towns in Uttar Pradesh were engulfed by Hindu-Muslim violence.[83] In Lucknow, however, Shia-Sunni strife continued.[84]

Just as the Muslim League failed to arouse the passions of the masses, so did the Hindu nationalists. At the mass level, both were effectively neutralized by the Congress Party. As partition approached in August 1947, the Hindu nationalists pledged to start a "direct action" movement to save India from "annihilation," to show that "the Hindu public is no more willing to tolerate the appeasement policy of Congress towards Muslims" and to "resurrect the Hindu nation."[85] On the first day of direct action, Hindu nationalists clashed not with Muslims but with Congressmen.[86] The Hindu nationalists' volunteers numbered only in the hundreds. Two days later, a gathering of 50,000 people heard G. B. Pant, head of the Congress government in Uttar Pradesh. "Where were these Hindu . . . leaders," thundered Pant, a religious Hindu himself but a leader of the party, "when the British imperialists were trying to crush . . . the freedom movement of the country?"[87] Quickly rising to an ideological challenge, the Congress Party far outmatched the mobilization by the Hindu nationalists. Communal violence did not take place.

CONCLUSION

Hyderabad before 1938 appears to have had a history of everyday Hindu-Muslim engagement similar to Lucknow's history. It is the political activity between 1938 and 1948 that decisively deviated from history, created new civic patterns, and brought about a divergence of future paths. Allowing the Congress Party to mobilize in 1938 was perhaps the principal way to give a solid associational foundation to the pre-existing communal harmony in Hyderabad.[88] The price was popular rule, with the prince as the titular head of government. It also required a gracious acceptance of the transition from feudal subjecthood to modern citizenship. The prince was unwilling to pay the price of transition. By electing to ban the interreligious Congress and crushing the organization that wanted popular rule and could have built Hindu-Muslim bridges in times of tension, the prince paved the way for a direct clash between the Hindu communalist Arya Samaj (which defied the ban) and the Muslim communalist MIM (which was never banned). No political organization occupied the middle ground; nor is there any evidence of autonomous associations. Organizations, newspapers, and political parties that extolled the virtues of the Nizam's rule were permitted, not independent organizations of any kind. Once polarized politics emerged after the 1937–38 movements, there were no civil associations to stem the communal tide. The move destroyed the everyday religious connections among the masses. The social elite continued to interact across the religious divide but not with the masses. A whole new era of bitterness and violence was inaugurated.

In Lucknow, contrariwise, no mass-based organizations engaged in communal campaigns could put down roots. It was the Shia-Sunni divide, not a Hindu-Muslim cleavage, that led to violence in Lucknow. The Muslim League, in principle, could have played the role the MIM played in Hyderabad. Being elite-based, it was unable to beat the mobilization power of sectarian organizations on one hand and the interreligious Congress Party on the other. The Hindu nationalists also could not match the cadres of the Congress Party. At independence, Hyderabad inherited sectarian calm and communal hostility and Lucknow its opposite. Historical legacies dramatically differed.

Chapter 8 Hindu Nationalists
as Bridge Builders?

Hyderabad and Lucknow have continued to follow different electoral and civic courses since independence. It is not, however, simply a continuation of pre-independence politics. Unlike the pre-independence days, when the franchise was limited, electoral politics since 1947 has been based on a universal franchise. Both Hyderabad and Lucknow have seen the rise of communal parties in India: the MIM in Hyderabad and the BJP in Lucknow. The outcomes, however, are very different for communal relations. Hyderabad has gone through a veritable communal nightmare, as communal politicians have promoted Hindu-Muslim violence as a way to create communal solidarity and win votes. Even more mainstream parties, ostensibly wedded to secularism and to Hindu-Muslim unity, have used communal violence in battles for power. In Lucknow, despite the convulsions of partitions and the destruction of a mosque, violence as a strategic tool has been missing in electoral politics. Hindu nationalists have increased their strength, but the city remains communally unpolarized. Why?

If electoral tendencies have favored Hindu nationalism, civic patterns have moderated the behavior of Hindu nationalists. Lucknow's biggest mass-based civic structure is economic. The embroidered textiles industry has boomed since independence, interlocking increasing numbers of Hindus and Muslims in relationships of engagement and interdependence. By now a large proportion of textile traders-cum-entrepreneurs are Hindu nationalists, but their workforce is primarily Muslim. Their political interests may lie in communal polarization, but if polarization gets out of hand and widespread rioting results, it may lead to the destruction of Hindu-Muslim links in the economy and to large economic losses, for traders as well as craftsmen. Civic links have thus induced a remarkable degree of moderation in Hindu nationalist politics. Unlike leaders in Hyderabad and Aligarh, Hindu nationalist leaders in Lucknow work for peace when communal tensions rise in the city. So do Hindus and Muslims in the neighborhoods, connecting for economic, political, and cultural reasons as well as prevention of riots and communal violence.

The sheer scale of post-independence expansion in the Chikan (embroidered textiles) industry explains how powerful its constraints on political behavior have become. The Chikan industry was born in the princely era. In the first half of the nineteenth century, it had flourished by supplying refined clothing for the courts and the nobles. After the British conquest of Lucknow in 1857–58, it was unable to compete with the machine-based textiles of Lancashire. The arrival of Indian independence, however, changed the situation again, for there was not only tariff-based protection from external competition for Indian textiles but also exclusive reservation of some sectors for small industry internally. The Chikan industry was one. Once their existence was legally guaranteed, the traders began to target the middle classes instead of the declining former aristocrats. The markets, as a result, became bigger, and a great deal of additional work was generated. In 1951, there were only about 4,200 workers in the industry in Lucknow.[1] By 1972, the number had increased to about 45,000 workers.[2] By the late 1980s, when the Hindu nationalists clearly became the biggest political force in the city, the workers numbered anywhere between 75,000 to 100,000.[3]

The implications of these statistics have already been discussed (Chapter 7). To recapitulate, if we assume a family size of six to seven with two workers per family—fair assumptions, given the descriptions of the industry[4]—about 200,000 to 300,000 workers are by now partially or wholly dependent on the Chikan industry in Lucknow. There are, in addition, thousands of traders. As indicated in the preceding chapter, anywhere between 30 and 50 percent of the entire Muslim population is engaged in the industry.

In Lucknow, as part of the informal eonomy, so many Muslims and Hindus do business entirely on the basis of trust in the local economy, and so many people in both communities are locked in associational or daily relationships in neighborhoods and workplaces, that the formation of neighborhood-level peace committees at the time of tensions is simply an *extension of the prior civic engagement.* The interests of Hindu nationalists at the state level may lie in a communal polarization, but at the local level, such a polarization will hurt them economically. Replacement of Muslim craftswomen by Hindu workers has high transition costs, since skills will have to be taught afresh whereas Muslim girls learn such skills at home from watching their mothers and sisters. Machines can't teach the skills of embroidery. Riots in Lucknow would entail loss of lives as well as a breakdown of the local economy. Those hurt will not only be the poor Muslims but also the rich Hindu nationalists, who are dependent on them. Thus, Hindu and Muslim political leaders also "naturally" come together to contain tensions and rumors, as do peace committees from below in the neighborhoods.

In Hyderabad, peace committees don't emerge from below but are put in place by the local administration from above. The administration tries to bring local political leaders into these committees, hoping their inclusion will calm the passions of the masses or discipline their cadres. These committees are ineffective. First, the top local leaders of the MIM and the BJP can't normally be brought together. They hate each other, are already committed to a political strategy of polarization, are prepared to charge each other with provoking violence but not ready to do business with each other, and have formed networks of thugs and wrestlers engaged in politically motivated killings. Second, in much of the old city, Hindus and Muslims do not meet in a civic setting—economic or social—where mutual trust can be formed. As explained in Chapter 7, the new-city elite is integrated but not linked to the old city, which makes its integrative impulses effective in the new city but not in the old. Lacking political support at the top and civic networks below, even competent police and civil administrators are unable to prevent a riot. The occasional peace committees from below consist essentially of civic-minded citizens, who don't have a prior citywide network of institutionally cultivated trust and engagement. Such peace committees are effective only in some neighborhoods, where the existing everyday contacts between Hindus and Muslims have somehow managed to stay robust. In the city as a whole, such micro-successes are few and far between.

DEEPENING CLEAVAGES IN HYDERABAD

Since 1948, Hindu-Muslim relations in Hyderabad have gone through three phases: an uneasy communal calm (1948–57); the re-emergence of communal violence (from 1957 to the mid-1970s); and institutionalized communal polarization and unrelenting communal carnage (since 1978). What stands out is not only the increasing level of violence and its utter gruesomeness but also the indubitable role of political parties, factions, and leaders in promoting communal violence as a political tool.

An Uneasy Communal Calm (1948–57)

With the defeat of the Nizam and the Razakars, an entire system collapsed. A new ideology of popular and democratic rule replaced hereditary rule. The ideological change had serious material consequences. The Nizam's bureaucracy was dismantled and reorganized, and the feudal estates abolished. As a result, for the Muslims in particular, the sources of income dried up substantially.

Of the six main occupational categories for Muslim occupations—work on feudal estates, domestic service for aristocratic families, public administration, the police force, the armed forces, industry, and trade—four were directly affected by the end of the Nizam's rule. The first two were undermined by the land reforms and the elimination of absentee landlords, and the next two by the overhaul of the Nizam's bureaucracy. The Nizam's armed forces were folded up between 1949 and 1950, and continuation in police and civil administration was made virtually dependent on evidence of lack of association with the Razakars. There were many unjust dismissals of officials for having suspected "ties" with the Razakars.[5] With the terror of the Razakars gone, a large number of personal scores were also settled, leading to considerable violence against the Muslims in the districts.[6] Since Hindus constituted a small proportion of the Nizam's police, army, and civil administration, the drastic alterations in the Nizam's bureaucracy hurt Muslims disproportionately.

The number of Muslims who lost their jobs cannot be directly ascertained from the available statistics. Indirect evidence of large-scale Muslim misery after the police action, however, is beyond doubt. In a 1956 survey, Muslims constituted 48 percent of the street beggars in Hyderabad city, more than the scheduled castes, and "the Police Action, abolition of jagirs, [and] disbandment of the regular and irregular forces" constituted a principal reason for the high Muslim incidence of begging.[7] Similarly, in 1960–61, a survey of cycle rickshaw drivers in Hyderabad city, who earn very small incomes, found that 68 percent of the drivers were Muslim and 32 percent non-Muslim.[8] Moreover, nearly 24 percent of the Muslim rickshaw drivers were previously employed by the Nizam's estates.[9]

Under the Nizam, mobility was primarily hereditary and employment principally dependent on patronage. Skills or levels of education that could provide alternative employment were missing. The fall of the Nizam thus left a lot of Muslims without any "respectable" livelihood. Oral histories and novels suggest that lesser, debt-ridden, absentee landlords were among those who took to rickshaw pulling, and women from some of these families turned to prostitution.[10] In the 1952 elections, Muslims overwhelmingly voted for the Communist Party because it was the only party in Hyderabad capable of beating the Congress, which most Muslims viewed as an adversary.

The fate of Muslims thus underwent a tragic metamorphosis. Some have argued that the tragedy was self-inflicted and that the Muslims felt after 1948 what Hindus did during the period 1944–48.[11] True as this argument may be, the reasons for the decline did not make it any more bearable. Resentment, agony, and bitterness marked the mood.

The Return of Communal Tensions and Violence (1957–75)

It was in this atmosphere that the Majlis (MIM), after its demise in 1948, was reborn in 1957. There were widespread protests at its rebirth.[12] The revival of the party could not be prevented under the law, for the new MIM quickly committed itself to the Indian constitution, and at least in its explicit pronouncements undertook to work not only for Muslim welfare but also for other "depressed communities."

Soon after its rebirth, the MIM became the party of Hyderabad Muslims. It contested elections at all three levels: municipal, state, and parliamentary. In the municipal elections, the MIM performed best. In 1960, its first electoral test after rebirth, the MIM contested 30 of 66 seats, winning 19 against the Congress's 33. In the process, it defeated 17 of the 21 Muslim candidates of the Congress Party, showing how "Congress Muslims" were viewed as "traitors" by the Muslim masses.[13] In the late 1980s, as explained below, the MIM became the largest party in the Municipal Corporation and ran the local government.

In the state assembly elections, the Majlis did not do as well, although it kept improving its position. It opened its account with one seat in 1962. In 1967 and 1972, it won three of eight assembly seats, all from the old city of Hyderabad. Finally, the MIM contested and lost the Hyderabad parliamentary seat in 1962 and 1967, increasing its vote share the second time.

The concentration of Muslims in the old city and the size of the constituency explain the difference in the MIM's performance in the local, state, and parliamentary elections. Since the size of the municipal constituency is smaller, Muslims are concentrated in the old city, and the MIM contests only from Hyderabad, the party does best in the municipal elections.[14]

With the reinvigoration of a reborn MIM, two more developments took place. First of all, the Hindu nationalist Bharatiya Jan Sangh (BJS), the BJP's predecessor, acquired a foothold in Hyderabad. In the 1952 and 1957 elections, the BJS had no presence there at all. After the MIM fought its first elections, becoming the second largest party in the Hyderabad Municipal Corporation in 1960, the BJS emerged on the political scene. It started with a small share of the popular vote in two assembly constituencies.[15] By the time of the next election (1967), one election after the rise of the MIM, the BJS finished second or third in eight of the ten assembly constituencies in Hyderabad.

A second development was the re-emergence of communal violence after a quiet decade in the 1950s. In the 1960s, there were riots in eight of ten years in Hyderabad. In the first half of the decade the riots were small in scale. Their frequency and size grew in the second half. On average, riots lasted 9 days in 1967, 36 days in 1968, and 11 days in 1970.[16] It is not clear whether the riots were linked to the MIM and the BJS feeding on each other's success. There did seem to be a correlation, however, if not a direct link.[17]

Riots and Cricket (1978–93)

These trends deepened after 1978. So powerful did the MIM become in the city that the Congress more or less left the old city to the MIM.[18] Indeed, the Congress sought an alliance with it whenever it was necessary to stabilize Congress governments. No fresh municipal elections were held between 1964 and 1986. In the late 1980s, the MIM emerged as the largest party. With the support of the Congress, it formed the municipal government. It maintained this status in the 1990s.

In the state assembly elections, the MIM more than held its ground, winning three to five seats consistently. In the parliamentary elections, it kept increasing its share of vote, but it was unable to win until 1984. It has won all six parliamentary elections since then—in 1984, 1989, 1991, 1996, 1998, and 1999.

The arrival of the MIM in India's parliament, even though it wins one seat only, has made it more visible than before. The emergence of a powerful regional party, the Telugu Desam Party (TDP), in Andhra Pradesh in 1983 contributed to this result. The TDP made contests in Hyderabad four-cornered. Since most Muslims continued to vote for the MIM, whereas after 1983 Hindu votes were split among the TDP, the BJP, and the Congress, it became easier for the MIM to win a parliamentary seat. Earlier, even though the Muslim municipal and assembly vote for the MIM remained intact, the larger size of the parliamentary constituency (and resultant lower Muslim proportion in the electorate) had made it only the second largest in Hyderabad city. This threshold was broken by the arrival of TDP.[19]

The BJP has also gained in Hyderabad. In 1983, it won its first assembly seat there and polled more than 20 percent in six other seats (Hyderabad had twelve assembly seats). Since 1985, the BJP has continued to win two to three assembly seats. It went on to win a parliamentary seat in 1991, 1996, and 1998. Since the 1980s, thus, the old city has been polarized—with the MIM winning three to five and the BJP two to three seats.

The trend toward communal violence has also taken a turn for the worse. The turning point was 1978. Clashing narratives make it very hard to establish what actually happened.[20] Eventually, police atrocity toward a Muslim couple became the issue over which riots broke out. Riots since then have taken place virtually every year, often many times in the same year. The partial exception is 1986–89, when the TDP, a regional party with no prior history in the Nizam's Hyderabad, ruled the state.

Table 8.1 presents a list of riots and of their immediate causes, which have ranged from elections, processions, and desecrations on one hand to petty quarrels and land deals on the other. The sheer frequency of riots since 1978 suggests the emergence of an institutionalized riot system. A gang of killers, generally organized under the leadership of wrestlers and ostensibly aimed at protecting communities, has been ready to launch into a wave of violence at virtually any possible pretext. Even trivial incidents such as a petty quarrel between two teenagers, or the arrest of a wrestler, have received a full-blown insertion into the narrative of communalism.

Violence increased along with votes for the MIM and the BJP, suggesting a link often proposed—that communal violence became a strategic tool in the hands of politicians. The more communal violence there was, the greater the polarization, and therefore the greater Muslim and Hindu identification with communal parties.

Table 8.1. Communal Riots in Hyderabad, 1978–95

Year	Month	Reported Cause
1978	March–April	Police atrocity toward Muslims
1979	July	Hindu temple near a mosque desecrated
1979	November	Muslim call for shopkeepers' strike after the forcible occupation of Mecca in Saudi Arabia by terrorists
1980	January	Around parliamentary elections, stabbing of Hindu boy followed by an emotional funeral procession with the body of the deceased draped in Janata party flag
1980	March	Petty quarrel
1980	September	Arrest of a wrestler
1981	July	Municipal elections due; playing of music before a mosque during the procession of Bonalu, a Hindu religious festival; elections postponed
1982	June	Marriage procession playing music in front of a mosque
1983	January	Election violence between MIM and BJP supporters
1983	May	Marriage procession playing music in front of a mosque
1983	September	Simultaneous occurrence of Ganesh procession and Id
1984	May	By-election clash between MIM and TDP workers
1984	July	Attack on Bonalu procession
1984	September	Violence during Hindu (Ganesh and Bonalu) and Muslim festivals
1985	March	Assembly elections
1986		Small skirmishes the year round, no major violence
1990	July	Land dispute between two speculators
1990	October	Small skirmishes
1990	December	Murder of a wrestler
1992–3	December–January	Destruction of Baburi mosque
1995	June	Tension in the old city

More direct evidence for the existence of such systems and political intentionality also exists. As a psychologist trying to understand the roots of communal violence in Hyderabad, Sudhir Kakar interviewed several wrestlers in Hyderabad and found that the institution of wrestling schools *(akharas)*—a wrestling leader, his disciples, and the ideology of physical discipline, courage, and combative defense of honor—had been turned into institutions of communal violence.[21] Called "criminal characters" *(goondas)* by the police, the wrestlers *(pehelwans)* were seen as valiant "warriors" by their neighborhoods. The "warriors" protected neighborhoods against, and took revenge for, the depredations of the police and other communities, and interceded between the police and the common folk, organized relief during riots, remaining "good" or "pious" Muslims or Hindus throughout. They took pride in their violence, saying it was for the defense of the community, religion, or *qaum* (nation). They flaunted their political connections, suggesting that the police couldn't touch them because they were protected by political parties. During riots, they stopped killing, they said, only when it was clear that they had killed more than had the wrestlers of the other community. Killing in riots, they said, was like a one-day cricket game: one stopped as soon as one had made more runs than the adversary. They were also sure that no one would dare testify against them in a court of law, making conviction impossible even when prosecutions could be brought. The distinction between crime and valor disappeared in the old city of Hyderabad.[22]

There is yet more evidence that communal violence is promoted by political parties. In 1989, after six years, the Congress Party returned to power in the state elections. The new chief minister of the state was M. Channa Reddy, an old party stalwart but a controversial figure. Ministerial berths were not given to a faction of the party. The adversarial faction decided to embarrass the government of its own party. As the ever-present communal rioting broke out, the adversaries of the chief minister smelled an opportunity. Riots remained out of control more or less continuously for three months (October–December 1990). Unable to restore law and order, the chief minister eventually resigned on December 13, 1990, and a new government, under a different faction leader, was sworn in. The riots, which had been raging for weeks, immediately stopped. There was no touch of subtlety in the transfer of power. The link was too obvious to be missed.[23]

COMMUNAL AMITY, SECTARIAN STRIFE

Lucknow has been living a paradox since independence. It has maintained its pre-1947 history of communal peace, despite a political novelty. Starting with the 1950s, the Hindu nationalist parties—first the Bharatiya Jan Sangh (BJS) and then its successor, the BJP—have been a major political force in the city. Moreover, headquartered in Lucknow, Hindu nationalists have twice been part of state government (the late 1960s and the late 1970s) and the sole rulers of the state twice in the 1990s. When, in December 1992, the Baburi mosque was torn down in Ayodhya, a town only eighty miles away from Lucknow, communal relations did deteriorate in the city. Yet the city remained free from communal violence. A similar pattern had prevailed at the time of partition.[24]Hindu nationalists may have become more powerful over time, but Lucknow has been free from communal violence.

Paralleling the pre-independence history, sectarian strife returned in the mid-1960s, producing several riots between the late 1960s and the late 1970s. In the 1980s and early 1990s, as Hindu-Muslim tensions peaked, there was a distinct decline in sectarian tensions. But the sectarian-communal equation has not been radically altered. Sectarian violence returned in 1996 and 1997. For the period after 1947 as well as the century as a whole, sectarian strife has been the prime wrecker of life and property in Lucknow, while, for all practical purposes, communal violence has been conspicuously absent. The rise of what is generally called a communal party in the city has made no difference to the historical pattern of sectarian strife and communal amity.

The Rise of Hindu Nationalists

At the time of partition, a Congress government was in power in Uttar Pradesh. It successfully dealt with the call for civil disobedience given by the Hindu nationalists to protest the formation of Pakistan. Two methods were adopted: preventive arrests and a quick political counter-campaign. Some of the leading members of the state Congress Party, for example, G. B. Pant, the head of the Uttar Pradesh government from 1946 to 1954, and Dr. Sampuranand, his successor from 1954 to 1960, have been called "closet" Hindu nationalists by scholars and political observers. In large political meetings, however, both attacked the Hindu nationalists, the latter declaring that "at the sight of freedom [they] proclaim themselves to be the champions of Hindu rights but were in the opposite camp during the long arduous struggle for freedom."[25] The Hindu nationalist campaign was quickly countered.

In 1952, the first post-independence elections were held. Hindu nationalists showed that they had already become a significant political force in Lucknow. The city has four state assembly constituencies. In the 1952 elections, the Congress won all four seats, but the BJS, a newcomer, finished second in three, receiving 20 percent of popular vote in two and 30 percent in the third. In 1957 and 1962, the BJS share of the popular vote ranged from 30 to 40 percent, although it still could not win any seats. In 1967 it finally won three of four seats, but returned to the second place in the next four elections.[26] In 1989, it won two seats again; and in 1991, 1996, and 1998, it swept all four.[27]

What explains the rise of Hindu nationalists in a city with no history of Hindu-Muslim bitterness? Three arguments can be given. First, as a result of partition, nearly 30,000 refugees arrived in Lucknow between 1947 and 1951. About 90 percent of the refugees were from West Pakistan, constituting up to 5 percent of the town's population in 1951.[28] Involuntary displacement, accompanied by loss of property and often loss of siblings and relatives, did arouse bitterness in most refugees and a desire for retribution in many. In the 1951 UNESCO survey in Lucknow, a large number of Muslims thought that "the refugees were out to create disturbances and riots in Lucknow, as they wanted to take revenge on Muslims and to take their property."[29] A majority of Hindus and "a greater majority of Muslims" also reported that the communal relations in Lucknow had been "adversely affected by the presence of refugees."[30] The presence of refugees was an important reason for the emergence of the BJS as a significant force.

Second, in 1952, land reforms abolished absentee landlordism *(zamindari)*. A study done in the 1960s concluded that, angry with the Congress for abolishing their privileges, the feudal lords joined the Hindu nationalist parties in large numbers.[31] The refugees may have supported Hindu nationalism because of their experiences in Pakistan. The landlords were hardly concerned with Hindu nationalism; they joined the BJS because it also supported the Hindu social hierarchy at that time, in which they were at the top. Many of the landlords lived in Lucknow city and still had a reasonably large following.

Finally, because government employment provided the biggest source of income, Lucknow also had a large concentration of upper castes, even though in the state in general the lower castes numerically dominated. A survey carried out in 1954–56 found that in Lucknow, "among the Hindus the upper castes are the most numerous, accounting for 31 percent of the total population."[32] The Hindu nationalist defense of the caste hierarchy, not its anti-Muslim beliefs, attracted many in the upper caste. The BJS that emerged in Lucknow, thus, was not driven by Hindu nationalist fervor but by a mixture of motivations.[33]

Resurgence of Sectarian Tensions

As routine compulsions of life overtook memories of partition, sectarian tensions started reappearing in Lucknow. In 1949, more than 250 people were arrested for defying orders concerning Muharram; in 1951, 120; and in 1952, "a large number."[34] In 1952, Shias and Sunnis applied for permission once again to recite Madh-e-Sahaba and Tabarra, only to be rejected by the administration. In 1953–54, the Sunni leaders went to the court, claiming that reciting Madh-e-Sahaba was permissible under freedom of religion, a fundamental right, but the High Court ruled that freedom of conscience was subject to considerations of public order. In the early 1960s a collective defiance of the court and administration was launched both sides. Large-scale rioting took place in 1969, 1974, and 1977.[35] Clashes took place in 1968, 1970, 1973, and 1979, after which the Muharram procession was banned for several years.

Communal Tensions, No Riots

In the 1980s, sectarian troubles declined and communal tensions began to surface, especially in the second half of the decade. A few days after the opening of the disputed mosque-temple site in Ayodhya in 1986, tensions ran high and minor clashes took place, but "at many places joint meetings by the members of different communities were held to restore normalcy."[36] Tensions peaked during Hindu nationalist mobilization for the "restoration" of Ram's birthplace in 1990 and after the destruction of Baburi mosque in December 1992.

As is well known, after the violence that accompanied partition in 1947–48, the period between 1990 and 1993 was the worst in India for Hindu-Muslim relations. Even in this period Lucknow experienced communal tensions but no riots. As already reported, symbolically charged provocations that have repeatedly precipitated riots in Hyderabad were also tried out in Lucknow during this period—by those who wished to foment riots. A sadhu was murdered, and a rumor circulated that a Muslim had killed him; it turned out that a Hindu had actually killed the holy man. Pork was thrown into a mosque, purportedly by Hindus; it was discovered that a Muslim had done it. Similarly, color was thrown into a mosque during the Holi festival of the Hindus. As is evident from table 8.1, if any of these events had taken place in Hyderabad they would have been used as an occasion by politicians to make provocative speeches and to touch off rioting. In Lucknow, relying on information provided by networks, the district administration was able to catch the culprit quickly and preempt escalation. The trouble-makers in Hyderabad are rarely caught.

Thus, as in Hyderabad, communal tensions do appear in Lucknow and nasty rumors also spread. But the same provocations have different outcomes. There are mechanisms in Lucknow that prevent the transformation of tensions and rumors into full-scale rioting but not in Hyderabad.

What are these mechanisms? The district magistrate formed peace committees that had Hindu as well as Muslim leaders, frequently consulting with them; he acted on every rumor and was able to neutralize most of them with quick investigation. Second, Hindu-Muslim peace committees emerged in neighborhoods from below, worked together, and kept peace.

The district magistrate argued that without political cooperation, at the top and at the local level simultaneously, he would not have succeeded, especially after the mosque was torn down. "If the political masters want a riot, an administrator can't prevent it; he can only check its magnitude."[37] Several key political leaders of the BJP were willing to help him discipline the cadres. Equally important was the fact that peace committees could include key local political leaders of both communities—something that Lucknow's historic tradition facilitated. Thus, owing to cooperation above and below, yet another political earthquake, the biggest after partition, could not undermine Lucknow's intercommunal edifice; only some cracks appeared.

The key questions are: Why were the Hindu nationalists willing to cooperate? Why did they not want riots? Why did they discipline cadres? The answers are provided by the Hyderabad-Lucknow comparison. They relate to the variance in political intentionality induced by local civic structures.

Variance in Political Intentionality and Its Civic Links

Politicians in Lucknow, even when communal tensions have emerged, have sought to bridge the Hindu and Muslim communities. Even Hindu nationalists have not promoted communal violence. Part of the reason simply is that they did not need polarization in order to be a force. The Muslim community had internal differences to the extent that some key Shia leaders supported the Hindu nationalists every now and then. Moreover, the dispossessed landlords and their dependents, and a large proportion of upper castes after 1947 provided the BJS with a base for many years in Lucknow. These groups cared more for the traditional social hierarchy than for Hindu nationalism or communalism. A more desperate set of local Hindu nationalists may have tried to polarize the area; a BJS or a BJP doing quite well could do without sowing division.

The MIM, on the other hand, thrives on polarization. Hyderabad is its only focus. Since the Muslim population is concentrated in the old city, the strategy of polarization has many electoral payoffs and few risks. If the MIM develops state-level ambitions, it will have to examine whether polarization in Hyderabad causes losses in constituencies where Muslims are fewer in number. The MIM did not have to ask this question because, for all practical purposes, it made Hyderabad the be-all and end-all of its life.[38] With its larger political ambition, the BJP asks both local and state-level questions, and increasingly, national questions as well. The local, the state, and the national wings of the party may see their interests differently. If the state-level politicians create a polarization for state-level electoral needs, the local politicians may resist it in their constituencies to protect their own interests. If the local politicians see a polarization as being in their interests, the state-level politicians may or may not fully cooperate, depending on how they see their interests. Polarization, in other words, is not necessarily in the interests of a party that has national ambitions and diverse tiers of functioning. Complex layers of intentionality are introduced at various levels.

So long as Hyderabad remains its focus, the MIM will not acquire any such complexity. If it begins to develop state-level ambitions, the acerbity of its communal rhetoric will almost certainly diminish. Muslims in the state of Andhra Pradesh as a whole constitute only 8 percent of the population as opposed to 37 percent in Hyderabad city. The MIM cannot win more seats with greater polarization. It will have to build alliances. Although both the MIM and the BJP are communal, their structure of intentionality differs.

The final question is, Why do Hindu nationalists look at their *local* interests differently? They may have won in the 1980s and 1990s, but they did not in the 1950s, 1960s, and 1970s. Why did they not try to polarize the city then? Moreover, even in the 1990s, Hindu nationalists did have ambitions beyond the local sphere. Many wanted not simply to win their seats but also a BJP government to rule the state. Several state-level BJP leaders come from Lucknow. Would a communal polarization in Lucknow, in which they could blame Muslims for creating disorder and instigating violence, not have been in their interest? Communal violence in the state capital, which has been an island of peace and whose peace has allegedly collapsed due to the misbehavior of Muslims, could in principle be symbolically significant.

So why did the Hindu nationalists not incite riots? First, the attempt communally to polarize a peaceful city can boomerang, depending on what the press, the civic groups, and the other political groups say. Unless the press and civic associations are firmly entrenched in a crime-politics-communalism nexus, who gets the blame for violence, what the press says, and who is legally or politically punished cannot be predicted. The radical uncertainty of the consequences constitutes a deterrent. The ability to create riots and also profit from them is not a function of voluntarism. If anti-violence civic structures exist, they can curtail the freedom to maneuver. Second, at least one consequence can easily be anticipated as a near certainty. If communal riots were to break out, the local economy would collapse. The links between Muslim workers and Hindu traders that constitute the bedrock of the local economy would be broken. Shia-Sunni riots do not have this implication. Given the crafts-based, not machine-based, nature of the textile industry, there are no clear, short-to-medium-run substitutes for Muslim workers. So many thousands of Muslims are involved in the textiles industry that an attempt to foment anti-Muslim riots—whatever larger political benefit they might bring—would almost certainly be accompanied by huge economic losses as well. The losses would accrue not only to the workers but also to thousands of Hindu nationalist traders.

If the dangers are so obvious and the gains so radically uncertain, why play the high-stakes game of rioting for the small chance that the party would benefit from it in the state as a whole? Mass-level intercommunal civic structures thus have the effect of moderating the communal right wing. Where is the room for a passionate argument for Muslim disloyalty to the nation and a "targeting" of Muslims for "punishment" if one depends on Muslims for profits, for a living, and for civic order?

Part III **Local Variations**

Ahmedabad and Surat: How

Civic Institutions Decline

Chapter 9 Gandhi
and Civil Society

Analytically speaking, the comparisons thus far have been across space, not across time. During the times in question, the four cities examined in the previous chapters have had a virtually unchanging character. Communal riots in two cities—Aligarh and Hyderabad—took place repeatedly, and communal peace in the other two—Calicut and Lucknow—was rarely broken. The trends were established in the 1920s and 1930s, and they endured after independence. The rise of mass politics and the political transformations of 1920s and 1930s laid the foundations of civic interaction between Hindus and Muslims or of its absence; and demonstrating path-dependence, the post-1947 civic life continued the pre-1947 trends. Cities were either riot-prone or peaceful for much of the century.

Ahmedabad and Surat, the cities now being compared, break this analytic and narrative structure. They do share two large similarities with the other pairs. First, at 12–15 percent, the percentage of Muslims in their populations has been roughly the same since independence.

And, second, at least since the late 1960s, Hindu-Muslim relations have been quite different in the two cities. With one exception discussed later, Surat has been peaceful, whereas Ahmedabad has had endemic violence.

Of greater analytic significance, however, is a new dimension of comparison. The pattern of communal relations has dramatically changed in Ahmedabad over time. Between 1920 and 1969, the city was on the whole communally peaceful, but since 1969 it has been among the most riot-prone cities of India. The year 1969, thus, introduces an *intertemporal* variation not present in other pairs. One should add that after staying calm for more than 60 years, the communal peace of Surat was also finally broken. Following the destruction of the Baburi mosque in Ayodhya in December 1992, Surat experienced the horrors of communal violence for the first time since 1927–28.

Thus far, we have only analyzed what makes violent and peaceful trends possible. We have not inquired into the conditions under which, once established, civic structures of peace—or institutionalized peace systems, as I have called them—break down. These two cities—Ahmedabad after 1969 and Surat after 1992—can enlighten us as to how and why that happens.

Ahmedabad and Surat also constitute the most tightly controlled pair in this study. The first two pairs compared northern and southern cities: Lucknow and Aligarh are in the north, Hyderabad and Calicut in the south. The third pair not only shifts the focus to western India, where so much of the communal violence has taken place after independence (Chapter 4), but also to the same state: Gujarat, where both Ahmedabad and Surat are located. The two cities, a mere 158 miles apart, have been exposed to an identical context of state politics since 1960, when the state of Gujarat, as it stands today, was founded.[1] Indeed, the similarity of state politics stretches back further. After 1810, when the British took over western India and located their headquarters in the city of Bombay, calling the area Bombay Presidency, Ahmedabad and Surat were made part of the province.[2] The context of state or provincial politics has been the same for both cities for nearly two centuries, a condition that holds for no other pair in this study.[3]

The 1969 carnage in Ahmedabad was the nation's single worst Hindu-Muslim riot between 1950 and 1995. About 630 people were killed in five days of mayhem and chaos, and many more injured and made homeless. Even during 1992–93, when communal violence scaled a new peak in post-independence India, no single riot, or city, had so many deaths. Ironically, only a year before the 1969 carnage in Ahmedabad a historian of the city had confidently written:

"The most tragic problem of modern Indian political history—the communal problem—has fortunately had only a small role in the history of Ahmedabad."[4] Rioting since 1969 has been frequent and often excessively brutal.

Until 1992–93, Surat was a study in contrasts. After the 1969 riots, when much of Gujarat burned in what appeared to be a chain reaction, Surat remained peaceful. Not a single life was lost, nor were there any serious injuries. A second wave of rioting rocked much of Gujarat during 1985–86, combining for the first time intra-Hindu caste riots with Hindu-Muslim violence, the latter following the former.[5] Ahmedabad was yet again the epicenter of both caste and communal violence, but Surat had no Hindu-Muslim clashes, only caste riots.[6] The 1992–93 riots in Surat finally ended this contrast. Just as it is important to understand why Ahmedabad, despite a history of communal peace, came apart in 1969, the 1992–93 riots in Surat also require an analytic probe.

Finally, the historic figure of Mahatma Gandhi lends this comparison a special edge. The rise of mass politics under Gandhi's leadership in the 1920s has been a common starting point for our analysis of all cities so far. In the current pair of cities, Gandhi's role is considerably more direct. Gujarat was Gandhi's home state, and Ahmedabad his adopted city. After he returned from South Africa in 1915, until he left for the Salt March of 1930, Gandhi made Ahmedabad his home, establishing his ashram there, creating and nurturing a large array of civic and political institutions, developing an enormous mass following, and leaving a formidable legacy of voluntary social service and communal harmony that was in many ways unique. Between 1920 and 1969, Ahmedabad took pride in Gandhian values of peace and nonviolence. Over the past three decades a metamorphosis has taken place. Violence, bigotry, and crime have taken over. A few Gandhian organizations are still fighting a dour battle for civic sanity and calm, but their attempts, though valiant, have not been able to reclaim Ahmedabad's lost civic heritage. The city's Gandhian soul has all but vanished.

Why did the pattern of Hindu-Muslim relations change in the two cities? This question underpins our analysis in this part of the book. The focus is on the changes across time in each city, not on the enduring dissimilarities across cities. The attempt is to understand how the structures of peace were undermined.

My argument is that, profoundly influenced by Gandhi, both cities witnessed a truly impressive level of civic activity during the national movement. Gandhi and his followers not only meticulously built a cadre-based Congress

Party, which succeeded as a mass-level organization to an extraordinary degree, they also formed labor unions and a whole variety for organizations for social change. In addition, a unique feature of the civic life of Gujarat was, and to some extent continues to be, its business associations. Though Bombay has been India's premier business city in modern times, Gujarat is the nation's leading business state, benefiting from a centuries-long commercial and trading tradition. Gujarat's business life has traditionally brought Hindus and Muslims together, forming bonds not only of commercial pragmatism and dependence but often also of trust.

Between 1920 and 1947, there were many provocations and occasions for big riots in the two cities, but the large array of civic associations, consisting of political, business, and social organizations, either successfully preempted communal rioting or controlled its spread. In contrast, Gujarat's vibrant and integrated civic structure has become quite fragile of late. Its capacity to resist and neutralize the riot-entrepreneurs has decreased. The "triggers" that could earlier be successfully contained have repeatedly touched off riots.

Since the intertemporal dimension is so critical in this part of the book, the sequence of narrative and analysis below departs from the pattern followed so far. The current chapter begins with a probe into the historical foundations of civic life in the two cities, focusing on the 1920s and 1930s. Then, to bring out the stark contrast with the pre-1947 period, the next chapter shifts the attention to the 1980s and 1990s, describing and analyzing the most recent phase of violence and asking what happened to the civic organizations that kept peace in the pre-independence period. Added to the analysis is a third and final chapter. Its purpose is directly to confront a central analytical question: Was the breakdown of intercommunal civic structures a consequence of communal violence, or was rioting a consequence of the weakening of intercommunal civic structures? In analyzing the relationship between civic organizations on one hand and violence and peace on the other, how does one sort out cause and consequence? This is the so-called question of endogeneity that any systematic causal analysis must necessarily probe.

THE FOUNDATIONS: GANDHI AT WORK

In the twentieth century, the *intercommunal* civic life[7] of urban Gujarat rested on four big organizational pillars.[8] First, after the 1920s, the Congress Party brought people of all communities together. As in many parts of India, the party became cadre-based in Gujarat in the 1920s and continued that way right until the 1960s. Gandhi directly led much of the Congress activity in Gujarat in the 1920s, and it is widely accepted that in the pre-independence period, the party was at its strongest in Gujarat.

Second, Gandhi's influence also created a vast array of social and educational agencies on a voluntary basis. They were formally independent of the Congress Party, although they often supported it politically. Since, as we have already noted, Gandhi's national movement had two aims—political independence from the British and social transformation of India—two different sets of organizations were created. The Congress Party was to be the vehicle of winning independence, but it would be only one of several organizations for social transformation. Voluntary agencies dealing with education, women's issues, welfare of the tribals and "untouchables," prohibition, self-reliance, and the "homespun" *(khadi)* movement were deeply concerned with "social" projects. Because of Gandhi's direct helmsmanship in Gujarat, these organizations attracted funds and a large following, becoming a remarkable presence on the state's civic scene.

Business associations constituted the third organizational pillar. At the turn of the century, Gujarat inherited a vibrant tradition of guilds *(mahajans)*. Using the weight of norms, not laws, the guilds supervised and enforced rules of business, punishing those who violated the customary standards of trust and rewarding good conduct. As the twentieth century progressed, the guilds were turned into modern associations. Offices were no longer inherited but elective. Instead of reliance on norms, the rules and purposes of the organization were explicitly codified. And voluntarism, rather than ascription, became the basis of association. The businesses or crafts that cut across communal lines provided extensive opportunity for intercommunal interaction.

Finally, as the century proceeded, there also came into being labor unions, cooperatives, and professional associations. The strength of labor unions in various cities depended on whether the business activity was primarily in the organized or the informal sector. Unions were formed more easily in the organized sector. Cooperatives have also been ubiquitous in Gujarat, penetrating labor unions and many other associations. Though plentiful, the professional associations—of doctors, lawyers, teachers, and so on—have on the whole not been as strong in Gujarat as the business associations have been. For centuries, Gujarat has been heavily business-oriented. It is quite common for doctors, lawyers, and teachers to have a business on the side.[9]

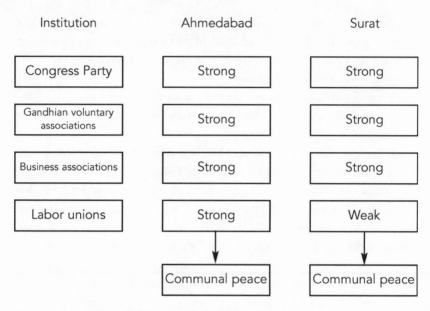

Institution	Ahmedabad	Surat
Congress Party	Strong	Strong
Gandhian voluntary associations	Strong	Strong
Business associations	Strong	Strong
Labor unions	Strong	Weak
	Communal peace	Communal peace

Figure 9.1 Associational Civic Structure in the 1920s and 1930s

The listing above is a generic one, applicable to all of urban Gujarat. We now need to examine the relative strength of these organizations in the two cities under study. Figure 9.1 summarizes the description below.

A CADRE-BASED CONGRESS PARTY

Both critics and admirers of the Congress Party agree that it reached the acme of its strength in Gujarat in the first half of the twentieth century.[10] Of all the cities studied in this project, Ahmedabad and Surat developed the most vibrant, disciplined, and cadre-based Congress Party organizations in the 1920s and 1930s.

This was partly because the Congress in Gujarat benefited from having some of India's tallest politicians during the freedom struggle. The two who contributed most were Mahatma Gandhi and his deputy, Sardar Patel. Both made Ahmedabad their home: Gandhi from 1915 to 1930 and Patel from 1913 to 1946. The combination of Gandhi and Patel was highly effective. Gandhi formulated the grand ideological design; Patel took care of the earthly organizational details.[11]

Before extending his ideas about mass politics and civil disobedience to all of

India, Gandhi experimented with them intensively in Gujarat. These were the experiments that he had so successfully tried out on a still smaller scale in South Africa. With rising success, as Gandhi became the undisputed leader of the national movement, moving out of Gujarat and traveling all over India, the management of party affairs in Gujarat fell increasingly to Patel.

Though never an ideological visionary like Gandhi, Patel is widely viewed by the scholars and observers of the Congress Party as an organizational genius.[12] He understood the value of discipline and also knew how to induce it in colleagues and cadres. Adversaries could win his personal affection, but not a place in the party hierarchy if they disagreed.[13] Inner democracy was for discussions and growth of the party, but once decisions were taken, the organization had to work like an army. Gandhi agreed with this view of organizational discipline: "Let us understand the functions of the Congress. For internal growth and administration, it is as good a democratic organization as any to be found in the world. But this democratic organization has been brought into being to fight the greatest imperial power living. For this external work, therefore, it has to be likened to an army. As such it ceases to be democratic. The central authority possesses plenary powers enabling it to impose and enforce discipline of the various units working under it."[14]

As a consequence of Patel's painstaking organizational efforts and Gandhi's charisma, a truly powerful Congress organization was born in Gujarat. By the late 1920s, the party reached all the way down to the neighborhood level and, in times of mass protest, to the street level.[15] Indeed, so remarkable was Patel's organization-building that he was elected again and again by the cadres to the state-level leadership of the party. Patel remained president of the Gujarat unit of Congress for two and half decades (1921–46), the longest such stint in the pre-independence history of the party.[16]

In Ahmedabad, Patel personally led many of the struggles.[17] A solid party organization was built in Surat as well.[18] In 1928, Patel orchestrated a widely known protest organized by the Surat unit of the party in Bardoli. Large numbers of people were mobilized. Their activities ranged from organizing demonstrations and marches to picketing liquor shops and boycotting stores that sold foreign textiles and clothing.

Were the Muslims directly involved in these activities? It has been noted that compared to the Hindus, even in Gujarat, the Congress was able to mobilize fewer Muslims.[19] From such differential mobilization, however, one should not conclude that Muslims were absent from Congress protests. The evidence indicates that their participation was quite considerable.[20] Stated differently, several civic bridges across the Hindu and Muslim communities were built, though not as many as the top-ranking Congress leadership would have wished for.

A half-success, however, was enough to keep peace, for the party was committed to Hindu-Muslim unity as a basis for nation-building. Even if Muslim participation was lower than expected, Hindu cadres of the Congress would simply not inflame communal passions. Indeed, along with their Muslim colleagues, these cadres would try to contain such passions, if they flared up for some reason and could lead to riots.

Communal peace did not require that intercommunal engagement involve *all* Hindus and Muslims—only that if some people or groups tried to disrupt the peace, substantial mechanisms be available for intercommunal communication and for organized intervention. The Congress Party, along with other organizations discussed below, provided such mechanisms. Gujarat was a very good example of the argument that, given a certain level of intercommunal interaction, the more committed the cadres were to Congress ideology and the more disciplined the organization was, the more salubrious would be the effect on peace.

GANDHIAN SOCIAL AND EDUCATIONAL INSTITUTIONS

According to Gandhian ideology, as we know, the British conquest of India was not simply military but partly based on India's own internal inadequacies, which had to be fought. A host of social organizations were thus created in the 1920s and 1930s, all raising their own funds from private sources and charities. Some sponsored the homespun movement, propagating Indian clothes and campaigning against British textiles. Others dealt with the welfare of the "untouchables," tribals, and women. Still others worked for the prohibition of alcohol consumption. Also important were the schools, which, through curricular reform, presented the new national vision and sought to instill national pride among the pupils.[21] Gandhi also established his Sabarmati Ashram just outside the city of Ahmedabad.[22] The ashram was to be a microcosm of the larger society envisioned by him.

The efforts of Gandhi and his followers to raise funds for such organizations were highly successful. Gujarat's business classes, which had a long-standing tradition of charity, came to their aid. By far the largest contributions were for educational institutions, which were to impart nationalist ideas. In 1920, a

Gandhi-inspired university, the Gujarat Vidyapith, was established in Ahmedabad. It educated the youth, trained teachers for schools, and ran secondary schools in much of Gujarat.[23]

The civic vigor generated by the educational mission was amply demonstrated in a widely noted case of educational restructuring during the civil disobedience of 1921. Since boycotting British schools was a major aim of the movement, Ahmedabad's municipal government, led by Sardar Patel, refused to accept a grant from the British government for the primary and secondary schools. For declining imperial generosity, the elected municipality was dismissed. Undeterred by British sanctions, the municipal leaders established a trust and ran the schools anyway. In 1922–23, a mere 5,200 pupils were registered in these schools. As Gandhians took over the schools, the enrollments rose four times in the next 10 years and six times in the next 15.[24]

Several other major education institutions were also founded during the 1930s: the Science College, the Arts College, the College of Commerce, and a public library.[25] Gandhi also vigorously defended instruction in the mother tongue (Gujarati). English, he argued, should be a taught as a language, but it should not be a medium of instruction. This move brought a very important institution, the Gujarati Vernacular Society, under his influence. Founded in the nineteenth century, the society's aim was to promote local literature and language. Once put into practice, the vernacularization of education had a remarkable long-run impact. Vernacular writings reached many more people than was possible through English, and they could later also be used for dissemination of nationalist ideas.

In Surat, the educational undertakings of Gandhians were less spectacular, but only because Ahmedabad's developments were so exceptional. A preexisting education society was taken over by Gandhians, and many colleges, high schools, and middle schools were founded.[26] By making education possible in the vernacular in Surat as well, the Gandhians were able to attract thousands of students to these institutions.

Ahmedabad also started a press, which published two of Gandhi's several newspapers, one in Gujarati *(Navjivan)* and another in English *(Young India)*. The former was established to reach out to a vast vernacular clientele in Gujarat; and the latter enjoyed an all-India circulation for the English-speaking nationalist elite. Political and cultural ideas were debated in these papers, the rationale of campaigns explained, questions and readers' objections answered, and strategies discussed. As a result, a formidable culture of debate and discussion emerged in Gujarat in which large numbers of people participated.

Finally, being a lawyer himself, Gandhi also penetrated the existing association of lawyers, called Gujarat Sabha. It used to be staunchly loyal to the British. Under Gandhian influence, the Sabha became nationalist in ideology. It also became engaged in social work with poor peasants, the tribals, and the untouchables.[27]

BUSINESS ASSOCIATIONS

Business communities, not the scholarly or priestly Brahmins, have long dominated Gujarat's social and political landscape. The notion of a "merchant prince," rare in the subcontinent, where princes almost never came from business communities, was in all probability developed in Gujarat.

A great deal of folklore has developed around the role of business in Gujarat's culture and life. Consider the following self-description by a Gujarati writer who uses exaggeration and wit as literary devices to capture the business orientation of Gujarat: "Wherever there is money or even possibility of money, there always is a Gujarati. The lure of money takes him to all parts of the world and to all sorts of things. . . . He goes on buying and selling, investing and reinvesting, and creates, by his own concentration and perseverance, heaven on earth, if not for all, at least for his family; if not for his family, at least for himself. This is not a mean achievement."[28] In contemporary language, the description above will almost certainly be viewed as an essentialization and hence as an inadmissible, even objectionable, exercise. The beauty of the statement, however, is that it is rarely contested by Gujaratis themselves. The state's business culture is widely accepted.

Gujarat's business orientation is also linked to a much-noted and distinctive category of organizations: the guilds. Born in the pre-modern times, the guilds remained vibrant until the end of the nineteenth century. There is a consensus among the historians of Gujarat that the guilds were a mainstay of social order until the nineteenth century.

What did the guilds do? Their function was to supervise the conduct of business in each major trade, to fix prices and determine wages, to derive and enforce rules about who could participate in the trade and who had to be excluded, and to safeguard the interests of members against encroachment by rulers. The guilds of merchants and financiers were known as *mahajans* (and those of artisans as *panch*). The biggest family in a specific trade would typically provide the customary head *(sheth)* of the guild. Until a new family overtook the leading family in a business or product line, leadership would normally be transferred by heredity.

In trades that attracted multiple communities, the guilds were intercommunal.[29] But a large number of professions were traditionally intracaste or intracommunal. In the textile sector, for example, the Muslims entered mostly as weavers, the "ex-untouchables" largely as spinners, and the Jains or Hindu Vaishyas as traders and manufacturers. Their respective guilds, therefore, had an in-group character. They did not offer opportunities for civic interaction across the caste or religious groupings.

As the twentieth century dawned, Ahmedabad and Surat inherited different kinds of business guilds. For historical reasons, Surat became the home of Muslim business communities—the Bohras, the Khojas, and the Memons, especially the first two.[30] Between the sixteenth and eighteenth centuries, Ahmedabad was the administrative headquarters of Mughal rule in Gujarat, but Surat was the business capital. In fact, Surat was western India's premier port city, until Bombay burst on the scene as one of British India's favorite business centers.[31] Surat's business potential had historically attracted Muslim traders and businessmen.[32]

Like the rest of India, Surat had two kinds of Muslims: the local converts and the immigrant Muslims, who claimed West Asian lineage and were part of the Mughal ruling class in pre-British India. The difference, however, lay in the fact that the local converts in Surat were not only poor artisans and servicemen but also traders, large and small. Especially important was the Bohra community of traders.[33] The Bohras vigorously interacted with Hindu businessmen and consciously distanced themselves from other Muslims. They were Shia by sect, whereas the former Muslim rulers as well as the poor Muslim artisans were Sunni.[34] Moreover, they practiced a special brand of Shi'ism rigorously supervised by their local priestly hierarchy and local institutions.[35] The Shia-Sunni divisions, among other things, brought the Bohras close to the Hindus. Other business communities of Muslims also developed extensive commercial contacts with the Hindu community.[36]

In Ahmedabad, the economic structure of the Muslim community was different. Much like the northern Indian cities and quite in contrast to Surat, Ahmedabad's Muslim community had a dualistic structure. At the top were the Muslim aristocrats previously dependent on the court, now in decline, and at the bottom a large mass of poor Muslim artisans and weavers.[37] In the middle of the two extremes, Ahmedabad did *not* have a large concentration of Muslim business communities.[38] In 1900, when the 26 textile mills in Ahmedabad became the center of the city's economic life, not a single mill was Muslim-owned.[39] Contrariwise, all 3 of Surat's textile mills were Muslim-owned.[40] Indeed, there was only one Muslim industrialist in Ahmedabad until 1900.[41] In Surat, though they ceased to be the big mill owners in the 1910s,[42] Muslims kept growing as traders, maintaining their ties with Hindu traders, and continuing to be an important part of the city's commercial life.

Thus, the historical backgrounds of the two cities were different. As the twentieth century began, Surat had the makings of an intercommunal associational life in the business sector, but Ahmedabad did not. The contrast stemmed from the long presence of Muslim business communities in Surat and their relative absence in Ahmedabad.

The structures of production differed as well. In the first half of the twentieth century, textile mills dominated Ahmedabad's economy and business life. In contrast, small manufacturing and trade marked Surat's economy. The composition of business communities in each town and the structures of production had serious implications for Hindu-Muslim relations.

Textile Networks

For much of the twentieth century, Ahmedabad was called the Manchester of India. In 1921 and 1941, the textile mills employed 43,515 and 76,357 workers, respectively, and the total population of the city for those two years was 274,007 and 591,267.[43] Thus, in this period, if we assume a family size of five, then anywhere between 65 and 80 percent of the population in the city was partially or wholly dependent on the mills; and if we assume a family size of six, the proportion rises to 77–95 percent.[44] With such dominance, the organizations of the textile sector, both capital and labor, inevitably came to play a major role in the civic life of the city.

The industrialists were organized under the Ahmedabad Millowners Association (AMA). Formed in 1891, the AMA went through a huge expansion in the early decades of the century. Between 1914 and 1935, the number of textile mills rose from 49 to 84. Two communities—the Hindu Banias and the Jains—controlled most of the mills. The first and only Muslim-owned mill was founded in 1912, but it collapsed in the 1920s.[45]

In other words, the leading association of the Ahmedabad elite experienced little direct Hindu-Muslim engagement. The AMA's character, however, had two *indirect* implications. First, the mill owners were heavily influenced by the preexisting business traditions of Gujarat, marked by a long-standing framework of conciliation and arbitration.[46] The guilds regulated competition and ensured reliance on negotiation and arbitration if disputes arose. Business competition did exist, but group confrontation and violence were not used as strategic tools of economic competition. The AMA continued the tradition of peace.

Second, and more important, there also existed a history of giving and institution-building. Traditionally, charity was by and large for religious purposes but, in the first half of twentieth century, large amounts were given to the Congress Party and to the Gandhian social and educational institutions discussed above. Gujarat's tradition of charity was, in fact, an important reason Gandhi chose Ahmedabad as his adopted home.[47] Surat had similar traditions.[48] The only difference was that Surat, not having mills and wealthy mill owners, simply had less money to offer than did Ahmedabad.

To the extent that the institutions and organizations associated with the mill owners served the cause of inter-communal engagement, they indirectly contributed to communal harmony in Ahmedabad. The leading business families sponsored and nurtured many institutions, especially in education. Civic contact between Hindus and Muslims was established on a large scale in these institutions.[49]

In Surat, owing to the historical presence of Muslim trading communities, business links between Hindus and Muslims were much more direct. Surat specialized in handlooms and silk embroidery (*Jari*), catering to the high-income market segment. By 1910, Surat had become India's leading center of silk embroidery. In 1921, when it had a population of about 115,000, the entrepreneurs in the industry numbered between 8,000 and 10,000, supported by a labor force of approximately 30,000–35,000 workers.[50]

The manufacturing and marketing of embroidered silk in Surat was driven by trust, not contracts. A large number of Muslims were involved at two points in the production process: winding and embroidery. Since each link in the production process was dependent on the other and Hindus and Muslims on the whole specialized in different parts of the process, extensive symbiotic relationships emerged in the economy.[51] From the laborer to the silver dealer, there were a series of what Haynes calls "transactional" and "multiplex ties."[52] Hindus and Muslims were interlocked in an economy of trust.

Compared to Ahmedabad, the guilds lasted longer in Surat and modern associations emerged later.[53] In the late 1930s and 1940s, the first modern business organizations to emerge in the Surat textile industry were the cooperatives of weavers. The change in organizational form was a consequence of technical change in the industry. As electricity was introduced in Surat in 1925–26, looms driven by electric power began to replace the hand-operated looms. Power looms increased the *total* costs of production, but by increasing production they also made the *unit* costs lower. It made sense, therefore, to switch to power looms. To deal with the higher capital requirements of the new age, many small weavers started pooling in their resources, creating cooperatives that would provide capital, services, and information.[54]

A chamber of commerce was finally established in 1941. Based on voluntary subscriptions, it worked as an apex body representing all trades and industries. The various cooperatives became its institutional members.[55] Modern business organizations were thus finally born in Surat. They did not break the traditional linkages between Hindus and Muslims. They simply gave these relationships a different form, better suited for the changing times. Under both the guilds and the cooperatives, business linkages between Hindus and Muslims remained strong.

LABOR ORGANIZATIONS

What the AMA was to businessmen in the city, the Textile Labor Association (TLA) was to the working class of Ahmedabad. Given the size of the textile-based working class, the TLA became a truly formidable mass-based organization. Surat's industrial base was different, consisting of small-scale and informal firms. As a consequence, unionization of labor was harder there, and no comparable labor organization emerged there.

A Legendary Trade Union

Like many civic institutions already discussed, the TLA was also founded by Gandhi in 1920.[56] Between 1920 and 1939, despite serious efforts by the Communist trade unions to make inroads, the TLA attracted 35–40 percent of all textile workers to its membership. Over the next decade, its membership rose further, covering 60 percent of the workforce.[57]

The TLA, to be precise, was not a union but a federation of unions that were organized around crafts. The spinners and weavers, for example, had their own unions. The latter, in turn, were members of the TLA, elected representatives to it, and were subject to its supervision and control.[58]

Hindu-Muslim relations in the workforce were shaped by the organizational structure of the TLA. Because of long-standing and hereditary specialization, most Muslim workers were weavers (though all weavers were not Muslim).

Hindus and Muslims thus interacted closely in the weavers' union, which, in turn, was linked to the other craft unions, all under the TLA umbrella. Through such linkages, the TLA was able to put together a large mass of Hindus and Muslims in an organizational network. Finally, because of Gandhian influence, Hindu-Muslim unity became one of the operative principles of the union.[59]

Two additional features of the TLA had a significant bearing on intercommunal relations and peace. First, true to Gandhian beliefs and much to the chagrin of Communist trade unions coveting control of textile workers, the TLA turned conciliation and nonviolence into its political creed. Violence and strikes were abhorred. If problems arose between workers and management, the first attempt was to negotiate a settlement, failing which arbitration by a board was accepted as a solution. The mill owners were also persuaded by Gandhi to make a similar commitment to arbitration. Strikes and lockouts were the last option, to be used if and only if everything else failed. As a consequence, a commitment to peace marked the overall work atmosphere.[60]

Second, the TLA was also wedded to the idea of "total transformation." It was not only concerned with wages and conditions in the work place but also with goals such as higher worker literacy, better family lives, the uplifting of women and children, better housing and living conditions, and a campaign against alcohol, communalism, and untouchability. Between the early 1920s and late 1930s, the TLA developed a whole gamut of institutions to deal with virtually all aspects of a worker's life.[61] Under what came to be called educational activities, it ran adult literacy schools for workers, primary schools for children, and scholarship schemes for secondary schooling. It created reading rooms and libraries, girls' dormitories, and women's welfare centers. Training classes were designed for workers to learn alternative crafts. A large number of housing, credit, and consumer cooperatives were also organized. Finally, social and cultural centers were created to provide meeting places for cultural programs, and neighborhood inspection committees were formed to deal with day-to-day complaints. Several hundred full-time staff members of the TLA were in charge of running these schemes, and tens of thousands of workers and their families were covered.

Funded primarily by workers' subscriptions,[62] the TLA maintained close contact with the Congress Party but remained organizationally distinct. This link provided huge benefits to the TLA, giving it greater power than the other trade unions that were trying to win control of workers. In 1937, when the first indigenous provincial elections under the British were won by the party and a

Congress government was formed in the Bombay province, the TLA was rewarded for its loyalty. The government legalized the concept of a "representative union." Any union to which at least 25 percent of the workforce in an industry subscribed would be a representative union. Other unions could exist in the industry, but only a representative union could officially negotiate with the owners or state agents on behalf of workers.[63] Until that time, the TLA's membership had covered no more than 30 percent of the workforce. After becoming a representative union, its membership rapidly rose in the 1940s, covering 60–70 percent of the workforce.

What do we know about the state of Hindu-Muslim relations in the union? As indicated above, Muslims were concentrated in the weavers' unions, which had both Muslims and Hindus. Weavers' unions, moreover, were also linked to the other craft unions that made up the larger TLA confederation. Were such organizational links substantial or effective?

There is evidence to suggest that on occasions when the TLA was unable to strike good wage bargains with the mill owners, the weavers, a large proportion of whom were Muslim, stayed away from the TLA.[64] But the weavers as a whole separated on such occasions, not just the Muslim weavers. In the 1930s and 1940s, the larger Hindu-Muslim divisions of the country did not undermine the TLA as an organization. Its Gandhian ideology was partly responsible. Moreover, even if the wage bargains did not suit the interests of weavers, the TLA had a great deal to offer by way of education, credit, and disaster relief.[65] It simply did not make any pragmatic sense to leave the union. By and large, Muslim workers remained in TLA.

Decentralized Industry and Unorganized Labor

Mainly because of the nature of production, labor organizations in Surat lagged far behind those in Ahmedabad. Surat's business was dominated by small firms and dependent on family labor. In firms that became bigger and had to hire nonfamily labor, recruitment was based on caste and kinship networks. The owners of such firms would be among the most influential members of their caste. Their downward links would provide an in-group workforce, and caste solidarities would facilitate social control over workers. In such an environment, it was hard for unions to emerge.

In 1945, 20 years after the birth of the TLA in Ahmedabad, the first trade union was born in Surat.[66] It was, in part, a consequence of technical change introduced by electricity in the early 1930s. Power looms had started replacing handlooms, increasing the size of production units and making dependence on hired labor necessary.

In the 1940s, a labor movement finally emerged.[67] In the late 1940s and early 1950s, textile workers came under the influence of the TLA, which opened a branch in Surat. A small number of workers joined CITU, a Marxist union.[68] Neither union was based on communal recruitment; both sought the membership of Hindu and Muslim workers.

Thus, by the 1940s, in Surat too, unions had started creating bonds between workers of different communities. Their scale, however, was much smaller than in Ahmedabad. Their impact on Hindu-Muslim relations, though positive, could not have been very extensive.

DID COMMUNAL VIOLENCE OCCUR?

As we have already noted, the period between the 1920s and 1940s was especially turbulent for communal relations in India. In several cities, as in Aligarh and Hyderabad, discussed earlier, a new era of communal polarization and violence was born in this period. In Ahmedabad and Surat, this did not happen. The civic institutions built by the Gandhians gave the two cities a remarkable capacity to resist the national-level "shocks."

The developments in Ahmedabad were especially striking. Just as Aligarh, owing to its symbolic importance as the center of Muslim separatism, was the special target of Hindu nationalist anger, Gujarat in general and Ahmedabad in particular were the objects of Muslim separatist attention. The reason was quite simple. If, *in Gandhi's city and state,* one could demonstrate that the Hindus and Muslims were at war with each other, it would vindicate more than anything else the view that Hindus and Muslims were simply too divided to form a united India. If Gandhi could not unite Hindus and Muslims in his home, where else could he?

Therefore, serious attempts were made to disrupt the peace of Ahmedabad and Surat, especially the former, on the symbolically important occasions: the first and second civil disobedience movements in the 1920s and 1930s, the Pakistan Resolution of 1940, the Quit India Movement of 1942, the 1946 provincial elections, and most of all, during India's partition in 1947.[69] Some communal violence did erupt in Ahmedabad and Surat, just as it did in the other peaceful cities of this study. What stood out, however—as in the peaceful cities examined earlier—was the ability of Surat and Ahmedabad to check a possible contagion of violence. Both returned to the old equilibrium of peace. The violence that ensued remained small or episodic. It did not endure.

Ahmedabad's riots took place in 1941 and 1946. Instead of spiraling to engulf large parts of the city, they were brought under control by the pre-existing networks. Congressmen worked hard to prevent their spread.[70] On occasion, some Congressmen, committed to the party's ideology of Hindu-Muslim unity, went to the extent of risking their own death to stop the killers.[71]

On its part, the TLA kept the workers peaceful. The city's middle classes were affected, but the workers did not participate in communal violence. Given how large the working population of Ahmedabad was, the ability of the TLA to maintain peace in the working class was a great success. Indeed, once alarm bells had rung in 1946, and it had become clear that the rioters would like nothing more than to bring communal violence to Gandhi's Ahmedabad, so effective was the preparation that there were no riots in the city at the time of partition, when so much of India burned. The TLA could legitimately take pride in keeping the mammoth body of workers from participating in the national trend toward communal violence. "The [TLA's] broader outlook and its practice in day-to-day activity is responsible to a very large extent for keeping peace among the working class when the communal sentiments are running very high throughout the country. . . . Ahemadabad's working class has been saved from the communal fury even when the city was afflicted by this disease more than once."[72]

Earlier, during yet another decade of rising communal violence in India, attempts were made to undermine the harmony of Surat. The city had small outbreaks of violence in 1927 and 1928, in which both Hindu and Muslim communalists were involved.[73] Peace, however, returned quickly. The rioters were frustrated by three factors: the divisions within the Muslim community, the strength of business linkages between Hindus and Muslims, and the organizational strength of the Congress Party.

In Surat, the attempt at communal polarization was led by the former Mughal nobility, declining economically but important symbolically.[74] The business communities of Surat—the Bohras, the Khojas, and the Memons— did not respond to the aristocrats' call for a united Muslim community. If accompanied by violence, such unity entailed the possibility of a rupture of business links with Hindu businessmen, for which the Muslim business communities were not ready.

Moreover, there were sectarian differences between the Sunni Muslims on one hand and the Bohras and Khojas, who were largely Shia, on the other. The Khojas, by tradition, do not even follow the Shariat.[75] And, considering the Bohras a heretical sect, the Sunni Mughal nobility in Gujarat had often persecuted them in pre-British times.[76] The Bohras have historically kept themselves quite distinct from the Sunni mainstream.[77] Such were the hostilities as late as 1910 that a riot broke out between Sunni Muslims and Shia Bohras.[78] The differences between the the Sunni mainstream and the Bohras were simply far too historically embedded to succumb to quick erasure by Hindu-Muslim disputes over processions, graveyards, and cow-slaughter in the 1920s.[79]

Finally, the second civil disobedience movement (1930–34) and the depth of Congress organization[80] ensured that the 1927 and 1928 riots did not set off a new trend of communal violence. At the time of partition, the atmosphere in the city was remarkably calm. Even the Muslim League leaders of Surat, who supported the Pakistan movement, did not leave for Pakistan.[81] Their links with the Hindu community and their roots in the city provided no cause for alarm.

To sum up, all three Muslim business communities of Surat—the Bohras, the Khojas, and the Memons—had extensive links with the Hindus, and two of them also had sectarian differences with the Muslim mainstream. To make its project of communal polarization successful, the erstwhile Mughal nobility had to undermine the formidable civic links of Surat Hindus and Muslims. That was not to be.

CONCLUSION

Between 1920 and 1940, the civic activity witnessed in Gujarat was quite monumental, especially in Ahmedabad. Although that was a period of organization building elsewhere in the country as well, the historic presence and creativity of Mahatma Gandhi gave Gujarat an edge. Making the argument that the fight against the British was not simply about winning independence but also about rebuilding Indian society, and by including Hindu-Muslim unity as a primary goal, Gandhi put in place arguments and inspiration for a cadre-based political party and a whole host of social and educational institutions, which sought to integrate Hindus and Muslims. In Ahmedabad, this effort was enhanced substantially by his role in building labor unions as well, and in both Ahmedabad and Surat, the business associations added sharper teeth to the integrative efforts. As a consequence, the two cities substantially escaped the larger national trend toward Hindu-Muslim rioting. Some small riots did take place, but their spread was successfully contained and their frequency limited. The sturdiness of the newly built civic organizations and associations was the primary reason why rioting remained episodic or small and why communal peace on the whole prevailed.

Chapter 10 Decline of a Civic Order and Communal Violence

Surat's communal peace lasted until the early 1990s.[1] In December 1992, after the Baburi mosque was torn down in Ayodhya, ghastly riots took place for five days. According to police records, 197 people were killed, 175 of whom were Muslim.[2] All deaths took place in the shantytowns; no lives were lost in the old city, although it witnessed some arson and looting. Of the many riots that broke out in the aftermath of the Baburi mosque demolition, only Bombay's violence surpassed the brutality, arson, and plunder witnessed in Surat.

Ahmedabad also had riots in December 1992 and January 1993. At least 70 people were killed.[3] Although bloody, the Ahmedabad riots were less shocking than those in Surat, partly because Ahmedabad, in contrast to its pre-1947 history, has lost its reputation as a communally peaceful city. In the 1980s, Ahmedabad had riots with alarming frequency: during January 1982, March 1984, March–July 1985, January, March, and July 1986, January, February, and November 1987, April, October, November, and December 1990, January, March, and April 1991, and January and July 1992.[4] The 1980s, in fact, resumed a trend

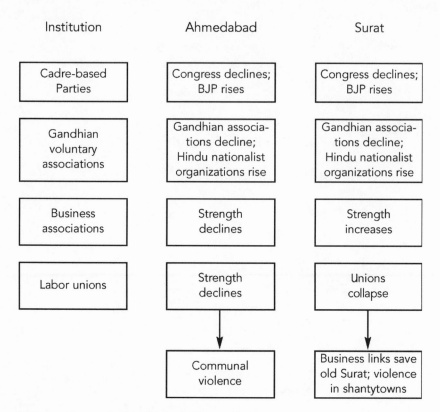

Figure 10.1 Associational Decline in the 1980s and 1990s

first signaled in 1969 when Ahmedabad's Hindu-Muslim peace was shattered for the first time since independence. The riots of 1969 were followed by communal violence in 1971, 1972, and 1973.[5] After 1973, there was a lull in the violence.[6] Communal rioting resumed with ferocity in the 1980s.

What role did the civic institutions play in Ahmedabad and Surat in the 1980s and 1990s? Figure 10.1 depicts the current state of civic institutions in both cities and also diagrammatically sums up the argument of the chapter. The Congress Party, Gandhian social institutions, labor unions, and business associations were the four organizational pillars of Gujarat's urban civic life identified in Chapter 9. Of these, this chapter will show, the first two have undergone massive erosion in both cities. The labor unions were, to begin with, not as strong in Surat as in Ahmedabad. By the 1980s, they had collapsed in Surat and markedly declined in Ahmedabad. Ahmedabad's once mighty TLA has more or less crumbled by now. A spent force, it seems incapable of revival.[7]

Departing partly, and only partly, from this overall trend of decline are the business associations. In Ahmedabad, the powerful Millowners' Association has lost influence. A number of smaller business associations have emerged, but they do not integrate Hindus and Muslims in large numbers. In contrast, the business associations of Surat continue to be highly intercommunal as well as vibrant. After the decline of the Congress Party and Gandhian social institutions, Surat's business life and associations have come to be the mainstay of the city's communal peace. Indeed, as I argue in this chapter, Hindu-Muslim engagement in Surat's old city and its business life explain why, despite shocking riots in the slums in 1992–93, the old city remained relatively peaceful. Prior interaction and communication between the two communities in the inner city were highly effective in deterring those who had a vested interest in starting riots in the old city. The shantytowns did not have the immune system provided by the intercommunal civic engagement. The riots, when they finally came to the slums in December 1992, consumed lives, charred homes, separated families, and destroyed livelihoods.

HINDU NATIONALISTS OR THE CONGRESS: WHO HAS CADRES NOW?

In Gujarat, its historic heartland, the Congress Party has lost its vigor and vitality. As the generation of leaders involved with the national movement passed away, the Congress, which continued to be in power and had state resources to distribute, began attracting politicians interested in the pursuit of power alone, not in ideological campaigns, organizational work, or mass mobilization. The more the party prospered in power, the more its civic vigor weakened.

This process, set in motion with the passing of the pre-independence generation in the 1960s, was accelerated after mid-1969, when a factional battle broke out between Prime Minister Indira Gandhi and the organizational bosses. The battle was over who would wield greater power, the prime minister or the party bosses, and which way the policies of a Congress government would go. Charging her with defying party discipline, the party bosses orchestrated a vote to expel Mrs. Gandhi from the party. Some of the key organizational figures engaged in the battle were from Gujarat. They had a solid hold over the party organization in their state. When the formal split between Mrs. Gandhi and the organizational bosses came, most of Gujarat's Congressmen stayed with the latter.

Before long, however, it became clear that although they controlled the organization, the party bosses did not have the same power over the electorate. They could not match Mrs. Gandhi's popularity with the masses. As the elections proved that the expelled leader was more popular, increasing numbers of Congressmen joined Mrs. Gandhi's electoral bandwagon. Of the two forces pulling on party members organizational and electoral—the latter finally triumphed, and the party of the expelled leader became the real successor to the original Congress.

Although Mrs. Gandhi's Congress could win elections in the 1970s and 1980s, her victories were due less to the organizational work done by party leaders and cadres than to an ingenious electoral strategy that she and her associates devised in Gujarat. In order to defeat the organizational bosses, Mrs. Gandhi turned explicitly toward the lower castes and minorities, both in the election campaigns and in the choice of personnel. She could, thus, portray herself as the real inheritor of the Congress ideology of social justice and present the upper-caste dominance of Gujarat Congress as a perversion of Congress ideals worthy of an electoral rebuke by the masses. Given that the lower castes, combined with the minorities, far outnumbered the upper castes, Mrs. Gandhi's strategy was a winner.[8]

The strategy, however, was purely electoral. In order to consolidate her hold over the party, Mrs. Gandhi ended the tradition of intraparty elections in the Congress. Bitten once by the organization, Mrs. Gandhi was twice shy about rebuilding it. The long-standing principle of intraparty elections was given up and mobility within the party ranks now depended on proximity to Mrs. Gandhi, whose successfully cultivated pro-subaltern image and charisma would deliver electoral victory to her party and its members. The organizational vibrancy of the Congress Party, premised as it long was upon internal elections and ideologically grounded organizational work at the grass roots, slowly withered away.[9]

Once the Congress lost its organizational vitality at the local levels in Gujarat, it also lost the vast reservoir of trained and disciplined party cadres, committed to party ideology and ready to take up organizational work. As this process went further, Congress leaders no longer had the ability to lead the cadres and citizens in the battle for communal harmony in a state where they were once famous for it. Indeed, many seem to have no ideological commitment to communal harmony.

The BJP has filled the organizational void created by the Congress. It has the

Table 10.1. Vote Shares of Hindu Nationalists and the Congress Party
in State Assembly Elections, Gujarat

Year	Hindu nationalists (percentage of votes)	Congress Party (percentage of votes)
1962	1.4	50.8
1967	1.9	46.0
1972	9.3	50.9
1975	8.8	40.7
1980	14.0	51.0
1985	15.0	55.5
1990	26.7	30.7
1995	42.5	32.8

cadres and the ideological commitment.[10] What was true of the Congress as an organization earlier is true of the BJP today.

In gathering political strength in the state, the BJP's rise has coincided with the decline of the Congress (table 10.1). In the 1950s, when Mahatma Gandhi was no longer alive but Gandhians were still strong, the Hindu nationalists were hardly visible in Gujarat. In the 1960s, too, they polled less than 2 percent of popular vote. In the 1980s, their share of state vote rose to 14–15 percent. In 1990 and 1995, their vote share finally climbed to 27 and 42.5 percent, respectively. The BJP came to power in Gujarat in 1995.[11] In the late 1980s and 1990s, it also captured control of the Ahmedabad and Surat municipal governments.

The BJP's political fortunes in the cities of Ahmedabad and Surat have more or less followed the statewide pattern (tables 10.2 and 10.3). Our 1995–96 survey provides further evidence of the decline of the Congress.[12] The respondents were asked which political party was their "favorite party" and whether their favorite party had changed at all in recent years. The Congress used to be the favorite party of 28 percent of the respondents in Ahmedabad and of 60 percent in Surat; in 1995–96 only 13 percent in Ahmedabad and 32 percent in Surat were still willing to call it their favorite party. In contrast, the proportions of those calling the BJP their favorite party had risen up from 39 percent to 55 percent in Ahmedabad and from 8 percent to 28 percent in Surat. Thus, the BJP has risen as the Congress has declined, but until recently the BJP has not been as popular in Surat as in Ahmedabad[13] and also that it has not fully displaced the Congress in either city.

Table 10.2. Vote Shares of Hindu Nationalists and the Congress Party
in State Assembly Elections, Ahmedabad

Year	Hindu nationalists (percentage of vote)	Congress Party (percentage of vote)
1952	3.0	60.3
1957	—	41.5
1962	3.1	46.5
1967	1.6	40.1
1972	13.9	54.8
1975	12.2	61.9
1980	15.8	58.4
1985	20.2	53.4
1990	43.2	24.4

The rising organizational strength of the BJP and the commitment of its cadres are amply reflected in the party's mobilization capacity. Between 1983 and 1992, the Hindu nationalists launched six mass mobilizations in Gujarat: all except one were aimed at "liberating" the birthplace of Rama in Ayodhya. In three of these mobilizations, the BJP participated as a political party. The other three were led by the BJP's sister organization, the Vishwa Hindu Parishad. The numbers mobilized in Ahmedabad during 1989–90 are reported to have compared with Gandhi's monumental Salt March of 1930.[14] Given how diametrically opposed Hindu nationalism has historically been to secular nationalism, one would have expected the Congress Party to launch a countermobilization.

Table 10.3. Vote Shares of Hindu Nationalists and the Congress Party
in State Assembly Elections, Surat

Year	Hindu nationalists (percentage of vote)	Congress Party (percentage of vote)
1952	0.4	57.8
1957	0	79.3
1962	0.6	67.5
1967	1.7	62.9
1972	8.8	50.8
1975	9.0	38.1
1980	20	54.7
1985	23.8	60.8
1995	52.1	42.3

That did not happen, for the Congress has lost its ideological stamina and much of its organizational strength.

Thus, while cadre-based political parties continue to flourish in Ahmedabad and Surat, the great difference now is that, unlike the Congress, the BJP tries to build bridges only across the various castes of Hindu society. From a Hindu-Muslim perspective, the civic activity of Hindu nationalists is disruptive, not integrative. Their aim is Hindu unity across the various castes, not Hindu-Muslim unity.

Although substantial, the success of BJP in gaining lower-caste support is not complete. In some parts of Gujarat, the lower castes and scheduled tribes have partially halted the BJP's march.[15] In Surat, a survey conducted in May–June 1993, a mere six months after the demolition of the mosque, showed that although a large number of people expressed their primary identity in religious terms, caste was still the single most important identity: twice as many people gave priority to caste as to religion.[16] The BJP gets more votes and has come to power in the state, but its ideological triumph is less than complete.

Despite the effervescence of lower-caste consciousness in some parts of Gujarat, however, lower-caste parties have not emerged, as they did in southern India in the first half of the twentieth century and as they have in Uttar Pradesh and Bihar since the late 1980s. Why this is so remains unstudied. Were such parties to emerge, the master narrative of caste would challenge religious nationalism in mass politics much more resolutely, and Hindu-Muslim violence would decrease, as it historically has in southern India and has of late in Uttar Pradesh and Bihar, and the decline of a cadre-based Congress Party would be felt less by those who champion communal peace.

DECLINE OF GANDHIAN SOCIAL INSTITUTIONS

Before independence, even if Gandhian social institutions did not attract as many Muslims as the activists ideally wanted, they used to promote communal peace. Hindu-Muslim unity was part of the ideology of Gandhian workers, whether they were engaged in nationalist education, campaigns for prohibition of alcohol, promotion of homespun clothes, or uplifting of the untouchables, tribes, and women.

These social institutions have declined in Ahmedabad and Surat. The evidence of their erosion is compelling. Gandhi's Ashram at Sabarmati is more of a tourist site today than a living source of community building. Gandhi's press, which educated millions for *political* action through newspapers and debates, is now primarily a source for providing Gandhian literature to libraries for *academic* pursuits. Gandhi's university—Gujarat Vidyapith—has become an institution that students avoid, for they want a degree that can be used in the job market. It is no longer a place for thousands to learn the values of nonviolence and communal harmony, nor a site for building networks of ideologically committed students and teachers. Moreover, since the government funds the institution, the university is not dependent any more on fund-raising by its faculty and benefactors. Successful fund-raising was earlier dependent on campaigns, on building networks of support, and on convincing people to give money and time.

A similar affliction has hit the vast network of personnel and stores selling "homespun" clothes, the *khadi bhavans.* The stores as well as the entire homespun industry were taken over by the government after independence. Government funding was a mark of respect for the father of the nation, but it defeated a basic civic purpose of Gandhian work: the khadi bhavans used to raise funds by conducting mass campaigns. The more they raised consciousness and the more they popularized the idea of self-reliance, the greater would be the availability of funds. In post-independence India, government patronage for the homespun industry made it unnecessary for the activists to enlarge the circle of contacts and run campaigns. The Gandhians were flattered by the new governmental attention after independence. Seeking financial security, they did not on the whole resist government patronage, unconsciously contributing to their own fall.

The place of Gandhian institutions has been taken up primarily by three kinds of civic bodies: social organizations of Hindu nationalists; charities and organizations set up by bootleggers; and new development-oriented NGOs. The first two have no interest in Hindu-Muslim unity. The third, still substantially influenced by Gandhian principles, are in a position to promote Hindu-Muslim unity, but the focus of NGOs is by and large rural development, not urban peace. They have little impact on communal violence, which is primarily urban.

The Rise of Bootleggers

The rise of bootleggers in Gujarat's political and social landscape emphatically demonstrates the erosion of Gandhian ideology and institutions. Earlier, in Gujarat, the Gandhians had vigorously campaigned for prohibition, calling the use of alcohol a moral affliction. They, of course, did not fully succeed. The British government, for one, would not impose prohibition just because the

Gandhians wanted it. Moreover, not everybody could be persuaded to give up alcohol. But the campaign did influence large cross-sections of Gujaratis. Partly as a consequence, alcohol merchants were unable to enter politics.

Paying homage to Gandhi after independence, successive state governments have imposed prohibition in the state. A predictable consequence is the rise of bootlegging. Illegal pubs have sprung up all over Ahmedabad and Surat, becoming an alternative center of civic networks for many. A government-appointed commission of inquiry noted that bootlegging had deeply penetrated Gujarat's civic life: "There is . . . evidence to show that a bootlegger is able to build up a social and economic position for himself in the locality of his operation, by utilizing part of his income in catering to the economic and social needs of the locality and by making contributions to charities, maintenance of widows, orphans, the decrepit, the old and the infirm."[17]

Moreover, fueled by graft, strong links between the police and bootleggers have emerged. "But for [police] connivance or active cooperation," reported the same government commission, "the illegal traffic in liquor selling cannot take place or cannot thrive—on a large scale."[18] Connections between politicians and bootleggers have also been formed. "A bootlegger," the commission continued, "is also able to build up a certain political influence for himself which enable him to establish contacts with the high echelons whose shield can be invoked in times of difficulties."[19] Indeed, the nexus in both cities has by now gone a step further. Instead of relying on politicians to save them in times of legal trouble, many bootleggers have become politicians themselves. They have built a political base, for they "sponsor public functions, float voluntary organizations, and make donations to schools, hospitals and religious organizations."[20]

This "new civicness" has dangerous consequences for peace. The voluntary organizations sponsored by bootleggers, rag-tag groups built for friends and dependents, have a mercenary character. They have no ideology, no agenda for social change, no committed cadres. They exist to raise the acceptability of bootleggers as leaders. If the interests of bootleggers require violence or rioting, these organizations do not try to prevent it. Unless they grow and are professionalized, breaking their umbilical connection with the founders, they can not build enduring defenses against violence.

The Gandhians may have failed in their efforts to ban alcohol use, but their campaigns ensured that alcohol merchants were never in the forefront of cultural, social, or political life. Today, alcohol is banned in Gujarat, but bootleggers have become leaders. The contrast could not be sharper.

The New NGOs

Although on the whole weaker than before, the Gandhian civic institutions are not entirely moribund. New-style developmental NGOs, many with a Gandhian ideology, have mushroomed in the last two decades. Indeed, Ahmedabad is the headquarters of a famous and relatively new such NGO: the Self-Employed Women's Association (SEWA). Often considered a model of nongovernmental civic activity by international development agencies, SEWA organizes poor women in the informal sector. Since it functions primarily as a labor union, I will examine it later at length. I focus here on the more typical new NGOs, whose basic features can be easily summarized. Most of them concentrate on rural development, not on urban issues.[21] This was true even when the civic groups were not called NGOs and Gandhian groups such as Sarvodaya dominated Gujarat's civic scene. Their emphasis was on rural work. While reflecting on the 1969 riots in Ahmedabad, Jaya Prakash Narayan, one of the tallest Gandhians of the century, had ruefully commented that "most of Gandhian and Sarvodaya workers work only in rural areas."[22]

The new NGOs, too, continue to work with landless laborers, tenants, tribals, and smaller peasants. Land rights, the environment, irrigation, and rural wages are the issues that occupy them. Rightly or wrongly, they have singled out villages as sites most in need of help. As a result, the impact of NGO activity is felt in the countryside, not in the city. They cannot play an effective role in communal conflicts, for such conflicts are primarily urban.

The Nonelectoral Wings
of Hindu Nationalism

Just as Gandhian social institutions at one time complemented the Congress Party in mass-contact campaigns, education, and social work, the BJP has a whole host of allied organizations today, especially the RSS and the VHP. Their activities include running ideological camps for the youth, schools and dispensaries for the tribals and scheduled castes, and organizations for women.[23] When the floods wreak havoc on ordinary people, many of the RSS and VHP activists do relief work, winning an increasingly larger number of recruits and sympathizers for their organizations. Congressmen used to be very good at such work in the past; they are now typically missing from places of distress. Moreover, just as the Gandhians used to excel at using newspapers to disseminate their ideology among the middle classes, Hindu nationalists have penetrated Gujarati newspapers and magazines. Compared to the pre-independence era, the middle classes today are considerably larger, and the circulation of vernacular newspapers much higher: indeed, the per capita circulation of newspapers in Gujarat is second only to that in Kerala.[24] Hindu nationalist writings and ideas enjoy wide dissemination.[25]

BUSINESS ASSOCIATIONS: DECLINE
IN AHMEDABAD, VIBRANCY IN SURAT

The textile industry has been the heart of local economies in both cities, but their fortunes have differed remarkably since the early 1970s. For much of the twentieth century, India's textile sector had two large components: the organized sector, consisting of mills, in which Ahmedabad has historically specialized; and the small-scale, unorganized sector, comprising the power looms and hand looms, which have been Surat's stronghold. Since the 1960s, the mill sector has declined, and the decentralized power loom sector has gained in its place.

In the 1950s, the mills accounted for 70–80 percent of the total amount of cloth produced in India, and the power looms and hand looms produced 20–30 percent. By the 1980s, the situation was reversed. In 1981, the mill sector was manufacturing a mere 25–28 percent of the total cloth produced, and the small sector more than 70 percent.[26] Since the 1980s, the mill sector has declined further.

The reasons for these divergent trajectories need not detain us. Briefly, developments in textile technology have made decentralization possible and undermined the viability of the centralized, Fordist model of production; with the rise in incomes of a poor society, consumer preferences have changed in favor of polyester-based clothing and moved away from cotton, in which the composite mills of the organized sector had specialized; and finally, on grounds of equity, independent India's laws have progressively favored the small, decentralized sector.[27]

These developments have led to the decline of Ahmedabad and the rise of Surat as textile centers. The civic consequences of such divergent industrial trajectories have also been vastly different, with implications for Hindu-Muslim relations that are clearly identifiable.

Organized Textile Networks in a New Era

As the mills have declined, the Ahmedabad Millowners' Association (AMA), the city's leading business association for decades, has been adversely affected.[28] In the late 1950s, there were 71 mills in Ahmedabad and 66, including the largest, were members of the AMA. In the mid-1990s, only 35 mills were functioning, of which 28 were members of the AMA.[29] Its membership lower, its clout is also smaller.

Moreover, in the earlier times, the leading textile industrialists, virtually all AMA members, were based in the city. In contrast, many of the city's new-generation industrialists are located in metropolitan Bombay, 340 miles south of Ahmedabad. The new technologies of communications make it possible to have long-distance management.[30] Working out of Bombay, they can still conduct business in their Gujarat plants. The civic consequences of the locational shift have been negative, however. Older industrialists had supported a wide array of social and educational institutions in the city. The new industrialists, not living in the city, have fewer stakes there and little interest in playing prominent civic roles.

With the decline of the old millowners, smaller manufacturers have mushroomed. Power looms, engineering goods, and chemical industries are their principal product lines. Being small, their financial resources, customary social standing, and organizational networks simply cannot match the AMA's former clout. Whether the smaller manufacturers can contribute to communal peace essentially depends on how interlinked they are with Muslims in their respective businesses, and how much of the city's population they cover through such networks. Earlier, the hold of millowners over the key institutions of the city—especially education and local government—was such that even though their numbers were not large, they could facilitate peace though their institutional networks.

In 1996, of the various trade and business associations registered with the Gujarat Chamber of Commerce, membership data were available for 52 associations. Muslim participation in business associations was low. Muslims constituted 14 to 15 percent of the city's population, but a mere 4 percent of all members of these associations.[31] Qualitative information collected on other associations also suggests a similar figure for Muslim representation.[32] The professional associations are even less integrated. The Muslim proportion of the membership of professional associations—of civil engineers, chartered accountants, and lawyers—ranged between 1 and 2 percent.[33] In Ahmedabad's business and professional life today, large-scale associational interaction between Hindus and Muslims simply does not exist.

Flourishing Decentralized Textile Networks

The Surat story is dramatically different. Building on the tradition of decentralized production, Surat businessmen have profited immensely from the fall of the organized sector. They have used the opportunity to buy power looms from the closing mills and expanded production many times. Surat has become the capital of small-scale textiles in India.

The growth in the number of power looms in Surat has been quite spectacular.[34] In 1970, the city had 19,025 power looms; in 1995, the number had exceeded a quarter million.[35] In 1996, the industry was estimated to have 65,000 to 70,000 entrepreneurs, big and small, and Muslims constituted roughly 15 percent of all entrepreneurs.[36] Since the Muslim proportion of the city's population is also 15 percent, it indicates a proportionate level of Muslim representation in the power loom sector.

Moreover, the textile business associations are intercommunally integrated. In the four biggest associations,[37] for example, Muslims account for 10 to 15 percent of members, another reasonable proportion given the Muslim share of the city's overall population. An independent study of Memons, by far the richest Muslim business community in the city, also reached similar results: 65 percent of Memon businessmen reported membership in intercommunal business organizations.[38]

Linkages also exist between Hindus and Muslims who are not part of associations, for different communities specialize in different parts of the production process. Muslims are involved in the industry as financiers, transporters, packers, and yarn brokers, not simply as manufacturers and traders. These various activities form interdependent links in a long chain. Where associations do not exist, symbiosis does.

Finally, credit continues to be personal and informal. Banks or stock markets are not the primary sources of credit for a large number of Surat businessmen. Informal credit functions on trust. "Millions worth of our goods," reported a leading Muslim business figure in the city, "are in [Hindu] processing houses; millions worth of their goods in our shops."[39] All businessmen interviewed in the city agreed that Hindus and Muslims in Surat's business life were highly integrated, both at day-to-day and associational levels.[40]

WEAKENED LABOR UNIONS

The changing business fortunes of the two cities, paradoxically, have had an identical impact on labor organizations. Both boom and bust weakened labor unions in the 1980s and 1990s. With the decline of textile mills in Ahmedabad, the TLA, a major organizational site of interaction between Hindu and Muslim masses, has been immeasurably weakened. In Surat, unions were never strong, and they continue to be weak. Industrialization in Surat has substantially advanced, but labor unions have not. Thus, Ahmedabad has for all practical purposes lost one of its powerful mass-based organizations, and Surat has not been able to create one.

A Collapsing Giant

In Ahmedabad, the once-mighty Textile Labor Associations has been crippled by the developments in the industry. At its peak in the late 1950s and early 1960s, Ahmedabad's textiles used to employ 125,000 to 135,000 workers[41] and the TLA had more than 100,000 members. There are a mere 30,000 to 35,000 workers left in the industry today, and no more than 25,000 to 28,000 of them are members of the TLA.[42]

Although the long-term decline of the composite textile sector can be dated to the mid-1960s, the problems of the industry reached a flash point only in the early 1980s.[43] The year 1983–84 saw the closure of 17 textile mills;[44] between 1984 and 1990, another 15 mills closed down. An estimated 40,000 workers were made jobless in a matter of two years between 1983 and 1985, the largest shock to the city's labor market in the twentieth century.[45] Since then the numbers laid off have increased further, as more mills have closed down.

Only a few laid-off workers received compensation; most either became part of the informal sector or could only find part-time work.[46] The TLA tried to persuade the government to take over the sick companies and pay workers, but its attempts, given in part the scale of the problem, mostly failed.[47] Since the closure of the mills, the TLA's hold over a very large proportion of the city's population has dissipated.

Estimates of the Hindu-Muslim breakdown of the laid-off workers suggest that Muslims and scheduled-caste Hindus formed about two-thirds of the retrenched workforce. A large proportion, unable to find work, joined the flourishing underworld driven by prohibition.[48] In the communal riots of 1984–85, the laid-off workers participated heavily, and a number of workers' neighborhoods were affected.[49] The TLA's moderating influence was absent from these riots. An organization that took pride in keeping workers free from communal violence had simply lost its power to do so.[50] Indeed, riots since the mid-1980s have repeatedly broken out in workers' neighborhoods. In the 1940s, small riots did take place, but never in working-class areas.

A Gender Gap?

This bleak landscape features a luminous exception. A relatively new union, built along Gandhian lines, has literally burst on the scene in recent years.

Called the Self-Employed Women's Association (SEWA), it is highly acclaimed in international development circles.[51] It organizes women who are "self-employed," the union's preferred term for the "informal sector." Remarkable though it is, SEWA does not wield the same power and influence over the working class as the TLA used to. The reasons are primarily gender-based.

The association seeks to overcome two structural sources of disadvantage—sector and gender—in the workforce.[52] The informal sector does not have the same legal protections for workers as in the organized sector, and women have greater disadvantages than do men. To transcend the two handicaps for self-employed women, SEWA has formed women's unions that fight exploitative work conditions and wage discrimination, built cooperatives that eliminate the middlemen from many crafts in which women specialize, created banks that provide facilities for deposit and loans, and founded educational institutions that make poor women literate as well as seek to change their consciousness about their rights.

Since the decline of textile mills, the informal sector has become considerably larger than the organized sector in Ahmedabad. Thus SEWA's potential clientele is vast. In 1995, it had 55,000 members in the city of Ahmedabad.[53] It is the largest union in the city today, far exceeding the numbers organized under the TLA in the 1990s. Muslim women constitute a third of its membership, and the remaining two-thirds come from the lower Hindu castes.[54]

In principle, the associational links between large numbers of Muslim and Hindu women should offer a bulwark against violence, at least in the neighborhoods where the female union members live. The association's members did indeed organize for peace in the 1980s and rid some neighborhoods of violence during riots, but when the crunch finally came—during the Ayodhya agitation in October 1990 and the demolition of the Baburi mosque December 1992—the Hindu nationalists managed to intimidate SEWA's women and staff into submission. If they organized for communal harmony on a large scale, they were told, the offices of SEWA and its workers might not be safe.[55] It was obvious to SEWA that if it wanted to fight Hindu nationalist militants, the union's infrastructure would inevitably become a target of the militants' wrath.

These calculations were a sign not of cowardice but of realism. The association's workers are, first of all, poor. They need the union's support for a whole variety of things. Second, arson and violence in the pernicious environment of December 1992 were quite possible. Finally, given the low speed of Indian court proceedings, legal remedies, if sought against Hindu nationalist militants, would take a long time to come through. Meanwhile, Hindu nationalists could make the short-term consequences of peace activism disastrous for the organization. Concerned about their future and opting for safety, SEWA's "sisters" *(behnein)* concluded that they would rather lie low and secure their own homes than organize for peace on a bigger scale.

It is unlikely that a male union of such large membership—a union like the TLA in earlier times—would have felt intimidated. As in 1946 and 1947, discussed in the previous chapter, the retaliation would have been swift, and the union's efforts for peace would have remained undiminished. The link between gender and raw physical power was frighteningly illustrated during the Ayodhya agitation (1989–92) in Ahmedabad.

Work Versus Workers' Rights

As noted in Chapter 9, there were no big labor unions in Surat in the 1920s and 1930s. In the 1950s and 1960s, a serious attempt was made to organize workers.[56] Following the Ahmedabad model, the TLA became the "representative union" in Surat, too. It organized workers, ran low-cost clothing stores for them, and managed schools, hospitals, and cooperative banks. The TLA in Surat appeared to gain some strength in the 1960s but, with a split in the early 1970s, its decline began. In the 1980s and 1990s, the decline continued further, and no other large unions emerged to fill the gap.

There are two reasons for the weakness of labor unions in Surat. First, the phenomenal growth since the mid-1970s has been in the informal and small sector, not in the organized sector. Because the workers are dispersed and split among a large number of small factories, it is tough to organize them in the informal sector. Moreover, labor in the informal sector does not have the same legal rights under Indian law as in the organized sector, where jobs are permanent, worker benefits must be paid, and the legally stipulated length of a workday must be maintained. The need for unions may be greater in the informal sector, but the possibilities are smaller.

Another factor militates against workers' collective action. Given the incentives for small-scale industry in India, a large industrial unit can for legal purposes be registered as a set of small units with the collusion of government officials of the labor department. This allows the owners to claim all kinds of tax benefits on grounds of size and makes it possible to avoid paying worker benefits and to hire and fire with impunity. Under India's labor laws, the last is not possible in the organized sector, but it can be done in the informal sector.

This creates a serious dilemma for workers in the informal economy. They would obviously like greater job security, but lacking support from the bureau-

cracy, living in a labor-surplus national economy, and aware of the legal freedom with which Indian workers can migrate from a depressed part of the country to one that is booming, they typically prefer the availability of work to
workers' rights. In Surat, too, estimates made in the 1980s showed that a mere 3
percent of workers in the power loom industry were part of unions.[57] "Although the majority of workers are aware of one or the other labor law, no complaints are registered for fear of losing the job. . . . The majority of workers
have no faith in factory inspectors, labor commissioners or the trade union-
ists."[58]

Second, language has presented a serious difficulty for unions that might
wish to organize workers. As Surat has boomed, thousands of outsiders have
poured into the city from various linguistic zones of India. They speak different
languages and live according to home-based customs and traditions. The migration was so quick, the numbers so large, and the cultural diversity so wide-
ranging that building any kinds of labor associations was a forbidding task.[59]
Any possible resurrection of organized labor was simply overwhelmed by the
sheer scale and diversity of migration.

SURAT RIOTS OF 1992–93:
TWO CONTRASTING NARRATIVES

The discussion above helps us understand and explain the outbreak and pattern of communal riots in Surat in 1992–93. In December 1992, after the
mosque was torn down in Ayodhya, the rioting that took place in Surat was
gruesome and shocking. In four days of bloodshed, 197 people were killed—22
Hindus and 175 Muslims. There was intermittent violence between January
and March 1993 as well, claiming another 16 lives, 8 Hindu and 8 Muslim.[60]
The riots in Surat surprised most scholars, journalists, and observers. "A bastion of communal amity crumbles," wrote India's leading commentator on
Hindu-Muslim relations.[61]

The pattern of violence was quite striking. All deaths took place in the shantytowns, none in the old city. The city of Surat has two very different parts today. The recent migrants live mostly in the shantytowns. Working 12-hour days
and six- to seven-day weeks—an illegal but widespread practice—they have
little possibility of developing systematic links with members of other communities. Shantytown migrants are connected primarily to in-group members,
both in the workplace and at home. In contrast, the old city remains integrated.
Its neighborhoods are mixed, and everyday relations common across religious

lines. A highly integrated old city is surrounded by a vast sea of migrants at the outskirts. The city's Hindu-Muslim business links are also very strong.

The Shantytowns: A Narrative
of Desperation and Violence

We have already noted that Surat has gone though an economic boom since the 1970s. The boom is, paradoxically, also responsible for the city's misery and misfortune. Because almost everyone can get work in the city, there is little unemployment. Most migrants can and do find jobs in the informal sector. In 1991, the city's population was about 1.5 million, and the workforce was estimated at 1 million. About 700,000 jobs were in the informal sector, of which nearly 40 percent were in the textile sector alone.[62]

The fact that Surat has become a magnet for migrants, attracting job-seekers from the many economically depressed parts of the country, has also led to a proliferation of slums. A census of Surat slums in 1991–92 found that nearly 450,00 people, constituting as much as 30 percent of the entire population of the city, lived in about 300 slum neighborhoods.[63] Close to 80 percent of slum-dwellers were born outside the city. They came not only from the neighboring states but also in large numbers from several thousand kilometers away, including the distant states of Orissa and Uttar Pradesh.

What do we know about life in the slums and the connections that might exist between migrants? Surat slum dwellers are predominantly young, male, and single. In 1991, about 60 percent of the migrants reported arriving single, and the average age was 15 to 25 years.[64] The slums are also heavily male-dominated. In 1961, there were 910 women per 1,000 men in the city; by 1981, Surat's female-male ratio had dropped to 840:1,000; and by 1991, it had declined even further. In 1991, at 930 women to 1,000 men, India's average female-male ratio was considerably higher. Considering that India's female-male ratio is widely known to be lower than that of most developing countries,[65] it is clear that the female-male ratio of Surat slums is abysmally low.

The labor market is highly ethnically segmented. It operates through the networks of labor contractors, or "jobbers" *(mukaddams)*, who recruit in some villages, some castes, and some religious groups only, or through the networks of "loyal workers," who provide kinship contacts to their places of origin. Thus, of the 90,000 migrants from Orissa by 1984, as many as 90 percent were from just one district (Ganjam), nearly all from Hindu middle castes, and none were Muslim.[66] The labor recruitment policy of employers aims at discipline and control because, among other things, such control is necessary if labor laws are to be violated. And tough middlemen recruiters, or loyal workers, make it easier for the employers to exercise control.

Job turnover is high. Less than one-third of slum dwellers in 1991 reported still being with their first employers.[67] Part of the reason is simply a search for higher wages by enterprising migrants, who make contacts after living in the city for a time. But much of the high turnover is also because workers are fired at the slightest sign of noncompliance or on grounds of ill health, which in turn is inevitable given the work conditions. "It is sad to note that in a majority of factories, even first-aid facilities are not provided," even though "electric shocks, chemical burns, physical injuries due to fall, etc." are common.[68] Fired workers, after recuperation, can, of course, easily find work, but employers can also find replacements for workers with ease. The effect is that the workplace is quite volatile in its composition. It is difficult for workers to form stable links with colleagues on the job.

If the workplace is not ideal for establishing social relationships, can such links be formed in the neighborhoods? We know that migrants of the same ethnicity, often recruited together, also tend to live together. Neighborhood links tend to be intraethnic or intracommunal. Many migrants rent sleeping time and berths, not homes. In the textile industry, for example, "three quarters of them live in accommodation of less than 49 square feet. . . . Many bachelors among the migrants huddle together in a congested space . . . these billets [are] so small that the eight, ten, or even more inhabitants could not at all be present at the same time. They sleep in turn, the night shift preparing a meal for day shift workers before starting their own work, and vice versa."[69]

Moreover, there are few common sites where the migrants of other communities can also congregate. About the only common site for entertainment is the illegal liquor den *(adda)*, where porn videos often accompany the eating and drinking. Such an "alternative civic site" does not provide a solid basis for forming ties. Routine illegality, a brutish and drunken atmosphere, and a nearly perpetual threat of violence make these places quite unfit for lasting civic contact. The dens are managed by thugs, often using force.

Studies are also available on the Hindu-Muslim composition of the slums. In 1991, Muslims constituted 18 percent of the slum-dwelling population, a proportion slightly higher than their 14 percent share in the city as a whole.[70] Unlike Muslims of the old city, however, Muslim migrants live in highly segmented areas in the slums. They also constitute a very small proportion of the workforce in the textile industry, Surat's principal economic sector, which remains highly integrated. Whereas 35 percent of all Hindu slum dwellers worked in the textile sector in 1991–92, only 12.6 percent of Muslims did.

Also, more than 60 percent of Muslim migrants in 1991–92 were in the self-employed category, compared to about 30 percent for the Hindus. Muslims were mostly coolies, rickshaw drivers, handcart pullers, and the sellers of vegetables, meat, iron, and plastic scrap. If unions were to exist in the self-employed sectors, Hindu-Muslim links could perhaps be forged. There are, however, no SEWA-like organizations in Surat, for males or females. For all practical purposes, Hindus and Muslims inhabit very different universes.

In this environment, once the news of the destruction of Baburi mosque spread and the rumors of rape and violence started circulating in December 1992, the mayhem was uncontrollable. Muslims were killed at random by Hindu thugs, in many cases with crowds spurring them on.[71] Indeed, some of the pockets where Muslims lived were wiped out completely.[72] Gang rapes were reported from the slums.[73] In the ensuing panic, the city witnessed a vast exodus of migrants who had been living and working there for years. Many months later, when it became clear that peace had returned, and the need for work did not run up against the clear possibility of violent death, the outflow was finally reversed.

During the riots, no organized action for peace was witnessed in the slums, and the police found the situation unmanageable. There were reports of some individuals saving their neighbors by hiding them, if they belonged to the Muslim community, but such expressions of life-saving compassion were rare. When the embers of violence finally cooled down, four days of reckless killings had taken place. Muslims were injured and killed with grisly impunity, and their homes and businesses, mostly small, destroyed.

The Old City: A Narrative of Interaction and Understanding

As the slums were burning, the old city had a very different experience. It was exposed to the same shock, namely, the attack on the Baburi mosque. It heard the same rumors that circulated in the slums about rapes, violence, and desecration. Indeed, a day after the mosque was torn down, some Muslims had organized a demonstration in the old city. To protest the illegal destruction of the mosque and the inability of the government to save it, several hundred Muslims gathered in front of the main building of the Municipal Corporation. Their protest touched off all sorts of rumors and "retaliation" in the far-away shantytowns,[74] but not in the old city next door. In the latter, peace committees of Hindus and Muslims sprang up in the neighborhoods and started working together to keep violence away. They were highly successful. The old city lost no lives. It only witnessed minor arson and looting.

Hindu and Muslim businessmen, who had worked together for years, were able to call on each other's time, contacts, and goodwill.[75] They took it upon themselves to squash rumors. They would investigate quickly whether a temple or mosque had indeed been attacked, women assaulted or raped, houses or shops burned. They would tell communities in their neighborhoods how false the rumors were and would also inform the local administration of the likely trouble spots and potential trouble-makers. Many of the Hindu businessmen involved in such peace committees were sympathizers of Hindu nationalism, but they were unwilling to break their age-old business connections for the sake of a political benefit. For some the issue of protecting the life of neighbors or colleagues was moral. For others, the concerns were more mundane but equally effective. They were simply not ready to risk disruptions in business. Hindus and Muslims are too tightly integrated in the city's economic life.

Special mention should be made of a truly nasty rumor. It aptly illustrates how rumors are planted in such situations and how civic networks function to keep peace, despite the great possibility of violence. The rumor grew out of a truly sick imagination, one reeking of vicious prurience and aimed at humiliating Muslims in the most degrading terms and provoking violence. This rumor suggested that Hindu goons had not only gang-raped Muslim women, but a video was made of the repulsive act, and it was added in some quarters that the video was being widely shown for entertainment in the illegal liquor dens of Bombay and Surat.[76]

A rumor of this kind, if believed, can drive a community into a state of rage and retaliation, as it did in the city of Aligarh, discussed in Chapter 5. In the old city, however, a leading Muslim businessman of Surat (and the intercommunal peace group of which he was a member) did not believe it and decided to investigate.[77] Having resources and credibility, he announced a prize of Rs 100,000—equivalent to US$3,000 at that time, a large sum in India—to any one who could bring or send the video to him, no questions asked. Having trade and contacts in Bombay, the businessman announced the award there as well.

No video arrived, then or later. Systematic attempts were made to procure it by others as well, but the video remained elusive.[78] The conclusion was obvious. The outrageous story was meant to provoke anger. Meanwhile, Hindu and

Muslim businessmen kept working together and helped keep peace in the neighborhoods and adjoining markets.[79] It is because of the stirring efforts of this kind, several in number and made possible by prior engagement, that not a single life was lost in the old city, even as violence engulfed the slums, and rumors, each as bad as the other, kept making the rounds.

The biggest textile associations, with Hindu and Muslim members, also launched neighborhood-level work. They succeeded in utilizing the services of their offices and members for peace. They used their associational links to ensure that violence did not spread to the old parts of the city, where most association members lived.[80] Their main clientele was not in the shantytowns, where the workers and the smaller and newer businessmen lived. The slums were beyond their reach. They could contribute significantly to peace in the old city but were unable to prevent rioting in the slums.

Gujarat's police officers provide an interesting clash of perspectives on the argument above. Surat's police commissioner when the riots broke out, P. K. Datta, sharply dissents.[81] For his inability to control riots, he was transferred by government even before the riots ended. But he disagrees that civic links were primarily responsible for peace in the old city, and the absence of such links the bane of the slums. If only a large enough police force had been made available to him and politicians had fully supported his efforts, he argues, he would have stopped riots in the slums as well.

In contrast, P. K. Bansal, brought in as Datta's successor right in the middle of the December riots, and others who have served Surat since, make a case for "civic links."[82] That the police force of Surat was inadequate when the riots broke out is not a claim they dispute. But they believe that although the size of the police force matters, it is rarely decisive in such violence-prone situations, and it would not have been decisive in Surat. According to their understanding of Surat, peace committees emerged in the old city because there were prior links, especially business links, between Hindus and Muslims, and the existence of prior communication helped the police maintain peace. No such mechanisms were available in the slums. Peace committees were formed by the administration, but they did not "have the same command and control over the population, for prior respect and prior links matter."[83] A more connected society, they argue, makes it easier for the police to perform its duties, and is therefore more conducive to peace. They "can't work without civic leaders or influentials."

This discussion yet again illustrates the distinction between peace committees from *below* and peace committees from *above*. When the civic connections between Hindus and Muslims are weak, the same officials who succeed else-where fail miserably. They do not all of a sudden lose their administrative abil-ities. The competence of Police Commissioner Datta, a highly respected offi-cer, was never in doubt. Civic links in the shantytowns, however, were entirely missing, making it inordinately difficult, if not impossible, for him to check ri-ots. Our survey provides further evidence for this claim. When asked why Surat used to be peaceful, close to 75 percent of the respondents cited prior under-standing and links between the two communities, not the size of the police force.

CONCLUSIONS

Two conclusions emerge from the discussion above. The first is relatively straightforward. The decline of intercommunal civic organizations built in the pre-independence period is quite comprehensive in both cities. Other organi-zations have emerged, but they are not as communally integrated as the ones before. Business organizations of Surat are the major exception. Their inte-grated character was highly effective in keeping riots confined to the shanty-towns.

Second, the police and local administration are much more effective when strong intercommunal links already exist in the civic sphere. A synergy between the local wings of the state and civil society keeps peace. In all violent cities in this study, including Ahmedabad, the local administration would invariably put together a city-level peace committee, consisting of the leading local politi-cians and citizens. Equally certainly, these committees would either become sites of interminable recrimination or be entirely ineffective. Even if the lead-ing local politicians advocated formal adherence to peacekeeping, they would actually be already committed to a strategy of political polarization and vio-lence. The leading civic figures would helplessly watch the exchange of bitter charges between politicians. They would not be able to push them toward con-crete suggestions for peace.

In peaceful cities, in contrast, the peace committees tend to form from be-low, at the neighborhood and associational level. Prior communication and contact between Hindus and Muslims facilitates the formation and function-ing of such crisis-managing institutions, and in their presence the police are more effective in maintaining law and order. Politicians, even if committed to polarization, are unable to undermine the reservoir of intercommunal commu-nication.

Chapter 11 Endogeneity?

Of Causes and Consequences

The preceding two chapters have presented two rather different profiles, disjointed in time. Our first profile came from the period between the 1920s and the 1940s (Chapter 9). The intercommunal civic structures of Ahmedabad and Surat were sturdy, and communal riots by and large did not take place; and if riots did break out, their spread in the two cities was successfully contained. Our second profile shifted attention to the 1980s and 1990s (Chapter 10), when we noticed that the integrative strength of civic structures had declined and riots took place frequently in Ahmedabad and managed to break the peace of Surat as well.

One could argue that these two profiles do not illustrate the larger point about the role of integrated civic structures in keeping peace at all. Indeed, rather than such structures containing or pre-empting riots, one could suggest that riots undermined the civic structures, especially in Ahmedabad. If so, my analysis must plead guilty to what methodologists call endogeneity: that is, the presumed causes were, in fact, the consequences, and vice versa.[1] What is considered a cause should be exogenous, not endogenous. It must precede the consequence.

If I have indeed mixed up the causes and consequences, the correct conclusion would be exactly the opposite of what I have argued thus far. The civic structure—associations and everyday life—would be intercommunal in a city that did not have communal riots for a long time; and if riots did take place, they would tear the integration apart. In such an analytic scenario, riots would be exogenous, and the civic structure endogenous: riots would precede the weakening, or disappearance, of integrated civic organizations, not vice versa.

If we advance further along this line of methodological reasoning, we could also say that the other cities examined so far were not good sites for sorting out the problem of endogeneity, even though that has been my claim so far. For, between the 1920s and 1990s, those cities did not substantially change in aspects that would matter. Either riots took place quite frequently both before and after independence (Aligarh and Hyderabad), or peace prevailed in both phases (Calicut and Lucknow). At no point were the integrated civic structures of the latter challenged by riots. How can we be so sure that the civic structures preempted riots when they were not challenged by the outbreak of one? Perhaps the dogs did not bark because there was nothing to bark about.

By this logic, Ahmedabad should provide the true test for my argument, for the city, Gandhi's home for years, had a solid intercommunal civic structure in the pre-independence period, but the integrative forces later weakened and riots took place regularly.[2] One may also add that the intercommunal fragility of the civic structure in the 1980s, to which the preceding chapter drew attention, is not sufficient for the purposes of showing cause and effect, for the civic weaknesses of the 1980s came *after* the 1969 riots in the city, not before. Could it be that that Ahmedabad's 1969 riots undermined the city's intercommunal organizations, namely, the Congress Party, the labor unions, the business associations, and the Gandhian social institutions? If so, the causation in the argument should be reversed. What I call a cause is in fact a consequence.

I argue below that such a conclusion, if drawn, would be entirely incorrect. It is not simply that the integrated organizations began to lose their character in the 1980s, but they did so *before* the 1969 riots. To make this point in adequate empirical detail, this chapter concentrates on showing the deepening fragility of Ahmedabad's integrated civic organizations in the 1960s and also seeks to locate its causes.

The Ahmedabad riots of 1969 took place because the two most formidable mass-based organizations, the Congress Party and the labor union, had lost their civic vibrancy and Gandhian social organizations had also declined in the 1960s *for reasons that had nothing to do with riots*. Riots took place because of the crippling weakness of the integrated civic organizations, long in the making; riots did not break up organizations that were as strong as they used to be before independence. Although the main purpose of this book is to explain why riots take place, not why integrated civic structures decline, I will also identify—in a necessarily brief way—the causes of Ahmedabad's civic decline and demonstrate that such decline both preceded the riots and was independent of them.

THE AHMEDABAD RIOTS OF 1969:
WHAT HAPPENED?

The immediate cause of the Ahmedabad riots was no different from the provocations or triggers witnessed so often elsewhere in the country. Characteristically, the event that led to the 1969 riots was small, but the repercussions were entirely out of proportion, primarily because it was seen as a symbol of larger forces and plans.[3]

On September 18, 1969, a large number of Muslims had assembled for an *urs* (celebration) at the tomb of a Muslim saint, as they always had on that date. The tomb is located near the Jagannath temple, a place of considerable importance for the local Hindus. At about 3 P.M., the *sadhus* (holy men) of the temple were returning with their cows, as they did every single day at that time. When the cows, led by the sadhus, tried to make their way through the crowd, a skirmish ensued. A few cows as well as some Muslims were hurt. In the confusion that ruled, the sadhus were apparently attacked for being unmindful of Muslim religious sentiment. Also damaged later were the windows of the temple. Realizing that an unnecessary attack on the sadhus had been made, some Muslim leaders issued an apology the same evening, blaming thoughtless and unduly excitable Muslim youths for the attack.

The next morning, the local newspapers reported in detail how the temple was attacked but did not report the apology. Later on that day, angry that a nearby grave had been desecrated, some Muslims gathered in front of the temple and shouted slogans. About the same time, a false rumor began to circulate in the town that the head priest *(mahant)* of the Jagannath temple had been attacked.

By the afternoon of September 19, rioting and killings had begun, primarily in the working-class neighborhoods. The violence worsened immeasurably the next day, the police admitted their complete failure to restore order, despite a curfew, and the army was called in. By September 23, the rioting had ceased, but in four days of violence, more than 600 people had been killed, many more injured and made homeless, and a large number of businesses destroyed. Muslims had suffered a great deal more than the Hindus.

The number of deaths was staggering. Since India's partition, no other riot in the country had led to so many deaths, nor indeed has any single riot in a city reproduced such a large number of casualties since 1969. The destruction of lives and property was deadly and wanton. For four to five days, utter mayhem ruled Gujarat's premier city, also the capital of the state at that time.

More than 600 lives lost in just a few days of uncontrolled rioting would be an awful development for any government responsible for law and order. What made the riots symbolically even more chilling was that 1969 was also the centenary of Gandhi's birth. The city had been preparing for a gala celebration on October 2, Gandhi's birthday. The riots took place barely a fortnight before the planned celebrations. Morarji Desai, India's second most powerful politician at that time, a well-known Gandhian and a native of Gujarat, expressed the horror thus:

> The orgy of violence that the city of Ahmedabad witnessed during the last four days is a matter of shame for any city, society or civilization. . . . Was the sacrifice of the father of the nation at the altar of non-violence in vain? . . . Bapu [Gandhi] lived here for about two decades and gave his message of peace to the world from here. Can this very city . . . stain his message in blood and that too when we are celebrating his centenary?[4]

The rioters also damaged Gandhi's ashram and assaulted its Muslim inmates. The rioters clearly wanted to attack the spirit of the occasion as well as what was once an inviolable site and the greatest symbol of harmony in the city.

Tensions had been building for some time. The literature notes the following background to the riots: the India-Pakistan war of 1965, when the plane carrying the state's chief minister was shot down by Pakistan and he was killed; an agitation against cow slaughter by Hindu religious leaders in 1967; a big rally of Hindu nationalists led by the RSS in 1968 in which speeches on why India was a Hindu nation were given, with large audiences listening; a huge Muslim procession to protest the attack on the Al Aqsa mosque, located in the Middle East, in 1969; the episode in which a Hindu police officer pushed a Muslim cartpuller, which led to the Quran that was placed in the cart falling in a ditch, also in 1969; and finally, in some sort of reverse replay, an incident a week before the riots when a Muslim police officer, in the process of implementing the law, ended up hitting the Ramayana.[5]

Seen as provocations and triggers for riots, these incidents cannot be called any more serious or significant than the build-up for India's partition in 1947, when Ahmedabad in fact did not have riots, or the events leading up to the Ayodhya mobilization of 1990–92, when it did. By themselves, these events can not explain why Ahmedabad had riots in 1969.

We need to know what the civic organizations and associations did when faced with such "shocks," for in 1947, these organizations, especially the Congress party and the TLA, were able to stave off riots when many other cities had them. After the India-Pakistan war of 1965, they had enough time to anticipate a worsening of Hindu-Muslim relations: Gujarat was, after all, one of the fronts where the war was fought. And as more incidents accumulated after the war, they had even greater reason to prepare for the worst.

Did they? What did the Congress Party and the TLA, the two biggest mass-level organizations of pre-independence years, as well as the other integrated civic organizations, do? What explains their inaction, if they indeed were passive and uninvolved?

STATE POWER AND GRASSROOTS WORK:
HOW A PARTY LOSES ITS CIVIC EDGE

The customary account of the organizational decline of the Congress dates back to the middle of 1969, when the party formally split. One faction went away with Indira Gandhi, another with those who had control over the organizations.[6] Does the split of the Congress a couple of months before the Ahmedabad riots have any significance for our analytic purposes?

The faction that dominated Gujarat was not with Mrs. Gandhi. In her bid for the national leadership of the party, she had in fact locked horns with stalwarts from Gujarat. As shown in Chapter 10, in order to defeat her opponents in the party, Mrs. Gandhi went over the heads of organizational bosses to appeal directly to the masses. Thinking her charisma enough to win power for her party, she abandoned the Congress tradition of having internal elections for party offices. She also gave up the well-established principle of decentralizing power within the party and dispersing it to the state and district levels. Instead, to ensure that no alternative source of power emerged, she started nominating state-level party leaders who were, as a consequence, beholden to her.

With this strategy, it is argued, commenced the organizational decline of the Congress Party, even as it continued to win elections owing to the charismatic appeal of its leader. The state-level leaders were now politicians who had no independent base of their own, who had not risen through the ranks, who had no long or distinguished experience of political work at the grassroots level. They were adept at "backroom politics" and at constructing alliances of convenience. As a consequence, the party, despite winning, lost its organizational coherence and vibrancy at the local level.

This standard account of the Congress Party requires amendment. As an *electoral* body, its organizational decay may have become transparent after the 1969 split, in India as well as Gujarat, but as a *civic* organization, its decline goes back much further. We need to ask what happened to the civic activities of the party if we wish to understand why it was so helpless in preventing the 1969 riots in Ahmedabad.

As we know from our previous discussion, after the party's turn to mass politics in the 1920s, Congressmen were involved in two arenas: governmental politics and social reconstruction. The former often required electoral politics so that governmental power—at the local and, subsequently, state levels—could be captured; and the latter, a child of Gandhian ideology, entailed civic activity such as grassroots work for Hindu-Muslim unity, *swadeshi* campaigns, nationalist education, and the uplift of women, tribals, peasants, and untouchables. The civic tasks were undertaken by all Congress leaders at some point or the other, and a large band of cadres committed to the ideology was thus created.

After independence, Gandhi wanted the Congress to give up its governmental role and focus entirely on social reconstruction. But those who had fought for independence for three decades were unlikely to heed the call, and they did not. Admiring Gandhi but not particularly inclined toward his call for self-abnegation, they thought that after the British left, they deserved to be in power. The top leadership of the Congress firmly believed that, even after independence, the party could continue to perform both roles: civic and governmental. The party chose to run governments and sought to build cadres, taking up the unfinished task of social change.

Gandhi's insight, however, turned out to be prophetic. *The decline of the party as a civic body accompanied its rise in power.* The more the party ran governments, the more it attracted people interested in sharing the spoils of power, not cadres committed to ideology and grassroots work. Those who joined the Congress when it was fighting the British against all odds did not do so because power was readily available. If anything, a jail sentence was more likely than a stint at ruling. An ideological commitment to the goals of the movement was an important motivating factor, and a great deal of social mobilization and work with the masses followed as a corollary. In contrast, those who joined the party after independence could see power within their reach. Governmental power was not precariously perched on distant horizons, realizable only after months or years in jail. Being a Congressman now meant enjoying the fruits of power. Reaping the harvest of its pre-independence political struggle, the party now was running all governments at all levels virtually all over the country.

As time wore on, the new Congressmen did not have to engage in "constructive activities." They could rise in the party if they delivered votes at the time of elections through manipulation of "vote banks"—making of shrewd alliances with caste and community leaders by promising them what they wanted, regardless of ideological considerations.[7] After independence, the party increasingly became a patron-client machine, not an organizational vehicle of ideological and social change.

Because the civic aspects of Congress activity were so pronounced in Gandhi's home state, the process outlined above was first sharply noticed in Gujarat. The ways in which rising power and declining civicness were integrally related became transparent as early as the mid-to-late 1950s. In Gujarat, a wide array of civic bodies were formed during the national movement, in which Congressmen had participated in large numbers. In the heartland of Gandhian ideology, a deviation from the civic projects of Congressmen was simply sharper than elsewhere and more manifest.

Indeed, watching the civic decline, the Congress Party had felt so concerned that in 1957 a committee was constituted to investigate the problems of party organization in Gujarat, where, after all, "some of the epoch making events of the . . . freedom movement were launched," and where Gandhi and Patel had "created a solid flank of Congress workers devoted to constructive work as well."[8] The committee did not deem it "proper to measure the strength or weakness of the Congress merely by the yardstick of the results of elections,"[9] for organizational health was analytically distinguishable from winning elections.

After extensive interviewing with party workers, the committee noted that "circumstances have changed after the achievement of independence"; that "the craze . . . for power and position [has vitiated] the atmosphere"; that "Congress workers at the base have lost contact with the people, . . . their discipline has become loose, . . . they indulge in mutual rivalries for occupying offices and . . . their . . . mode of living has considerably changed."[10] And with respect to "constructive activities," the findings of the committee were unmistakable: "During the struggle for independence under the guidance of Gandhi constructive activities were . . . made part and parcel of the movement. . . . The state of affairs today is that many Congress members believe that the sphere of

activity for the Congress is restricted to its organizational and parliamentary activities only."

What, then, could be done? What were the normative conclusions that the
committee drew? And what were its predictions? Arguing presciently, the committee said that " if this tendency is not checked, it will prove dangerous to the
stability and efficiency of the organization." In particular, the committee
warned that "*to combat the evils of communalism,* it is necessary to establish
properly functioning village, Ward or mohalla [neighborhood] Congress committees."[11]

A restructuring at the grass roots and a re-emphasis on civic activities were
thus necessary. They did not take place. Like many reports of the Congress
Party after independence, this one too gathered dust. The short-term attrac-
tions of power simply overwhelmed the long-term need for ideological and organizational reinvigoration. Corrective action, even if intended, was not finally
taken.

It should now be clear why the Congress Party played very different roles in
the city during the 1941 and 1946 riots on one hand and the 1969 riots on the
other. During the 1941 and 1946 riots in Ahmedabad, Congressmen had
worked hard to prevent the spread of violence, and they had the cadres and
commitment to succeed (see Chapter 9). Even more striking, working with the
TLA, they were able to ensure that no riots took place in Ahmedabad at the
time of India's partition. In contrast, when the riots broke out in September
1969, Congressmen were nowhere to be seen. Neither the leaders nor the cadres
were active in containing communal violence. It was the first such episode of
inactivity in a city known for Congress politicians' commitment to Hindu-
Muslim unity.

At the level of leadership, a split in the Congress had already taken place in
July 1969. As we know, the right-of-center Congress faction had broken away
from Mrs. Gandhi and had also taken most of the cadres with it in Gujarat.
Moreover, to keep itself in power after the split, the right wing had actually
struck an alliance with the Hindu nationalists. Thus, the leaders were hopelessly compromised: they were dependent on Hindu nationalists, who had led
the mobilization against the Muslims for having violated the sanctity of the Jagannath temple. Morarji Desai, Gujarat's main leader after Gandhi and Patel
and Mrs. Gandhi's rival in Delhi, arrived in the city only on the fourth day of
riots, when nearly 400 lives had already been lost. In the past, as shown in
Chapters 9 and 10, either the leaders would organize campaigns against communalism or, even if the major leaders were busy elsewhere, as in 1946, the lo-

cal leaders and cadres were well enough trained to fight communal violence. More than a few lives simply could not be lost in riots.

Desai's arrival was too late, and it was also rather disingenuous, at that point, to announce an indefinite fast until violence stopped.[12] After taking its full bloody course, violence was already on its way out under the army's supervision.[13] Other leaders of the Congress were no better; most were ministers in state government. In more activist and committed times, they would have resigned for having failed to save hundreds of lives in the state capital. In 1969, they hung on to power.

With leaders unable to give up the temptations of state power, it was left entirely to the cadres to do something. There is, of course, no evidence that Congress cadres were actively involved in killing. But the acts of omission were all too obvious. It is highly unlikely that a horrendous act such as the one described below could have taken place—of all places—at Gandhi's ashram if the ideological and organizational strength of the Congress had still been intact:

> A gang armed with axes, rods and stones stormed the world famous Sabarmati ashram. . . . The target of this blood-thirsty gang was 70-year old . . . Ghulam Rasul Qureshi, a [Muslim] inmate of Sabarmati ashram, an old associate of Gandhi. . . .
>
> The gang was crying for blood of a man who had worked all his life for communal harmony and independence of India, and who was assaulted by Muslim League members in 1939 as he had pleaded for a nationalist measure in Ahmedabad municipal [government]. The sanctity of this historical Ashram was of no use to this gang. . . . The doors of the . . . Ashram were damaged and the house of [Mr.] Qureshi . . . stoned, but his life was saved as other inmates of the Ashram rushed to his help. But the houses of two sons of Mr. . . . Qureshi were set aflame in Navrangpura.[14]

Saving Gandhi's ashram and the house and family of a lifelong Muslim Gandhian from attack does not take military preparation on the scale of war. A few committed cadres, with their organizational might, have often saved prominent buildings and key men in many riots in India. Congressmen, both leaders and cadres, were entirely missing from the scene.

Similarly, lurid, offensive, and provocative rumors, falsely printed by local newspapers, were also not neutralized in time. As other chapters have shown, this is something quite easy if an organization with networks in the neighborhoods is available and decides to investigate the rumor.[15] Such civic activities were traditionally an integral part of being a Congressman and used to come naturally after enough grassroots-level organizational work had been done.

To conclude, the civic decline of the Congress did not begin with the split of 1969 but in the 1950s, and it was not caused by communal riots. Instead, it was driven by the increasing association of the Congress with state power and the decreasing significance of constructive activities in the party's political priorities. The more the Congress allied itself with the state, the smaller became its role as a builder of civil society. The spark that triggered riots in 1969 only showed how much the Congress had already deteriorated.

THE OTHER SIDE OF CORPORATIST PRIVILEGES:
HOW A MIGHTY UNION DEVELOPS
FEET OF CLAY

In addition to the Congress, the TLA was the other great mass-based civic organization in pre-independence Ahmedabad. We know, however, that working-class neighborhoods suffered some of worst rioting in 1969.[16] The TLA did post-riot relief work but played no pre-emptive role. This was quite contrary to its historical role. In the pre-independence period, it had kept workers away from communal violence.

Throughout the 1960s, the TLA had been deteriorating as a civic body. The reasons for its decline were internal as well as external. Internally, the consequences of the TLA's monopoly of labor representation, rarely challenged, were disastrous for its civic vigor; externally, the impact of new migration of workers into the city in the 1950s and the economic downturn in the 1960s had a deleterious effect. Unlike those who had come in the previous decades, a large proportion of the migrants who entered the textile workforce in the 1950s and 1960s came from outside the state of Gujarat, especially from the non-Gujarati-speaking areas of the country.[17] Their assimilation into the union culture required special efforts on the part of TLA. Its organizational monopoly of labor representation, however, made the TLA too self-assured of its own power and too ill-equipped to undertake its customary civic tasks.

As discussed in Chapter 9, the TLA was the only "representative union" in Ahmedabad textiles by law. According to the Bombay Industrial Relations Act (1946), applicable to the entire Bombay Province, of which Gujarat was a part, there were three kinds of "approved" unions: representative, primary, and qualified. Any union was "approved" if its membership was "regular" (meaning sta-

ble), if it kept a record of its meetings, and if it was willing to allow the government to audit its accounts. If, following the above rules, a union could enlist 5
percent of workers in an industry to its membership, it would also be a qualified union; if the proportion enlisted was 15 percent, it would become a primary union.

But when would a union become representative? The criteria were pre-
dictably more stringent. A representative union was one that (a) had 25 percent
of workers in an industry as its members, (b) committed itself to conciliation
and arbitration as the routine methods of dispute resolution between workers
and employers, turning to strikes only if legal recourse had been exhausted, and
(c) agreed that strikes would be called only after a majority of its members in a
secret ballot had voted in favor of the extreme measure. Only a representative
union had the legal authority to represent workers in courts and in negotiations
with employers and government.

Power essentially belonged to a representative union, not to others. Since the
formulation of the law in 1946, the TLA had been the only representative
union in Ahmedabad textiles. Indeed, the legislation was aimed at giving the
TLA an advantage over the Communist-inclined unions when the latter
seemed to pose a challenge, first in the 1930s and then in the 1940s.[18]

The TLA's monopolistic status, a case of corporatism if we use the language
of interest representation,[19] turned out to be its undoing. It progressively became a hollow giant, for the size of its membership was no reflection of its civic
vibrancy. Even if the TLA attracted as many as 70 to 80 percent of all textile
workers, as it actually did through the 1950s and 1960s, peaking in the early
1960s with more than 100,000 members in a workforce of 130,000, its mammoth size could be quite deceptive.[20]

The workers did not have any realistic option except to join the TLA, for no
other unions could easily become representative unions.[21] The issue was not
simply that a sizable proportion of workers would have to be enrolled, but also
that unions had to demonstrate commitment to conciliation and arbitration as
methods of dispute resolution and abjure the use of strikes. Typically, a new
union would show its strength and popularity by staging a successful strike.
That was the best way to attract members, but if it did so, it would lose the
chance of becoming a representative union for having encouraged strikes.

Thus, workers had very little incentive to join anti-TLA unions because they
could not legally represent them; social and welfare services are all they could
normally provide. In comparison, the TLA could provide both welfare services

and legal representation. Alternative unions could flourish only against all odds.

Under the best of circumstances, organizations are rarely a perfect expression of their guiding ideologies. So long as the TLA had to compete with other unions, as in the 1930s, it was forced to undertake organizational work for survival. Once corporatism ruled the scene, only an unflinching ideological commitment by its leaders could keep its ethos of work alive. The union's popularity no longer depended on organizational work and ideological dissemination. The TLA could attract members even if the gap between its commitments and actions widened, for other unions were badly disadvantaged.

As the first generation of truly committed leadership passed away, the TLA became a victim of its own success. Its new leaders did not have to work as hard, and the bureaucratized top and middle of the organization increasingly lost touch with the base.[22] By the 1960s, much against the Gandhian principles, some of its leaders had started living lavish lives; in the name of conciliation, they had also developed collusive relations with mill owners; and they were no longer responsive to workers' interests.[23]

Associational vitality was further weakened by the new migration in the 1950s, when Ahmedabad's textile sector was still booming. In 1961, 50.9 percent of the city's population consisted of migrants, the highest proportion ever.[24] The new migrants came increasingly from areas that did not speak Gujarati, had inherited traditions of Hindu-Muslim tensions and violence, and had not developed commitments to Gandhian ideology with the same intensity as Gujarat had.

Moreover, a commitment to Gandhian methods in industrial relations was something specific to Gujarat, especially Ahmedabad. Outside Gujarat, Gandhi's influence marked nationalist activity in general, not industrial relations per se. In a mobilization for political independence and self-rule, it is one thing to take the blows of a policeman and not hit back; to be hit or abused by an employer or workplace boss, and yet follow the principles of nonviolent resistance, is another matter altogether. The new migrants needed adequate socialization into the Gandhian ideology of labor unionism, which included, among other things, a commitment to communal unity. But, having secured a monopoly status, the TLA leadership had few incentives to undertake the arduous task of socialization.

The year 1963–64 provided compelling evidence of the TLA's organizational weaknesses. It suffered a humiliating defeat in its own bastion. Aware that dissatisfaction with the TLA was mounting, a left-wing union, led by Indulal Yagnik, who had been at the helm of the movement for a Gujarat state in 1956–57, started mobilizing workers for higher, inflation-based allowances and bonuses.[25] Support for the Yagnik-led union increased rapidly. A strike call was given in August 1964 that began to attract considerable popular attention.[26] Yagnik's ideological thrust was Marxist, not Gandhian: "There is fire in the hearts of workers. The fire is getting deeper and deeper. . . . The workers will take law in their hands and create a revolution just as there were revolutions in Russia and France. . . . Unless workers do something nothing will be gained. Nobody is prepared to give you [anything] unless you show your power."[27] Violent clashes took place between Yagnik's supporters and TLA activists, the latter trying to ensure that the strike was unsuccessful. The police opened fire, leading to six deaths and many injuries. Yagnik and other leaders of the movement were jailed for inciting workers, but in the process they also became the new heroes of Ahmedabad's working class.

A year later, in the 1965 municipal elections, the TLA's candidates lost badly. The TLA contested 27 of 78 seats, but it lost all of them. (In 1962, it had fought 31 seats and won 29.)[28] Yagnik's supporters won a majority and ran the municipal government.[29] "After a long time," said a stunned TLA, referring to the losses, "the voice of Ahmedabad labour ceased to be heard in the [municipal] council."[30] Officially, the union attributed the defeat to false "propaganda" on the part of the Communists. Internally, the TLA leaders knew that reinvigoration was necessary.[31] The revitalization, however, did not come about.

By far the biggest evidence of the TLA's failure was the widespread rioting in working-class neighborhoods. Textile workers killed one another on grounds of religion: "All his life my husband worked, fought and gave sacrifices for the textile workers of Ahmedabad. He was thrown out of employment several times for championing the cause of workers, Hindus as well as those belonging to other communities. But during this riot he was killed by his fellow workers just because he was a Muslim. Our house and all our belongings were burnt and today we are destitute."[32]

In the past, tensions and bitterness—and they occasionally were present—would never turn into an orgy of violence. Such tensions would be managed by union activists and their vast network; and if violence did ensue, it would be contained. It was because of such civic consciousness and involvement that the 1946 Ahmedabad riots had simply not been able to reach working-class neighborhoods. And no riots took place at the time of partition. A vigorous union at that time knew what it meant to keep people together. By the late 1960s, it was strong enough to run relief camps after riots and persuade workers to return to work about a week after the riots had ceased[33] but not vibrant enough to *prevent* riots, even in working-class neighborhoods.

The TLA's problems were not simply organizational and migration-related. The obstacles that the TLA faced in its path of recuperation were also beginning to take economic form. In the mid-1960s, the downturn of the organized textile sector had begun. Although the crisis, as analyzed in Chapter 10, would come to a climax only in the 1980s, the problems in the late 1960s were serious enough to close down several mills. A sizable retrenchment of workers took place.[34] The ideological and organizational recuperation had also to take place in an adverse economic situation. The TLA was simply not up to the challenge. It had grown too used to its power and privileges.

To conclude, the riots did not cause the decline of TLA; its prior civic decline allowed the riots to take place.

GANDHIAN SOCIAL INSTITUTIONS AND BUSINESS ASSOCIATIONS

At this point one could ask a question about the state of the other two associational pillars of Ahmedabad's civic life: the Gandhian social organizations and the powerful AMA. Could they have made up for what the TLA and the Congress had lost?

The deterioration of the Congress was accompanied by the decline of Gandhian civic activities in general. By the late 1960s, Gandhian ideology had lost much of its earlier power. As Chapter 10 noted, some of the activities, like the homespun movement, were, after independence, patronized officially by government subsidies, which made it unnecessary to launch campaigns and raise funds for sustenance. Others, like prohibition, were being overtaken by newer values in society, and bootleggers were beginning to make their presence felt.[35] Still other activities like nationalist education had lost their original rationale, because independence had already been achieved. Post-independence education was in any case nationalistic, and equally important, the bulk of primary, secondary, and higher education had been taken over by the government. Imparting the right kind of education did not require campaigns for raising finance and restructuring curricula, as was the case before independence.

The premier business organization, the AMA, still had most of the business magnates and families that had earlier exerted such control over the city's life. The collapse of textiles, after all, came in the 1980s, not in the 1960s. The AMA in 1969 was a powerful association.

There were, however, two reasons why it could not wield the influence it had in the past. First, the large-scale migration of the 1950s had made the city bigger and more diversified. The business leaders did not have the same status for the new, non-Gujarati migrants as they did for the earlier migrants, who came from Gujarat. Second, the AMA was not a civic body of the masses but of the elite. It could play a powerful role if mass organizations shared similar interests and ideologies. The Congress Party and the TLA, in earlier times, used to be close to the AMA. After Gandhi and Patel, the Congress increasingly developed an anticapitalist and populist ideology. The earlier relationship between the Congress and business did not exist any longer. Gandhi's economic ideology was both pro-poor and pro-business; Nehru's was pro-poor but anti-business.

If the mass organizations were no longer working for Hindu-Muslim harmony, the AMA's peace-making abilities were entirely insufficient. As in Hyderabad (see Chapter 8), an integrated elite association is not as important for communal peace as mass-level organizations that successfully integrate the two communities. The declining vigor of integrated associations and organizations explains why, despite quite considerable everyday engagement between Hindus and Muslims, Ahmedabad had such ghastly riots. Neighbors still tried to save neighbors, irrespective of religion, but such human warmth and compassion was powerless in the face of organized gangs of killers who came from outside the neighborhood. The scene described below was typical.

> I met an old woman in a refugee camp. She was sitting in a corner with a blank face and murmured, Oh God, what a catastrophe *(Ya Allah Kya ghazab ho gaya)*. . . . With great difficulty she narrated her tale of woe. Only a few days back, we were a happy family of seven, but today I am the only person alive. . . . We were living happily. My husband and son were earning, my daughter was studying, and I used to look after my two grandchildren and my daughter-in-law used to look after our home. . . . We were staying in a mixed locality, our relations were so close. . . . We used to share our joys and sorrows; we used to attend each other's cultural, religious and social festivals. But on the night of September 20, a crowd attacked our house, poured petrol over it and set it to fire; they savagely threw my husband and son and the grandsons into the fire, and took away my daughter and daughter-in-law. In the meantime, some of my neighbors came to my rescue and saved me. My husband, son and son-in-law were roasted alive, and I have not heard of my daughter and daughter-in-law. I wish I had also been roasted alive.[36]

SURAT, 1969

A comparison with Surat in 1969 further highlights the importance of broad-based civic organizations. First, Ahmedabad's AMA had 100 large mill owners as members in 1969, whereas Surat's business associations were made up of thousands of small manufacturers. Second, the Congress Party of Surat was organizationally in a much better shape than in Ahmedabad and still had a much greater following. Although the party had declined in both cities, it is widely recognized that the deterioration in Surat was less serious.[37] It is also worth noting that in the 1950s and 1960s, the Congress vote in Surat was consistently higher than in Ahmedabad (see Chapter 10 and table 10.3). Finally, Surat in the late 1960s was still a small town, not full of migrants from all parts of India. The strength of both mass organizations, the Congress Party and the business associations, was enough to keep a city of Surat's size peaceful.

Thus, even as Ahmedabad was burning and had also touched off riots in several other Gujarati towns, Surat's mayor, confident of his organizational abilities and the business integration of the city, allowed a Hindu religious procession to take place. He was sure that he had little to fear. A religious procession of that size in Ahmedabad would have almost certainly led to violence. In Surat, it went off peacefully.[38] In 1992, when the Congress in Surat was no longer what it used to be, the much larger and still heavily integrated business associations were still able to ensure peace in the old city of Surat.

In short, although all integrated civic organization have a role to play, the mass-level organizations are a much more powerful bulwark against violence than are elite associations. Integrated Rotary and Lions Clubs can be helpful, but their capacities are not the same as those of trade unions, traders associations, small business associations, and cadre-based political parties (or mass-level film and reading clubs as in southern India).

CONCLUSION

In Ahmedabad, the post-independence decline of integrated associations was not a consequence of communal riots; riots were a consequence of a prior decline of organizations that bound Hindus and Muslims together in large numbers. These organizations deteriorated for reasons not related to riots. Of the two large mass-based organizations, the Congress Party declined because its association with the state led to a a de-emphasizing of its role as a civil society organization, which was one of its key tasks before independence. And the TLA went down because, in the absence of any challenge to its monopoly of labor representation, it developed civic lethargy. A vibrant union would have socialized the new workers to the ethos of the city, but the TLA was no longer alert. Once the organizational sources of civic integration had so weakened, the sparks and skirmishes that used to be managed earlier through grass-roots work led to a ghastly communal conflagration.

Part IV **Conclusions**

Chapter 12 Ethnic Conflict,
the State, and Civil Society

In its search for factors contributing to ethnic violence and peace, this book has concentrated on the significance of intercommunal or interethnic civic engagement[1] and on the greater value of associational, as opposed to everyday, engagement. It is because of such engagement that, despite having the same demographic proportions of Hindus and Muslims, some cities remain peaceful but others have repeated communal violence. And it is because the utility of everyday engagement declines with size that quotidian civicness may suffice to keep villages in peace but typically fails to prevent violence in cities, making integrated associations more valuable.

My argument about the relationship between associational life and communal peace excludes *intra*communal or *intræ*ethnic associations. The claim is not that such associations are undesirable on the whole, only that they were not found useful for purposes of ethnic or communal peace.[2] In short, for communal peace, intercommunal civic engagement is better than no engagement or only intracommunal engagement; and within the former category, as the size of the locality increases, associational engagement is better than everyday engagement. The key determinant of peace is *inter*communal civic life, not civic life per se.

In this chapter I would like to consider three related and hitherto only partly examined issues. First, to make the theoretical thrust of this book clear, I revisit—briefly—a question discussed in Chapter 2, namely, in what ways is my argument about civic linkages across ethnic communities different from the existing theories of ethnic violence? In particular, I compare my arguments with the institutional arguments, which have become very important in the field. Second, if civic linkages across communities are so important, I ask, can they be built where they don't exist or have been undermined? While addressing both of these issues, I also discuss the role of the state in making ethnic peace or in creating the conditions for ethnic violence. What the state can, does, or should do has often been an important concern in intellectual debates about ethnic or communal violence. The debate can be taken further if we compare the respective roles of civil society and the state in ethnic conflicts. We not only need to know what the states did or failed to do but also what would make them perform their functions better. Can civil society aid or impede that process? Finally, I briefly discuss whether my argument is India-specific or also applicable to other societies or other types of conflict—racial, linguistic, and so on. Is the Hindu-Muslim relationship *sui generis* by any chance? How might one think about the portability of the argument?

In answering these three questions, I seek to explore how far my argument can go and what its limits might be. Since a civil society thrust is relatively new in the field of ethnicity and nationalism, I wish to present my conclusions as part of a cumulative process of inquiry. What can we learn as we proceed further with a civil society thrust in our research? And what questions would carry forward such a research program? Underlying these questions is also a concern for the practical implications of my argument. Can we, as researchers, say something useful about how to prevent riots and loss of human lives, in India and elsewhere?

NEW THRUST

Chapter 2 lists the four existing traditions of inquiry in the field of ethnicity and nationalism: essentialist, instrumentalist, constructivist, and institutionalist. All four, I argued, suffer from, inter alia, two deficiencies. First, they do not distinguish between ethnic conflict and ethnic violence (and some unwarrantably read off ethnic *conflict* from ethnic *identity*). If conflict takes place in the institutionalized channels of the polity, it is likely to be mostly nonviolent. Such conflict is natural in a multiethnic society. If, by intent or consequence, public policy or the functioning of the state is ethnically biased, such conflict is highly likely, provided groups are free to organize and protest. Competitive polities routinely allow expressions of particularistic demands, and considerations of social justice may also require that ethnic groups articulate their sense of deprivation if they feel deprived.

When conflicts turn violent and exact a price in terms of human lives, they are, and often should be, a matter of concern. Ethnic peace may not be a desirable equilibrium, especially if peace means maintenance of unjust ethnic hierarchies and keeping some groups permanently down, socially, economically, or politically. But violence leading to death and destruction does invite reflection on why precious human lives should be lost in the resolution or management of ethnic differences. There is no compelling reason, empirical or theoretical, to believe that conflicts simply cannot be managed in a way that minimizes the loss of human lives. Such a distinction between conflict and violence, driven both by empirical and normative considerations, suggests that ethnic peace should be conceptualized as an absence of violence, not as an absence of conflict. Conflict is both natural and often desirable, for it allows groups to negotiate and manage their differences.

Second, all four traditions of inquiry, I also argued, are pitched at a high level of aggregation—global or national. As a result, they are unable to solve a lasting empirical puzzle in the field, namely, why is it so often the case that ethnic relations in some cities or regions explode into violence and riots, whereas the same communities in other cities or regions *of the same country* stay peacefully together, or at any rate, manage their tensions without allowing them to degenerate into rioting and killing? Why is intranational variation in ethnic violence so typical? Ethnic violence tends to be locally or regionally concentrated. Short of nationwide civil wars, it tends not to be evenly spread across a country. Violence tends to exist in pockets.

Civic linkages across communities provide a solution of the puzzle. The key lies in realizing that such links tend to differ locally or regionally. Although the concern with civil society has risen tremendously in recent times, the relevance of civic links to understanding the patterns and causes of ethnic conflict has not yet been researched or highlighted. Such links deserve serious attention. Simply put, local (or regional) variations can best be explained with local (or regional) variables, not with national or global factors, which are, by definition, constant across local settings. To explain variation with what is constant would be methodologically fallacious. Global or national-level factors may provide a *context* for the violence, but unless they are joined with local variables, they cannot constitute the *cause* of locally concentrated violence. Precisely because all existing traditions present the argument at a high level of generality, whereas understanding why ethnic violence has specific theaters requires an examination of local factors as well, local or regional variations in ethnic violence are an insoluble puzzle in each existing tradition of theory.

One should not overstate the importance of civic links, however, and call the existing theoretical traditions, and the systemic and general factors they emphasize, entirely irrelevant. Civil society may explain what other factors cannot, but the opposite may also be true: civic factors, in and of themselves, may not be able to explain what other factors do. Systemwide factors—national-level political or electoral institutions, for instance—matter. In what precise ways they do so is a more relevant question than whether they do.

The level of analysis is a key issue here. Because political or electoral institutions are typically systemwide (an entire polity is either federal or unitary, consociational or liberal, parliamentary or presidential), institutional factors can easily explain why violence in a given country on the whole increases or decreases once the new institutions are introduced or older ones abrogated. If the comparison is at a national level, such systemwide institutions can indeed be a helpful tool in our work.

Consider an example. It is often remarked that despite early concerns,[3] a linguistic reorganization of Indian federalism in the 1950s and 1960s significantly reduced the level of violence between *linguistic* groups in India.[4] Each linguistic group received a state of its own in the federal polity, which in turn diminished the anxieties and fears of most language groups. Compared to the political passion and the rioting associated with it in the 1950s and 1960s, language has by now become a minor issue in Indian politics.

In contrast, because of language issues, Tamil-Sinhalese relations in Sri Lanka moved from bad to worse after the late 1950s.[5] It is suggested that the absence of federalism made Sri Lankan conflict increasingly violent.[6] Much of the Tamil minority in the country is concentrated in the north and could therefore have found a limited measure of self-governance, provided by federalism, a moderating force. The political elite of the Sinhalese majority, however, continued to insist on a unitary political system, offering federalism far too late as a solution to the political aspirations of the Tamil minority.

In other words, when we compare national-level aggregation of ethnic violence in India and Sri Lanka, a hypothesis based on the effects of a federal ver-

sus a unitary polity is likely to go very far.[7] But if we were to move from national-level variation in violence to one within a nation, an explanation that invoked systemwide institutional factors would be quite inadequate. Such a
hypothesis would not be able to explain, for example, why ethnic riots in Sri
Lanka were concentrated repeatedly in some parts of the island. To explain
them, we have to rely on factors that vary locally or regionally.

Another example is relevant here. In British India, Muslims were given
countrywide separate electorates, in which only Muslims could be the electors
and the elected. These were to be distinguished from general electorates, where
others voted and fought for elective office. This institutional innovation, introduced by the British, was ostensibly aimed at answering the concerns of Muslim leaders, who had argued that if a typical liberal polity were allowed to exist
in India, the Muslim minority would be overwhelmed by a Hindu majority.
With franchise expanded after 1919, separate electorates did indeed become increasingly relevant to the polity, but instead of peace resulting from such institutional engineering, Hindu-Muslim riots continued to erupt. Riots, however,
were not evenly spread. Some towns and regions continued to be the center of
violence, even though separate electorates were instituted all over British India.

Why was that so? Did the distribution of violence depend on some locally
specific factors? This is where civil society comes in. Being highly local in its intensity and texture, it begins to explain how connections between groups provide a city, town, or region with, as it were, an immune system that can take
exogenous shocks (or "viruses") from outside, as systemwide changes with respect to local settings by definition are. Conversely, the absence of such links
makes a city or town highly vulnerable to such shocks. Local-level factors can
not be read off the systemwide institutions. They have a life of their own.

Beyond the level of aggregation, the other difficulty with institutional explanations, and its implication for our purposes, should also be noted. The check-
ered career of consociationalism, an idea developed precisely to provide security to minorities in a multiethnic society,[8] best illustrates the point. Making a
polity consociational may well give a considerably greater sense of participation
to ethnic groups, but such outcomes do not always obtain. Consociationalism
appears to have calmed ethnic relations in post-1969 Malaysia, but as a formula
it did not work in Lebanon, among other cases.[9]

Consociational arguments were also a constant source of trouble and violence in pre-1947 India. After 1937, the Muslim League and its leaders wanted
to be the "sole spokesman" of all Muslims in the polity, but the Congress Party
did not believe in a one-community-one-party principle. It wanted individu-

als, rather than religious communities, to choose political parties,[10] and argued that political parties could and should be multireligious in their programs and representation. Indeed, even after the consociational arguments of the Muslim League acquired popularity, many Muslims continued to be among Congress Party's supporters, and some were its leaders, too. A great deal of violence resulted from the contestation over how to represent the Muslims of India—in a Westminster liberal or in a consociational way. Debates about representative arrangements were not a source of peace in late British India.

Thus, even at the aggregate level, the relationship between institutional designs, on one hand, and violence, on the other, may not be clear-cut or determinate. More important, why the relationship varies may have a great deal to do with the overall state of civic relations in a multiethnic country. An attempt at consociationalism, *even when a multiethnic society is integrated in many areas of civic life,* may lead to greater violence, not less. Consociationalism may have a better chance of success if a society is not simply multiethnic but also highly segregated in its civic life.[11]

If civic factors—associational or quotidian—were not so spatially differentiated and were also constant across time, they would play roughly the same role as systemwide political institutions. That is why in societies where civic organizations are decimated by the state and no autonomous public space for human organization and deliberation exists, almost the entire society can go up in flames when the state begins to weaken. Alternatively, the entire society may look very peaceful when the state is strong. A totalitarian polity, normally opposed to autonomous nonstate spaces, is thus typically a clay-footed colossus, as so many states of the former Soviet bloc discovered after the late 1980s. Civil society, if present and especially if vibrant, can provide self-regulating mechanisms, even when the state runs into a crisis.

India's repeated encounters with ethnic violence of all kinds (religious, linguistic, caste) and its equally frequent returns from the brink have a great deal to do with the self-regulation that its largely integrated and cross-cutting civil society provides. Local structures of resistance and recuperation, as well as local knowledge about how to fix ethnic relations, have ensured that even the worst moments—1947–48 and 1992–93—do not degenerate into an all-out collapse of the country into ethnic warfare. A Rwanda, a Burundi, a Yugoslavia are not possible in India unless the state, for an exogenous reason such as a protracted war, kills all autonomous spaces of citizen activity and organization. A more powerful state in India is likely to make the country more vulnerable to ethnic warfare, not less.

A BETTER STATE? DIRECT VERSUS
INDIRECT MECHANISMS

The line of reasoning above has serious implications for a recurrent theme in debates on ethnic conflict. The role of the state in ethnic conflict has often been a focus of intellectual and popular attention. If the state, it is frequently said, were ethnically neutral or conscientious enough to perform basic duties such as the maintenance of law and order and protect the lives of its citizens, there would be no large-scale communal violence in the first place.

In keeping with this larger intellectual and political thrust, whenever a major communal riot takes place in India, two kinds of reactions typically set in: academics, activists, and journalists write reports on the riots, and an inquiry commission is instituted by the government, sometimes only after enough citizen pressure has been exerted. The failure of the local organs of the state—the police and civil administration—in maintaining law and order is invariably noted, and the state is criticized for its failings or ethnic biases and exhorted to do better.

With respect to prevention of future riots, the inquiry commissions and research reports typically present the following conclusions, all focusing on what the government should do: state governments should not undermine or interfere with local law enforcement; speedy and firm action to control rioters should be taken at the first sign of trouble; prosecutions of offenders should not be withdrawn by the state for political reasons; communal political parties should be banned or regulated by the state; civil and police officers in service should not be transferred for reasons other than the requirements of service; the police force should be made professional so that its communal biases are eliminated; the press should be stopped by the state from making false and deliberately inflammatory statements; and the state should cleanse school textbooks of communal interpretations of history.[12]

All inquiry commissions so far have investigated the causes of riots by focusing on riots alone, not on what we might call nonriot cases.[13] The same is true of researchers. A principal argument of this book is that this strategy is fundamentally inadequate, if not entirely useless. That the state somehow failed to protect the lives of its citizens or targeted the lives of one particular ethnic group is a conclusion predetermined by such a strategy of inquiry. If the researchers and judges only investigate violence, the failure of state organs in preventing riots, for a whole variety of reasons, is bound to be a foregone conclusion. There is no mystery to be unraveled here.

Normatively speaking, much of what the inquiry commissions recommend should happen, but they do not specify clearly how to make it happen. Their exhortative reasoning begs an analytical as well as a practical question: why is the state, which so often fails in riot-prone cities, effective in preventing riots in peaceful cities, even when the times are rough and tensions reach alarming heights, as they did in 1947–48 and 1992–93? Irrespective of the provocation, many towns and cities, after all, do not have riots, despite having substantial populations of both Hindus and Muslims.

If we study violence and peace together, a different conclusion, along with a new point of entry for practical action, emerges. If the state was able to keep peace in so many places, even though several other cities and towns burned, it is only fruitful to disaggregate the state into its local organs—the police and the civil administration—and ask why these organs function better in some places than in others. Is it due to the greater professionalism and ethnic neutrality of the police and civil administration in some places than in others? Is it that, compared to the riot-prone Ahmedabad, the police were more thorough in the city of Surat, peaceful until 1992? If so, how did the professionalism of Surat police disintegrate in 1992 and 1993, when riots did break out after nearly 70 years of communal peace in the city? Likewise, did the police and civil administration of Lucknow, a communally peaceful city in Uttar Pradesh, have no communal biases, whereas in Aligarh, a riot-prone city of the same state, the police and civil administrators consistently had an anti-Muslim bent?

This is an impossible line of inquiry. In India, the police and civil administrations are branches of state, not local, government. Throughout their professional lives, civil and police officers in a state are transferred from one town to another. As a consequence, no town is permanently patrolled by one set of officers. And although the people on the lower rungs of the civil and police administrations can be kept in one place for longer periods of time, it will be extremely hard to prove that on a matter as critical as law and order during mass disturbances, the lower staff, whose promotion depends on the positive recommendation of the bosses, can repeatedly defy those bosses and continue to express their communal biases during period of communal tension. With so much flux at the level of personnel in any given town, the biases and quality of administration and policing do not stay the same for long periods of time. Moreover, riot-prone cities often get some of the most competent police and administrative officers and the peaceful ones some of the least able. *If neither staff abilities nor the quality of administration and policing systematically vary be-*

tween peaceful and riot-prone cities, it is not possible to link the difference between peaceful and violent towns to policing or administrative factors.

The fundamental reason for riots lies elsewhere. It is the environment of a peaceful city that makes the police and administration perform its law-and-order functions better, irrespective of the biases or the level of professionalism. As far as riots are concerned, a communally integrated place is simply better policed and administered. The local organs of the state function better when there are robust links between Hindus and Muslims in civic life—associational in the cities and quotidian in the villages.[14]

This argument implies neither that the local organs of the state should not be more professional nor that there should be lower citizen pressure on the state. It simply calls attention to a different and indirect mechanism of citizen oversight and pressure. An attempt to rebuild or strengthen civic links between Hindus and Muslims is a method that, although indirect, is more effective in keeping the state accountable for the life of its citizens. To dwell on the failings of the state and to remind the state authorities about their duties may often be necessary, but such approaches have so far yielded limited returns. Tens of inquiry commissions and even more numerous findings and critiques of researchers since 1947 bear testimony to the ineffectiveness of a method that is directly exhortative. It is an insufficiently imagined intellectual stance. An integrated civil society seems to have much greater potential for changing the behavior of the state than a critique that demands but is unable to procure such a change.

If this argument is right, an important set of questions logically follows. Can intercommunal civic links be built over the short run? Who can build them—the state or civic groups—and why? Are civic networks "path-dependent," depending on long historical legacies, not short-term human action? For those practically inclined, these are perhaps the most important questions associated with the research undertaken for this book. If it is not easy to build interethnic civic networks in the absence of historical legacies, the practical implications of my argument would be quite limited.

CAN CIVIC LINKS BE FORGED?

In the historical materials examined in this book, we found that the post-independence civic institutions and patterns of Hindu-Muslim interaction were put in place between the 1920s and 1940s, during India's independence movement. The origins of communally integrated associations were thus part of the great social and political transformations brought about by the movement. They were linked to Mahatma Gandhi's ideology, which placed great emphasis on voluntary associations and on the general importance of nonstate, civic spaces of human life. To bring about social and political transformation, the ideology relied more on civic action and capacity than on state policy.[15]

Should we then conclude that associational life is dependent on historically transformative political movements? If so, one will also have to argue as a corollary that the room for human volition and activism is limited and that one has to wait for a great political transformation to take place before new civic structures can be built. We know that such movements do not come about every day.

An important question thus is: Can movements smaller than India's independence movement forge intercommunal civic networks where associations and everyday life have continued to be highly segregated? Are Aligarh, Hyderabad, and Ahmedabad, the three highly segregated and riot-prone cities of our study, beyond redemption? How should we interpret the role for smaller acts of human agency in the building of civil society?

Fortunately for future research as well as practical action, pre-independence civic transformations in India can be read in two different ways. As argued above, one could, of course, say that such path-breaking movements do not emerge easily; hence one should be pessimistic about the possibility of human intervention in the civic process. But a second, more nuanced, interpretation is equally possible. Although India's independence movement, given the role of Gandhi and his emphasis on civil society, was undoubtedly unique, a movement does not have to be so monumental in order to bring about civic changes. In some parts of southern India, for example, a much smaller movement aimed at ending caste injustice within Hindu society and capturing governmental power through elections had remarkably positive implications for Hindu-Muslim relations. As the Brahmin–non-Brahmin divide—an intra-Hindu, not a Hindu-Muslim, issue—became the driving force of southern politics, a large space was created for the lower Hindu castes and Muslims to come together.

Smaller acts of human agency thus matter. On the basis of available evidence, such acts can be divided into three categories: movement politics aimed at electoral politics, nonelectoral civic interventions, and initiatives led by the local administration. Of the three, the first two are civil society based, and the third state-based. Since the state and civil society are fundamentally different from, and sometimes opposed to, each other, the third category is by far the most counterintuitive and quizzical. In the discussion below, I briefly deal with the first two categories but concentrate quite heavily on the puzzling third.

Movements and Electoral Politics

As far as the impact of social movements on civic life is concerned, the example of the lower-caste movement in southern India has already been given. In various small localities, the beginnings were made with a fight for social dignity and a battle against the hierarchy of the caste system. Over time, these locally launched struggles became a movement, spreading to the whole region. Subsequently, the movement turned into a cadre-based party and sought to capture power at the state level through participation in electoral politics.

As the movement transformed social relations, integration of Hindus and Muslims emerged as a by-product. The Brahmins were seen and presented as the primary adversary of the lower-caste movement. As a result, the Brahmins, not Muslims, were increasingly excluded from the associational life established by the lower-caste movement—in political parties, unions, film clubs, reading clubs, business associations, and so on.[16]

In parts of northern India, lower-caste movements also emerged in the late 1980s and early 1990s. In Bihar, India's second largest state, the rise of lower-caste parties in the 1990s also led to a serious decline in communal violence, precisely when some of the worst rioting took place in the nation as a whole. In contrast, between 1960 and the early 1980s, the state of Bihar used to have frequent Hindu-Muslim riots.

The new lower-caste movement has brought Hindus and Muslims together at the mass level and has made it extremely hard for politicians to polarize the state population on Hindu-Muslim lines. Indeed, the Hindu nationalists themselves appear to be heading toward incorporating the lower castes, if not Muslims, in their parties and political coalitions. How lasting the effect of this political shift will be on Hindu-Muslim relations depends on what kinds of civic institutions are put in place. We know that lower-caste parties are playing an integrative role. More research along the lines followed here can indicate whether other civic institutions are being transformed. Be that as it may, the decade-long Hindu-Muslim peace in a state often rocked by communal riots in the past is both unmistakable and remarkable.

The Utility of Small Steps

Examples less ambitious than the lower-caste movement also exist. Capturing power has not been their purpose. They are not about electoral politics. Rather, they have aimed at providing better and more sustained livelihoods and work to poor people. Since both Hindus and Muslims are part of such organizations, we find that understanding routinely created during work has acted as an integrative force at the time of communal tensions.

Undertaken by NGOs, most such experiments are not as grand as the institutional restructuring of a polity or a national or regional movement, but, we should note, the grander alternatives are harder to realize, and smaller interventions easier to undertake. More such small-scale, highly localized interventions will also save many more lives. In riots during which even a small number of precious human lives may be worth saving, the utility of such small steps should not be understated. I shall give two instances, each led by an NGO.

Disha is a women's NGO working in Saharanpur, Uttar Pradesh. Disha's workers *(sakhis* and *sahayoginis)* are drawn from both religious communities, and women workers usually work in pairs. As part of the state's Mahila Samakhya (MS) initiative, Disha worked to improve women's education and awareness about a wide range of social issues.

> Where relations between the two communities have been strained or nonexistent they have played an extremely positive role. . . . In Bateda., before MS started, the women from the Muslim "mohalla" [neighborhood] did not speak to the women from the Hindu "basti" [neighborhood]. In the initial stages of building relationships . . . , the *Sakhis* and the *Sahayoginis* [women workers] realised the importance of drawing the two communities together, but had the foresight not to force the issue prematurely. They therefore held separate meetings in the two hamlets. They did, however, make it a point to casually mention snippets of information and interesting stories that had been related in the other meeting. Gradually, a relationship of trust was built. As a result of this groundwork the *Sakhis* and *Sahayoginis* did not find it difficult to mobilize the two communities on a common basis like ration cards. Once the barrier was broken there was no going back. Now joint meetings are held, alternatively in each "basti." They are even supported by the men in their efforts.[17]

Such contacts helped stop communal violence in the autumn of 1990. Women mobilized by the NGOs were active in stopping the national controversy over the Baburi mosque from destroying local communal harmony. Hindu women who had met Muslims through Disha's social work persuaded local Hindus to reassure Muslim families—who were about to flee their homes—that they would be in no danger if they stayed.

Another example is SEWA, an organization discussed in Chapter 10. Even as the communal atmosphere in the city of Ahmedabad deteriorated, SEWA was able to build an organization of working and poor women, both Hindu and

Muslim. The association's women may not have been able to reverse the communal trend in the entire city, but in the neighborhoods where they lived, they were able to work for and keep peace, even as communal fires raged outside. It is difficult to estimate how many more lives would have been lost in the city if the moderating influence of SEWA had not been present in the neighborhoods. But it is necessary to raise this counterfactual scenario, if only to underscore the point that without SEWA, the loss of lives would undoubtedly have been greater, not smaller. It not only provided a better livelihood to the poor; it also saved lives during riots.

The Bhiwandi Experiment

The example of a state-led initiative—our third category of human intervention—is far and away the most dramatic. Bhiwandi, a town just outside Bombay, was infamous for Hindu-Muslim riots in the 1970s and 1980s. In the late 1980s, the local police took the initiative in putting a stop to riots. The turning point was the arrival in June 1988 of a police chief for a three-year term.[18] In those three years, Bhiwandi was transformed from a town whose capacity for rioting had become legendary to one that could meticulously work for and keep communal peace, even in the worst of times, as between 1988 and 1993. The key was building Hindu-Muslim contacts in an organized way and around common issues of concern. We do not yet know how long Bhiwandi's communal peace will last, but peace has prevailed since 1988, a remarkable turnaround for a town known for its relentless communal hostility and frequent violence. The experiment raises a whole range of important issues about the possibility of local-level intervention in the building of civil society.

The town of Bhiwandi is a rather unlikely site for healthy and robust civic engagement. A center of small textile manufacturing, most of which exists in the informal sector, Bhiwandi is full of "sprawling hutment colonies, narrow streets, the never-ceasing rattling of powerlooms," and "the town's civic amenities are bursting at the seams under the increasing demands of the shanties mushrooming all round."[19] Moreover, Hindus and Muslims tend to live in segregated neighborhoods.

Undeterred by this setting and the town's history of violence, the police chief argued that instead of fighting the fires when they broke out, it was better for the police to bring Hindus and Muslims together to create mutual understanding. The aim was to set up durable structures of peace. If the Hindus and Muslims could meet each other often enough and discuss common problems, a reservoir of communication and perhaps trust would be created, which in turn would play a peace-making role at the time of communal tensions. Thinking that "to be forewarned is to be forearmed,"[20] the police chief decided to put together neighborhood committees *(mohalla samitis)* for the whole town, under his supervision.

Since segregated living was the norm in the town, each committee covered two adjacent neighborhoods and consisted of an equal number of Hindus and Muslims, selected on the basis of local knowledge. The committee members were those who "wielded considerable influence in their respective mohallas and had a clean record." Special care was taken to ensure that "no communalist or known criminal" lacking a "genuine desire for peace" was selected. For every two or three committees, one police officer was appointed to act as liaison officer. Wherever available, the committee members included highly respected professionals such as doctors and advocates. But in the poorest neighborhoods, where no such professionals were present, the committees consisted of "coolies and even housewives."[21] Whether professionals, coolies, or housewives, the only condition was that committee members be respected by their neighbors for probity and goodwill, for which local knowledge was used, and have no criminal records, for which police data were checked.

Seventy such committees were created to cover the entire town. They would discuss "matters of mutual concern." They would meet as necessary, at least once a week normally but daily in times of tension, with a police officer presiding. And as time wore on, they turned out to be so successful that even non-members started attending important meetings, thus broadening "the base of mutual confidence."[22]

During 1988–91, the nationwide mobilization sponsored by the Hindu nationalists for the destruction of the Baburi mosque and "liberation" of Ram's birthplace was at its peak. As a consequence, communal tensions in much of India were high, and there were many moments of tension and bitterness in Bhiwandi as well. But "when passions ran high, members on both sides came together and voluntarily undertook the task of patrolling the streets for nights on end. Rumours were suppressed on the spot and rumour-mongers handed over to the police. . . . [As a result], the evil-doers preferred to lie low . . . [and] were totally isolated by the constant vigilance against them by committee members."[23]

In 1991, as the police chief left Bhiwandi for his next posting, his successor did not dislodge the committees. He sought instead to continue the arrangement. The utility of continuation was soon brilliantly illustrated. By the time the Baburi mosque was torn down in December 1992, Bhiwandi's citizens, both

Hindus and Muslims, had developed such mutual understanding, confidence, and resolve that they successfully kept the peace of their neighborhoods and town. Not a single life was lost.

Bhiwandi's peace in the aftermath of the mosque demolition was a remarkable development—not only because it had such an awful past but also because it was the period of India's worst post-partition violence. Moreover, rioting came as close to Bhiwandi as the neighboring city of Bombay. In December 1992 and January 1993, Bombay witnessed massive riots. Given the proximity of Bombay, rumors of the worst kind floated in and out of Bhiwandi, but they failed to trigger riots. A fierce communal storm thus passed Bhiwandi by, without shaking its new civic edifice.

Were the Bhiwandi police communally biased against the Muslims? If they were, how was peace kept? The police chief freely admits that "many among the rank and file in the police were victims of communal propaganda."[24] But that did not prevent him from either working with these policemen in undertaking the experiment or from achieving success. We don't know for sure whether the educational campaigns launched by the police chief were able to transform the hearts and minds of the rank and file.[25] It is, however, manifestly clear that even the biased policemen could not vitiate the final results, for they operated under two sets of constraints: leadership from above and public pressure from below. The visionary boss, given the hierarchical structure of the police, could not be defied, and once committees acquired a force of their own, the erring policemen, not simply the criminals, could be easily brought to book by citizen vigilance and pressure. With such pressures from above and below, the biases of the police, even if they remained, became more or less irrelevant.

Inferences

What should one conclude from these examples? First, although it may too simplistic to say that Hindu-Muslim civic links can be forged at will, it would be equally wrong to suggest that one must wait for transformative political moments, created by large social or political movements, before civil society can be rebuilt or desperately violent cities can be turned around. These examples generate confidence in the idea that small acts of human agency have a role of their own in the creation of integrative civic links. Indeed, intercommunal civic linkages can be forged even in highly unfavorable circumstances, such as Bhiwandi, and such bridges, if built, can provide a town with a strong immune system to deal with communal shocks.

Second, the view that blames the biases of the state officials, especially the police, for riots needs an important amendment. That biases exist is perhaps beyond doubt. But the argument that they are primarily responsible for riots, or for the state's failure to prevent them, is flawed. Police biases should, of course, be worked upon, or exposed when witnessed, but one does not have to wait until the biases disappear to work for and secure peace. One can effectively constrain the operation of biases if the right kinds of institutional pressures are created.

Third, the Bhiwandi experiment, in particular, questions the conventional wisdom that there is an adversarial relationship between the state and civil society. As argued above, civil society is a *non*state, not an *anti*state, space of our life whose vigor can be, though is not necessarily, promoted by the state. Civil society is typically antistate when the state, intentionally or not, begins to undermine civic life. Because civic linkages were forged on the initiative of the local organ of the state, the Bhiwandi experiment suggests fruitful possibilities of a state–civil society synergy for stemming endemic violence. With a strong civic edifice in place, the state can prevent riots with considerable ease. Without building such an edifice, even the ablest state officials may not be able to prevent riots.

Further research, among other things, will clarify the boundaries that need to be put around the observations above. It will, for example, be very useful to learn whether the Bhiwandi experiment is exceptional or replicable. Although the main thrust of the Bhiwandi experiment is consistent with the principal arguments of this book, there is, in a methodological sense, a fundamental and important difference. The six cities selected in this book for in-depth analysis either maintained their violent or peaceful character through much of the twentieth century or in one case, Ahmedabad, where a decisive change did take place, it was in the direction of decline—from peace to violence. Because of what it set out to do, the book's research design did not include a city where a transformation from endemic violence to peace took place, at least none as unambiguous as Bhiwandi.[26] Of the six, no city was riot-prone for as long as Bhiwandi was (the 1970s and 1980s) and then also moved toward peace for as long.

There is an important and generic issue here that suggests potentially fruitful lines of future inquiry. The way to turn violence-torn towns around is a problem not yet systematically investigated and understood by researchers and activists. A research design that selects such towns and cities and examines the transformative mechanisms in a methodologically defensible way should clarify the general lessons that can be drawn from the Bhiwandi experiment.

But, whatever we learn from future research, one thing is certain. There is no evidence in our materials that the state alone can bring about lasting peace in violence-torn areas. The state should begin to see civil society as a precious potential ally and think of the kinds of civic linkages that can promote the cause of peace.

BEYOND INDIA

In the end, we might wish to ask whether the conclusions of this book are India-specific or have resonance elsewhere. Although disaggregated statistics, as I noted in Chapter 2, on local or regional dispersions of ethnic violence have not been systematically collected for many countries, the data that we do have— for example, for the United States or Northern Ireland[27]—show roughly the same larger pattern that exists in India. On the whole, ethnic violence tends to be highly locally or regionally concentrated. A countrywide breakdown of ethnic relations is rare. We tend to form exaggerated impressions of the destructive power of ethnicity because violence is what attracts popular attention, especially the attention of media. The quiet continuation of routine life may be important for research, but it is not "news," and hence is unimportant for the media. In contrast, large riots or major acts of violence make "good copy" and are widely reported. In the process, we end up getting the impression that ethnic violence is normal and ethnic peace rare in the world, whereas the reality is the other way round.

If we systematically investigate the links between civil society and ethnic conflict, we can achieve a better understanding of violence in general as well as of its local or regional variations. Although such research, as I have repeatedly argued, has not yet been done on an extensive scale, some potentially powerful indications are available in the existing literature.

Consider first the former Yugoslavia, a country often presented in the media as having been heavily ethnically integrated until the civil war broke out in the 1990s. If true, the implications of the Yugoslav civil war would run contrary to the argument of this book. Is the popular impression correct?

Specialists who study eastern Europe have long argued that in Communist societies, civic organizations independent of the state were not allowed by the rulers. Thus, prior *associational* engagement between different ethnic communities—the more important determinant of peace than everyday engagement in this study—becomes more or less irrelevant to the analysis of ethnic conflict in most former Communist countries. It also means that (a) once Communism ended, the absence—or utter weakness—of associational civic life made the former Communist countries highly vulnerable to ethnic shocks and (b) the variation in ethnic violence could be seen to a substantial extent as a function of the intensity of everyday engagement between ethnic groups.

The available studies seem to support both of these derivations. Research on two widely noted Yugoslav civic bodies—the self-managed industrial societies and local self-governments—shows that the Communists had completely penetrated these organizations, turned them into appendages of the state, killed the interests of ordinary citizens in participating in them, and robbed them of their civic role.[28] The evidence on the second point—everyday interethnic engagement—is also supportive but quite in contrast to the popular discourse about the former Yugoslavia. A high incidence of interethnic marriage in the country in general, and Bosnia in particular, is often cited as an example of everyday interethnic integration. In the literature on ethnicity, interethnic marriage is indeed considered to be the highest form of everyday integration.[29]

Contrary to popular wisdom, statistics indicate that (a) the rates of interethnic marriage were very not high in Yugoslavia (12–13 percent only, not the oft-cited 30 percent) and did not increase at all between 1961 and 1989 and (b) Bosnian intermarriage rates were no different from the overall Yugoslav averages (13 percent). The region recording the highest interethnic marriage rates was Vojvodina (28 percent), which also remained peaceful during the civil war in Yugoslavia. Serbia (minus Vojvodina) had the lowest intermarriage rates.[30]

These statistics are regionally disaggregated, not locally. For more rigorous study, further disaggregation of violence will be necessary. Town-level disaggregation of Yugoslav violence is not available, however, and given what we know about data on civil wars, it may never be unearthed with any accuracy. But even at the current level of disaggregation, the data, rather than undermining my India-based conclusions, are by and large consistent with them. The relation between ethnic violence and interethnic civic engagement is inverse.

Consider Northern Ireland now. The available data on post-1969 Catholic-Protestant violence there, as opposed to Yugoslavia, are disaggregated at the town level.[31] And, despite the larger conflict, some towns have indeed remained peaceful. What explains the variance?

The existing studies have dealt at length with conflict and discourse at the national level, not with why there was variance at the lower levels of aggregation. Among the few exceptions is that of John Darby, who studied three local communities in Greater Belfast—Kileen-Banduff, the Upper Ashbourne Estates, and Dunville.[32] All three communities analyzed by him have mixed populations, but the first two have had a lot of violence since the late 1960s, whereas the third has been quiet. Darby found that as expected, churches, schools, and political parties were segregated in all three communities, but Dunville had some distinctive features not shared by the other two. In contrast to the segregated voluntary groups in the first two communities, Dunville had mixed Rotary and Lions Clubs, as well as clubs for soccer, bowling, cricket, athletics, boxing, field hockey, swimming, table tennis, and golf. There was also a vigorous and mixed Single Parents Club. These results, too, are quite consistent with my findings.

Studies of racial violence in the United States are also of interest. From the perspective of a cumulative research program, however, the comparative relevance of American materials is potentially highly challenging.

There is no good theory emerging from these studies that can explain city-level variance in racial violence in the 1960s. Why were Newark, New Jersey, Detroit, Michigan, and Los Angeles, California, which together accounted for a very large proportion of all deaths in the 1960s riots, so violent? And why did southern cities, though politically engaged, not have riots in the 1960s?[33] The studies show that economic inequalities between African and white Americans explained neither the *timing* nor the *location* of riots, but no firm alternative explanations have been provided. Lieberson and Silverman's work comes reasonably close to what I am arguing for India: they emphasize local integration, especially African American participation in the local government structures.[34] But no scholar, to my knowledge, has investigated whether civic associations—labor unions, churches, PTAs, and so on—were on the whole racially better integrated in the peaceful cities.[35]

If they were not—and here lies the innovative potential of American race relations in a comparative sense—we might need an initial distinction in our theory between (a) multiethnic societies that have a history of segregated civic sites (unions, churches, schools, business associations)—for example, the United States and South Africa—and (b) multiethnic societies whose ethnic groups have led an intermixed civic life—for instance, India. Interracial or intercommunal civic engagement may be a key vehicle of peace in the latter but, given the relative absence of common black-white civic sites in countries like the United States, there may not have been any space for interracial associational engagement historically, leading to puzzles about the precise mechanisms of peace in a different historical and social setting.

Indeed, if we think further about this distinction, it may actually be more accurate to say that some *groups* in a society may be historically segregated, not *societies* as a whole. In India, where political parties, unions, business associations, film clubs, and voluntary agencies are by and large ethnically quite mixed, segregation has marked relations between the scheduled castes, who were "untouchable" for centuries, and the upper castes, who were ritually and socially "superior." Historically, there have been no associational sites where the upper castes and the untouchables could come together. Similarly, Protestants, Catholics, and Jews could eventually find common civic sites in the United States, but blacks and whites on the whole could not.[36]

"Self-policing," a mechanism of peace theoretically proposed by Fearon and Laitin but yet to be empirically examined, may well be relevant to such segregated settings.[37] In the terminology developed in this book, it means intraethnic, or intracommunal, policing. If exercised by elders, by an ethnic association, or by civic organizations such as black churches, intraethnic policing may lead to the same result that interethnic engagement does in India. Future research must take such alternative possibilities seriously. Much remains to be learned.

Appendix A. Questionnaire for the Project on Hindu-Muslim Relations in India

Neighborhood:
Hindu-Dominated/Muslim-Dominated/Mixed:
Peaceful/Violence-prone/Had violence/Tensions in 1992–93

I. BIOGRAPHICAL

A. Personal

1. Name
2. Gender: M/F
3. Religion: Hindu/Muslim
4. Age
5. Caste/Zat/Biradari:
6. Education (if any):
7. Occupation:
8. How long have you lived in this mohalla/locality?
9. Where did you live prior to moving here?
10. If a migrant into the city, where did you come from? And when?

B. Family

1. Could we talk about your family?
Children/siblings/parents
Living with you?

Age
Education
Occupation
(Names not necessary)
a.
b.
c.
d.
e.
f.
g.
h.
i.
j.

C. Economic

1a. May we now talk about the economic condition of your family? Compared to the past, is your economic condition
    i. better
    ii. worse
    iii. the same

1b. When, in your view, did it become better or worse, and why? If the same, why hasn't it changed?

2. What was the traditional occupation of your family?

3a. May we talk to you about the economic condition of your community in this mohalla/ locality?
    Compared to the past, in your view, are they
    i. better
    ii. worse
    iii. the same

3b. If better or worse, when did it change and why? If no change, why no change?

4. Have some castes/zats/biradari done economically better, or the entire Hindu/Muslim community in the mohalla or locality?

5. Are there many in your family or neighborhood who went to the Middle East in the last 10–20 years? They must be better off. Are their children also better educated, or is there no impact on education?

6. Do you own a:
    i. scooter/motorbike/moped
    ii. bicycle
    iii. car?

D. Education

1. Could you please tell us about the educational levels of your family? Have/Do your parents/children gone/go to school?

Highest grade attained
Gender
Type of school
Medium of
Highest grade attained
sibling/parent
Instruction
Highest grade planned
Type of school:

    a. Madarsas

    b. Government

    c. Public/convent

    d. Private

Medium:

    i. English

    ii. Hindi

    iii. Urdu

    iv. Gujarati

    v. Telugu

    vi. Malayalam

2a. Do you read newspapers? If yes, which ones?

2b. If not (or even if yes), how do you get news?

    i. Radio

    ii. TV

    iii. Others

2ci. What sorts of programs on radio/TV interest you? (get 2–3 titles, and briefly describe whether related to films, serials, business, sports, news, etc.).

2cii. Did you watch Ramayana, Mahabharata, and Tipu Sultan on TV? What do you think of them?

    Ramayana

    Mahabharata

    Tipu Sultan

2d. Do the programs on TV/radio present a balanced or good picture of your community? Do they give more attention to other communities?

3. Ask literate families. In your view, should girls be educated as much as boys? If the answer is not, please ask why.

Ask illiterate families:

4a. Did you want to send children, both girls and boys, to school? Or was it not possible at all?

4b. If you have the opportunity, will you send both boys and girls to school?

II. CULTURAL AND RELIGIOUS CONCERNS

Could we talk to you about religious and cultural matters?

1. Are you religious? Do you worship/do namaz? If yes, daily/weekly/irregularly?

2. In your view, has your community become more religious than before? Explain (are there more mosques/moadarsas/temples in the area? Do more people go to them?)

3. For what matters (marriages, property matters, education, politics) do you consult a Maulvi/Pandit, if at all?

4. Should there, in your view, be a common civil code about marriage and property for all communities in this country, or should different communities have different personal laws? Why?

5. It is often said that when a cricket match takes place between India and Pakistan, some people applaud Pakistan. Do you remember any such thing? How do you feel about it?

Muslim Respondents only:

6a. When you get together for Friday prayers, does the Maulana/Maulvi talk about only religious matters or other matters as well? If other matters, what are those?

6b. Do you have an exchange of views with other co-religionists when you get together for Friday prayers? If yes, on what matters?

7a. Does the Tablighi Jamaat, or some other Jamaat (or Anjuman) come to your area for religious preaching? Which ones?

7b. What do they say?

7c. Do you agree with their views about religion?

7d. Do other people in the locality agree with them?

8. Are there differences among the Muslims of your locality on zat/biradari? What kind?

9. Islam allows up to four wives. When Prophet Mohammed announced this in the seventh century, it was a revolutionary step because men before that used to have many more wives and women's rights were not well-defined. In today's conditions, can or should polygamy be practiced?

III. INTERCOMMUNITY RELATIONS

1. Which events/periods of the nation's or your regional/local history do you find most significant? Why? (Even illiterate people should be asked this question. Note what they say.)
     i. Before the British period
        Local and/or national events
        Local and/or national heroes
        Local and/or national villains
     ii. During the British period
        Local and/or national events
        Local and/or national heroes
        Local and/or national villains
     iii. Independence and after
        Local and/or national events
        Local and/or national heroes
        Local and/or national villains

(For local history, seek in Hyderabad and Lucknow views on the Nizams and Nawabs; in

Calicut, on Malabar rebellion; in Gujarat, Somnath and Gandhi's message of Hindu-Muslim unity; in Aligarh, AMU)

2. How did you learn about these events?

    i. from elders

    ii. books/newspapers

    iii. TV/radio

    iv. others

3. Do people of other religions live in your locality/mohalla? Which religions? Can you tell us about your relations with them?

    i. Do families visit each other?

    ii. Are festivals jointly celebrated (which ones), or do families visit each other during festivals?

    iii. Do you eat together—sometimes, often, once in a while, never?

    iv. Do children play together in the neighborhood?

    v. Do your children feel any religion-based discrimination in schools? If yes, describe.

    vi. Does the history taught in schools present a fair image of your community? Give instances.

    vii. Are there people of other religions in your workplace? How would you describe your relations with them?

    viii. Are you a member of any associations or clubs? What kind (business, trade union, professional, social)?

    ix. Are there members of other religious communities in these associations/clubs? Which communities?

    Do you interact with them?

Questions 4–7 for the 60 plus age category only:

4. Can we have you recall your childhood for us? How were the Hindu-Muslim relations in the 1930s and 1940s?

    i. in the locality/mohalla (please give instances)

    ii. in the workplace (please give instances)

5. Do you remember the events of 1947–48? Did the relations change at that point?

6. Did many people leave for Pakistan in your locality?

7. What happened to Hindu-Muslim relations in the 1950s?

    a. improved

    b. deteriorated

    c. no change

Questions 8–16, for everyone. Question 8 may not be answered by those younger than 38–40:

8. Do you remember the Indo-Pak wars of 1965 and 1971? Did those wars affect Hindu-Muslim relations in your locality, school, or workplace? If yes, in what ways?

9. What about the last ten years? How have the Hindu-Muslim relations been in the locality, school, and workplace?

10. Will Hindu-Muslim relations improve in the future?

11a. Have there been any riots or tensions in this locality?

11b. Who helps you most during times of riots or tensions?
> i. neighbor, irrespective of religion
> ii. political leaders
> iii. administration and police
> iv. social workers

12. Why, in your view, do riots take place, if they do in your city/locality?

13. Are there, in your locality/mohalla, committees/associations/organizations that have both Hindus and Muslims and that deal with social or cultural life or matters such as electricity, sanitation, and water?

14a. Do these committees/organizations/organizations/clubs try to maintain peace in times of Hindu-Muslim tensions?

14b. Do they succeed?

15a. Do people form Hindu-Muslim peace committees in times of tensions in your locality? (Note that this question is different from # 13, which is about pre-existing committees for purposes other than peace.)

15b. Do these committees wind up when tensions are over, or do they continue even after tensions end?

16. What, in your view, should be done to stop riots, if they take place in your city?

17. Why, in your view, were Hindu-Muslim relations peaceful in your city?

18. Have the relations been peaceful since 1993, or has the violence of 1992–93 altered relations forever?

IV. ADMINISTRATION AND POLICE

1. Which government offices have you needed, or do you need, most?
> i. municipality
> ii. police
> iii. courts
> iv. district collector
> v. banks

2. Do you face any difficulties in getting work done? Do you feel any biases in the way government offices deal with you?

3. Do the police help you when you need them? What biases, if any, did you notice in police behavior?

4. Do you find any differences between the PAC and the police?

5a. Is your community well-represented in the police and administration?

5b. If the numbers of officers belonging to your community go up in the police and administration, will it make a difference to you? Will it benefit the community?

V. POLITICAL MATTERS

Could we talk about political matters?

1. Are you interested in politics? At what level, and why?
> i. mohalla
> ii. caste/zat/biradari

    iii. municipality
    iv. state
    v. nation

2. Do you vote? How many times have you voted in elections?

3. Do you have a special affection for a particular party? Why?

4. Have you always voted for this party, or have you changed? If yes, what accounts for the change?

5a. What considerations matter to you when you vote?

    i. caste
    ii. religion
    iii. party
    iv. qualifications of the candidate
    v. others

5b. Do you consult some people before voting?

    i. family head
    ii. caste/zat/biradari leaders
    iii. religious leaders on the area
    iv. party leaders
    v. any others

6. Some people say that if in politics an alliance between the Muslims and "backward" castes emerges, as it has in U.P. and Bihar, it will best serve the interests of both Muslims and lower castes. What do you think?

For Muslim Respondents Only (Questions 7–14)

7. Some people say that Muslims should have a national party of their own. What do you think?

8. Some people say that there should be job reservations for Muslims. What do you think?

9. Do you find any differences between the Congress and the BJP? (to be asked everywhere except Kerala)

10. Ask only in Hyderabad and Calicut: Do the leaders of the Muslim League (Kerala)/ MIM (Hyderabad) work for the Muslim community or only for their own personal interests? Please give reasons.

11. If the answer is they are only self-interested, ask: why do you vote for them if you do?

12. Do the Muslim leaders in the Congress Party work for the community?

13. Are there any national or state-level Muslim leaders you trust?

14a. Are there enough Muslim leaders in your municipal corporation/state assembly/parliament?

14b. If there were more Muslim members, would it help the community?

14c. Are there any Hindu leaders who can benefit, or have benefited, the Muslim community? Explain how.

14d. What, in your view, are the most pressing issues for Indian Muslims? Maximum attention should be placed on which of these issues? (Ask them to prioritize)

    i. education, health, and employment
    ii. physical security
    iii. religion and language

Why?

For all respondents

15. Some people argue that Muslims are pampered in this country. Do you agree? If yes, tell us why you think so.

16a. Do you have any problems or complaints with the Hindu/Muslim community?

16b. If yes, what should they do that will please you?

Context and date of the interview:

Appendix B. Data Entry Protocol
for the Riot Database

Definition of Event: What is a communal riot? Following Olzak's work on race conflict in the United States, we might identify an event as a communal riot if (a) there is violence, and (b) two or more communally identified groups confront each other or members of the other group at some point during the violence. In other words, Hindu riots against the police would not count. Nor would PAC or police shooting of Muslims if there was no Hindu-Muslim violence before or after. If the event is police versus a single group, we should not enter the case as either probable or definite, but instead enter it in the "Police versus single group" box. In events involving one communally identified political group (Muslim League, BJP) and some group X, not necessarily the police (for example, violence between the Muslim League and Congress or violence between the Muslim League and CPM), unless we have reason to believe otherwise, the event *should* be classified as a probable (strong/small likelihood).

Town/City: Enter the name as given in the newspaper. Then check it later to see if the spelling conforms to the official spelling given in the index to the Oxford Atlas of India. We'll use the official spelling as standard, which may involve, e.g., changing "Ahmedabad" to "Ahmadabad"

Village:

District: Enter when given

State: Note the present-day state as well as the state name at the time of the riot.

For example, a riot in 1968 in Mysore state should be marked "Karnataka, Mysore." Where there have been boundary changes or where there is general uncertainty about the name of the state in which a riot occurs, mark "Yes" in the "Coding Question" category and mark the specific query next to an asterisk in the "Notes" section.

Population: This data will be entered later from census data.

Year: Year in which riot takes place. If a riot covers two years, enter as follows: "1971, 1972."

Month: Use the drop-down menu. "Month in which riot takes place." If a riot covers two months, hit the "other" category in drop-down down menu and enter as follows: "May, June."

Day: The day on which the riot was reported to have begun. As reports usually come out one or two days after the initial incident, it is important to count back to the original day.

Reported Cause: The purpose of this section is to specify general categories under which the causes of communal riots can be grouped. The list is self-explanatory and hopefully comprehensive. When a reported cause does not fit any of the categories on the list, enter it as "other" and list the cause concisely in no more than five words. For example, "Other: Forced Singing of Vande Mataram." We should be consistent as far as possible in the wording we use here, so that if the same event turns up more than once as a candidate for "other," we can later incorporate it as a new category without having to go back and standardize individual descriptions.

Local Precipitating Events: If the local precipitating event is the same as the reported cause, enter it as such where the categories are identical. For example, if a land dispute is both the reported cause and the precipitating event, the entry in both cases will be economic interest (land) and economic interest (land). In three cases, (1) public ritual/festivities, (2) political, and (3) criminal, the reported cause categories are not replicated in the list of precipitating events but broken down further. Public ritual/festivities is broken down into (a) Namaz/puja/aarti, (b) religious procession, (c) marriage procession, or (d) consecration of religious site. Political is broken down into (a) bandh, (b) demonstration, or (c) factional fight. There is one common category in the list of precipitating events that covers both public ritual and a political event: speech by political/religious leader. Finally, "criminal" is broken down into (a) gang violence, (b) attack, or (c) theft. In these cases when reported cause and precipitating event are the same, the categories used to describe them will be different—the broader category will be used under reported cause and the more specific category under precipitating event. One example: when a tazia procession is both the reported cause and precipitating event, it will be entered as public ritual/festivities (other) in "reported cause" and as religious procession under "local precipitating event." When a speech by Sadhvi Rithambara at a VHP rally is both the reported cause and the precipitating event, it will be listed as *both* political (agitation) and public ritual/festivities (other) in the "reported cause" section and as speech by political/religious leader under "local precipitating event."

When the local precipitating event is different from the reported cause, there is no cause for worry. We just use the categories that seem most relevant in each case.

Hindu-Muslim: The purpose here is merely to identify whether an event involved Hindu-Muslim conflict, or alternatively, e.g., involved Shiah-Sunni or Hindu-Buddhist conflict. Unless specifically asked by Varshney or Wilkinson to list these conflicts, you should only mark "yes" in this box.

Probable Case: Your usual entry will be "Definite Case."

Coding Question: If some information in a particular case is ambiguous, and the coder feels that a new category/term should be added to accommodate it, or some discussion is required before categorization, enter "yes" here. Then in a note at the bottom state your question. Use the following example as guide: "*Event connected with state political conflict in Lucknow. Should I include within 'Political conflict (state politics)' or create a separate heading?"

A *definite case* is one where the following conditions apply: *If the riot was reported at the time of the event, or subsequently,* as "communal" in nature, unless there is good reason to believe that another competing mobilization (such as caste or ethnicity) may have been responsible for the violence. For example, in Ahmedabad in 1985, the violence was simultaneously motivated by caste and communal identity. When this situation occurs (i.e., violence is reported as "communal" and as, e.g., "caste" or "tribal") then we mark the event as "strong likelihood."

As well as the above conditions, where there is no room for ambiguity, all cases involving unspecified "group clashes" and the following precipitating events should also be regarded as "definite" unless they occur in Punjab. (In Punjab, because of the minuscule Muslim population, we assume all unspecified group clashes are Hindu-Sikh. In 1971 only 114,447 people of 13,551,960 were Muslim, and of these only 42,306 were classified as "urban." In no place did Muslims account for more than 1 percent of a town's population. Source: *Census of India 1971,* Series 17-Punjab, Part II-C (i) and Part V-A, Distribution of Population by Religion and Scheduled Castes, pp.11–23.)

where "cow slaughter" is the precipitating event for the riot/group clash

where "music in front of mosque" is the precipitating event for the riot/group clash

where "music in front of religious building/place of worship" is the precipitating event for the riot/group clash

A *strong likelihood* case is (a) one where an event is reported as "communal" but there is good reason to believe that another competing mobilization may have been responsible for the violence. For example, in Ahmedabad in 1985, the violence was simultaneously seen as motivated by caste and communal identity. When this situation occurs (i.e., violence is reported as "communal" and as, e.g., "caste" or "tribal") then we mark the event as "strong likelihood." (b) One where an event is not reported as "communal," but the group clash occurs in an area where "communal violence" was reported shortly before or after the event. (c) As well as the above conditions, all cases involving unspecified "group clashes" and the following precipitating events should also be marked as "Strong likelihood":

where "pig slaughter" is the precipitating event for the riot/group clash

where a more general phrase such as "animal slaughter" is the precipitating event for the riot/group clash

where "Use of public space for religious ritual" is the precipitating event for the riot/ group clash

where "Procession" is the precipitating event for the riot/group clash

where "Construction" is the precipitating event for the riot/group clash, and the construction *does* involve a building used for religious purposes where "Illegal Attack on Building" is the precipitating event for the riot/group clash, and the attack *does* involve a building used for religious purposes

where "Demolition/Attempted Demolition" is the precipitating event for the riot/group clash, and the demolition or attempted demolition *does* involve a building used for religious purposes

A *weak likelihood* is found in the following situations: If unspecified "group clashes" are mentioned in connection with the following events, they should always be entered as "weak likelihood":

where "Accident" is the precipitating event for the riot/group clash

where "Fight" is the precipitating event for the riot/group clash

where "Quarrels over women (eve teasing)" is the precipitating event for the riot/group clash

where "Quarrels over women (rape)" is the precipitating event for the riot/group clash

where "Quarrels over women (intermarriage)" is the precipitating event for the riot/group clash

where "Construction" is the precipitating event for the riot/group clash, and the construction does not involve a building used for religious purposes

where "Illegal Attack on Building" is the precipitating event for the riot/group clash, and the attack does not involve a building used for religious purposes

where "Demolition/Attempted Demolition" is the precipitating event for the riot/group clash, and the demolition or attempted demolition does not involve a building used for religious purposes.

Duration in Days: Count from the beginning of the riot to the last day on which violence was reported to have taken place. If there is a lull ("lull" defined as no reported incident of violence) in violence of a day or more separating incidents of violence in the same town (e.g., June 1–7, June 9–12), then enter this as two separate cases.

Killed, Injured, Arrested: The most accurate numbers available from the *Times of India*. In general these numbers will be the last figures quoted, which may be printed a week or even some months after a riot has actually ended (particularly if the figures are reported from the findings of a subsequent riot inquiry). In some cases, however, a specific figure will be quoted at the end of five days of rioting (e.g., "local officials report 43 killed, 128 injured, 405 arrests") but a week later only general figures will be given (e.g., "In the recent riots in x, an estimated 50 people were killed, and more than 500 injured"). In this case note that we should use the higher figures of 50 and 500 and make a note of the lower figures. Always list all "final" figures and their sources.

Source: Enter appropriate source from drop-down menus.

Source Dates: If more than one, enter using American-style notation, as follows: "3/8/71, 3/23/71."

Officials: The names of all the officials named in press accounts as being connected with the event in their official capacities, as well as their ranks, e.g., Mr. Ram Sharma (DM), Mr. J. N. Chaturvedi (SP). Information on any action these officials took (or didn't take) which may have alleviated or intensified the riot should be entered in the notes. The following abbreviations are acceptable: SP (Superintendent of Police), DM (District Magistrate), IG (Inspector General), and DIG (Deputy Inspector General). At present, all other ranks should be entered in full form in brackets after the name of the official. New abbreviations may be used only after consultation.

Officials Transferred/Suspended: The rank of the official(s) should be listed. Abbreviation rules are as above.

Type of Policing Arrangement: Mark all police forces used, e.g., in a serious riot we may have "Police, PAC, BSF, Army." The term "police" is the default for local police. If a force was used in an area before the first day of violence (i.e., not ordered to an area but actually used in an area), enter it in this way: "PAC before, Army before." Normally the PAC, etc. only arrives after the outbreak of violence, so the default is simply "PAC" to save ourselves from typing "PAC after" every time. It is important for searching purposes that the space between, e.g., "PAC" and "before" is typed as option space rather than just a space.

Link Made to Outside Event: If a link is reported in the newspaper to events outside the city where a riot takes place (e.g., a communal riot nearby), then mark "yes"; if not then mark "no." After this write in the nature of the outside event, e.g., "Communal Riot" using the same terms (complete with option space entries) that are used for the "reported cause" section.

Police vs. Single Group: If an event fits only this category (i.e., the police do not attack Muslims after a Hindu-Muslim riot has already broken out), then write "yes" in this space.

Dalit/Muslim: Mark "yes" if an event fits this category; otherwise ignore.

Notes: A specific citation should always be given after each note, e.g., "TOI, 3/24/78."

The following information should always be entered when available: Hindu/Muslim residential and employment patterns, RSS/Jamaat involvement, or the involvement of any other organizations.

Appendix C. Regression Results:

Hindu-Muslim Riots, 1950–1995

The large-n data set allows us to run regressions and test some hypotheses in a systematic way. Given their popularity or relevance, we tested three hypotheses about the determinants of Hindu-Muslim riots in India. The first one is that higher levels of literacy are correlated with lower rates of riot incidence (Sen Hypothesis). The statistical tests employed here reveal that the relationship between the literacy level of a city and the number of deaths it had in riots, or the number of riots it witnessed, is insignificant.

The second hypothesis has to do with feelings of "psychological insecurity of the majority community" (one version) and "greater assertiveness of the minority community" (a second version). It expects a higher incidence of riots in towns with a greater percentage of Muslims. The test results here largely seem to deny a significant correlation between the percentage of Muslims in a town and its riot incidence.

Finally, the third hypothesis is put forward by the antimodernists, which would indicate that larger cities are more likely to be riot-prone than smaller ones. They argue that a culturally chauvinistic backlash is more likely in a setting of modernity, which tends to erode cultural heritages. Another interpretation is possible, however. A larger city is also likely to lead to weakened face-to-face interaction, unless organizations or associations are built to bring people together. A smaller city with a greater sense of community is less likely to have a high incidence of rioting. It turns out that all the statistical tests find a positive correlation between the size of the population and the dependent variables used as proxies for riot-proneness and riot intensity.

STANDARD LEAST SQUARES REGRESSION RESULTS

The first basic set of regressions was run with "number of deaths" and "number of incidents" as dependent variables and "lit" (literacy rate), "mus" (percentage of Muslims), and "populati" (population) as the independent variables. The figure for "number injured" was not used as a dependent variable, because as explained in Chapter 4, this statistic was not covered consistently across regions by the Bombay edition of the *Times of India* (the source for the data). The results are summarized in tables App.C.1 and App.C.2.

We can see quite clearly that the literacy variable (lit) is insignificant for both dependent variables that can be consistently used to proxy riot incidence. The percentage of Muslims is not significant for the first (number of deaths) and is barely significant for the second (number of incidents). On the other hand, the population variable is clearly significant for both dependent variables.

Although results using "number of deaths" and "number of incidents" are useful, however, they do not indicate whether a city should be considered riot-prone. For instance, a city with many small skirmishes but with hardly any deaths would be overrepresented in the second category and not have a presence in the first. Also, it is not clear if such a city should be considered to be highly riot-prone. On the other hand, it is also true that some towns have one or two serious riots with high fatalities but have remained peaceful for the rest of the 46-year period under consideration.

What we need, therefore, is a definition of "riot-proneness" that incorporates both of the above features and that will identify the cities that are particularly susceptible to riots for fur-

Table App. C.1. Riot Deaths in Relation to Literacy Rate, Muslim Percentage, and Size of City

Source	SS	df	MS
Model	625222.739	3	208407.58
Residual	1649538.95	64	25774.0461
Total	2274761.69	67	33951.667

Deaths	Coefficient	Standard Error	t	$P > |t|$	[95% Conf. Interval]	
lit	.0823038	3.201945	0.026	0.980	−6.314317	6.478924
mus	2.927024	1.80401	1.623	0.110	−.6768999	6.530948
populati	.0410712	.0088886	4.621	0.000	.0233142	.0588282
cons	−40.90201	254.9974	−0.160	0.873	−550.3178	468.5138

Note: All lines starting with a (.) are stata commands.
Number of obs = 68 $F(3, 64) = 8.09$ Prob > F = 0.0001 $R^2 = 0.2749$ Adj. R^2 = 0.2409   Root MSE = 160.54

Table App. C.2. Number of Riots in Relation to Literacy Rates, Muslim Percentage, and Size of City

Source	SS	df	MS
Model	3648.33824	3	1216.11275
Residual	7677.47058	64	119.960478
Total	11325.8088	67	169.041923

Incident	Coefficient	Standard Error	t	$P > \lvert t \rvert$	[95% Conf. Interval]	
lit	.1148477	.2184448	0.526	0.601	−.3215459	.5512413
mus	.2459815	.1230741	1.999	0.050	.0001127	.4918503
populati	.0030837	.0006064	5.085	0.000	.0018723	.0042951
cons	−9.155028	17.39656	−0.526	0.601	−43.90866	25.5986

Number of obs = 68 $F(3, 64) = 10.14$ Prob > F = 0.0000 $R^2 = 0.3221$ Adj. R^2 = 0.2904   Root MSE = 10.953

ther analysis. Since such a definition must necessarily be arbitrary (there is no prescribed standard in the literature), it is advisable to apply progressively stronger conditions to the different "cut-off" conditions for a town to be considered riot-prone.

LOGISTIC REGRESSION RESULTS

Four definitions, listed in Chapter 4, are used for the following analysis. The weakest definition (rp1) is that a town is considered riot-prone if it has had at least 15 deaths spread out over at least 3 riots and over 2 five-year periods. Since the classification of riot-proneness assigns a town a value of either 1 (if riot-prone) or 0 (if not riot-prone), rp1 (along with and rp2, rp3, and rp4) is a discrete dependent variable.

A town is considered riot-prone under rp2 if it has had at least 20 deaths over at least 4 ri-

Table App. C.3. Riot-Proneness in Relation to Literacy Rate, Muslim Percentage, and Size of City (RP1)

Log Likelihood = −29.365904

rp1	Coefficient	Standard Error	z	$P > \lvert z \rvert$	[95% Conf. Interval]	
lit	.0810143	.0549895	1.473	0.141	−.0267631	.1887918
mus	.1602692	.0481273	3.330	0.001	.0659415	.2545969
populati	.000672	.0003088	2.176	0.030	.0000667	.0012772
cons	−10.13634	4.723092	−2.146	0.032	−19.39343	−.8792526

Number of obs = 68   chi2(3) = 31.74   Prob > chi2 = 0.0000   Psuedo $R^2 = 0.3508$

Table App. C.4. Riot-Proneness in Relation to Literacy Rate, Muslim Percentage, and Size of City (RP2)

Log Likelihood = −27.789341

rp2	Coefficient	Standard Error	z	P > | z |	[95% Conf. Interval]	
lit	.02182	.0539106	0.405	0.686	−.0838429	.1274829
mus	.1232096	.0413212	2.982	0.003	.0422217	.2041976
populati	.0008037	.0003333	2.411	0.016	.0001505	.0014569
cons	−5.626409	4.491866	−1.253	0.210	−14.43031	3.177488

Number of obs = 68   chi2(3) = 30.03   Prob > chi2 = 0.0000   Psuedo R^2 = 0.3508

ots and over 3 five-year periods. It meets the conditions for rp3 if it has had at least 25 deaths over a minimum of 5 riots over 4 five-year periods. Finally, the most stringent condition for a city to be called riot prone is under rp4, which requires that the city in question have at least 50 deaths over a minimum of 10 riots over at least 5 five-year periods.

But this time, we cannot use a standard least squares regression because the dependent variable is discrete and can only take on the values 0 and 1. So, we have to use a logistic regression wherein a positive coefficient for an independent variable indicates that an increase in that variable implies an increase in the probability that the dependent variable have value 1 (table App.C.3).

As we can see, the logit regressions also support the notion that literacy rates are not significant determinants of riot-proneness and that high populations do significantly imply a higher probability of being riot-prone. The Muslim variable is a little bit unclear. It is significant in the less stringent classifications of riot-proneness (rp1 and rp2) and not so in the more stringent classifications (rp3 and rp4). At the higher levels of lethality (rp3 and rp4), the percentage of Muslims ceases to be a dominant factor and we must look at other explanations for the data.

Table App. C.5. Riot-Proneness in Relation to Literacy Rate, Muslim Percentage, and Size of City (RP3)

Log Likelihood = −30.047404

rp3	Coefficient	Standard Error	z	P > | z |	[95% Conf. Interval]	
lit	.016745	.0520455	0.322	0.748	−.0852623	.1187523
mus	.0434926	.0278563	1.561	0.118	−.0111047	.09809
populati	.0006855	.0002843	2.411	0.016	.0001283	.0012427
cons	−4.083352	4.173058	−0.979	0.328	−12.2624	4.095692

Number of obs = 68   chi2(3) = 16.38   Prob > chi2 = 0.0009   Psuedo R^2 = 0.2142

Table App. C.6. Riot-Proneness in Relation to Literacy Rate, Muslim Percentage, and Size of City (RP4)

Log Likelihood = −13.666236

rp4	Coefficient	Standard Error	z	P > |z|	[95% Conf. Interval]	
lit	−.0961294	.087699	−1.096	0.273	−.2680163	.0757574
mus	.0347261	.0414447	0.838	0.402	−.046504	.1159562
populati	.0009442	.0003556	2.655	0.008	.0002472	.0016412
cons	2.477201	6.583626	0.376	0.707	−10.42647	15.38087

Number of obs = 68   chi2(3) = 21.93   Prob > chi2 = 0.0001   Psuedo R^2 = 0.4451

Notes

CHAPTER 1. INTRODUCTION

1. For an analysis of how ethnicity, on the basis of a myth of common ancestry, can take so many forms (language, race, religion, and sometimes even dress and diction), see Donald Horowitz, *Ethnic Groups in Conflict* (Berkeley: University of California Press, 1985), pp. 41–54.

2. Ibid., pp. 21–24.

3. This is not to say that community life *within* ethnic groups, as opposed to conflict *between* ethnic groups, has not been studied as part of civil society. A striking, though not the only, example is Michael Walzer, *What It Means to Be American* (New York: Marsilio, 1992). The view that ethnic (or religious) community life can be called civic is, of course, contested by many. The debate is summarized and evaluated in the next chapter.

4. In *Making Democracy Work: Civic Traditions in Italy* (Princeton: Princeton University Press, 1993), Robert Putnam has used the term "social capital" for civic networks. My use of the term "networks of engagement" differs from Putnam's in two ways. First, my focus is on intercommunal civic ties, not civic ties per se. Because it is correlated both with violence and peace, the term "social capital" must be distinguished from intercommunal networks of engagement. Communal organizations, focusing on a single religious group only, can be shown to have a great deal of trust among its members. If they exist in plenty, such organizations, by Putnam's definition, can endow a town with a

high degree of social capital. These organizations, however, are not only often incapable of preventing Hindu-Muslim riots, but they are also associated with the escalation of communal violence. What matters for communal violence is not whether communal life or social capital exists but whether social and civic ties cut *across* the Hindu and Muslim groups. Stated differently, intercommunal, not intracommunal, networks are critical to communal peace. Second, although civic engagement in Putnam's work rightly includes both formal and informal interactions between individuals and families, the difference between the two forms should be noted as well. For ethnic peace, everyday engagement between ethnic groups may be better than no interaction at all, but it is also qualitatively different from the more formal, organized engagement. Everyday interethnic engagement may be enough to maintain peace on a small scale (villages or small towns), but it is no substitute for interethnic associations in larger settings (cities and metropolises), as I will argue later at length (Chapter 2). In his more recent work, Putnam has started speaking about varieties of social capital—e.g., "bridging" and "bonding." See Putnam, *Bowling Alone* (New York: Simon and Schuster, 2000), ch. 1.

5. Among the exceptions are James Fearon and David Laitin, "Explaining Ethnic Cooperation," *American Political Science Review* (December 1996): 715–35; Horowitz, *Ethnic Groups in Conflict;* Myron Weiner, *Sons of the Soil: Migration and Ethnic Conflict in India* (Princeton: Princeton University Press, 1978); Crawford Young, *The Politics of Cultural Pluralism* (Madison: University of Wisconsin Press, 1976).

6. The need for variance in social science research has been emphasized by Gary King, Robert Keohane, and Sydney Verba, *Designing Social Inquiry* (Princeton: Princeton University Press, 1993).

7. The data set was put together in collaboration with Steven Wilkinson, whose own work, based on the statistics thus collected, formed the basis of his Ph.D. dissertation, "The Electoral Incentives for Ethnic Violence: Hindu-Muslim Riots in India" (Political Science Department, MIT, 1998). The preliminary results of our collaboration were reported in Ashutosh Varshney and Steven I. Wilkinson, "Hindu-Muslim Riots (1960–93): New Evidence, Possible Remedies," Special Paper Series (Delhi: Rajiv Gandhi Foundation, June 1995).

8. The last two cities are not normally viewed as riot-prone. But they have had so many small riots, and some large ones in the 1950s, that they are unable to escape the list of worst cities in a long-term perspective (1950–95). In a 1970–95 time series, Calcutta is unlikely to figure; Delhi may also disappear.

9. To ensure international standardization, the terms "town" and "city" will be used interchangeably in this book. In terms of population size, what is called a city in Europe may look like a town by Asian standards. On the other hand, in terms of civic amenities, many of India's cities would be comparable to towns in Europe.

10. Lloyd Rudolph and Susanne Rudolph, *In Pursuit of Lakshmi* (Chicago: University of Chicago Press, 1987), p. 196.

11. L. K. Advani, a leader of the BJP, interviewed in *Sunday* (Calcutta), July 22, 1990.

12. Syed Shahabuddin, a prominent Muslim leader, has often made this argument in lectures, discussions, and political speeches.

13. Rudolph and Rudolph, *In Pursuit of Lakshmi*, p. 195.

14. Peace committees are also sometimes imposed from above by the local administration. Such committees may or may not be effective. My argument is primarily about the committees that emerge as citizen initiatives.

15. M. N. Srinivas, *Remembered Village* (Berkeley: University of California Press, 1979).

16. These connections can be proved social-scientifically, not legally. The latter requires establishing *individual* culpability, not obvious links between politicians and gangs *as groups*.

17. Paul Brass, *Theft of an Idol* (Princeton: Princeton University Press, 1997).

18. Alternatively, one could also use a medical analogy. When civic engagement is vibrant and cuts across the two communities, it provides a city with enough strength to resist most viruses, if not all. If it is absent or weak, the city becomes vulnerable to small viruses, becoming sick at the slightest exposure or provocation.

19. For a lucid explanation of the two theories, see Paul Krugman, "The Economics of Qwerty," in Krugman, *Peddling Prosperity* (New York: Norton, 1995), pp. 221–44.

20. The violence is primarily confined to the old city in Hyderabad. The new city is not much affected.

21. This reasoning also suggests a third difference with Putnam's *Making Democracy Work,* in which the existence of social capital differentiated good governance from bad. The relationship between social capital and communal violence yields a different formulation. If my argument is right, civic networks determine the presence or absence of riots, but they are politically constructed in the long run. Putnam's study emphasized the independent role of social capital both in the short and the long run.

22. To be more technically specific, as the details below will make clear, the sampling was "disproportional stratified," not "proportional stratified." For a clear and concise explanation of the conditions under which such samples introduce economy without sacrificing reliability, see Herbert Blalock, *Social Statistics* (New York: McGraw Hill, 1979), ch. 21, esp. pp. 560–67.

23. Stratifying according to income or class could have been another way of reaching the subaltern, but data on income and class are notoriously hard to come by.

24. Since it is not the main theoretical concern of this project, I have not taken up postmodern arguments in detail here. A more thorough discussion appears in Ashutosh Varshney, "Ethnic Conflict and Postmodernism: A Passage to India," *Comparative Politics* (October 1997).

25. James Scott, *Weapons of the Weak* (New Haven: Yale University Press, 1984).

CHAPTER 2. WHY CIVIL SOCIETY?

1. For the United States, see Stanley Lieberson and Arnold Silverman, "The Precipitants and Underlying Conditions of Race Riots," *American Sociological Review* (December 1965); for Northern Ireland, see Michael Poole, "Geographical Location of Political Violence in Northern Ireland," *Political Violence: Ireland in Comparative Perspective,* ed. John Darby, Nicholas Dodge, and A. C. Hepburn (Belfast: Appletree, 1990).

2. Among the first to make this claim was Karl Deutsch, *Nationalism and Social Communication* (Cambridge: MIT Press, 1953), and among the latest, Eric Hobsbawm, *Nations*

and Nationalism Since 1780: Programme, Myth, Reality (Cambridge: Cambridge University Press, 1989).

3. See the discussion of "subcultural dualism" in Robert Dahl, *Polyarchy* (New Haven: Yale University Press, 1971); Walker Connor, *Ethnonationalism* (Princeton: Princeton University Press, 1994), ch. 2.

4. Myron Weiner, "Affirmative Action: An International Perspective," *Development and Democracy* (May 1993); Thomas Sowell, *Preferential Policies: An International Perspective* (New York: William Morrow, 1990); Timur Kuran, *Private Truths, Public Lies* (Cambridge: Harvard University Press, 1997).

5. The bargain was shifted further in favor of the Malays after 1969. See, e.g., James Jesudason, *Ethnicity and the Economy: The State, Chinese Business, and the MNCs in Malaysia* (Kuala Lumpur: Oxford University Press, 1989).

6. Language as a political issue briefly surfaced again in the 1960s, but that was the last time it determined politics in many states. For reasons why language politics generated the results it did, see David Laitin, "Language Policy and Political Strategy in India," *Policy Sciences* (fall 1989).

7. A classic, essentialist-instrumentalist debate is that between Paul Brass and Francis Robinson on Muslim identity in India. See their exchange in *Political Identity in South Asia,* ed. Malcolm Yapp and David Taylor (London: Curzon, 1979). See also the succinct review of such debates in the introduction to *The Politics of Cultural Pluralism,* ed. Crawford Young (Madison: University of Wisconsin Press, 1995).

8. Robert Kaplan, *Balkan Ghosts: A Journey Through History* (New York: St. Martin's, 1993).

9. Clifford Geertz, "The Integrative Revolution: Primordial Sentiments and Civil Politics in the New States" in *The Interpretation of Cultures* (New York: Basic, 1973).

10. Connor, *Ethnonationalism,* pp. 199–201.

11. Charles Taylor, "Nationalism and Modernity," in *The Morality of Nationalism,* ed. Robert McKim and Jeff Taylor (New York: Oxford University Press, 1997).

12. Russell Hardin, *One for All: The Logic of Group Conflict* (Princeton: Princeton University Press, 1995); Ronald Rogowski, "Causes and Varieties of Nationalism: A Rationalist Account," in *New Nationalisms of the Developed West,* ed. R. Rogowski and E. Teriyakia (London: Routledge, 1985); Michael Hechter, "Explaining Nationalist Violence," *Nations and Nationalism.* 1, no. 1 (April 1995); Paul Brass, *Language, Religion, and Politics in North India* (Cambridge: Cambridge University Press, 1973). An instrumentalist earlier, Brass, as discussed later, is now a postmodernist.

13. Sometimes Ernest Gellner's *Nations and Nationalism* (Oxford: Oxford University Press, 1983) is also seen as a major instrumentalist text. According to Gellner, industrialization led to nationalism in history. The "low" oral cultures, he argued, could not have produced the standardization necessary to run an industrial economy; only "high" cultures with standardized modes of communication could have. I read Gellner more as a functionalist than an instrumentalist. For a clear statement of differences between functionalism and rational choice, see Jon Elster, "Game Theory, Functionalism, and Marxism," *Theory and Society* (fall 1980).

14. Thomas Schelling, *The Strategy of Conflict* (New York: Oxford University Press, 1963), p. 54.

15. Robert Bates, "Ethnic Competition and Modernization in Contemporary Africa," *Comparative Political Studies* 6 (January 1974).

16. See Donald Horowitz, *Ethnic Groups in Conflict* (Berkeley: University of California Press, 1990), pp. 99–135.

17. The point is analogous to Jon Elster's objection to an instrumental conception of norms: "Some argue that . . . norms . . . are tools of manipulation, used to dress up self-interest in a more acceptable garb. But this cannot be true. . . . . If some people successfully exploit norms for self-interested purposes, it can only be because others are willing to let norms take precedence over self-interest." In Elster, *Nuts and Bolts for the Social Sciences* (New York: Cambridge University Press, 1989), p. 118.

18. See Gyan Prakash, introduction to *After Colonialism: Imperial Histories and Postcolonial Displacements* (Princeton: Princeton University Press, 1995), p. 10. This section realizes heavily on my article, "Postmodernism, Civic Engagement and Ethnic Conflict: A Passage to India," *Comparative Politics* (October 1997).

19. For example, Richard Rorty, *Essays on Heidegger and Others* (Cambridge: Cambridge University Press, 1991); Jürgen Habermas, "Modernity versus Post-Modernity," *New German Critique* (winter 1981); Seyla Benhabib, "Epistemologies of Post-Modernism," *New German Critique* (fall 1984). A good overview is Stephen K. White, *Political Theory and Postmodernism* (Cambridge: Cambridge University Press, 1991).

20. Eric Hobsbawm and Terence Ranger, eds., *The Invention of Tradition,* (Cambridge: Cambridge University Press, 1983); Linda Colley, *Britons: Forging the Nation, 1707–1837* (New Haven: Yale University Press, 1992); Benedict Anderson, *Imagined Communities* (London: Verso, 1983).

21. Anderson, *Imagined Communities,* pp. 9–36.

22. Colley, *Britons.*

23. As is widely known, Foucault, Lyotard, and Derrida have provided the principal theoretical inspiration for the postmodern literature. A useful collection of their writings is Thomas Docherty, ed., *Postmodernism: A Reader* (New York: Columbia University Press, 1993). Internal differences exist within postmodern and poststructural scholarship, just as they do within the mainstream social sciences. For an overview of postmodernism and the differences within it, see Pauline Marie Rosenau, *Postmodernism and the Social Sciences* (Princeton: Princeton University Press, 1992).

24. Anderson, *Imagined Communities,* pp. 37–46.

25. For an exposition of this view—based on anti-Jewish pogroms in nineteenth- and twentieth-century Russia, Hindu-Muslim conflict in India, race riots in 1980s Britain, and racial violence in the United States—see Paul Brass, introduction to *Riots and Pogroms* (London: MacMillan, 1996).

26. Prakash, introduction to *After Colonialism,* p. 21.

27. Analogous arguments have been made about other ex-colonial societies. For Africa, see essays in Leroy Vail, ed., *The Creation of Tribalism in Southern Africa* (Berkeley: University of California Press, 1989); for Latin America, see Frederick Cooper, Allen Isaacman, Florencia Mallon, William Roseberry, and Steve Stern, eds., *Confronting Historical Paradigms: Peasants, Labor, and the Capitalist World System in Africa and Latin America* (Madison: University of Wisconsin Press, 1993).

28. The most widely read argument in this mode is Gyanendra Pandey, *The Construction of Communalism in Colonial North India* (Delhi: Oxford University Press, 1990). Also see Partha Chatterjee, *The Nation and Its Fragments* (Princeton: Princeton University Press, 1993).

29. To some, this would mean that the master narrative has acquired hegemony in a Gramscian sense—in that more and more "natives" have come to believe it. Others would make a distinction between hegemony and dominance, the latter term meaning imposition from above but not acceptance from below.

30. Paul Brass, *Theft of an Idol* (Princeton: Princeton University Press, 1997).

31. Elsewhere, instead of religion, some other division was chosen. For example, in the Yoruba region of Nigeria, ancestral city rather than religion was emphasized by the British. See David Laitin, *Hegemony and Culture: Religion and Politics Among the Yoruba* (Chicago: University of Chicago Press, 1986).

32. For the relation between essentialism and constructivism, see E. Valentine Daniel, *Charred Lullabies: Chapters in an Anthropology of Violence* (Princeton: Princeton University Press, 1996), ch. 2.

33. J. S. Mill, "Representative Government" in *Three Essays* (New York: Oxford University Press, 1990), pp. 385–86.

34. For other institutionally focused arguments about ethnic conflict, see Alvin Rabushka and Kenneth Shepsle, *Politics in Plural Societies: A Theory of Democratic Stability* (Columbus, Ohio: Charles Merrill, 1972).

35. The book that represents Lijphart's views best is *Democracy in Plural Societies: A Comparative Exploration* (New Haven: Yale University Press, 1977). Although, as already cited, Horowitz's principal work is *Ethnic Groups in Conflict,* the debate between the two became especially sharp regarding South Africa. When South Africa, before its transition to a post-apartheid era, was debating what political system to choose, Lijphart argued in favor of a consociational system, and Horowitz disagreed. For Lijphart's arguments, see his *Power-Sharing in South Africa* (Berkeley: Institute of International Studies, 1985). For Horowitz's, see his *A Democratic South Africa? Constitutional Engineering in a Divided Society* (Berkeley: University of California Press, 1991), esp. ch. 5.

36. The variations include, controversially, the argument that India is a consociational democracy. See Arend Lijphart, "The Puzzle of Indian Democracy," *American Political Science Review* (June 1996).

37. Horowitz, *Democratic South Africa,* pp. 184–203.

38. John Darby, *Intimidation and Control of Conflict in Northern Ireland* (Dublin: Gill and MacMillan, 1986). Darby used these fictitious names for actual communities.

39. For a review of some other definitions, see Alex Hadenius and Frederik Uggla, "Making Civil Society Work, Promoting Democratic Development," *World Development* (October 1996).

40. Milan Kundera, *The Unbearable Lightness of Being* (HarperCollins, 1984).

41. For the early history of the idea, including Marx's critique of Hegel, see Adam Seligman, *The Idea of Civil Society* (Princeton: Princeton University Press, 1992).

42. Jürgen Habermas, *The Structural Transformation of the Public Sphere: An Inquiry into the Category of Bourgeois Society,* trans. Thomas Burger and Frederic Lawrence (Cambridge:

MIT Press, 1989). For a debate built around the publication of the English translation, see Craig Calhoun, ed., *Habermas and the Public Sphere* (Cambridge: MIT Press, 1994).

43. See Charles Taylor, "Modes of Civil Society," *Public Culture* (fall 1990); Michael Walzer, "The Idea of Civil Society," *Dissent* (spring 1991); Jean Cohen and Andrew Arato, *Civil Society and Political Theory* (Cambridge: MIT Press, 1992); Joshua Cohen and Joel Rogers, eds., *Associations and Democracy* (London: Verso, 1995).

44. The most prominent empirically oriented exception of recent times is Robert Putnam, *Making Democracy Work: Civic Traditions in Italy* (Princeton: Princeton University Press, 1993). The debate generated by Putnam's work is also leading to empirically based scholarship. See Sheri Berman, "Civil Society and the Collapse of the Weimar Republic," *World Politics* (April 1997), the special issue on social capital of *America Behavioral Scientist* (April 1997), and Deepa Narayan and Michael Woolcock, "Social Capital: Implications for Development Theory, Research, and Policy," *World Bank Research Observer* 15 (August 2001). Also see the argument about how civil society can be related to both peace and conflict by Jack Snyder and Karen Ballentine, "Nationalism and the Marketplace for Ideas," *International Security* (fall 1996).

45. Ernest Gellner, "The Importance of Being Modular," in *Civil Society: Theory, History, Comparison,* ed. John Hall (Cambridge: Blackwell, 1995). This article is a good summary of a large number of Gellner's works on civil society, written in the reflective and the activist modes. Many of these writings, including some polemical essays, have been put together in Gellner, *Conditions of Liberty: Civil Society and Its Rivals* (New York: Penguin, 1994).

46. Gellner, *Conditions of Liberty,* p. 9.

47. For another argument of a similar genre, see Edward Shils, *The Virtue of Civility* (Indianapolis: Liberty Fund, 1997).

48. See John Hall, "In Search of Civil Society," in *Civil Society,* p. 19.

49. For pioneering work on the modernist uses of tradition and ethnicity, see Lloyd Rudolph and Susanne Rudolph, *The Modernity of Tradition* (Chicago: University of Chicago Press, 1967); Myron Weiner, *Sons of the Soil* (Princeton: Princeton University Press, 1978).

50. See the discussion of a southern Indian lower-caste movement in Chapter 5.

51. See, e.g., Barbara Wake Carroll and Terrance Carroll, "The State and Ethnicity in Botswana and Mauritius," *Journal of Development Studies* (April 1997).

52. In societies in which drinking in public is outlawed or is culturally discouraged, pubs tend to attract the criminally inclined, not the civic-minded. Violence is always possible—and always around the corner.

53. Dilip Menon, *Caste, Nationalism, and Communism in South India: Malabar, 1900–1948* (Cambridge: Cambridge University Press, 1994).

54. I have personally had some of the most interesting conversations about politics—local, state, national, and even international—in such neighborhood tea shops in India and have watched modern journalists interview citizens and write stories for their papers there. A rather informal and traditional site has been put to some remarkably modern uses.

55. For a discussion of gossip, folk tales, and social revelry in the Malaysian countryside, see

James Scott, *Weapons of the Weak: Everyday Forms of Peasant Resistance* (New Haven: Yale University Press, 1985).

56. See the brief but thoughtful discussion in Harry Boyte, "The Pragmatic Ends of Popular Politics," in *Habermas and the Public Sphere,* ed. Craig Calhoun (Cambridge: MIT Press, 1994).

57. Starting with E. P. Thompson's *The Making of English Working Class* (Harmondsworth: Penguin, 1968), such historical works are by now many. For a quick review of how they relate to Habermas, see Mary Ryan, "Gender and Public Access: Women's Politics in Nineteenth Century America," and Geoff Elly, "Nations, Publics, and Political Cultures: Placing Habermas in the 19th Century," in *Habermas and the Public Sphere,* ed. Craig Calhoun (Cambridge: MIT Press, 1994).

58. Jürgen Habermas, "Further Reflections on the Public Sphere," in *Habermas and the Public Sphere,* ed. Craig Calhoun (Cambridge: MIT Press, 1994).

59. For discussion of the ways in which civic activity in the United States has declined, see Robert Putnam, "The Strange Disappearance of Civic America," *American Prospect* (winter 1996); "Bowling Alone," *Journal of Democracy* (January 1995); and Putnam, *Bowling Alone* (New York: Simon and Schuster, 2000).

60. It has been argued that "self-policing" can also be a mechanism of ethnic peace. See James Fearon and David Laitin, "Explaining Interethnic Cooperation," *American Political Science Review* (December 1996): 715–35. In the terminology used in this book, self-policing essentially means *intra*ethnic policing, not *inter*ethnic engagement. For the relation between the Fearon-Laitin argument and my own, see the concluding chapter of this book.

61. Brass, *Theft of an Idol.*

62. Sara Dickey, *Cinema and the Urban Poor in South India* (Cambridge: Cambridge University Press, 1993).

CHAPTER 3. COMPETING NATIONAL IMAGINATIONS

1. This chapter synthesizes arguments made at length in four papers I have already published: "Contested Meanings: India's National Identity, Hindu Nationalism, and the Politics of Anxiety," *Daedalus* (Summer 1993); "Battling the Past, Forging a Future? Ayodhya and Beyond," in *India Briefing 1993,* ed. Philip Oldenburg (Boulder, Colo.: Westview Press for Asia Society, 1993); "The Self-Correcting Mechanisms of Indian Democracy," *Seminar* (January 1995); and "Is India Becoming More Democratic?" *Journal of Asian Studies* (February 2000).

2. Therefore, this usage differs from the postmodern interpretation of the term. In its latter version, master narratives are the principal prisms of interpretation promoted by the colonial powers about the colonies. See Gyan Prakash, ed., *After Colonialism: Imperial Histories and Postcolonial Displacements* (Princeton: Princeton University Press, 1995), especially the introduction. On how the very idea of nationalism in India is a colonial import, see two books by Partha Chatterjee, *Nationalist Thought and the Colonial World: A Derivative Discourse* (Minneapolis: University of Minnesota Press, 1993) and *The Nation*

and Its Fragments: Colonial and Postcolonial Histories (Princeton: Princeton University Press, 1995).

3. In the 1980s Sikh nationalism, a third type of religious nationalism, led to a decade-long insurgency in the state of Punjab. Sikh nationalism is currently quiet. It seems to have settled for a place in the federal system, as opposed to outright independence.

4. For a detailed analysis of northern Indian political trends with respect to the so-called lower castes, see the symposium in the *Journal of Asian Studies* (February 2000), containing articles by Varshney, Kanchan Chandra, Christophe Jaffrelot, and Stuart Corbridge.

5. Some may argue that there are two other candidates for master narratives: language and urban vs. rural. In the 1950s and 1960s, language was an extremely contentious issue in Indian politics, but its salience declined precipitously with a linguistic reorganization of Indian federalism. In the 1970s and the early 1980s, a narrative seeking to create an all-India rural coalition against the city, especially on economic issues, seemed to emerge and head for power. India, according to this narrative, lived primarily in the villages but cities had dominated the country's resources and developmental priorities. A reversal of priorities was necessary. The rise of religious and caste issues in the late 1980s basically overwhelmed this narrative. Like language, it faded away as a tool of mass mobilization. For its rise and decline, see Ashutosh Varshney, *Democracy, Development, and the Countryside: Urban-Rural Struggles in India* (New York: Cambridge University Press, 1995).

6. For an assessment of their performance in North India, see Christophe Jaffrelot, "The Rise of Other Backward Classes in the Hindi Belt," *Journal of Asian Studies* (February 2000). For an overall national assessment, see Varshney, "Is India Becoming More Democratic?" in the same issue.

7. There are several such parties. Arguments about lower-caste unity notwithstanding, the lower-caste–based parties tend to splinter.

8. For earlier scholarly attempts at defining India's national identity, see Rajni Kothari, *Politics in India* (Boston: Little, Brown, 1970), chs. 2, 7, and 8; Ravinder Kumar, "India's Secular Culture," in his *The Making of a Nation* (Delhi: Manohar, 1989); and Ainslie Embree, *Imagining India* (Delhi: Oxford University Press, 1989), esp. sec. 1. A more recent attempt is Sunil Khilnani, *The Idea of India* (New York: Farrar, Straus and Giroux, 1997).

9. Eric Hobsbawm, *Nations and Nationalism Since 1870* (New York: Cambridge University Press, 1990); and Anthony Smith, *The Ethnic Origins of Nations* (Oxford: Basil Blackwell, 1985). On the relationship between race and nation, see Anthony Marx, *Making Race and Nation* (New York: Cambridge University Press, 1998).

10. Stanley Hoffmann, "Thoughts on French Nationalism," *Daedalus* (summer 1993).

11. Samuel P. Huntington, *American Politics: The Promise of Disharmony* (Cambridge: Harvard University Press, 1981), ch. 2.

12. For a report, see Judith Miller, "Strangers at the Gate," *New York Times Magazine*, 15 September 1991; for an analysis, see Rogers Brubaker, *Citizenship and Nationhood in France and Germany* (Cambridge: Harvard University Press, 1992), esp. ch. 7.

13. Huntington, *American Politics*, p. 16.

14. Diana L. Eck, "The Imagined Landscape: Patterns in the Construction of Hindu Sacred Geography," in *Tradition, Pluralism, and Identity: In Honour of T. N. Madan,* ed. Veena Das, Dipankar Gupta, and Patricia Uberoi (New Delhi: Sage, 1999), pp. 23–46. Also see Ainslie Embree, ed., *Alberuni's India* (New York: Norton, 1971).

15. Urdu—a language combining Persian and Hindi, written in Arabic script—is a typical syncretistic language, developed under Muslim rule in medieval times. In Uttar Pradesh, Punjab, and Kashmir, several Hindus have acquired fame in Urdu poetry.

16. P. M. Currie, *The Shrine and Cult of Muin-al-Din Chishti of Ajmer* (Delhi: Oxford University Press, 1989); Susan Bayly, *Saints, Goddesses, and Cults: Islam and Christianity in South India* (Cambridge: Cambridge University Press, 1985).

17. These include Benaras, Tirupati, Rameshwaram, Puri, Haridwar, Badrinath, Kedarnath, and Ayodhya.

18. These include the Cauveri, the Ganga, and the Yamuna, the confluence of the last two in Prayag.

19. Some historians disagree. They argue that a Hindu identity is at best a creation of the past two hundred to three hundred years. Before that, there were different sects but no Hindu identity as such. For the ancient period, see Romila Thapar, "Imagined Religious Communities? Ancient History and the Modern Search for Hindu Identity," *Modern Asian Studies* 23, no. 2 (1989). For the modern period, see Robert Frykenberg, "Constructions of Hinduism at the Nexus of History and Religion," *Journal of Interdisciplinary History* 23, no. 3 (winter 1993).

20. M. S. Golwalkar, *We or Our Nationhood Defined* (Nagpur: Bharat, 1939). For a scholarly analysis of the ideology of Hindu nationalism and its evolution, see Christophe Jaffrelot, *The Hindu Nationalist Movement in India* (New York: Columbia University Press, 1996).

21. V. D. Savarkar, *Hindutva,* 6th ed. (Bombay: Veer Savarkar Prakashan, 1989). Savarkar, however, contests the notion that Hindutva is a religious term. For him, it has a cultural meaning. On how this distinction, worthwhile otherwise, is meaningless in Hindu nationalism, see below.

22. Worship at the graves of great Sufi saints resembles Hindu forms of piety in several ways: devotional music, deposition of flowers, and a priestly offering of the "sacred sweets" *(prasad)* bring the two together; idols (Hinduism) and graves (Islam) separate them.

23. Khushwant Singh, *A History of the Sikhs,* vol. 1 (Princeton: Princeton University Press, 1963), ch. 2.

24. Jawaharlal Nehru, *The Discovery of India* (Delhi: Oxford University Press, 1989), p. 62.

25. In a similar vein, Rajni Kothari writes: "In contrast to the great historical empires, the unity of India owed itself not to the authority of a given political system but to the wide diffusion of the cultural symbols, the spiritual values, and the structure of roles and functions characteristic of a continuous civilization. The essential unity of India has not been political but cultural" (*Politics in India,* p. 251). A contrast with another large multiethnic nation, the United States, can be drawn here. Several commentators argue that the unity of the United States lies in the political principles that founded the nation, although different communities evolved their distinctive cultures (represented by the hyphenation of most Americans—Italian-American, Japanese-American, Chinese-Amer-

ican, and so on). On America's pluralism of cultures but consensus on political ideas, see Michael Walzer, *What It Means to Be an American* (New York: Marsilio, 1993).

26. Of these, some are past rulers, others purely cultural figures. Kabir and Nanak were saints who inspired syncretistic beliefs and preached interreligious understanding and love. For a sampling of their ideas, see John S. Hawley and Mark Jurgensmeyer, *Songs of the Saints of India* (New York: Oxford University Press, 1988).

27. Nehru, *Discovery,* p. 270.

28. Ibid., p. 63. Also see his discussion of the role of *Dharti* (land) in the peasant conception of *Bharat Mata* (Mother India) in "The Search for India" and "Bharat Mata," pp. 57–60.

29. Jawaharlal Nehru, "Will and Testament," in *Jawaharlal Nehru: An Anthology,* ed. S. Gopal (Delhi: Oxford University Press, 1980), pp. 647–48.

30. For a fuller discussion of Kashmir, see Ashutosh Varshney, "India, Pakistan, and Kashmir: Antinomies of Nationalism," *Asian Survey* (November 1991), and "Three Compromised Nationalisms: Why Kashmir Has Been a Problem," in *Perspectives on Kashmir,* ed. Raju Thomas (Boulder: Westview, 1992).

31. Strictly speaking, such concessions do not affect the territorial principle, unless the concerned minority community is also geographically concentrated. In political discourse, however, as explained earlier, "national unity" and "territorial integrity" function as substitutes. Such "appeasement" is considered tantamount to promoting disintegrative tendencies. See Arun Shourie, *Religion in Politics* (Delhi: Roli, 1987), pp. 91–124.

32. Nanaji Deshmukh, *Rethinking Secularism* (Delhi: Suruchi Prakashan, 1989); H. V. Sheshadri, K. S. Sudarshan, K. Surya Narain Rao, and Balraj Madhok, *Why Hindu Rashtra?* (Delhi: Suruchi Prakashan, 1990). Deshmukh and Sheshadri are important functionaries of the Rashtriya Swayamsevak Sangh, the ideological fountainhead of Hindu nationalism.

33. I borrow this way of distinguishing the models from Ashis Nandy. One should emphasize that Nandy himself does not believe in the melting pot model. The metaphor of the salad bowl, according to him, best captures India's cultural essence.

34. H. V. Sheshadri, "Hindu Rashtra: What and Why," *Hindu Vishva* 25, no. 12 (Silver Jubilee Special Issue) (1989–90): 30. *Hindu Vishva* is the journal of Vishva Hindu Parishad (VHP).

35. Ibid.

36. L. K. Advani, interview, *Sunday* (Calcutta), 22 July 1990.

37. Frykenberg, "Constructions of Hinduism."

38. Savarkar, *Hindutva,* title page, elaborated further between pp. 110 and 113.

39. Deshmukh, *Rethinking Secularism.*

40. Savarkar, *Hindutva,* p. 113.

41. The hostility felt by Hindu nationalists toward the Christians, especially those who believe in conversion, has gone through several ups and downs. In the late 1990s, anti-Christian rhetoric surged once again, accompanied by a rise in anti-Christian violence, though it is yet to be clearly established who is behind the violence.

42. "You would be most welcome to the Hindu fold. This is a choice which . . . Mohammedan and Christian communities are free to make—a choice which must be a

choice of love." Savarkar, *Hindutva*, p. 115. Assimilation is also the theme of Deen Dayal Upadhyay, *Akhand Bharat Aur Muslim Samasya* (Noida: Jagriti Prakashan, 1992). Deen Dayal Upadhyay was the pre-eminent political leader of the Jan Sangh (BJP's predecessor) in the 1960s. It is interesting to note that accepting this argument, some Muslim politicians—for example, Sikandar Bakht—have been part of the BJP and have fought elections on BJP tickets. Sikandar Bakht's position on the demolition of Baburi mosque was explained in an interview in *Saptahik Hindustan* (Delhi), 20–26 December 1992.

43. Exclusivist Islam can be a personal faith or it may also enter the political sphere, thus becoming an ideology, displaying sometimes what are known as fundamentalist qualities. Ashis Nandy has very usefully suggested the distinction between faith and ideology in "The Politics of Secularism," *Alternatives* (fall 1989).

44. Maulana Abul Kalam Azad's speech as president of Indian National Congress in 1940, reproduced in *Sources of Indian Tradition,* ed. Stephen Hay, 2d ed. (New Delhi: Penguin, 1991), 2: 237–241.

45. For an excellent overview of the whole range of Muslim responses, see Rajmohan Gandhi, *Understanding the Muslim Mind* (New Delhi: Penguin, 1987). Also see Mushirul Hasan, *Legacy of a Divided Nation* (Delhi: Oxford University Press, 1997), esp. chs. 3–4.

46. A very large number of Muslims have been exponents of Indian classical music. Muslim playwrights and poets, writing in Hindi, have also existed. Similarly, some of the leading Urdu poets have been Hindu (e.g., Firaq Gorakhpuri). Even in the popular arts, the story is the same. Mohammed Rafi has been a leading singer; Naushad Ali, a leading music composer; Kaifi Azmi, Sahir Ludhianvi, and Shakeel Budayuni, leading song-writers; and Dilip Kumar, Mina Kumari, and Nargis, legendary Muslim film actors, acting also in films with distinct Hindu overtones. Mansur Ali Khan Pataudi and Azharuddin have led India's cricket teams. The tomb of Salim Chishti, a Sufi saint, is visited by millions of Hindus and Sikhs, not simply Muslims.

47. Nothing illustrates this better than one of his famous prayers, called *Ramdhun: Ishwar Allah Tere Naam, Sabko Sanmati de Bhagvan* (God and Allah are two names of the same entity. May God give good sense to every one).

48. Mahatma Gandhi, *Hind Swaraj* (Ahmedabad: Navjivan, 1938) pp. 45–46.

49. Ibid., p. 59.

50. Deen Dayal Upadhyay, *Akhand Bharat Aur Muslim Samasya,* p. 1. Also see M. S. Golwalkar, *Rashtra* (Nation) (Delhi: Suruchi Prakashan, 1982) esp. the chapter titled "*Musalman aur Bharat Rashtra*" (Muslims and the Indian nation).

51. The RSS does not participate in elections. The BJP, the electoral face of Hindu nationalism in independent India, called Bharatiya Jan Sargh until 1977, was born in 1952. For details, see Walter Anderson and Sridhar Damle, *Brotherhood in Saffron* (Boulder: Westview, 1986); Jaffrelot, *Hindu Nationalist Movement.*

52. The institutions of Hindu nationalism may have finally emerged in Maharashtra, but Hindu revivalism itself was born in Bengal in the writings of Swami Vivekanand and Sri Aurbindo and in the novels of Bankim Chandra. In 1952, West Bengal was also the birthplace of Jan Sangh, BJP's precursor in electoral politics. It was founded by Shyama Prasad Mukherjee, a prominent Bengali of the 1940s.

53. For a critical assessment, see Margaret Chatterji, *Gandhi's Religious Thought* (London: Macmillan, 1983).

54. The assassin argued thus in his defense: "Gandhiji while advocating his views always showed or evinced a bias for Muslims, prejudicial and detrimental to the Hindu community and its interests" (p. 19); "Gandhiji is being referred to as the Father of the Nation—an epithet of high reverence. But if so, he failed in his parental duty in as much as he has acted very treacherously to the nation by consenting to the partitioning of it. . . . He has proved to be the Father of Pakistan" (p. 111). Both citations are from Nathuram Godse, *Why I Assassinated Mahatma Gandhi* (Delhi: Surya Bharti Prakashan, 1993).

55. The RSS, a government investigation committee found, was not directly involved in the assassination; some RSS individuals were. In the eyes of the populace, this was not an important distinction. For details, see Bruce Graham, *Hindu Nationalism and Indian Politics* (Cambridge: Cambridge University Press, 1990), ch. 3.

56. For a nuanced and fieldwork-based account of the movement in the late 1980s and early 1990s as well as an ingenious narration of how people viewed Rama, in whose name the mosque was torn down, see Jonah Blank, *Arrow of the Blue Skinned God* (Boston: Houghton Mifflin, 1992).

57. See Rajni Kothari, "The December 6 Watershed," *Hindustan Times,* 27 December 1992; Salman Khurshid, "How Does One Repair a Damaged Hinduism?" *Indian Express,* 16 December 1992; Lloyd Rudolph and Susanne Rudolph, "Modern Hate," *New Republic,* 22 March 1993.

58. L. K. Advani, interview in *Newstrack,* January 1991.

59. L. K. Advani, "BJP Is Unequivocally Committed to Secularism," *Indian Express,* 27 December 1992.

60. Savarkar, *Hindutva.*

61. This is the famous speech that formed the intellectual bedrock for Pakistan. It was given on March 23, 1940 in Lahore and has been reproduced in several documents. See Jamil-ud-Din Ahmed, ed., *Some Recent Speeches and Writings of Mr. Jinnah* (Lahore: Ashraf, 1952), 1:138.

62. For discussion of why this is so, see E. Sridharan and Ashutosh Varshney, "Towards Moderate Pluralism: Political Parties and Party Politics in India," in *Political Parties and Democracy,* ed. Richard Guenther and Larry Diamond (Baltimore: Johns Hopkins University Press, 2001).

63. The best analysis of the partywise distribution of India's vote and the social, regional, and gender bases of party support in the elections of the 1990s has been done by Yogendra Yadav and his associates in Delhi. See especially the following: Yogendra Yadav, "Political Change in North India," *Economic and Political Weekly,* 18 December 1993; Yogendra Yadav and Alistair Macmillan, "How India Voted," *India Today,* 16 March 1998; Oliver Heath and Yogendra Yadav, "Social Profile of Congress Voters, 1996 and 1998," and Oliver Heath, "The Anatomy of BJP's Rise to Power," *Economic and Political Weekly,* 21 August–3 September 1999.

64. The BJP was part of the Janata coalition that ruled India between 1977 and 1979. L. K. Advani, who finally led the Ayodhya movement, was a cabinet minister in the Janata government. There was no talk of Ayodhya then.

65. For a fuller discussion, see my "Three Compromised Nationalisms."

66. Eugene Weber, *Peasants into Frenchmen* (Stanford: Stanford University Press, 1976).

67. The United States is perhaps the best example of multiethnic nation-building in the world. Ethnic strife has existed, as it is bound to in a multiethnic country, but since the Civil War of the 1860s, the territorial integrity of the United States has not been in question. To students of nationalism, the American nation is both puzzling and unique. It is not based on common descent, religion, or language. Nor does it appear to be primarily territorial. It seems to be more about citizenship and about the political principles underlying the origins of the nation. See Walzer, *What It Means to Be an American.*

68. Rogers Brubaker, *Nationalism Reframed* (New York: Cambridge University Press, 1997).

69. For an evocative account of the nonviolence of the national movement, see Denis Dalton, *Mahatma Gandhi: Nonviolent Power in Action* (New York: Columbia University Press, 1993).

70. For discussion of how this generalization might have to be qualified to reflect the nuances of different local settings, see Shahid Amin, "Gandhi as Mahatma: Gorakhpur District, Eastern UP, 1921–2," in *Subtaren Studies*, vol. 3, ed. Ranajit Guha (Delhi: Oxford University Press, 1989).

71. For an account of how the leadership styles of Nehru and Indira Gandhi had profoundly different consequences for the Congress Party as well as for the overall polity, see Ashutosh Varshney, "Why Democracy Survives," *Journal of Democracy* (July 1998).

72. The debate between those who argue that Mrs. Gandhi was a prisoner of social forces and those who argue that she led her party's decline is unlikely to be settled. See Atul Kohli, *Democracy and Discontent: The Crisis of Governability in India* (New York: Cambridge University Press, 1991).

73. Of late, there has been some disunity in the BJP, though it has not reached proportions that it did in the Congress.

74. "[T]he emergence of secularism in Europe . . . was not only an expression of repugnance towards the corruption of institutionalized religion but . . . the basis for the separation of state and church is also to be found in the New Testament itself. The privatization of religion, through the assumption by the individual of the responsibility for his own salvation without the intervention of church, was a later development. A similar ideology is, however, absent from the cultural traditions of India. The idiom in which to express the ideal of secularism has, therefore, yet to be constructed. This is not an easy task, because the great majority of the people of [South Asia] are adherents of one faith or another and also because in such matters borrowed ideas do not carry us very far." T. N. Madan, "Religion in India," *Daedalus* (fall 1989).

75. For an argument about modernity and Indian politics with a different flavor, see Sudipta Kaviraj, "Modernity and Politics in India," *Daedalus* (winter 2000).

76. "The roots of the crisis lay . . . at the beginning of the Modern Era, in Galileo and Descartes, in the one-sided nature of the European sciences, which reduced the world to a mere object of technical and mathematical investigation and put the concrete world of life . . . beyond their horizon. . . . The more [man] advanced . . . , the less clearly could he see either the world as a whole or as his own self, and he plunged further into what . . .

Heidegger called in a beautiful and almost magical phrase, 'the forgetting of being.'"
Milan Kundera, "The Depreciated Legacy of Cervantes," in *The Art of the Novel* (New
York: Harper and Row), 1988, pp. 3–4.

77. See Isaiah Berlin's *Against the Current* (New York: Penguin, 1980), especially "The
Counter-Enlightenment" and "The Divorce Between the Sciences and the Humanities"
(which mirrors Kundera's position); Leszek Kolakowski, *Modernity on Endless Trial*
(Chicago: University of Chicago Press, 1990), especially "Modernity on Endless Trial"
and "The Revenge of the Sacred in Secular Culture."

78. See especially Albert Einstein's essays on science and religion in *Ideas and Opinions* (New
York: Crown, 1982), esp. pp. 36–53.

79. Einstein, therefore, argued that science (or rationality) and religion deal with two different kinds of questions, and it is possible for scientists also to be religious. Einstein, *Ideas
and Opinions.*

80. See also the excellent paper by Chris Bayly, "The Pre-History of Communalism? Religious Conflict in India, 1700–1860," *Modern Asian Studies* 19, no. 2 (1985).

81. For details, see Mark Tully and Satish Jacob, *Amritsar* (London: J. Cape, 1984).

82. For details, see Paul Brass, *Language, Religion, and Politics in North India* (Cambridge:
Cambridge University Press, 1975).

83. There were other ways to deal with the problem: the Rajiv Gandhi government later
flushed out its targets by constructing a siege around the temple, not by desecrating it.

84. Ashis Nandy, "Indira Gandhi and the Culture of Indian Politics," in his *At the Edge of
Psychology: Essays in Politics and Culture* (Delhi: Oxford University Press, 1990).

85. Donald Eugene Smith, *Religion and Politics in South Asia* (Chicago: University of
Chicago Press, 1963). For a perspective on Indian secularism, especially as compared to
that in Israel and the United States, see Gary Jacobsohn, "Three Modes of Secular Constitutional Development," *Studies in American Political Development* 10, no. 1 (September 1996).

86. The Supreme Court also held that the *Shariat,* if read carefully, permitted alimony.
Muslims argued that a secular court had no business to pass judgments on religious matters. Strictly speaking, the second argument was not required for the judgment. Here
was yet another example of secular arrogance. For the political controversy surrounding
the Shah Bano case, see Asghar Ali Engineer, *The Shah Bano Controversy* (Delhi: Ajanta,
1987). For the legal and conceptual issues involved, see John Mansfield, "Personal Laws
or a Uniform Civil Code?" in *Religion and Law in Independent India,* ed. Robert Barid
(Delhi: Manohar, 1994).

87. For further implications, see Myron Weiner, *The Indian Paradox* (Delhi: Sage, 1989, ch.
7, esp. pp. 216–18. Also, on how the term "minority" is used in India, see Weiner's "India's Minorities: Who Are They? What Do They Want?" in the same volume.

88. Lloyd Rudolph and Susanne Rudolph, *In Pursuit of Lakshmi* (Chicago: University of
Chicago Press, 1987), p. 197–98.

89. Psephologists disagree with this view, but politicians on the whole continue to hold it.

90. For a rare statistical analysis of this subject, see Abusaleh Shariff, "Socio-Economic and
Demographic Differentials Between Hindus and Muslims in India," *Economic and Po-*

litical Weekly, 18 November 1995, pp. 2947–54. Also see N. C. Saxena, "Public Employ-ment and Educational Backwardness Among the Muslims in India, in *Religion, State, and Politics in India,* ed. Moin Shakir (New Delhi: Ajanta, 1989).

91. Gopal, *Anatomy of a Confrontation,* pp. 17–20.

92. Donald Horowitz, *Ethnic Groups in Conflict* (Berkeley: University of California Press, 1985).

93. For the ideological differences, going back to the Ayodhya movement, between the two leading lights of the BJP, A. B. Vajpayee (currently India's prime minister) and L. K. Ad-vani (presently India's home minister), see Atal Behari Vajpayee, "Advaniji aur Mere Matbhed to Hain," *Dharmyuga,* 16 January 16 1993. In a recent essay, Vajpayee has de-fended a view of India's national identity that is roughly the same as, not radically con-tradictory to, the typical secular nationalist view originally proposed by the leaders of the freedom movement. It is also very different from the position often taken by Advani on the same question, especially as cited in note 36 of this chapter. See Atal Behari Vaj-payee, "Time to Resolve Problems of the Past and Move On," *Hindustan Times,* 2–3 January 2001.

CHAPTER 4. HINDU-MUSLIM RIOTS, 1950–1995

1. The statistics for this chapter were compiled in partnership with Steven Wilkinson. Some of the results were reported in Ashutosh Varshney and Steven Wilkinson, "Hindu-Muslim Riots, 1960–1993: New Findings, Fresh Remedies," Special Paper Series (New Delhi: Rajiv Gandhi Institute of Contemporary Studies, May 1996).

2. As reported in Chapter 1, I will use the terms "town" and "city" interchangeably. This is to ensure international standardization. Speaking on the basis of population size, what is called a city in Europe may look like a town by Asian standards. On the other hand, if civic amenities are taken as a defining criterion, many of India's cities would be compa-rable to towns in Europe.

3. Gopal Krishna, "Communal Violence in India," *Economic and Political Weekly,* 12 Janu-ary 1985.

4. Interview with Justice Sardar Ali Khan, Chairman, Minorities Commission, *Times of India,* 9 July 1995.

5. *Annual Report of the Minorities Commission* (Delhi: Government of India, 1985–86), pp. 76–77.

6. Interview with G. P. Shukla, senior IAS officer, U.P. cadre, 15 December 1994.

7. The discussion in this paragraph and the next is based on research conducted for Ashutosh Varshney, *Democracy, Development and the Countryside: Urban-Rural Struggles in India* (New York: Cambridge University Press, 1995).

8. See, e.g., Gyanendra Pandey, *The Construction of Communalism in Colonial North India* (Delhi: Oxford University Press, 1993), ch. 2.

9. For compilation, the data for the period 1950–95 took about 1,400 hours of work. Ap-proximately 1,600 separate riots and possible riots were entered into a Filemaker Pro database.

10. The biggest case in point is the Surat videotape story, which concerned an alleged gang-

rape during riots in December 1992. Several researchers, including myself, have independently established that no such tape existed. The *Times of India* refused to run the story without firm proof of the tape's existence, unlike most other papers in India. For details, see the discussion of the videotape episode in Chapter 10.

11. The National Integration Council defines a major riot as one in which at least four people were killed.

12. The ratios for various states were as follows: Maharashtra (1.1), Gujarat (1.3), Andhra Pradesh (1.4), Karnataka (1.9), West Bengal (1.5), U.P. (0.9), M.P. (0.9), and Bihar (0.7). Thus, compared to the first two states, which are in western India neighboring Bombay, some distant states had higher ratios, others lower. No systematic reporting bias in favor of western India is noticeable.

13. *The Sixth Report of the National Police Commission* (Delhi: Government of India, 1981), p. 60.

14. Whether greater precision is possible in the future should be considered an open question at this point. It will require a multi-year, large-team project that goes through multiple newspapers to double-check the *Times of India*–based data presented here. Disaggregated official data and reports, if made available by the government, can also provide greater cross-checking. A multiple-year project of this kind has been carried out by Charles Tilly and his associates for France and England. See David Snyder and Charles Tilly, "Hardship and Collective Violence in France: 1830–1960," *American Sociological Review* 37 (1972); and Charles Tilly, "Contentious Repertoires in Britain, 1758–1834," *Social Science History* 17 (1993).

15. This statement is based on interviews not only with editors of the major dailies but also with tens of reporters from the field. All accept the possibility of some underreportage, but the degree necessary to invalidate the claim that rural India's share of riot deaths is minuscule is simply ruled out, given how information travels in a democracy endowed with a free press.

16. The same point can be statistically made by calculating the average number of deaths per year and the standard deviations. The graphic representation in the figures simply makes the point visual and more obvious.

17. It is often argued that the state of Bihar, otherwise riot-prone, was an exception in the period of the Ayodhya agitation. This argument is only partly true. Compared to the Bhagalpur violence in 1989, when a very large number of people died, the period 1990–93 did show a downward trend (see figure 4. 7). But if we consider the all of the 1980s, the period 1990–92 was not exceptionally peaceful. The most sensible conclusion would be that everyone expected Bihar to be much worse than it actually turned out to be. A conflagration was expected in Bihar, not in Bombay. Recent politics in of Bihar is based on a Muslim–backward caste coalition. It may deserve credit for preventing a conflagration in 1992–93. But it should be noted that a downward trend had begun to emerge in the 1980s before Bhagalpur plunged Bihar into unknown depths of communal horror.

18. The seven towns in Uttar Pradesh on the list account for 55 percent of the total deaths. In a state of more than 50 districts and more than 100 towns, these figures also show a high degree of concentration, though not as high as in Maharashtra, Gujarat, and Andhra.

19. Ashis Nandy, "The Politics of Secularism," *Alternatives* 13, no. 3 (1988); T. N. Madan, "Secularism in Its Place," *Journal of Asian Studies* (November 1987).

20. Among the first to deal with this possibility were Lloyd Rudolph and Susanne Rudolph, *The Modernity of Tradition* (Chicago: University of Chicago Press, 1967); Reinhard Bendix, "Tradition and Modernity Revisited," *Comparative Studies in Society and History* (April 1967); Rajni Kothari, "Tradition and Modernity Revisited," *Government and Opposition* (summer 1968). Building on this work, a widely noted attack on the presumed power of modernity came from Samuel Huntington, "The Change to Change: Modernization, Development and Politics," *Comparative Politics* (April 1971).

21. Unlike economic development, which is an income-based measure, the human development index includes literacy and health, in addition to income, each factor holding a third of the weight. For a larger discussion of how, and why, the concepts of human development and economic development are different, see United Nations Development ment Program, *The Human Development Report* (New York: Oxford University Press, 1992).

22. Amartya Sen, "Threats to Indian Secularism," *New York Review of Books*, 8 April 1993. In his more recent work on the subject, Sen appears not to make this claim too strongly, though on the left wing of scholarship the view continues to be important. For Sen's more recent position, see his "Secularism and Its Discontents," in *Unraveling the Nation*, ed. K. Basu and S. Subrahmaniam (Delhi: Penguin, 1996). In a roughly similar, modernist category can be placed another widely read treatise: Sunil Khilnani, *The Idea of India* (New York: Farrar, Straus and Giroux, 1997).

23. The statistics in this paragraph are from Ashis Bose, *Demographic Diversity of India: 1991 Census* (Delhi: B. R. Publishing, 1991), p. 62.

24. Based on Government of India, *India 1994* (Delhi: Ministry of Information and Broadcasting, 1995), pp. 16–18.

25. The distinction is necessary, for even though postmodernists have embraced the ideas of scholars such as Ashis Nandy regarding modernity, Nandy calls himself an antisecularist or an antimodernist, not a postmodernist.

26. Ashis Nandy, "The Politics of Secularism and the Recovery of Religious Tolerance," *Alternatives* 13, no. 3 (1988): 155 (emphasis added).

27. The numbers in these paragraphs are calculated from the 1991 census data.

28. See, e.g., Chris Bayly, "The Pre-History of Communalism? Religious Conflict in India, 1700–1860," *Modern Asian Studies* 19, no. 2 (1985).

29. For what backward caste movements represent and a critique of many of their demands, see Andre Beteille, *The Backward Classes in Contemporary India* (Delhi: Oxford University Press, 1992).

30. For a forceful argument on these lines, see Charles Taylor, *Multiculturalism and the Politics of Recognition* (Princeton: Princeton University Press, 1993).

PART III. LOCAL VARIATIONS

1. For a clear and brief statement on what social or "constructive" activities were necessary for nation-building, see Mahatma Gandhi, "Constructive Programme: Its Meaning and

Place," 13 December 1941, in *Collected Works* (Ahmedabad: Navjeevan Press, 1978), 75:146–66.

2. Gandhi, *Collected Works*, 84: 64.

3. It could, in principle, be argued that the analysis should be taken back even further and one should investigate the period before the 1920s to understand why different towns had different Hindu-Muslim relationships in place when the Gandhian moment in mass politics arrived. Something like this only sets up a trap for infinite regress. One needs to ask: What is the value-added of such an analytical move? And even if one went back to the nineteenth century to understand patterns available in the twentieth, some-one can always say that one should go back still further—let us say, a century earlier. Where we start is thus a conceptual and methodological question. In the materials in-vestigated in this book, the transformation of Indian society with the rise of a mass-based politics of protest and reconstruction constitutes such a start.

CHAPTER 5. ALIGARH AND CALICUT

1. *Dainik Jagran* (Aligarh edition), 16 April 1994.

2. *Chandrika* (Calicut), 3 August 1994.

3. Nicholas Dirks has argued that conflicts between Brahmins and the lower castes formed the master narrative in southern Indian politics, just as Hindu-Muslim divisions were the master narrative of northern India. See Dirks, "Recasting Tamil Society: The Politics of Caste and Race in Contemporary Southern India," in *Caste Today*, ed. C. J. Fuller (Delhi: Oxford University Press, 1997).

4. *Aaj*, 10 December 1990; *Amar Ujala*, 11 December 1990.

5. "For an Aligarh of Peace," interview with District Magistrate A. K. Mishra, *Frontline*, 22 December 1990, pp. 22–23.

6. Author's interviews with AMU vice-chancellor M. Naseem Farooqui, Delhi, 15 July 1994; several AMU professors, August 1994; and local journalists, August 1994. For a thoughtful review of all such reports appearing in local newspapers, see Namita Singh, "Sampradayitka ka khabar ban jana nahin, kahbron ka sampradayik ban jaana khatar-nak hai," *Vartaman Sahitya* (September 1991).

7. Author's interviews in Trivandrum with Amitabh Kant, district collector, Calicut, 1991–94, 20 July 20 1995; Shankar Reddy, police commissioner, Calicut, 1991–94, 22 July 1995; Siby Matthews, police commissioner Calicut, 1988–1991, 21 July 1995; K. Jayakumar, collector, Calicut, 21 July 1995; Rajeevan, police commissioner, Calicut, 1986–88, 21 July 1995. Politicians of the League and the BJP confirmed their participation in peace com-mittees. The political leaders interviewed were Dr. Muneer, Muslim League MLA since 1991, 23 July 1995; K. Sreedharan Pillai, president, Calicut District BJP Committee, Calicut, 25 July 1995.

8. "Kerala: A Dangerous Divide," *India Today*, 15 September 1992.

9. Author's interview, Sreedharan Pillai, president, BJP District Committee, Calicut, 25 July 1995.

10. Unless otherwise reported, the statistics here and below are from the project's survey, conducted in Calicut and Aligarh in 1995–96.

11. These numbers and the information below are based on extensive interviews with the president and the general secretary of the Kerala Vyapari Vyavasayi Ekopana Samithi (Samithi hereafter). The Samithi is a powerful all-state body, based in all towns of Kerala, that keeps records and statistics and has a professionally run office. It is rare to find a trade association in northern India being run so well.

12. Data supplied by the Samithi, Calicut Branch, July 1995.

13. Author's interview, K. Hassan Koya, general secretary, Samithi, Calicut, 25 July 1995.

14. Author's interview, V. Ramakrishna Erady, wholesale rice dealer, Calicut, 25 July 1995.

15. Information supplied by Mohammed Sufiyan, ex-president, Vyapar Mandal, Aligarh, August 1995.

16. Elizabeth Mann, *Boundaries and Identities* (New Delhi: Sage, 1992), p. 83. Mann's is an excellent ethnographic work on Muslim lives in Aligarh.

17. Ibid., pp. 101–2.

18. Ibid., pp. 84–85.

19. Exact numbers of union members and their religious distribution is almost impossible to find. Estimates based on the interviews are the best one can do. The description below is based on interviews with labor leaders in Calicut, especially a long and detailed interview with M. Sadiri Koya, state secretary, INTUC, 4 August 1993.

20. Dilip Menon, *Caste, Community, and the Nation: Malabar 1900–1948* (Cambridge: Cambridge University Press, 1995), pp. 145–49.

21. The state of Kerala has "a library or a reading room within walking distance of every citizen." K. A. Isaac, "Library Movement and Bibliographic Control in Kerala: An Overview," paper presented at the International Congress of Kerala Studies, Trivandrum, August 1994.

22. For some early larger movements along caste lines in southern India, see Lloyd Rudolph and Susanne Rudolph, *The Modernity of Tradition* (Chicago: University of Chicago Press, 1967).

23. Lord Kinross, *The Ottoman Centuries* (New York: Morrow Quill, 1977), ch. 39.

24. So striking was the cooperation that Swami Shraddhananda, a Hindu religious leader of the Arya Samaj, which had developed an anti-Muslim image, was allowed to address a Muslim crowd in the Jama Masjid (main mosque) of Delhi. For a first-hand account, see Swami Shraddhananda, *Inside Congress* (Bombay: Phoenix Publications, 1946), pp. 68–75.

25. Before the 1920s, there were other periods of *sporadic* rioting: the 1830s and 1850s, 1892–93, 1907–14, 1917–18. A systematic analysis of these riots is not yet available. A brief discussion of riots in the 1830s and 1850s is available in Chris Bayly, "The Pre-History of Communalism? Religious Conflict in India, 1700–1860," *Modern Asian Studies* 19, no. 2 (1985). For the 1890s, see John McLane, *Indian Nationalism and the Early Congress* (Princeton: Princeton University Press, 1977), ch. 10.

26. For the proselytizing movements of the period, see Mushirul Hasan, *Nationalism and Communal Politics in India* (Delhi: Manohar, 1991), ch. 8; G. R. Thursby, *Hindu-Muslim Relations in British India, 1923–1928* (Leiden: Brill, 1975), pt. 4. For Arya Samaj, see Kenneth Jones, "The Arya Samaj in British India, 1875–1947," in *Religion in Modern India,* ed. Robert Baird, 2d ed. (Delhi: Manohar, 1991), pp. 27–54.

27. Especially painful to the Muslims was an infamous pamphlet, *Rangila Rasul,* published by an Arya Samaj enthusiast. Written in awful taste, it dealt with the private life of Prophet Mohammed.

28. The lives of Swami Shraddhanand, leader of the Arya Samaj and the *shuddhi* movement, and Khwaja Hasan Nizami, priest at the shrine of Nizamuddian Auliya in Delhi, were threatened. The former was killed by a Muslim in 1926.

29. *Memoranda Submitted by the Government of India and the Indian Office to the Indian Statutory Commission,* vol. 4, pt. 1 (London: His Majesty's Stationery Office, 1930), pp. 99, 106. These numbers excluded the "minor occurrences."

30. In the North West Frontier Province, Khan Abdul Ghaffar Khan, who later came to be called "the Frontier Gandhi," created a nonviolent organization called the Khudai Khidmatgars (Servants of God) in the late 1920s. Like Gandhi's followers, the Khidmatgars, overwhelmingly Muslim, accepted nonviolence as a creed, not simply as a policy. See Joan Bondurant, *The Conquest of Violence* (Princeton: Princeton University Press, 1988), pp. 131–45.

31. For alienation of Uttar Pradesh Muslims, see Gyanendra Pandey, *The Ascendancy of the Congress in Uttar Pradesh, 1926–34* (Delhi: Oxford University Press, 1978), ch. 5., "The general Muslim aloofness," writes Pandey, "stands out in sharp contrast to the participation of masses of Muslims in the nationalists agitations of 1919–22 in many parts of India" (p. 115).

32. For the ancient and medieval history of Aligarh, see J. M. Siddiqui, *Aligarh: A Historical Survey* (New Delhi: Munshiram Manoharlal, 1981).

33. Chris Bayly, *Rulers, Townsmen, and Bazaars: North Indian Society in the Age of British Expansion, 1770–1870* (Cambridge: Cambridge University Press, 1983).

34. For details of British-Muslim relations in this period, see Francis Robinson, *Separatism Among Indian Muslims: The Politics of the United Provinces Muslims, 1860–1923,* 2d ed. (Cambridge: Cambridge University Press, 1993), pp. 98–104.

35. The best published account of the birth and first three decades of MAO College is David Lelyveld, *Aligarh's First Generation: Muslim Solidarity in British India* (Princeton: Princeton University Press, 1978).

36. Following the Cambridge-Oxford model, Sir Syed chose Aligarh as the location. Eighty miles away from Delhi, Aligarh was far enough from the corrupting influences of the big city but not too far from its conveniences.

37. Aga Khan III, *The Memoirs of Aga Khan* (London: Cassell, 1954), pp. 35–36.

38. M. S. Jain, *The Aligarh Movement* (Agra: Sri Ram Mehra, 1965).

39. Khalid Bin Sayeed, *Pakistan: The Formative Phase, 1857–1948* (Karachi: Oxford University Press, 1968).

40. "Higher values were discarded for the low; a few hundred acres of dusty land and buildings without character were exchanged for the infinite spaces of religious and moral speculation; the reconstruction of the social and economic life of a whole community was sacrificed to secure retirement in the lower grades of government service for the sake of a few hundred Muslim families." M. Mujeeb, *Indian Muslims* (London: George Allen and Unwin, 1967; Delhi: Munshiram Manoharlal, 1985), p. 451.

41. A rueful Nehru, known for his pro-Muslim sympathies, admiration for Urdu, and tren-

chant opposition to Hindu nationalism, wrote: "The tradition of Aligarh College was . . . conservative, both socially and politically. Its trustees came from among the princes and big landlords. . . . Under a succession of English principals, closely associated with government circles, it had fostered separatist tendencies and an anti-nationalist outlook. The chief aim kept before its students was to enter government service in subordinate ranks. For that a pro-government attitude was necessary and no truck with nationalism and sedition. The Aligarh college groups had become the leaders of the new Muslim intelligentsia and influenced sometimes openly, more often behind the scenes, almost every Muslim movement." Jawaharlal Nehru, *The Discovery of India* (Delhi: Oxford University Press, 1985), pp. 342–79.

42. Syed Sharifuddin Pirzada, ed., *Foundations of Pakistan: All-India Muslim League Documents (1906–1947)*, vol. 1 (Karachi: Royal, 1990), p. 6; The Agha Khan, *Memoirs*, pp. 75–77.

43. With the exception of Punjab and Bengal, the Muslim-majority states.

44. The Khilafat movement had stirred the conscience of students, but the university bureaucracy continued to be loyal to the British. Unable to break the hold of loyalists on the levers of power, the leaders of the Khilafat movement decided to found a new university, the Jamia Milia Islamia. It would later be called the home of *nationalist* Muslims, and Aligarh the home of *separatist* Muslims. On the whole, the older ideology of loyalty to the British returned after the collapse of Khilafat movement at AMU. For an account of this and other political tendencies at AMU, see Mushirul Hasan, "Nationalist and Separatist Trends in Aligarh, 1915–47," *Indian Economic and Social History Review* 22, no. 1 (1985).

45. A brief summary of Aligarh's municipal politics until 1920–21 is as follows. In 1868, municipal elections, based on property and taxation, were introduced to elect the Municipal Board for local self-governance. Despite the Indo-Islamic character of the town, historically dominated by Muslim aristocracy, the elective principles of property and taxation had made Hindus and Muslims equally represented on the Board. Of the 13 elected members in 1883, 5 were Hindu, 5 Muslim, and 3 other, all elected from general constituencies. Between 1880 and 1915, the Hindu-Muslim distribution was roughly in balance. In 1916, communal representation was introduced as an elective principle, freezing Muslim representation at a high level. "A History of Aligarh Municipality" (Aligarh: Aligarh Municipal Board, n.d.).

46. In the late 1880s and 1890s, Lala Lajpat Rai, an important leader of Arya Samaj, had started his political career with an attack on Sir Syed. Rai as a young man admired Sir Syed for his liberal religious views but was deeply disappointed by Sir Syed's alliance with the British. "Open Letters to Sir Syed Ahmed Khan," in *Lala Lajpat Rai: Writings and Speeches* (Delhi: University Publishers, 1966), 1:1.

47. For a detailed account of the first years of Jamia Milia through the biography of one of its leading stalwarts, see B. Sheik Ali, *Zakir Husain: Life and Times* (Delhi: Vikas, 1991), chs. 5–7.

48. Hasan, "Nationalist and Separatist Trends," pp. 5–8.

49. "India in 1930–31," statement prepared for presentation to Parliament, Government of India, Bureau of Public Information, Delhi, 1931, p. 470.

50. The account below relies on Hasan, "Nationalist and Separatist Trends."

51. "A UNESCO Study of Social Tensions in Aligarh 1950–51," report prepared by Pars Ram, edited with an introduction by Gardner Murphy (Ahmedabad: New Order, 1954), p. 172.

52. *The Times* (London), 12 April 1927.

53. *Aligarh Gazetteer*, 1962, p. 40. It was led by Malkhan Singh, later an important Uttar Pradesh politician. He was being sentenced to prison for leading the movement in Aligarh. *Indian Annual Register 1922* (Calcutta: Annual Register Office, 1922), 2:64–65.

54. Aligarh has a wealthy trading community called Barehsenis. Jwala Prasad Jigyasu, a wealthy Varshney trader, led the city's wing of the Congress in the mid-to-late 1930s. For details, see Zoya Hasan, *Dominance and Mobilisation: Rural Politics in Western Uttar Pradesh* (Delhi: Sage, 1989), ch. 4.

55. For details, see Zoya Hasan, "Congress in Aligarh," in *Congress and Indian Nationalism*, ed. Richard Sisson and Stanley Wolpert (Berkeley: University of California Press, 1988), pp. 334–38.

56. Census of India, 1991.

57. Census of India, 1991.

58. Except in the small principality of Cannanore in north Malabar in the sixteenth century. See K. K. N. Kurup, *The Ali Rajas of Cannanore* (Trivandrum: College, 1975).

59. For shared rural traditions, see Stephen Dale and M. Gangadhara Menon, "Nercca: Saint-Martyr Worship Among the Muslims of Kerala," *Bulletin of the School of Oriental and African Studies* 16, no. 3 (1978). Moreover, unlike the distinctly Persian or Arabic style of northern Indian mosques, the Moplah mosques borrowed heavily from the existing temple and church styles. Indeed, to an untutored eye, the architecture of Moplah mosques until recently has been quite indistinguishable from that of a church or a temple. K. J. John, "The Muslim Arabs and Mosque Architecture in Malabar," in *Kerala Muslims: A Historical Perspective,* ed. Asghar Ali Engineer (Delhi: Ajanta, 1995).

60. This has led to some interesting results. Malayalam is a highly Sanskritized language. The Moplahs, therefore, end up using a great many Sanskrit words that in the north are unmistakably associated with Hinduism. In Kerala, they are seen as words of Malayalam, not of Sanskrit. Moplahs have also produced some of the giants of Malayalam literature. In an interview with me, M. T. Vasudevan Nair, a leading literary and cultural figure in Kerala today, called Vaikom Mohammed Bashir "one of the greatest figures ever in Malayalam literature" and N. P. Mohammed and K. T. Mohammed "major literary figures." Interview in Calicut, 2 August 1994.

61. Robert Hardgrave, "The Mappilla Rebellion, 1921: Peasant Revolt in Malabar," *Modern Asian Studies* 11, no. 1 (1977): 91. For alternative estimates, see Roland Miller, *Mappila Muslims of Kerala* (Delhi: Orient Longman, 1992), pp. 148–49.

62. R. H. Hitchcock, *A History of the Malabar Rebellion, 1921* (Madras: Government Press, 1925), pp. 126–37. Hitchcock was the district superintendent of police in Calicut at the time of the rebellion. Ernad and Walluvanad were the *taluks* (subdistrict administrative units) most affected. Both taluks were just south of Calicut.

63. Interview with Keshava Menon, then head of Malabar Congress, in M. Gangadhara Menon, *Malabar Rebellion, 1921–1922* (Allahabad: Vohra, 1989), p. 494; Hitchcock, *History,* pp. 156–57.

64. Hitchcock, *History*, pp. 32–4.

65. "Report of the Knapp Committee on the Moplah Train Tragedy," *Indian Annual Register 1922*, vol. 2 (Calcutta: Indian Annual Register Office, 1923), p. 833. The Knapp Committee was instituted by the government to inquire into the tragedy.

66. K. N. Panikkar, *Against Lord and State: Religion and Peasant Uprisings in Malabar, 1836–1921* (Delhi: Oxford University Press, 1992), ch. 2.

67. Ibid., pp. 179–82; Hardgrave, " Mappilla Rebellion," p. 86; Hitchcock, *History*, pp. 162–63, 324–25; E. M. S. Namboodiripad, *Kerala: Yesterday, Today, and Tomorrow* (Calcutta: National Book Agency, 1967), pp. 148–49.

68. E. M. S. Namboodiripad, *Kerala*, p. 147. For the overall violence (murders, looting, and arson), see Hitchcock, *History*, pp. 141–52.

69. The causes of Moplah rebellion remain almost as controversial today as they were in the 1920s. The scholarly judgments of the historians of the Malabar rebellion remain split into two camps: those supporting the theory of Moplah religious fanaticism and those arguing that a combination of anti-British and anti-landlord sentiments led to the revolt. These views are best represented in Stephen Dale, *Islamic Society on the South Asian Frontier: The Mappillas of Malabar, 1498–1922* (Oxford: Clarendon, 1980); Panikkar, *Against Lord;* D. N. Dhanagre, "Agrarian Conflict, Religion, and Politics: The Moplah Rebellions in Malabar in the 19th and 20th Centuries," *Past and Present* (February 1977); and Menon, *Malabar Rebellion*, esp. pp. 423–84.

70. "The Moplah outbreak," wrote Gandhi, "has disturbed the atmosphere, as nothing else has since the inauguration of noncooperation." *Young India*, 8 September 1921.

71. It is sometimes argued that the invasions of Mysore Sultans, Hyder and Tipu, had caused a communal divide temporarily in the late eighteenth century. Miller, *Mappilla Muslims*, pp. 88–93.

72. Kenneth Jones, "Socio-Religious Reform Movements in British India," in *The New Cambridge History of India*, vol. 3, pt. 1 (Cambridge: Cambridge University Press, 1994), p. 194; R. K. Ghai, *Shuddhi Movement in India* (New Delhi: Commonwealth, 1990), pp. 83–88; J. T. F. Jordens, *Swami Shradhhananda: His Life and Causes* (Delhi: Oxford University Press, 1981), pp. 125–27; G. R. Thursby, *Hindu-Muslim Relations in British India: A Study of Controversy, Conflict, and Communal Movements in Northern India, 1923–28* (Leiden: Brill, 1975), pp. 136–45; J. F. Seunarine, *Reconversion to Hinduism Through Shuddhi* (Madras: Christian Literature Society, 1977), p. 36.

73. Madan Mohan Malaviya, Presidential Address, All India Hindu Mahasabha (1922), *The Indian Annual Register, 1923* (Calcutta: Annual Register Office, 1923), 2:132. Though the Arya Samaj was against idol-worship and many of the leaders of the Mahasabha, such as Madan Mohan Malaviya, were old-style Hindus *(Sanatanis)*, the new situation brought the two wings of Hinduism together. Given the renewed threat of conversions to Islam, they thought it pointless to fight internal battles for reform.

74. Lala Hans Raj, cited in Thursby, *Hindu-Muslim Relations*, p. 142.

75. The Ezhavas today constitute more than 20 percent of the population of Kerala state. Precise percentages for the 1920s are not available, partly because Kerala was not a state at that time. Malabar was part of the Madras Presidency of British India.

76. The Ezhavas are called Tiyas in Malabar. To simplify the narrative, I will continue to use the term "Ezhava."

77. G. Rajendran, *The Ezhava Community and Kerala Politics* (Trivandrum: Academy of Political Science, 1974), pp. 23–24.

78. Dilip Menon, *Caste, Nationalism, and Communism in South India: Malabar, 1900–1948* (Cambridge: Cambridge University Press, 1994), p. 73.

79. The Brahmins were called the Namboodiris in Kerala. Thursby, *Hindu-Muslim Relations,* pp. 143–44. Elsewhere, Namboodiris objected to the conversions the Arya Samaj had already made. They were not ready to accept the lower caste converts back into their ranks. See Menon, *Caste, Nationalism, and Communism,* p. 80.

80. Namboodiripad, *Kerala,* pp. 151–52, emphasis added.

81. For a compelling argument that this merger facilitated the emergence of a Communist movement, see Menon, *Caste, Nationalism, and Communism.* While talking about the peasants and workers, the Communists could repeatedly use caste issues, which had great resonance in Malabar.

82. E. M. S. Namboodiripad, *A Short History of the Peasant Movement in Kerala* (Bombay: People's Publishing House, 1943), pp. 20–27.

83. E. M. S. Namboodiripad *Reminiscences of an Indian Communist* (New Delhi: National Book Agency, 1987), pp. 75–90.

84. Namboodiripad, *Kerala,* p. 189.

CHAPTER 6. VICIOUS AND VIRTUOUS CIRCLES

1. Paul Brass, *Theft of an Idol* (Princeton: Princeton University Press, 1997).

2. In 1997, in the Varshney College Teachers Association, 97 percent of members were Hindu and 3 percent Muslim; and in the AMU Teachers Association, 85 percent of members were Muslim and 15 percent Hindu. Proportions were calculated on the basis of membership lists.

3. In 1997, in a town of more than 35 percent Muslim population, the Bar Association had 7.5 percent Muslim members and more than 90 percent Hindu members. Proportions were calculated from the list of members.

4. In 1997, there were two trade associations: Aligarh Mahanagar Udyog Vyapar Sangh and Aligarh Udyog Vyapar Mandal. The former was bigger and BJP-supported: in 1996, only 4 percent of its members were Muslim. The latter was considerably smaller and had more than 20 percent Muslim members.

5. The smaller business association, the Aligarh Udyog Vyapar Mandal, is allied with a party that promotes a lower caste–Muslim alliance. The Samajwadi Party is led by Mulayam Singh Yadav, a highly popular leader of the lower castes and Muslims in Uttar Pradesh.

6. Gopal Kumar, "The Popular Science Movement in Kerala," *Bulletin of Concerned Asian Scholars* (fall 1997).

7. K. Ramachandran Nair, "Trade Unionism in Kerala," in *Kerala's Economy,* ed. B. A. Prakash (New Delhi: Sage, 1994).

8. Kumar, "Popular Science Movement."

9. Ashis Bose, *India's Urban Population: 1991 Census Data* (New Delhi: Wheeler, 1993), p. 409.

10. What follows is a summary of thirty-five interviews conducted with the poor and illiterate Muslims out of fifty Muslims selected in the town sample.

11. For a fascinating ethnographic account of the emotional and cultural issues among the Aligarh Muslims, see Elizabeth Mann, *Boundaries and Identities: Muslims, Work, and Status in Aligarh* (New Delhi: Sage, 1992). With subtlety and empathy, Mann re-creates the world of Muslims who are poor or have only recently been upwardly mobile.

12. Based on *Census of India,* Uttar Pradesh, 1971, 1981, and 1991.

13. For further details of the likely caste breakdown and the political affiliations of different castes, see Violette Graff, "Religious Identities and Indian Politics: Elections in Aligarh, 1971–1989," in *Islam, Politics, and Society in South Asia,* ed. Andre Wink (Delhi: Manohar, 1991). There are two large business *(vaishya)* castes: the Barehsenis (12 percent of the population) and the Agarwals (6 percent). It is also believed that the latter traditionally supported the Congress but in all probability have switched to the BJP by now. The former have been big supporters of Hindu nationalism for a long time.

14. Pars Ram and Gardner Murphy, "Recent Investigations of Hindu-Muslim Relations in India," *Human Organization.* 11 (summer 1952): 13–16.

15. For details, see Theodore P. Wright Jr., "Muslim Education in India at the Crossroads: The Case of Aligarh," *Pacific Affairs* (spring–summer 1966).

16. Zakir Hussain's speech at the 1951 convocation (graduation) of the university, in B. Sheik Ali, *Zakir Hussain: Life and Times* (Delhi: Vikas, 1991), p. 204.

17. The violence was important enough for Prime Minister Nehru to take up the matter in his confidential fortnightly memos to the chiefs of state governments. He urged caution because Muslim communalism was again on the rise. Nehru, *Fortnightly Letters to Chief Ministers, 1947–64,* vol. 4: *1954–57* (Delhi: Oxford University Press, 1988), p. 436.

18. "By and large the Aligarh University still continues to be the center of that very mentality which resulted in the partition of this country. . . . We think it continues to be a plague spot in India. Until and unless this plague spot is cleared of its plague symptoms and made a national organization, there will be danger." Balraj Madhok, arguing on behalf of the Bharatiya Jan Sangh in parliament. *Lok Sabha Debates,* 2d ser., 11 August 1961, pp. 1722–23.

19. Ram, *UNESCO Study of Social Tensions in Aligarh, 1950–51* (Ahmedabad: New Order Book Company, 1954), p. 172.

20. Ibid.

21. Ibid.

22. *Dainik Prakash,* 16 September 1956.

23. For example, *Dainik Prakash,* 15 and 19 April 1957.

24. *Times of India,* 3–5 October 1961; *Hindustan Times,* 6 October 1961.

25. Mann, *Boundaries and Identities,* p. 79.

26. "Therefore the responsibility of the riot goes to the Muslims of Upperkot. . . . Even when the news of violence reached the head office of [the Congress candidate, he and his colleagues] did little to control the situation" (p. 86). My translation from the Hindi.

Uttar Pradesh Rajya ke Aligarh Nagar Mein 2 March, 1971 and Uske Baad Huey Sampra-dayik Upadravon Ke Sambandh Mein Jaanch Ayog Ki Report [Report of the Commission for Inquiry into Communal Disturbances of Aligarh, U.P., on March 2, 1971, and After] (Allahabad: Superintendent of Printing and Publishing, 1975). Justice D. S. Mathur was asked by the state government to make an investigation.

27. *The First Annual Report of the Minorities Commission* (Delhi: Government of India, 1979), pp. 75–77.

28. Namita Singh, *"Aag Abhi Bhi Jal Rahi Hai"* [The Fire Is Still Burning], *Dinmaan,* 26 November–2 December 1978, pp. 24–28.

29. "Janata Chief's Version of Aligarh Riots Contested," *Times of India,* 21 October 1978; "Janata Silent on RSS Role in Aligarh," *Times of India,* 17 November 1978; "RSS Is Not Involved: Chandra Sekhar," *Times of India,* 20 November 1978; "Janata Plans to Give Clean Chit to RSS in Aligarh," *Times of India,* 24 November 1978; "UP Janata Threatened by Aligarh Issue," *Indian Express,* 18 November 1978; "UP Janata Rift over RSS Role in Aligarh," *Indian Express,* 24 November 1978; "PM's Stand on RSS Wishywashy: Madhu Limaye," *Indian Express,* 30 November 1978.

30. *First Annual Report,* p. 80; "Aligarh Riots," Report of the Study Team of the People's Union of Civil Liberties (PUCL), *Economic and Political Weekly,* 18 November 1978, p. 1883–84.

31. *Times of India,* 14 August 1980.

32. After the 1961 riots in Aligarh, the scheduled castes and Muslims had come together to deliver a stunning defeat to the Congress in the 1962 assembly and parliamentary elections. The alliance lasted only for an election. It did not become institutionalized as a lower caste–Muslim political coalition. For details, see Paul Brass, *Factional Politics in an Indian State* (Berkeley: University of California Press, 1965), pp. 106–11.

33. There are several parties that emerged from the Janata umbrella of 1977–79: the Janata Dal, the Samajwadi Party, the Bahujan Samaj Party, the Samata Party, and the Rashtriya Janata Dal.

34. They create fatigue only in the long run when curfews do not seem to end; the schools, markets, banks, and ration shops do not open; and the routine life of the town is completely disrupted for long periods of time.

35. The Bahujan Samaj and the Samajawadi Parties, electoral and government partners between 1993 and 1995, fell out in June 1995.

36. The exit polls done after the 1991 and 1993 elections in Uttar Pradesh showed that the BJP was able to get a sizeable chunk of the lower-caste vote.

37. For a good discussion of the various considerations, see Sukumar Panikkar, "The Muslim League in Kerala," Ph.D. diss., Department of Political Science, University of Kerala, Trivandrum, 1977, pp. 334–42, 402–4. Each year in April, Malappuram *nercha* is celebrated in commemoration of *Shahids* (martyrs) of the Malabar rebellion.

38. For a history of this demand, see Abdul Azeez, *Rise of Muslims in Kerala Politics* (Trivandrum: CBH, 1992), ch. 4.

39. In 1947, the government reported that of 117 officers posted at the subdistrict level in Malabar, only 4 were Moplahs. For these and later estimates, see Miller, *Mappillas,* pp. 192, 194.

40. There was only one university in Kerala at that time, based in Trivandrum.

41. Panikkar, "Muslim League," p. 329.

42. Ibid, p. 365.

43. Between 1947 and1950, the Indian Communists were engaged in an insurrection. They did not believe in parliamentary communism at that time.

44. Ronald J. Herring, *Land to the Tiller* (New Haven: Yale University Press, 1983), ch. 7.

45. E. M. S. Namboodiripad, "Presidential Address," International Congress of Kerala Studies, 27–29 August, 1994, *Addresses and Abstracts,* vol. 1 (Trivandrum: AKG Center for Research and Studies, 1994), p. 2.

46. T. J. Nossiter, *Communism in Kerala: A Study in Political Adaptation* (Berkeley: University of California Press, 1982), p. 357.

47. Ibid., p. 345.

48. Miller, *Mappillas,* p. 188.

49. Interview, P. K. Kunhalikutty, Muslim League, Industry Minister, Congress-led government, Trivandrum, 20 July 1995.

50. Ibid.; interview, M. K. Muneer, M.L.A. from Calicut, Calicut, 23 July 1995.

51. Once the Ezhavas achieved free entry to temples in the 1930s and the walls of deference started coming down, they renegotiated their relationship with Hinduism and ceased to "stand outside." After the self-respect movement, they also did not convert to other religions.

52. The other percentages are as follows: scheduled castes and tribes (8.8 percent), Brahmins (1.8 percent), other castes (9 percent). *Report of the Backward Classes Reservation Commission, Kerala* (Trivandrum: Government of Kerala, 1970), p. 441.

53. John Oommen, "Politics of Communalism in Kerala," *Economic and Political Weekly,* 18 March 1995, p. 545.

54. Ibid. This meaning goes all the way back to the earlier writings on Kerala communalism. See, e.g., K. S. Nayar, "Communal Interest Groups in Kerala," in *South Asian Religion and Politics,* ed. Donald Eugene Smith (Princeton: Princeton University Press, 1966).

55. The ideology of equality has reconstructed, not obliterated, caste in Kerala. Because ritual purity and pollution have been abandoned, caste associations such as the Nair Service Society (NSS) and the SNDP have been desacralized. These traditional and ascriptive organizations provide useful modern services to their members.

56. As, for example, in Hyderabad during the 1948 police action and in Ahmedabad in 1969.

CHAPTER 7. PRINCELY RESISTANCE TO CIVIL SOCIETY

1. A small riot also took place in July 1940, but it was controlled within a day. *The Pioneer,* 8, 9, and 10 July 1940.

2. For details, see Gopal Krishna, "Communal Violence in India," *Economic and Political Weekly,* 12 January 1985, p. 66.

3. The first book-length treatment of the Chikan industry is Clare M. Wilkinson-Weber, *Embroidering Lives: Women's Work and Skill in the Lucknow Embroidery Industry* (Albany: SUNY Press, 1999).

4. Wilkinson-Weber, ibid., surveys the various estimates.

5. V. B. Singh et al., "Problems of Select Urban Handicrafts in Uttar Pradesh (A Survey): Chikan, Lucknow" (Lucknow: Giri Institute of Economic Development and Industrial Relations, 1975), pp. 8–9.

6. Uttar Pradesh Minorities Financial and Development Corporation, "A Survey of Chikan Industry" (n.p., n.d.), p. 3.

7. The production process has the following stages: cutting, stitching, printing, embroidery, washing, and pressing. Different artisans are involved in different parts of the process.

8. Robert Putnam, *Making Democracy Work* (Princeton: Princeton University Press, 1994).

9. This information is based on field interviews with and a survey of traders.

10. Wilkinson-Weber, *Embroidering Lives,* p. 190.

11. Amartya Sen, "The Profit Motive," in *Choice, Welfare and Measurement* (Cambridge: MIT Press, 1984).

12. James Scott, *Moral Economy of the Peasant* (New Haven: Yale University Press, 1978).

13. Author's interview, president, Andhra Pradesh Chamber of Commerce and Industry, Hyderabad, 12 August 1994.

14. *Directory of the Hyderabad Chamber of Commerce and Industry,* 1994.

15. Afzal Mohammed, "Role of the Informal Sector in Urban Communities: A Case Study of Hyderabad City" (Hyderabad: Centre for Economic and Social Studies, 1994), typescript.

16. The state of Andhra Pradesh, formed in 1956, merged the Telugu-speaking parts of the Nizam's Hyderabad and the former Madras Presidency. On grounds of linguistic federalism, the Kannada- and Marathi-speaking parts of the Nizam's state were merged with Maharashtra and Karnataka.

17. Authors's interview with Vande Matram Ramchandra Rao, 23 October 1993, Hyderabad. In his youth, Rao had participated in the Vande Matram movement against the Nizam.

18. For an understanding of the meaning of Muharram rituals for the Shias, see Keith Guy Hjortshoj, "Kerbala in Context: A Study of Muharram in Lucknow" (Ph.D. diss., Cornell University, 1977), especially chs. 3 and 4.

19. Rosie Llewellyn-Jones, *A Fatal Friendship: The Nawabs, the British and the City of Lucknow* (Delhi: Oxford University Press, 1992).

20. For an insightful analysis of these points, see Hjortshoj, "Kerbala in Context," ch. 3.

21. C. M. Naim, "The Art of Urdu Marsiya," in *Islamic Society and Culture,* ed. Milton Israel and N. K. Wagle (New Delhi: Manohar, 1983). For an English translation of a well-known marsiya of Mir Anis Ali, Lucknow's leading marsiya writer, see David Matthews, *The Battle of Karbala* (Delhi: Rupa, 1994).

22. Hjorthhoj, "Kerbala in Context," ch. 4; Census of India "Muharram in Two Cities: Lucknow and Delhi" (1961).

23. Some of the everyday Hindu-Muslim engagement can be seen during both Hindu and Muslim festivals, when families of both communities visit and greet one another. The contrast between the new and old cities can be visually quite dramatic on such occasions. My own field research in Hyderabad coincided with the Dussehra festival of the Hindus. It was clear that many Hindu households in the upscale Banjara Hills had a regular

stream of Muslim visitors, but the old city at the same time was remarkably full of bitterness, recrimination, and complaints.

24. The Nizam Club, for example, is 30 percent Muslim, based on the 1996 Directory of Members. There were 985 Muslim members and 3,343 total members in 1996. These numbers and proportions change only marginally from year to year.

25. Especially remarkable is a film, *Is Shahar Ko Kay Hua?* (What happened to this city?).

26. This figure was calculated from the list of employees and unions. The railways had 6,281 employees in 1996; 632 were Muslim. These numbers, too, change only slightly over time.

27. This figure was calculated from the membership directory of the Avadh Bar Association, 1992–93.

28. One may argue that a mixed, educated workforce demonstrates middle-class integration, not elite-level integration. This reasoning, although right on the whole, would require some modifications in Lucknow. In a city where more than half of Muslims may still be illiterate, higher education ipso facto places one at the elite level.

29. Harriet Ronken Lynton and Mohini Rajan, *The Days of the Beloved* (Berkeley: University of California Press, 1974). For Lucknow, see Abdul Halim Sharar, *Lucknow: The Last Phase of an Oriental Culture,* trans. E. S. Harcourt and Fakhir Hussain (Delhi: Oxford University Press, 1975).

30. Raja Kishen Prasad, for example, served as a prime minister, the highest official post, under the sixth Nizam (1901–12) as well as under the seventh (1927–36).

31. The three largest religious groups were the Hindus (84.3 percent), the Muslims (10.6 percent), and the Christians (1 percent) . These are 1931 figures. Until 1948, there was no significant change in the percentages reported here. See Census of India, 1931, vol. 23, pt. 1, Hyderabad State (Hyderabad-Deccan: Government Central Press, 1933), p. 232.

32. Linguistically, the state had four large groups. Telugu was the mother tongue of 48.3 percent of the population, Marathi that of 26.2 percent, Kannada that of 11.2 percent, and Urdu that of 10.4 percent. Census of India, 1931, p. 229.

33. The feudal lord *(jagirdar)* in many cases had the right to keep his own police and armed forces and run judicial, educational, and public health systems. The *jagir,* in other words, was a state within the state.

34. A. M. Khusro, *Economic and Social Effects of Jagirdari Abolition and Land Reforms in Hyderabad* (Hyderabad: Osmania University Press, 1958), pp. 1–12.

35. C. V. Subbarao, "Industrial Capital and Technology in Hyderabad State, 1875–1950," report submitted to the Indian Council of Social Science Research, Delhi, 1988, p. 62.

36. As far as I know, the idea of differing historical narratives has never been applied to Hyderabad's history. A brief indication of it appears in a seminar report. See Vasant Bawa's incisive comments in Helen Butt, *The Composite Nature of Hyderabadi Culture,* rapporteur's report on a seminar (Hyderabad: Osmania University, 1990), pp. 69–70.

37. Bilkees Latif, *Her India: The Fragrance of Forgotten Years* (Delhi: Arnold Heinemann, 1984), pp. 44–5; see also Mirza Ismail, *My Public Life* (London: Allen and Unwin, 1954), p. 103.

38. For a fascinating discussion of the Mulki–non-Mulki conflict between the 1850s and the 1930s, see Karen Leonard, "Hyderabad: The Mulki–non-Mulki Conflict," in Robin Jef-

frey, *People, Princes, and Paramount Power: Society and Politics in the Princely States* (Delhi: Oxford University Press, 1978).

39. Syed Abid Hasan, *Whither Hyderabad?* (Hyderabad: The Nizam's Subject League, 1935), p. 43.

40. Swami Ramananda Tirtha, *Memoirs of the Hyderabad Freedom Struggle* (Bombay: Popular Prakashan, 1967), pp. 49–50. A follower of Gandhi, the Swami was among the first politicians to introduce Hyderabad to mass politics at a time when politics was predominantly aristocratic and court-related. For similar memoirs of the time, see D. G. Deshpande, "Political Developments and the Situation in Hyderabad State During the Period 1925–1940," in *History of Hyderabad District 1879–1950,* ed. M. Radhakrishna Sarma, K. D. Abhyankar, and S. D. Moghe (Hyderabad: Bharatiya Itihasa Sankalana Samiti, 1987). In addition, I conducted long interviews with three participants in the anti-Nizam movement in Hyderabad: Vande Matram Ramchandra Rao, 23 October 1993; the late Gopal Rao Ekbote, education minister in the 1950s, 25 October 1993; and M. Channa Reddy, former chief minister, Andhra Pradesh, 10 March 1995.

41. James Scott, *Domination and the Arts of Resistance* (New Haven: Yale University Press, 1990); James Scott, *Weapons of the Weak* (New Haven: Yale University Press, 1984).

42. The English translation of the two would be Society of Pure Hindus (Arya Samaj) and Council for the Unity of Muslims (MIM).

43. Even government documents accepted this, though their number seem to be on the lower side. See *Report of the Reforms Committee 1938,* appendix 1 (Hyderabad: Government Central Press, 1938).

44. For the circumstances surrounding the MIM's birth, see Munir Ahmed Khan, "Muslim Politics in Hyderabad" (Ph.D. diss., Hyderabad: Osmania University, Hyderabad, 1980), pt. 2.

45. A fifth group, the Mulki League, fell by the wayside as mass politics took over. The elite nature of the Mulki League became very clear in this period. The League was unable to mobilize the masses.

46. There was a Communist uprising in the 1940s. It made some headway in rural areas but not in the city. See Mohan Ram, "The Communist Movement in Andhra Pradesh," in *Radical Politics in South Asia,* ed. Paul Brass and Marcus Franda (Cambridge: MIT Press, 1973).

47. A good sampling of the lurid campaign slogans is available in Lucien Benichou, "From Autocracy to Integration: Political Developments in Hyderabad State, 1938–1948" (Ph.D. diss., University of Western Australia, 1985), chs. 3–4.

48. Ian Copeland, "Communalism in Princely India: The Case of Hyderabad, 1930–40," in *India's Partition,* ed. Mushirul Hasan (Delhi: Oxford University Press, 1993).

49. N. Ramesan, *The Freedom Struggle in Hyderabad* (Hyderabad: Hyderabad State Committee for Compilation of History, 1956), ch. 11. The list of Samaj complaints against the government was long: a ban on the entry of major Samaj preachers from British India; desecration of Samaj temples, *Om* flags, and *havan kunds* (places for fire worship); banning of Samaj schools, gymnasiums, and newspapers; and restrictions on its public meetings. The Hyderabad government called the Samaj subversive; the Samaj called the government communal.

50. "The ultimate goal of the Hyderabad State Congress is the attainment of Responsible Government built on a strong foundation of our basic loyalty to the ruler and the Asaf Jahi Dynasty and the creation of sincere unity and harmony among all communities . . . diverting thus the present consciousness . . . from the communal trend to the progressive and national path of patriotism." Ibid., pp. 134–35.

51. *Report of the Reforms Committee 1938,* ch. 2.

52. Khan, "Muslim Politics," chs. 3–4; and Benichou, "From Autocracy," chs. 4–5.

53. Khan, "Muslim Politics," p. 80. The MIM organizations emerged in sixteen districts of the state.

54. Benichou, "From Autocracy," p. 167.

55. The story of this "intricate relationship" is analyzed by Benichou, "From Autocracy," ch. 4. Dispossession of Bahadur Yar Jung's titles in 1943 was the high point of the Nizam's disapproval of the MIM.

56. For a detailed account from Delhi's side, see V. P. Menon, *Integration of the Indian States* (Hyderabad: Orient Longman, 1956). For inside details from Hyderabad, see Ali Yavar Jung, *Hyderabad in Retrospect* (Bombay: Bennet, Coleman, 1949); Mir Laiq Ali, *Tragedy of Hyderabad* (Karachi: Pakistan Cooperative Society, 1962). For the British side, see Alan Campbell Johnson, *Mission with Mountbatten* (Bombay: Jaico, 1951). Menon negotiated on behalf of Delhi; Yavar Jung was part of the Nizam's government until late 1947; Laiq Ali was Hyderabad's prime minister between December 1947 and September 1948; and Campbell Johnson represented Viceroy Mountbatten.

57. See Jung, *Hyderabad in Retrospect,* pp. 25–28.

58. From the speeches of Kasim Razvi, the chief of the Razakars, cited in K. M. Munshi, *End of an Era* (Bombay: Bharatiya Vidya Bhavan, 1957), pp. 140–42. See similar citations in Ramanand Tirtha, *Memoirs,* p. 188–90. K. M. Munshi, Delhi's agent-general at Hyderabad, has also quoted Razvi using even more vituperative language in his speeches. Since I have not been able to confirm them independently, I have used only texts cited by authors from very different political quarters.

59. Fareed Mirza, *Pre and Post Police Action Days in the Erstwhile Hyderabad State: What I Saw, Felt, and Did,* pamphlet published by the author, 1976, p. 3; author's interview with Fareed Mirza, 16 November 1994, Hyderabad.

60. Mirza, *Pre and Post Police Action,* p. 13. As already stated, Muslim dissidents were also the object of the Razakars' wrath. The Muslim editor of an Urdu newspaper, *Imroz,* one of only two newspapers critiquing the Razakars, was killed in a highly symbolic and gruesome manner. For chilling details, see Mirza, p. 25; Jung, *Hyderabad in Retrospect,* pp. 38–41. Mirza also read out to me the unpublished pages from his diary, pages he wrote on the day the editor of *Imroz* was murdered. The narrative was about his fear of approaching death and his prayer to Allah. Mirza had been publicly identified by Razvi as a Muslim renegade. Luckily for him, before he could be attacked the Hyderabad state fell to Indian forces, and with it fell the Razakars.

61. Veena Talwar Oldenburg, *The Making of Colonial Lucknow* (Princeton: Princeton University Press, 1984).

62. Symbolizing the Hindu-Muslim amity of Lucknow is a rather striking image. According

to legends and popular history, the city of Lucknow was founded by Lakshman, the younger and loyal brother of the Hindu Lord Ram. A hillock, called Laskmantila, marks the founding event. The Aurangzebi mosque stands at the hillock today. The mosque is said to have been constructed in the late seventeenth century by the Mughal emperor Aurangzeb on a site that previously had a Hindu tower-cum-temple. Sites such as Laksh-mantila have touched off political passion and violence elsewhere. In Lucknow's history, however, there is no evidence yet of violence over the site, nor any politically passionate disputes.

63. The classic popular history of Lucknow nawabs and their times is Abdul Halim Sharar, *Lucknow: The Last Phase of an Oriental Culture* (London: Elek, 1992), esp. pp. 29–75.

64. David Pinault, *The Shiites: Ritual and Piety in a Muslim Community* (New York: St. Martin's, 1992).

65. Francis Robinson, "The Emergence of Lucknow as a Major Political Centre, 1899 to the Early 1920s," in *Memories of a City: Lucknow,* ed. Violette Graff (Delhi: Oxford University Press, 1997).

66. Chowdhry Khaliquzzaman and the Raja of Mahmudabad were Lucknow-based. The latter was also a financier of the League. See Raja of Mehmudabad, "Some Memories," in *India's Partition: Process, Strategy and Mobilization,* ed. Mushirul Hasan (Delhi: Oxford University Press, 1993).

67. Sandria Freitag, *Collective Action and Community: Public Arenas and the Emergence of Communalism in North India* (Delhi: Oxford University Press, 1990), ch. 8; Imtiaz Ahmed, "The Shia-Sunni Dispute in Lucknow, 1905–1980," in *Islamic Society and Culture,* ed. Milton Israel and N. K. Wagle (Delhi: Manohar, 1983); Mushirul Hasan, "Traditional Strife and Contested Meanings," in *Memories of a City: Lucknow,* ed. Violette Graff (Delhi: Oxford University Press, 1997).

68. H. R. Nevill, *Lucknow: A Gazetteer,* District Gazetteers of the United Provinces of Agra and Oudh, vol. 37 (Allahabad: Government Press, 1904), pp. 65–69.

69. Official note of the Deputy Commissioner, 12 September 1924, General Administration, File no. 479/1924, Uttar Pradesh State Archives, Lucknow.

70. Deputy Commissioner to the Commissioner, 14 September 1924, General Administration, File no. 479/1924, Uttar Pradesh State Archives, Lucknow.

71. Deputy Commissioner to the Commissioner, 24 September 1924, General Administration, File no. 479/1924, Uttar Pradesh State Archives, Lucknow.

72. The citation is from *The Leader,* 1 October 1924. For earlier statements, see *The Indian Daily Telegraph,* 13–26 September 1924.

73. *Haqiqat,* 17 September 1924.

74. Deputy Commissioner to the Commissioner, 13 November 1924, General Administration, File no. 479/1924, Uttar Pradesh State Archives, Lucknow.

75. H. A. Lalljee, *Shia Muslims' Case* (Bombay: Jawahir Press, 1946), pp. 38–9.

76. For a summary of the 1905–9 dispute, see Mushirul Hasan, "Sectarianism in Indian Islam: The Shia-Sunni Divide in the United Provinces," *Indian Economic and Social History Review* 27, no. 3 (April–June 1990).

77. "The Sunni Civil Disobedience movement goes from strength to strength. *Jathas* [orga-

nized groups] are coming in from other places in the province and from other provinces as well." Deputy Commissioner to Harper, 24 March 1939. General Administration, File no. 65/1939, Uttar Pradesh State Archives, Lucknow.

78. Superintendent of Police Lucknow to Deputy Inspector General of Police, United Provinces, 7 July 1939, General Administration, File no. 65/1939, Uttar Pradesh State Archives.

79. Note, District Magistrate, Lucknow, 6 April 1939, General Adminsitration, File no. 65/1939, Uttar Pradesh State Archives, Lucknow.

80. For the widespread rioting necessitating police firing in March and July, see Superintendent of Police to D.I.G., 31 March and 7 July 1939, General Administration, File no., /65/1939, Uttar Pradesh State Archives, Lucknow.

81. The riots stopped in 1943, but arrests for defying prohibitory orders were made every year until 1952.

82. Deputy Commissioner to the Commissioner, 13 March 1939, General Administration, File no. 65/1939, Uttar Pradesh State Archives, Lucknow. Some Shia organizations took an explicit stand against the "Sunni character" of the Muslim League and against the demand for Pakistan. Lalljee wrote, "Why [are] the Shias opposed to Pakistan? . . . Shias . . . are in a minority amongst the Mussalmans. . . . [T]heir principal oppressors [are] their own brethren in faith, the Sunni Mussalmans. What will be their position under the absolute Sunni rule in Pakistan can well be imagined" (*Shia Muslims' Case*, p. 32).

83. See *The Pioneer*, 7 July 1947.

84. "A Note on Shia Sunni Trouble in Lucknow," Lucknow Administration, typescript (n.d.).

85. *The Pioneer*, 8 July 1947.

86. *The Pioneer*, 2 August 1947.

87. See *The Pioneer*, 4 August 1947.

88. A similar conclusion is reached by Carolyn Elliott, "Decline of a Patrimonial Regime," *Journal of Asian Studies* 34, no. 1 (November 1974).

CHAPTER 8. HINDU NATIONALISTS AS BRIDGE BUILDERS?

1. V. C. Sharma, *Uttar Pradesh District Gazetteers* (Lucknow: Government of Uttar Pradesh, 1959) 37:148–49. Of this number, 3,500 workers were in Chikan, 700 in Zardozi.

2. V. B. Singh, P. D. Shrimali, and R. S. Mathur, "Problems of Select Urban Handicrafts in Uttar Pradesh (A Survey): Chikan Lucknow" (Lucknow: Giri Institute of Economic Development and Industrial Relations, 1975), p.16.

3. Clare M. Wilkinson-Weber, *Embroidering Lives: Women's Work and Skill in the Lucknow Embroidery Industry* (Albany: SUNY Press, 1999), surveys the various estimates.

4. Singh, Shrimali, and Mathur, "Problems," pp. 8–9.

5. During my field research, I met a score of Muslims in their late sixties and seventies who were suspended from service after police action, only to be reinstated several years later when the charges of complicity could not be proved. Several recalled the hardships with

transparent pain and agony. Forty percent of the sample in the survey was more than sixty years of age, which yielded a large number of such accounts.

6. For details, see Fareed Mirza, *Pre and Post Police Action Days in the Erstwhile Hyderabad State: What I Saw, Felt, and Did,* pamphlet published by the author, 1976. Some highly exaggerated accounts of the violence are also available. See especially the accounts that emerged from Pakistan: Nawab Moin Nawaz Jung, *Hyderabad in Fetters* (Karachi: Karwan-e-Adab, 1952); Qutubuddin Aziz, *The Murder of a State* (Karachi: Islamic Media Corporation, 1993); and Mir Laiq Ali, *Tragedy of Hyderabad* (Karachi: Pakistan Cooperative Society, 1962). Citing an unpublished report by Sunderlal and Abdul Ghaffar, Omar Khalidi, editor of a widely used reference on Hyderabad, argues that "at least 200,000 Muslims were killed" (*Hyderabad: After the Fall,* [Wichita, Kan.: Hyderabad Historical Society, 1988], p. 205), which therefore made it into a "holocaust." If we use the census figures for statistical trend analysis, one can show that this figure is absolutely beyond the realm of statistical probability.

7. *A Socio-Economic Survey of Street Beggars in Hyderabad* (Hyderabad: Indian Institute of Economics, 1956), p. xiii.

8. *A Socio-Economic Survey of Rickshaw Drivers in Hyderabad City* (Hyderabad: Indian Institute of Economics, 1962), p. 7.

9. In contrast, only 12.5 percent Hindus had taken to rickshaw pulling after losing jobs as "domestic servants or hotel boys," ibid., p. 15.

10. Author's interviews; M. Ranga Rao and J. V. Raguvendra Rao, *The Prostitutes of Hyderabad* (Hyderabad: Association for Moral and Social Hygiene, 1970); Jilani Bano, *Aiwaan-i-Ghazal* (Delhi: Shabdkaar, 1980). The last is an Urdu novel that deals with Hyderabad's aristocratic life between the 1920 and the 1950s. For the impact of police action, see especially pp. 324–25.

11. "However it may have arisen, the Muslims' *hubris,* the overweening pride that led them to extravagant folly, brought them down, as in a Greek drama, to disaster. That their fate was to some degree deserved, their suffering therefore self-inflicted, is integral to the tragedy" (p. 51): William Cantwell Smith, "Hyderabad: Muslim Tragedy," *Middle East Journal* 4 (1950), reproduced in Khalidi, *Hyderabad,* p. 25.

12. For a larger discussion, see Theodore P. Wright Jr., "Revival of the Majlis Ittehad-ul-Musilimin of Hyderabad," *Muslim World* 53 (1963): 234–43, also reproduced in Khalidi, *Hyderabad.*

13. For a fuller discussion, see Rasheeduddin Khan, "Muslim Leadership and Electoral Politics in Hyderabad: A Pattern of Minority Articulation," *Economic and Political Weekly,* 10–17 April 1971.

14. Roughly eight to ten municipal constituencies equal one assembly constituency, and five to six assembly constituencies make a parliamentary seat. As a result, thirty to forty municipal seats won by the MIM add up to three or four assembly seats.

15. V. B. Singh and S. Bose, *State Elections in India* (Delhi: Sage, 1988), table I.1.3.

16. For details, see Gopal Krishna, "Communal Violence in India," *Economic and Political Weekly,* 12 January 1985.

17. Meanwhile, another old issue—Mulki versus non-Mulki—rocked Andhra politics,

leading to mass mobilization. It died out in a few years. For the causes of its rebirth and decline, see Myron Weiner, *Sons of the Soil: Migration and Ethnic Conflict in India* (Princeton: Princeton University Press, 1978).

18. For an exhaustive discussion of the old city of Hyderabad today, see Ratna Naidu, *Old Cities, New Predicaments: A Study of Hyderabad* (New Delhi: Sage, 1990).

19. For a longer discussion, see Omar Khalidi, "Muslims in Indian Political Process: Group Goals and Alternative Strategies," *Economic and Political Weekly,* 2–9 January 1993.

20. Ramiza Bi, a prostitute according to the police and a helpless woman according to Muslim narratives, was arrested by the police late one night. When she did not return home, her husband went to the police station next morning. Muslim narratives suggest that Ramiza Bi was raped by Hindu policemen; the police deny it, adding that two Muslim policemen were on duty that night. An altercation took place between the husband and police. The husband, a heart patient, died of heart failure, according to the police; he was beaten to death, according to Muslim narratives.

21. Sudhir Kakar, *The Colors of Violence* (Chicago: University of Chicago Press, 1995).

22. This is also the theme of Javeed Alam, "Changing Grounds of Communal Mobilization: The Majlis-e-Ittehad-ul-Muslimeen and the Muslims of Hyderabad," in *Hindus and Others,* ed. Gyan Pandey (Delhi: Oxford University Press, 1993).

23. In an interview with the author, Channa Reddy confirmed the link but did not expand on it. Interview in Hyderabad, 10 March 1995. According to the account of the newspapers, the factional battle was encouraged by the Delhi headquarters of the Congress Party.

24. Data for the early 1950s were collected by the UNESCO and are reported in the *UNESCO Report on Communal Tensions (Hindu-Muslim)* (Lucknow: Laboratory of Experimental Psychology, 1952). They are also summarized in Gardner Murphy, *In the Minds of Men: A Study of Human Behavior and Social Tensions in India* (New York: Random House, 1953), pp. 155–61.

25. This statement is based on a reading of *The Pioneer,* a Lucknow daily, July–October 1947. The quotation is from *The Pioneer,* 2 August 1947.

26. The exception was 1969, when it dropped to the third place, losing the second place to BKD, a party created by Chowdhry Charan Singh, a veritable agrarian ideologue in Indian politics, after he broke away from the Congress in 1968.

27. As for Lok Sabha elections, Lucknow has had one seat. The BJS was second in 1952, 1957, 1962, and 1971. In 1977, 1980, and 1989, it made adjustments with its coalition partners. In 1969 and 1984, it lost badly, but it won the seat in 1991, 1996, and 1998.

28. V. C. Sharma, *Uttar Pradesh District Gazetteers* (Lucknow: Government of Uttar Pradesh, 1959) 37:70–71. The numbers are for the district of Lucknow, but it is widely assumed that most of them settled down in Lucknow city.

29. *UNESCO Report,* p. 51.

30. Ibid., p. 40.

31. Angela S. Burger, *Opposition in a Dominant Party System* (Berkeley: University of California Press, 1969).

32. "Next come the intermediate castes with 23.5 percent of the total households. The lower castes account for only 12 percent of the total households." Radhakamal Mukherjee and

Baljit Singh, *Social Profiles of a Metropolis: Social and Economic Structure of Lucknow 1954–56* (New York: Asia Publishing House, 1961), p. 41.

33. Burger, *Opposition,* p. 246.

34. "Note on Shia-Sunni Trouble," Lucknow Administration (n.d.), p. 7.

35. The 1969 riots, in which, according to official sources, six lives were lost, 43 shops and 104 houses were burnt, and 148 people including 67 policemen received injuries, lasted six days. In 1974, 8 lives were lost, 25–30 shops and houses burnt, and 84 persons were injured. See "Note," pp. 10–11.

36. *Times of India,* 16 February 1986.

37. Author's interviews with the late Ashok Priyadarshi, district magistrate, Lucknow, 1989–92, 21 November 1993, and 21 August 1994.

38. Author's interview with Sultan Salahuddin Owaisi, president of the MIM, 24 October 1995, Hyderabad. For an earlier perception, see G. Ram Reddy, "Language, Religion, and Political Identity: The Case of MIM in Hyderabad," in David Taylor and Malcolm Yapp, *Political Identity in South Asia* (London: Curzon, 1979).

CHAPTER 9. GANDHI AND CIVIL SOCIETY

1. Gujarat as a cultural entity has been in existence for centuries, but as a state in modern times, it was founded only in 1960.

2. The British took Ahmedabad and Surat in 1818.

3. Within Gujarat's boundaries exist two different kinds of territories, ex-British and ex-princely. Ahmedabad and Surat were part of British India, not princely India, which is another point of similarity.

4. Kenneth L. Gillion, *Ahmedabad: A Study in Urban Indian History* (Berkeley: University of California Press, 1968), p. 171. Though Gillion failed to notice them in his historical research, Ahmedabad did have communal riots in 1941 and 1946. These riots were small, however, and their spread was successfully contained. He is generally right that communalism played a small role in the city.

5. This includes the city of Baroda (Gujarati: Vadodara), which falls between Ahmedabad and Surat. Baroda is only 70–80 miles away from Surat. It had many riots in the 1980s.

6. Justice V. S. Dave Commission, *Report of the Commission of Inquiry, Violence and Disturbances in the State of Gujarat, February 1985–July 1985* (Ahmedabad: Government Press, April 1990), pp. 2–5.

7. As in the discussion of other cities, I will concentrate only on intercommunal civic life. And as before, the implication is not that Gujarat had no intracommunal or in-group civic life. Indeed, like other parts of India, Gujarat has had a whole series of traditional, caste-, and religion-based organizations. But these latter organizations were not built for intercommunal or intercaste engagement. Members of a given caste or religious community formed such organizations to preserve group traditions and promote in-group interaction and cohesion. Their presence is not central to my argument; the presence of intercommunal interaction and organizations is.

8. To be sure, there were other organizations, but these four types of organizations accounted for a vast bulk of Gujarat's intercommunal associational life. Smaller examples

of intercommunal civic interaction would make the argument empirically fuller but, analytically speaking, we need not go any further to understand the patterns of communal peace or violence. The value-added of a greater enumeration of organizations is minimal.

9. Organized sports, lacking roots, have also not been an important locus of civic activity in Gujarat.

10. For a critical perspective from a Gujarat Congressman who left the party but admitted that the Congress was a truly formidable organization, see Achyut Yagnik, *Atma Katha* (Autobiography [1955–73]), trans. Devavrath Pathak (New Delhi: Nehru Memorial Museum and Library, n.d.), esp. vol. 3, sec. 1. Yagnik became an arch-opponent of the Congress in the 1950s and 1960s. See also Pattabhi Sitaramayya, *History of the Indian National Congress,* vol. 1 (1885–1935) (1935; Delhi: Chand, 1969). One should add that the discussion here applies to British Gujarat only, not princely Gujarat. Princely India was not the focus of Congress politics. There were five districts in British Gujarat, of which Surat and Ahmedabad were two.

11. Makrand Mehta, "The Leader and His Milieu: Gandhi and Ahmedabad, 1915–1920," in *Regional Roots of Indian Nationalism,* ed. M. Mehta (New Delhi: Criterion, 1990); Howard Spodek, "Sardar Vallabhbhai Patel at 100," *Economic and Political Weekly,* 13 December 1975.

12. Myron Weiner, *Party Building in a New Nation: The Indian National Congress* (Chicago: University of Chicago Press, 1967), pp. 38–39 and ch. 4. Also see David Hardiman, *Peasant Nationalists of Gujarat: Kheda District 1917–1934* (Delhi: Oxford University Press, 1981).

13. Yagnik, *Atma Katha,* especially vols. 3 and 5.

14. Gandhi's statement is cited by Yagnik, *Atma Katha,* 2:2.

15. For detailed accounts, see Narhari Parikh, *Sardar Vallabhbhai Patel,* vols. 1 and 2 (Ahmedabad: Navjivan, 1953).

16. He moved finally to Delhi in 1946 to prepare for the Congress takeover of national government after the impending departure of the British.

17. Patel was a municipal councilor in Ahmedabad between 1917 and 1922. He led a boycott of British schools during the 1921 noncooperation movement and was thrown into jail. From 1924 to 1928, he was chairman of municipal government, when a large number of civic institutions were forged.

18. Again, even critics testify to the local power of the Congress in Surat. See Dinkar Mehta's testimony, "The Oral History Project," Delhi: The Nehru Memorial Museum and Library, 1978, especially pp. 9–15, 63–65. Mehta, who belonged to Surat, was a Congressman to begin with but switched to Communism by the mid-1930s. Along with Indulal Yagnik, he came a leading left-wing politician of Gujarat after independence.

19. David Hardiman, "The Quit India Movement in Gujarat," in *The Indian Nation in 1942,* ed. Gyan Pandey (Calcutta: K. P. Bagchi, 1988).

20. Gopal Krishna, "The Development of the Indian National Congress as a Mass Organization, 1918–23," *Journal of Asian Studies* 25, no. 3 (1966): 421–22.

21. For a listing of such organizations, their history, and their membership in Ahmedabad, see *Gujarat State Gazetteers: Ahmedabad District* (Ahmedabad: Government of Gujarat,

1984), pp. 881–93. For Surat, see *Gujarat State Gazetteers: Surat District* (Ahmedabad: Government of Gujarat, 1962), pp. 909–28. See also Usha Bhatt, "Women's Organizations and National Awareness in India: A Case Study of Jyotisangh, Ahmedabad (1934–47)," in *Regional Roots of Indian Nationalism,* ed. M. Mehta (New Delhi: Criterion, 1990).

22. For a fuller discussion of why Gandhi chose Ahmedabad as his home, see Lloyd Rudolph and Susanne Rudolph, *The Modernity of Tradition* (Chicago: University of Chicago Press, 1968); Howard Spodek, "On the Origins of Gandhi's Political Methodology," *Journal of Asian Studies* 30, no. 2 (February 1971).

23. For details, see *Gujarat State Gazetteers: Ahmedabad District,* pp. 701–96.

24. Census of India, 1961, *Special Report on Ahmedabad City,* vol. 5, *Gujarat,* pt. X-A (I), pp. 182–83. Prajakiya Kelvani Mandal, a voluntary association, was founded for financing and running these schools.

25. *Gujarat State Gazetteers, Ahmedabad District,* p. 750.

26. The name of the organization was Sarvajanik Education Society. Founded in 1912, it came into the hands of Gandhians by the 1920s. For the list of institutions created by the society, see *Gujarat State Gazetteers: Surat District,* 912–13, and *Supplement to Surat District Gazetteer,* p. 169.

27. Makrand Mehta, "Leader and His Milieu," pp. 127–35.

28. Yashodhar Mehta, "About Ourselves with Apologies. We Gujaratis," cited in Kenneth L. Gillion, *Ahmedabad: A Study in Urban Indian History* (Berkeley: University of California Press, 1968), p. 4.

29. For a classic treatment of the guilds at the end of the nineteenth century in Gujarat, see E. Washbrook Hopkins, *India: Old and New* (New York: Charles Scribner's Sons, 1896), pp. 169–205.

30. For a description of all three communities, see Asghar Ali Engineer, *The Muslim Communities of Gujarat* (Delhi: Ajanta, 1989).

31. Between 1810 and 1947, Surat's decline under the British coincided with the rise of Bombay as a port city.

32. Trading alone may not have been the reason Muslim businesses flocked to Surat. Surat is also the religious home of Daudi Bohras, one of the three Muslim business communities noted above. It is, however, unclear whether Surat became a Bohra religious center because it was also their business stronghold, or vice versa.

33. The Bohras are divided into several groups: Daudis, Sulemanis, Alavis, and Atba-e-Maliks. The Daudis are the biggest, and unless otherwise specified, I will use the term Bohras to mean Daudi Bohras. For a detailed description, see Asghar Ali Engineer, *The Bohras* (Delhi: Vikas, 1980).

34. There is also a Sunni Bohras community. Compared to that of the Shia Bohras, it is very small.

35. For a careful recent discussion, see Jonah Blank, *Mullahs on the Mainframe: Islam and Modernity Among the Daudi Bohras* (Chicago: University of Chicago Press, 2001).

36. Douglas Haynes, *Rhetoric and Ritual in Colonial India: The Shaping of Public Culture in Surat City, 1852–1928* (Berkeley: University of California Press, 1992), ch. 4.

37. E. G. Fawcett, *Report on the Collectorate of Ahmedabad, 1849.* Selections from the Record

of the Bombay Government, n.s., vol. 5 (Bombay: Education Society Press, 1854), pp. 70–71.

38. Makrand Mehta, "Business Environment and Urbanization: Ahmedabad in the 19th Century," in *Studies in Urban History,* ed. J. S. Grewal and Indu Banga (Amritsar: Guru Nanak Dev University, 1981), pp. 132–33; Gillion, *Ahmedabad,* pp. 54–56; *Ahmedabad Gazetteer,* 1979, 4:293–94.

39. Makrand Mehta, *The Ahmedabad Cotton Textile Industry* (Ahmedabad: New Order, 1982), appendix 1.

40. Haynes, *Rhetoric and Ritual,* p. 41.

41. A Muslim started a match factory in 1895. See Gillion, *Ahmedabad,* p. 89.

42. By 1914, all three Surat textile mills owned by Muslims had gone into liquidation. The three mills were owned by the former Mughal nobles.

43. Figures on the number of workers are from Census of India, 1961, *Special Report on Ahmedabad City,* vol. 5, *Gujarat* (1961), p. 10, and the population figures are taken from other census reports.

44. Because of the possibility of multiple jobs in the same family, the available statistics do not allow us to estimate the exact number of people partially or wholly dependent on textiles. The approximate estimates, however, are enough to show the dominance of textiles in Ahmedabad.

45. Mehta, *Ahmedabad Cotton Textile Industry,* appendix 2.

46. Howard Spodek, "Traditional Culture and Entrepreneurship: A Case Study of Ahmedabad," *Economic and Political Weekly,* Review of Management, February 1969.

47. M. K. Gandhi, *An Autobiography,* 2d ed. (Ahmedabad: Navjivan, 1969), p. 297.

48. Douglas Haynes, "From Tribute to Philanthropy: The Politics of Gift-Giving in Western Indian City," *Journal of Asian Studies* 46, no. 2 (May 1987).

49. For a brief listing of these institutions, see *Special Report on Ahmedabad City,* pp. 187–88. It should be added that the AMA was not the only business association in the city, although it was certainly the most important. Many other business and trade associations were established in the 1920s and 1930s (*Gujarat State Gazetteers,* Ahmedabad District, pp. 443–45). These associations indicate possibilities for civic interaction in the business sector, but no firm conclusions about Hindu-Muslim engagement can be drawn, for no information on their social composition is available. Inferences about the mill owners indirectly promoting such engagement, through their funding of organizations and schools, can be more confidently made.

50. The size of the embroidered silk industry is reported in Douglas Haynes, "The Dynamics and Continuity in Indian Domestic Industry: Jar Manufacture in Surat, 1900–1947," in *Cloth and Commerce: Textiles in Colonial India,* ed. Tirthankar Roy (New Delhi: Sage, 1996). The description below relies heavily on Haynes's fine-grained historical research, including his "Artisanal Origins of Surat's Industrialization," paper presented at the I. P. Desai Memorial Seminar at the Centre for Social Studies, Surat, November 1994. One should add that there were several other industries, each considerably smaller than embroidered silk, in terms of both production and workforce. A listing of such industries, along with the dates of origin, appears in the *Surat Gazetteer,* 1962, ch. 6.

51. In addition, traders and merchants, coming from Hindu and Muslim communities, stood at the beginning and the end of the production process as suppliers of raw materials and as sellers of final products.
52. Haynes, "Dynamics and Continuity," p. 311.
53. Haynes, *Rhetoric and Ritual,* pp. 60–76.
54. Those who had enough capital of their own were able to make the switch sooner. See *Surat Gazetteer,* 1962, p. 450.
55. Ibid., p. 619.
56. Mahatma Gandhi, "Speech at Meeting of Mill-Hands," 25 February 1920, *Collected Works* (Ahmedabad: Navjeevan, 19xx), 27:47–51.
57. For these calculations, the workforce numbers were taken from Census of India, *Special Report on Ahmedabad City,* and the TLA membership figures from the various annual reports of TLA.
58. For organizational details, see Subbiah Kannappan, "The Gandhian Model of Trade Unionism in a Developing Economy: The TLA in India," *Industrial and Labor Relations Review* 16, no. 1 (October 1962).
59. Interviews with Arvind Buch, 10 August 1996, Ahmedabad, and Ela Bhatt, 8 August 1996, Ahmedabad. Both have been important TLA figures. Also see Mahatma Gandhi, "Letter to Shapurji Saklatvala," 10 May 1927, *Collected Works,* 40:302.
60. This mode of functioning was a product not only of the Gandhian commitment to nonviolence but also of the principle of trusteeship that Gandhi developed and promoted. Industry, according to the latter principle, was considered a partnership in which both owners and workers were involved. Being a partnership, negotiation and persuasion, not confrontation, were keys to successful functioning. See especially "Speech at Meetings of Mill-Hands, Ahmedabad," 25 February 1920, 17:47–50; "Mill-Owners of Ahmedabad," 6 April 1930, 43:196–98 in Gandhi, *Collected Works.*
61. For a fuller discussion, see Sujata Patel, *The Making of Industrial Relations: The Ahmedabad Textile Industry, 1918–1939* (Delhi: Oxford University Press, 1987), esp. pp. 81–86.
62. E. Daya, "The Ahmedabad Experiment in Labour-Management Relations," *International Labor Review* 26, no. 4 (1959); and S. Kannappan, "Gandhian Model."
63. This was in part done in response to the challenge Communist unions had begun to pose in Ahmedabad to TLA's control over workers. For details, see Patel, *Making of Industrial Relations,* pp. 126–36.
64. Salim Lakha, *Capitalism and Class in Colonial India: The Case of Ahmedabad* (Delhi: Sterling, 1988), ch. 6.
65. The TLA, for example, provided financial assistance and free schoolbooks to poor Muslim children though a Muslim organization. See William Albright Dawson, "Trade Union Development in West Indian Textiles" (Ph.D. diss., University of Wisconsin, 1971), pp. 219–20.
66. *Surat Gazetteer, 1962,* p. 467.
67. Between 1920 and 1930, the number of looms in Surat had only slightly increased—from 100 to 185. Between 1930 and 1940, the number increased from 185 to 2,079. P. C. Mehta and R. S. Gandhi, *Man Made Textile Industry of Surat* (Surat: Manmade Textile

Research Association, 1986), p. 10. The MANTRA is the official research organization of the decentralized textile industry in India.

68. There is no documentary material on the labor unions of Surat. Nor has the TLA of Surat kept records the way its Ahmedabad counterpart did. These statements, therefore, are based on interviews with labor leaders of the city: Hakumat Desai, former labor leader and activist during the 1950s, 4 August 1996, and Naishadh Desai, TLA president, Surat, 4 August 1996.

69. See, e.g., Hardiman, "Quit India Movement," p. 92.

70. Gandhi, *Collected Works,* 84:4.

71. Known for being excessively harsh to himself, Gandhi was, however, acutely saddened by the rioting in Ahmedabad. That it was much smaller than rioting elsewhere was less important to him; that it happened at all was more significant. For the 1941 riots, see his *Collected Works,* 74:10–11, 26–29. For the 1946 riots, see *Collected Works,* 84:40–41, 30–32, 396, 426–27.

72. Khandubhai Desai, *Textile Labor Association, Ahmedabad: An Indigenous Experiment in Trade Union Movement* (Ahmedabad: TLA, 1948), p. 15. Desai was among the leading lights of the TLA. In the 1950s and 1960s, he went on to become a labor minister in Nehru's cabinet in Delhi.

73. For details, see *The Times* (London), 5 May 1927; *The Times* (London), 1 October 1928. For Gandhi's reaction, see Mahatma Gandhi, *Collected Works,* 37:171.

74. Haynes, *Rhetoric and Ritual,* ch. 12.

75. Engineer, *Muslim Communities,* pp. 9–10. Khojas have several sub-sects. The Ismailis (owing allegiance to the Agha Khan) and Isna-Asharis are the best-known and the biggest.

76. Engineer, *Bohras,* pp. 108–9.

77. *The Gazetteer of Bombay Presidency,* 1877, vol. 2, *Gujarat,* "Surat," "Broach."

78. The British census always categorized the Bohras as a group separate from the Muslim community. Also see Haynes, *Rhetoric and Ritual,* p. 261.

79. As for the Memons, who did belong to the Sunni sect and could, in theory, have joined the Mughal nobility in its polarizing effort, business reasons again turned out to be significant. Their commercial links with the Hindus in the textile sector have also been historically very strong. See Garrett Menning, "The City of Silk: Ethnicity and Business Trust in Surat City, India" (Ph.D. diss., University of California, Santa Barbara, 1996), pp. 258–64.

80. Dinkar Mehta, "Oral History Project," pp. 63–64.

81. Based on interviews in Surat with senior citizens, especially Vaikunth Desai (former mayor, Surat), 12 December 1993, and Justice D. A. Desai (retired judge, Supreme Court), who practiced law in Surat (1946–60), 3 August 1996. Abdul Qadir Sheikh, president of Muslim League in Surat, stayed back.

CHAPTER 10. DECLINE OF A CIVIC ORDER

1. In October 1990, triggered by the mobilization for the destruction of Ayodhya mosque, Surat had a small riot. Muslim property was destroyed in several parts of the city, but there were no deaths. See *Times of India,* 1 November 1990 and 22 April 1991.

2. In the next four months, there were several smaller incidents in which a few more people were killed. See *Times of India,* 18–26 January 1993 and 22 April 1993.

3. *Times of India,* 24 December 1992, and 9, 10, and 18 January 1993.

4. *Times of India,* various issues. For the 1985 riots, also see Justice V. S. Dave, *The Report of the Commission of Inquiry* (Ahmedabad: Government of Gujarat, 1990), 1:225–32, and vol. 2.

5. For the only study of communal tensions of this period, see Ghanshyam Shah, "Anatomy of Urban Riots: Ahmedabad 1973," *Economic and Political Weekly,* annual number, February 1974.

6. The city's attention was occupied first by a movement aimed at cleaning up public life and, subsequently, by a campaign launched to oust Mrs. Gandhi from power, followed by her declaration of emergency (1975–77).

7. In a thoughtful analysis of the 1985 riots in Ahmedabad, Howard Spodek has also focused on "the failure of local institutions for conflict resolution." If the historically created institutions had been vibrant, he argues, the riots would not have broken out in Ahmedabad. See Howard Spodek, "From Gandhi to Violence: Ahmedabad's 1985 Riots in Historical Perspective," *Modern Asian Studies* 23, no. 4 (1989): 765–95.

8. For a detailed treatment, see Ghanshyam Shah, "Strategies of Social Engineering: Reservation and Mobility of Backward Communities of Gujarat," in *Diversity and Dominance in Indian Politics,* ed. Ramashray Roy and Richard Sisson (Delhi: Sage, 1990).

9. Atul Kohli, *Democracy and Discontent* (New York: Cambridge University Press, 1990), chs. 3 and 9.

10. See Ghanshyam Shah, "BJP's Rise to Power," *Economic and Political Weekly,* 13–20 January 1996; Achyut Yagnik, "Hindutva as Savarna Purana," in Ashis Nandy, Shikha Trivedy, Shail Mayaram, and Achyut Yagnik, *Creating a Nationality: The Ramjanmabhumi Movement and the Fear of the Self* (New Delhi: Oxford University Press, 1995).

11. For details, see Shah, "BJP's Rise to Power."

12. The Ahmedabad survey was conducted in Kalupur, Naranpura, Raikhad, Navrangpura, Paldi, Dani Limda, Jamalpur, Shahpur, Khdia, Gomitpur, and Naroda. In Surat, given the smaller size of the city, the sample size was also smaller. The areas surveyed were Rander, Nanpura, Zampa Bazaar, Machhli Peeth, Ved Road, and Athwa Lines.

13. This has been true since the late 1950s. Between the 1957 and 1967 elections, the Congress consistently got more votes in Surat than in Ahmedabad. See John R. Wood, "British versus Princely Legacies and the Political Integration of Gujarat," *Journal of Asian Studies* 44, no. 1 (November 1984).

14. Yagnik, "Hindutva," p. 109.

15. For a thoughtful analysis, see Ghanshyam Shah, "The BJP and Backward Castes in Gujarat," *South Asia Bulletin* 14, no. 1 (1994).

16. Ghanshyam Shah, "Identity, Communal Consciousness and Politics," *Economic and Political Weekly,* 7 May 1994, p. 1134. No such survey has been held for the whole state.

17. *Report of the Laththa Commission of Inquiry (Second),* (Ahmedabad: Government of Gujarat, 1978), p. 34. The commission, headed by Justice N. M. Miabhoy, was constituted to inquire into the causes and consequences of bootlegging in Ahmedabad city. Similar evidence can easily be produced for Surat.

18. Ibid., p. 65.

19. *Report of the Laththa Commission (First)* (Ahmedabad: Government of Gujarat, 1978), p. 34.

20. Ghanshyam Shah, "Economy and Civic Authority in Surat," *Economic and Political Weekly,* 8 October 1994, p. 2674.

21. No census of NGOs is available. Information on NGOs is, therefore, primarily interview-based. Discussions and interviews with Achyut Yagnik (January 1994 and August 1996) were especially instructive. Yagnik runs an NGO in Ahmedabad, writes about NGOs and their advantages and pitfalls, and is among the most knowledgeable observers of Gujarat politics.

22. Jaya Prakash Narayan, "The Crime in Gujarat," *Searchlight,* 28 October 1969.

23. In order to "assimilate" the scheduled castes, the RSS has started an organization, Samajik Samrasta Manch. Bharat Sevashram and Hindu Milan Mandir work among the lower castes in general. Women are organized under the various Mahila organizations, students under Akhil Bharatiya Vidyarthi Parishad, and workers under Bharatiya Mazdoor Sangh.

24. Robin Jeffrey, "Gujarati: Cheque-book Journalism in Reverse," *Economic and Political Weekly,* 15 February 1997.

25. I might add that in my interviews for this book in different parts of the country, the Hindu nationalist fervor I encountered in Gujarat was, far and away, much higher than elsewhere in the country.

26. To be more precise, the dominance of "composite mills" was over. The mills were of two types: spinning and composite (spinning and weaving). Spinning mills produced the yarn, which used to be supplied to the decentralized sector, whereas composite mills used their own yarn. The latter have declined, not the spinning mills. Much of the expansion of spinning mills has taken place in southern India, and the center of gravity in Indian textiles has shifted from the west to the south.

27. For a longer discussion, see S. R. B. Leadbeater, *The Politics of Textiles* (New Delhi: Sage, 1993).

28. The AMA is now called ATMA (Ahmedabad Textile Manufacturers' Association). In keeping with the modern norms of functioning, the name was changed in the mid-1980s.

29. The list was supplied by the ATMA, August 1996.

30. The Ambanis, currently one of India's leading business families, exemplify this trend.

31. The membership lists of 52 associations were checked to derive a Hindu-Muslim ratio. Given their importance in the city, the businesses covered included manufacturers of engineering goods, dyestuff, and power looms; auto dealers; transporters; printers; and grain, paper, cloth, and timber merchants.

32. For associations that did not or could not provide membership lists, interviews with the officers of the association were conducted.

33. This information is based on the membership lists of professional associations registered with the Gujarat Chamber of Commerce and Industry, such as the Income Tax and Sales Tax Bar Associations, the Tax Advocates' Association, the Chartered Accountants' Association, and the Gujarat Institute of Civil Engineers.

34. Diamond-cutting and polishing is the other industry to have grown in recent years in Surat, but the size of its workforce is less than a one-fourth that of textiles. There are few Muslim entrepreneurs (or workers) in the diamond-cutting industry. The power loom industry is where the Muslims are primarily involved.

35. The 1970 figure is from P. C. Mehta and R. S. Gandhi, *Manmade Textile Industry of Surat* (Ahmedabad: MANTRA, n.d.), p. 10. The 1995 figure is an estimate based on interviews with officers of textile industry associations.

36. The industry has three main parts: weaving, processing, and marketing. It is estimated that there are about 30,000 entrepreneurs involved in the first, approximately 400 plants in the second, and 35,000 traders in the third. Interview with Arunbhai Jariwala, president, Surat Art Silk Manufacturers Association, 9 August 1996, and B. C. Naidu, president, Surat Management Association, 4 August 1996.

37. They are the Surat Art Silk Manufacturers' Association, the Surat Art Silk Producers' Cooperative Society, the Surat Vankar Sahakari Sangh, and the Surat Weavers Cooperative Producers' Society, each having 1,400 to 2,000 members. Muslim proportions were calculated from the membership lists.

38. Garrett Menning, "City of Silk: Ethnicity and Business Trust in Surat City," Ph.D. diss., University of California at Santa Barbara (December 1996), p. 205.

39. Ibid., p. 315.

40. Given their wealth and activities, some Muslim entrepreneurs are also counted among the business leaders of the city and have been playing a highly visible role in business associations as well as the civic life of the city.

41. These figures are based on the various *TLA Annual Reports,* 1958–62, Ahmedabad.

42. Interview, Arvind Buch, general secretary, TLA, Ahmedabad, 10 August 1996.

43. For causes of the crisis, see Leadbeater, *Politics of Textiles.*

44. Sujata Patel, "Nationalization, TLA and Textile Workers," *Economic and Political Weekly,* 7 December 1985.

45. Supriya Roy-Chowdhry, "Industrial Restructuring, Unions, and the State: The Case of Textile Mill Workers in Ahmedabad City," Working Paper no. 1269 (Ahmedabad: Indian Institute of Management, July 1995).

46. B. B. Patel, *Workers of Closed Textile Mills* (New Delhi: Oxford and IBH Publishing, 1988); and Sujata Patel, "Contract Labour in Ahmedabad Textile Industry," *Economic and Political Weekly,* 11 October 1986.

47. S. Vasavada and Pankaj G. Patel, "Role of Trade Unions," in S. S. Mehta and Vinod Shanbagh, *Indian Textiles: An Intersectoral Perspective* (New Delhi: Oxford and IBH Publishing, 1990).

48. Achyut Yagnik, "Hindutva as a Savarna Purana," in Ashis Nandy, Shikha Trivedy, Shail Mayaram, and A. Yagnik, *Creating a Nationality* (Delhi: Oxford University Press, 1995).

49. Sujata Patel, "Communal Riots in Ahmedabad 1985," typescript, 1990.

50. Interview, Arvind Buch, 10 August 1996.

51. Studies of SEWA are growing. See Kalima Rose, *Where Women Are Leaders* (London: Zed Press, 1992); Howard Spodek, "The Self-Employed Women's Association (SEWA) in India: Feminist, Gandhian Power in Development," *Economic Development and Cultural Change* 43, no. 1 (October 1994): 193–202. Some interesting additional materials

are available in Virginia Appell, "The Self-Employed Women's Association: Ideology in Action," Ph.D. diss., University of British Columbia, 1996; and Rohini Narendra Patel, "The Pressure Group Role of Voluntary Associations: A Case Study of the Ahmedabad's Women's Action Group and the Self-Employed Women's Association," Ph.D. diss., Pennsylvania State University, May 1995.

52. The associations' members and their activities fall into three categories: "hawkers and vendors" (small sellers of vegetables, fruit, housewares, and clothes); "home-based workers" (weavers, potters, paper rollers, embroiderers, and other craftswomen); and "manual labor and service providers" (construction workers, headloaders, cart pullers, launderers, and domestic workers). *SEWA 1995* (Amehdabad: Self-Employed Women's Association, 1995), p. 1.

53. It had approximately 219,000 members in India overall, of which all but 158,000 were in the state of Gujarat. Compare *SEWA 1995*.

54. Interview, Ela Bhatt, general secretary, SEWA, Ahmedabad, 8 August 1996.

55. For a claim like this, I must protect my sources both for their safety and as part of routine interviewing norms.

56. There is no published study of labor unions in Surat. The materials below are based on interviews with two labor leaders: Naishabh Desai, president, Majur Mahajan, Surat, 4 August 1996, and Hakumat Desai, former labor leader, 4 August 1996.

57. Vidyut Joshi, "Casualization of Labour in Textile Industry," in S. S. Mehta and Vinod Shanbagh, *Indian Textiles: An Intersectoral Perspective* (New Delhi: Oxford and IBH Publishing, 1990), p. 155.

58. R. S. Gandhi, Y. C. Mehta, and A. B. Talele, *Decentralized Sector of the Indian Textile Industry* (Surat: National Information Centre for Textile and Allied Subjects, 1985), p. 133.

59. Naishabh Desai, interview.

60. The numbers were supplied by P. C. Pande, police commissioner, Surat (1994–97). Police statistics are likely to be an underestimate, but not by a wide margin. While counting deaths, the police included all bodies that could be identified. Some bodies, however, simply could not be recovered, and if the relatives did not report them to the police, the police estimate would not include such cases. It is unlikely that there are many cases of the latter kind, because Muslim politicians, still visible and powerful in the city, ensured that a proper count of Muslim deaths was made. Even if afraid of the police, Muslim citizens could reach several Muslim politicians, who in turn had sufficient power over the police to induce proper counting, though not enough to prevent riots. Interview, Kadir Pirzada, Muslim ex-mayor, Surat, 6 August 1996. Hence police estimates of riot deaths, although doubtful in parts of India where Muslim politicians are not powerful at all, are more or less accurate in Surat.

61. Asghar Ali Engineer, *Economic and Political Weekly*, 13 February 1993.

62. Jan Breman, *Footloose Labor: Working in India's Informal Economy* (Cambridge: Cambridge University Press, 1996), p. 54.

63. Biswaroop Das, *Socio-Economic Study of Slums in Surat City*, report of the Center for Social Studies, Surat, 1994. Unless otherwise noted, the numbers below are from the remarkable census of slums conducted by Das.

64. The numbers in this paragraph come from Breman, *Footloose Labor*, pp. 49–50.

65. Jean Dreze and Amartya Sen, *India: Economic Development and Social Opportunity* (Delhi: Oxford University Press, 1996).

66. Bishnu C. Barik, "Unorganized Migrant Labour in the Textile Industry of Surat—a Case Study," in *Migrant Labour and Related Issues,* ed. Vidyut Joshi (New Delhi: Oxford and IBH Publishing), 1987.

67. Breman, *Footloose Labor,* p. 69.

68. Mehta and Gandhi, *Manmade Textiles Industry,* p. 129.

69. Breman, *Footloose Labor,* p. 64.

70. Unless otherwise stated, the numbers on Muslims migrants are based on Biswaroop Das, "A Socio-Economic Profile of Muslim Households Living in the Slums of Surat City" (Surat: Center for Social Studies, 1996, typescript).

71. Although for the account here I have primarily relied on my own research, mention should also be made of some other excellent reports and analyses. See especially Sudhir Chandra, "Of Communal Consciousness and Communal Violence," *Economic and Political Weekly,* 4 September 1993; Harish Khare, "The Surat Explosion," *Times of India,* 12 January 1993; Lancy Lobo, "Communal Violence in Surat City," *Social Action* 43 (April–June 1993); and Ghanshyam Shah, "Surat 1993," *Seminar,* November 1993.

72. I personally saw a couple of such areas.

73. Kalpana Shah, Smita Shah, and Neha Shah, "The Nightmare of Surat," *Manushi,* no. 74–75 (1993): 52–53.

74. Interview, Mehmood Pardewala, former president, Bharatiya Minority Suraksha Sangh, 5 August 1996. Pardewala had organized the protest. He has contested elections for the municipal corporation, the state assembly, and parliament and also served time in jail. In August 1996, when I interviewed him, he was publisher of *Gujarat News.*

75. This information is based on many interviews conducted with businessmen in Surat. Some are individually cited below.

76. Originating apparently in a vernacular paper, *Gujarat Mitra,* the rumor first appeared as news among the national dailies in the *Indian Express.* See Darshan Desai and Bharat Desai, "Camera Unit Films Mob Stripping Women," *Indian Express,* 19 December 1992. Given new technologies of communication, the rumor was put on the wires as news and was believed in the Indian diaspora in the United States. It was also the subject of a panel in the annual meetings of the Association of Asian Studies, Los Angeles, in April 1993, which I attended as part of the audience. Unlike the *Indian Express,* Dileep Padgaonkar, editor-in-chief of the *Times of India* at that time, refused to carry the story until his correspondents in Surat had personally seen the video and confirmed its existence. Interview, Dileep Padgaonkar, Delhi, 20 July 1994. As it turned out, the *Times of India* reporters in Surat, despite trying hard for a week to get the video, were unable to confirm its existence. Interview, Nayeem and Rafat Quadri, correspondents, Times of India Group, Surat, 1 and 2 August 1994. Jan Breman, another long-time researcher in Surat, was unable to verify that the video was ever made. See Jan Breman, "Anti-Muslim Pogrom in Surat," *Economic and Political Weekly,* 17 April 1993, pp. 739–40.

77. Interview, Sheikh Mehmood Maniar, Surat, 12 December 1993. Maniar is a leading local businessman with significant business interests in Bombay as well.

78. See, e.g., Breman, "Ant-Muslim-Pogrom in Surat." Also unable to get the video was a

former mayor of the city :"I don't think the video exists. *Maine bahut kohish ki, Muhje video nahin mila.* (I tried very hard, but I could not get it)." Interview, Kadir Pirzada, 6 August 1996, Surat.

79. "*Peace Committee ke kaam ke liye bahut se sharif Hindu khul kar aye*"(for the peace committee work, many decent Hindus came openly and enthusiastically). Interview, Sheik Mehmood Maniar. Maniar's Hindu colleagues on the committee, as elsewhere in the old city, included people with whom he had conducted business for a long time.

80. "We may not be politicians, but our social status and links matter. We can police our neighborhoods without the police. Inside the old city, there are long-standing social and business links between the two communities." Interview, Arun Bhai Jariwala, president, Surat Art Silk Manufacturing Association, 9 August 1996, Surat.

81. Datta's view is available in his testimony to the Commission of Inquiry. It was also vigorously defended in his interview with me in Ahmedabad, 7 August 1996.

82. Interviews with P. K. Bansal, police commissioner in Surat from December 9, 1992 to January 20, 1993, and from June 1986 to June 1988, Ahmedabad, 7 August 1996; and P C. Pande, police commissioner, Surat, 1994–1997, Surat, 6 August 1996. Having been police commissioner of Surat earlier, Bansal was brought in to control riots after Datta's transfer. He remained there for forty days—until peace returned in January 1993.

83. Interview, P. K. Bansal.

CHAPTER 11. ENDOGENEITY?

1. For a concise explanation of the problem of endogeneity in the social sciences, see Gary King, Robert Keohane, and Sidney Verba, *Designing Social Inquiry* (Princeton: Princeton University Press, 1994), pp. 185–95.

2. If we use Eckstein's language, it is a "crucial" or "critical case," for it is the "least likely" place for communal riots. See Harry Eckstein, "Case Study and Theory in Political Science," in *Handbook of Political Science,* ed. Fred Greenstein and Nelson Polsy (Reading, Mass.: Addison-Wesley, 1975).

3. Ahmedabad's 1969 riots are among the most intensively researched riots of post-1947 India. My reconstruction of the main outlines below relies heavily on the *Times of India.*

4. Morarji Desai, broadcast on All India Radio, reported in the *Times of India,* 24 September 1969.

5. For a concise summary, see Ghanshyam Shah, "Communal Riots in Gujarat: Report of a Preliminary Investigation," *Economic and Political Weekly,* annual number, August 1970.

6. Myron Weiner, "Institution Building in India," in his *The Indian Paradox* (New Delhi: Sage, 1989); Atul Kohli, *Democracy and Discontent* (Cambridge: Cambridge University Press, 1990).

7. Myron Weiner, *Party Building in a New Nation* (Chicago: University of Chicago Press, 1968); Paul Brass, *Factional Politics in an Indian State* (Berkeley: University of California Press, 1965).

8. *Report of the Subcommittee Appointed by the Executive Committee of Gujarat Pradesh Con-*

gress Committee to Enquire into the Working of the Congress Organization in Gujarat (Delhi: All India Congress Committee, 1957), p. 1 (*Report* hereafter).

9. Ibid., p. 4.

10. Ibid., p. 42.

11. Ibid., p. 5 (emphasis added).

12. "Morarji on Fast to End Violence," *Times of India,* 23 September 1969.

13. "Ahmedabad Under Army Control: Peace Prospects Brighten," *Times of India,* 23 September 1969.

14. Sampradayikta Virodhi Committee, *Ahmedabad Riots X-Rayed* (New Delhi: Sampradayikta Virodhi Committee, 1970), p. 1.

15. The rumors about what happened at Jagannath temple were, of course, numerous and highly exaggerated. *Sevak,* an afternoon edition of *Sandesh,* a local vernacular newspaper, also printed a story about an alleged gang rape of Hindu women by Muslim men in Gomtipur. See Ajit Bhattacharjea, "Ahmedabad Riots," in Sampradayikta Virodhi Committee, *Ahmedabad Riots X-Rayed* (New Delhi: Sampradayikta Virodhi Committee, 1970).

16. "At the outskirts, Saraspur, Asarva, Naroda, Gomtipur, Chamanpura and Maninagar are the worst hit," *Times of India,* 21 September 1969. The eastern outskirts were the largely labor-dominated areas of the city. The participation of workers in riots was an object of commentary in many contemporary articles. See, e.g., Subrata Banerjee, "Ahmedabad: Myth and Reality," *Mainstream,* 1 November 1969; Iqbal Ahmed Ansari, *Ahmedabad Riots: Focus on Dark Corners* (Delhi: Radiance Book Depot, 1970), esp. p. 13.

17. In the 1930s, another great period of migration into Ahmedabad, the migrants came almost entirely from other parts of Gujarat. See Sujata Patel, *The Making of Industrial Relation.* (Delhi: Oxford University Press, 1987).

18. The fact that the TLA's secretary was also the labor minister in the provincial Bombay government after 1937 and that he had the support of the Congress Party made such a law possible.

19. Suzanne Berger, ed., *Organizing Interests in Western Europe* (New York: Cambridge University Press, 1981).

20. During its two best years of enrollments, the TLA had 104,046 members in 1960–61 and 101,135 in 1961–62. Compare *TLA Annual Reports,* 1961–62 and 1962–63 (Ahmedabad: Textile Labor Organization).

21. Other unions that tried to break in were Mill Mazdoor Sabha, Mill Kamdar Union, and Ahmedabad Miscellaneous Industrial Workers Union.

22. For a succinct analysis of the organizational problems, see Manju Parikh, "Labor Capital Relations in Indian Textile Industry," Ph.D. diss., University of Chicago, 1988, ch. 9.

23. For more details, see R. C. Goyal, "Trade Union Influence on Workers' Voting Behavior in Ahmedabad City," paper presented at the National Seminar on Industrial Relations in a Developing Economy, 20–23 September 1967, Chandigarh, sponsored by Shri Ram Centre for Industrial Relations.

24. For a thoughtful analysis of the new migrants, see B. K. Roy Burman, "Social Profile," *Seminar,* annual number, January 1970.

25. The union was called the Samyukta Kamdar Sangram Samiti. It allied with the Maha Gujarat Janata Parishad, led by Yagnik, to sponsor the strike.

26. This and the next paragraph heavily rely on the report of the committee appointed by the to inquire into the 1964 agitation. See Justice N. K. Vakil, *Report on the Incident of Police Firing at Ahmedabad on the 5th of August and Other Incidents of the 5th and 6th of August 1964* (Ahmedabad: Government of Gujarat, 1965).

27. Ibid., p. 177. For a fuller taste of Yagnik's rousing speeches and its effects, see pp. 173–90.

28. For a fuller analysis of the early to mid-1960s, see Goyal, "Trade Union Influence," 1967.

29. Yagnik's mistake was that although he capitalized on widespread worker disaffection, hurting the TLA, he did not put an alternative organization in place. The TLA returned to power in the next municipal elections, but that was because Yagnik's supporters, though able to win, failed to run the municipal government wisely and well: the TLA's return to power was rooted in a negative vote against the incumbents. Lacking a solid organization, Yagnik's men and his union simply disappeared from the political scene. Despite its victory, however, the TLA did not rebuild itself as an organization.

30. TLA Annual Report 1964–65, p. 7.

31. Goyal, "Trade Union Influence," 1967.

32. A victim's report to the Sampradayikta Virodhi Committee, *Ahmedabad Riots X-Rayed,* pp. 1–2.

33. "Ahmedabad City Wears a Normal Look," *Hindustan Times,* 30 September 1969.

34. "During the last few years, 7 mills in Ahmedabad have closed down and about 17,000 workers were thrown out of employment" (Burman, "Social Profile," p. 36).

35. Ajit Bhattacharjea, "Sparks That Set Gujarat Ablaze," *Hindustan Times,* 6 October 1969.

36. Sampradayikta Virodhi Committee, *Ahmedabad Riots X-Rayed,* p. 2.

37. See the careful discussion in John R. Wood, "British versus Princely Legacies and the Political Integration of Gujarat," *Journal of Asian Studies* 44, no. 1 (November 1984).

38. Interview, Vaikunth Shastri, mayor (1968–70), Surat, 15 December 1994.

CHAPTER 12. ETHNIC CONFLICT, THE STATE, AND CIVIL SOCIETY

1. Consistent with my usage so far, I will continue to deploy the terms "ethnic" and "communal" interchangeably. For a longer discussion of terms, see Chapter 2. I should also note that in an insightful essay on India's communal relations, Imtiaz Ahmed, as I do in this book, had emphasized the analytical necessity of a focus on "the dynamics of the local situation factors" as opposed to the "broad or universal causes." See Imtiaz Ahmed, "Political Economy of Communalism in Contemporary India," *Economic and Political Weekly,* 2–9 June 1984, pp. 903–6.

2. This finding, and the logic underlying it, does raise a question: Are there any conditions under which intraethnic, intracommunal associations can play a peaceful role? Given that so much of the world lives its spiritual and civic life in ethnic or religious associations, this is a tremendously important question, but it as yet not empirically explored, except partially in the consociational literature to be discussed later.

3. Selig Harrison, *India: The Most Dangerous Decade* (Princeton: Princeton University Press, 1963).

4. Myron Weiner, *The Indian Paradox* (Delhi: Sage, 1989), ch. 2.

5. For a brief overview, see E. Valentine Daniel, *Charred Lullabies* (Princeton: Princeton University Press, 1997), ch. 2.

6. Tamil activists in Sri Lanka have often made this argument.

7. This is not to say that language was the only issue in Tamil-Sinhalese conflict, only that it was very important and could have been handled through federalism.

8. Arend Lijphart, *Democracy in Plural Societies* (New Haven: Yale University Press, 1988).

9. For more counterexamples and detailed criticism, see Donald Horowitz, *A Democratic South Africa? Constitutional Engineering in a Divided Society* (Berkeley: University of California Press, 1990), ch. 5; Ian Lustick, "Stability in Deeply Divided Societies: Consociationalism versus Control," *World Politics* 31, no. 3 (April 1979): 325–44.

10. Ashutosh Varshney, "Why Democracy Survives," *Journal of Democracy* 9, 3 (July 1998).

11. Hence the oft-expressed discomfort with Lijphart's novel and provocative argument that India's communal peace between 1950 and the mid-1960s was dependent on consociationalism, and its greater violence since the mid-1960s a consequence of making the democracy more liberal. See Arend Lijphart, "The Puzzle of Indian Democracy," *American Political Science Review* 90 no. 4 (June 1996). Lijphart ignores the pre-1947 period of Indian democracy, when the system was indeed more consociational and violence too was greater. See Steven Wilkinson, "India, Consociational Theory and Ethnic Violence," *Asian Survey* 35, 5 (September–October 2000).

12. Ashutosh Varshney and Steven Wilkinson, "Hindu-Muslim Riots (1960–93): New Findings, Possible Remedies," Special Paper Series, Rajiv Gandhi Institute of Contemporary Studies, New Delhi, July, 1996.

13. This is not only true of inquiry commissions in India but also elsewhere. In the United States, the famous Kerner Commission only investigated cities where race riots took place in the late 1960s.

14. As Julius Ribero, one of India's most respected post-independence police officers, put it, he succeeded in keeping the towns he administered riot-free until he became the police commissioner of Bombay in the 1980s. There was something about Bombay's life that made it impossible even for an officer of his stature experience and abilities to keep communal peace in the mid-1980s. Author's interview with Julius Ribero, Bombay, 2 August 1996.

15. As already explained in Chapters 9–11, in all cities except one (Ahmedabad), the basic structures of Hindu-Muslim civic interaction set up during the independence movement lasted for decades thereafter.

16. India's independence movement and the anti-Brahmin movement of southern India clashed on several issues, but Hindu-Muslim relations were not one of them. See Marguerite Ross Barnett, *The Politics of Cultural Nationalism in South India* (Princeton: Princeton University Press, 1976); Narendra Subramaniam, *Ethnicity and Populist Mobilization: Political Parties, Citizens and Democracy in South India* (Delhi: Oxford University Press, 1999). For a fascinating account of the functioning of film clubs, see Sara Dickey, *Cinema and the Urban Poor in South India* (Cambridge: Cambridge University Press, 1993).

17. *Mahila Samakhya Uttar Pradesh: An Overview 1989–1991.* New Delhi: Mahila Samakhya

National Project Office, Department of Education, Ministry of Human Resources, September 1991, pp. 71–73. This instance was reported and analyzed earlier in Varshney and Wilkinson, "Hindu-Muslim Riots."

18. Three-year postings are customary for police and administrative officers at the state level in India, unless riots break out or some other politically significant events take place. Suresh Khopade, a police officer in Maharashtra state, was appointed deputy commissioner of police for Bhiwandi. In his unpublished memoirs, *Bhiwandi Riots and After* (n.d.), he has given a detailed account of initiatives he took between 1988–1991, a particularly violent period in India, during which the mobilization to destroy the Baburi mosque reached new heights. Khopade's achievements were widely hailed in political and journalistic circles, although the larger significance of his experiment—for the kinds of interventions that are possible and desirable in riot-prone towns—was not drawn. I will cite extensively from his memoirs and draw the larger implications. I am grateful to Julius Ribero, one of India's most highly respected police officers of the post-independence era, for sharing the manuscript with me. In Ribero's view as well, Khopade's was an extraordinary initiative. Author's interview with Julius Ribero, retired commissioner of police (Bombay), governor of Punjab, and ambassador to Romania, 2 August 1996, Bombay. For a report on Bhiwandi see A. R. Momin, "Bhiwandi Shows the Way," *Sunday Times of India,* 10 January 1993.

19. Khopade, *Bhiwandi Riots and After,* preface.

20. Ibid., p. 115.

21. Ibid., p. 116.

22. Ibid., p. 118.

23. Ibid., p. 119.

24. Ibid., p. 116.

25. Ibid., pp. 116–17.

26. Arguably, Calicut in the 1920s can be counted as a close parallel. After the Malabar rebellion of the early 1920s, there was no Hindu-Muslim violence at all. But the rebellion took place outside Calicut, not in the city. Some may also suggest that Ahmedabad after 1946 could be viewed as a comparable example. That would also not be a parallel, for the 1946 riots of Ahmedabad, compared to the Bhiwandi riots of the 1970s and 1980s, were minor.

27. For the United States, see Stanley Lieberson and Arnold Silverman, "The Precipitants and Underlying Conditions of Race Riots," *American Sociological Review* 31, no. 2 (December 1965); and for Northern Ireland, see Michael Poole, "Geographical Location of Political Violence in Northern Ireland," in *Political Violence: Ireland in Comparative Perspective,* ed. John Darby, Nicholas Dodge, and A. C. Hepburn (Belfast: Appletree, 1990).

28. Sharon Zukin, *Beyond Marx and Tito* (New York: Cambridge University Press, 1975); Ellen Comisso, *Workers' Control Under Plan and Market: Implications of Yugoslavia's Self-Management* (New Haven: Yale University Press, 1979).

29. Because the incidence of Hindu-Muslim marriages is known to be so low as to be virtually negligible, intermarriage statistics for India were not collected. Data on other forms of everyday engagement were.

30. Nikolai Botev, "Where East Meets West: Ethnic Intermarriage in the Former Yugoslavia," *American Sociological Review* 50, no. 6 (June 1994).

31. Poole, "Geographical Location."

32. John Darby, *Intimidation and the Control of Conflict in Northern Ireland* (Dublin: Gill and MacMillan, 1986).

33. Donald Horowitz, "Racial Violence in the United States," in *Ethnic Pluralism and Public Policy*, ed. Nathan Glazer and Ken Young (Lexington: Lexington Books, 1983).

34. Lieberson and Silverman, "Precipitants and Underlying Conditions."

35. The Kerner Commission Report had an excellent opportunity to give us an explanation. It missed the chance because it studied the riot-afflicted cities only, not the peaceful ones.

36. Nathan Glazer, *We Are All Multiculturalists Now* (Cambridge: Harvard University Press, 1996).

37. James Fearon and David Laitin, "Explaining Inter-Ethnic Cooperation," *American Political Science Review* (December 1996): 715–35.

Index

Abdullah, Sheikh, 64

Advani, L. K., 65, 71, 81, 320n. 11, 329n. 36, 331n. 64, 334n. 93

Aga Khan III, 137, 339n. 37

Ahmed, Imtiaz, 351n. 67, 368n. 1

Ahmed, Sir Syed, 136

Ahmedabad: associations, 222, 224, 240, 250; BJP, 240, 245; business associations, 229–30, 240, 249, 277; charity, 231; communal linkages, 250; communal structure, 229–30; Congress Party, 223, 240, 244, 266–71; M. Gandhi, 221, 226; Gandhian organizations, 226–27, 246, 275; Hindu nationalists, 244; history, 220, 228; labor unions, 223, 240; media attitudes and standards, 164; peace committees, 261; riot-proneness, 7, 103, 220; riots, 220–21, 236, 239–40, 264–66; TLA, 232–34, 236, 252, 271–275

Ahmedabad Millowners Association (AMA), 230–31, 249–50, 275–76

Akali Dal, 79

Akbar, 66, 68

Alam, Javeed, 354n. 22

Ali, Mir Laiq, 350n. 56, 353n. 6

Aligarh: associations, 128–130, 151; BJP in, 121, 161; civic engagement, 121, 122, 126–27; communalism, 136, 150; communal tensions, 157–58; economic ties, 128; educational segregation, 150–51; elites, 133; literacy, 108, 151, 153; media attitudes and standards, 119–20, 123; middle class, 121, 151; peace committees, 124–25; political cleavages, 122–23; political history, 132–34, 340n. 45; riot-proneness, 7, 121; riots, 158–162; trade unions, 129. *See also* Arya Samaj; Calicut; Muslim League

Aligarh Muslim University (AMU): and civic relations, 152–54; history of, 137, 155–58; and Muslim politics, 120, 130, 139

373